Writing Creative Nonfiction

Tilar J. Mazzeo, Ph.D.

PUBLISHED BY:

THE GREAT COURSES
Corporate Headquarters
4840 Westfields Boulevard, Suite 500
Chantilly, Virginia 20151-2299
Phone: 1-800-832-2412
Fax: 703-378-3819
www.thegreatcourses.com

Printed in the United States of America

Tilar J. Mazzeo, Ph.D.

Clara C. Piper Professor of English
Colby College

Professor Tilar J. Mazzeo is the *New York Times* best-selling author of *The Widow Clicquot: The Story of a Champagne Empire and the Woman Who Ruled It*, the story of the first international businesswoman in history, and *The Secret of Chanel No. 5: The Intimate History of the World's Most Famous Perfume*. *The Widow Clicquot* won the 2008 Gourmand Award for the best book of wine literature published in the United States.

Professor Mazzeo holds a Ph.D. in English and teaches British and European literature at Colby College, where she is the Clara C. Piper Professor of English. She has been the Jenny McKean Moore Writer-in-Residence at The George Washington University, and her writing on creative nonfiction techniques has appeared in recent collections such as *Now Write! Nonfiction: Memoir, Journalism, and Creative Nonfiction Exercises from Today's Best Writers.*

An experienced travel, food, and wine writer, Professor Mazzeo is also the author of *Back Lane Wineries of Sonoma* and *Back Lane Wineries of Napa*. Her travel essays have appeared in publications such as *Food & Wine* magazine, and her narrative nonfiction account of life in the Hotel Ritz in Paris during the Second World War is forthcoming from HarperCollins.

Professor Mazzeo divides her time between coastal Maine and the California wine country. ■

Table of Contents

INTRODUCTION

LECTURE GUIDES

Table of Contents

Table of Contents

Writing Creative Nonfiction

Scope:

Have you ever wished that you could capture a vivid memory or experience in words? Do you dream of writing about a historical or cultural figure who fascinated you? Is there a family history you have always wanted to share, or one of your life's adventures that you have always said to yourself would make a wonderful story? Have you ever wanted to launch a new career as a writer or wanted to explore writing as a private passion? Writing well is not only useful, but it helps us preserve our life experiences as they truly occurred or as we felt them. It lets us share stories in ways that others find compelling. Creative nonfiction can open whole new windows on the way you and your readers experience history—maybe *your* history.

This course will help you write effectively about the things that matter to you, and it will introduce you to the exciting and quickly growing field of creative nonfiction—the art of bringing all the traditional strategies of fictional storytelling to narrating real-life events. In this course, you will learn how to craft powerful memoirs and family histories, how to write a biography of a fascinating figure, the history of an inspiring moment, or a work of riveting travel writing.

This course takes you from the beginning to the end of the process of writing creative nonfiction: from finding your story and crafting great beginnings to finding an audience for your book and working through the revision process. It offers firsthand advice from a bestselling author on breaking into the world of publishing and plenty of hands-on exercises for anyone simply interested in learning how to write more powerfully about his or her personal experiences.

Along the way, you will also learn about how to write chapters that are page-turners, how to develop gripping characters, and how to find the right structure for your story. You will learn how to develop the research skills to support your writing and how to write about the lives of people you know in ways that will not make them uncomfortable. You will learn how to use cliffhanger endings that keep your readers on the edge of their seats, how to keep your reader imaginatively engaged in factual history, and how to avoid common pitfalls like mixed metaphors, purple prose, and stock characters. You will also learn about the ethics of writing about true experiences, biographies, and autobiographies and how to avoid—unlike some recent controversial authors—breaking what writers and editors call the nonfiction contract.

In this course, you will practice new writing strategies that will help you master the art of storytelling so you can tell the stories of your experience and of the world around you from new perspectives, with panache. You will learn how to revise and edit your own work with new insight and confidence, how to find a community of fellow writers, and the secrets of the seven habits that professional writers cultivate to keep on writing and to manage writer's block.

Your professor—an award-winning, *New York Times* best-selling author—will guide you through the genres of personal creative nonfiction writing that both interested amateurs and professionals can enjoy, including the memoir, cultural history, travel writing, personal essays, and biography. Lectures offer practical advice on selecting and organizing ideas, establishing the goals and themes of your work, and publishing finished products.

Your professor uses memorable examples from well-known authors and specifically tailored craft exercises to help you learn the secrets of great writing from personal experience. You will learn highly effective research techniques to help you pursue your personal interests in prose, as well as how to craft the nonfiction story you have always wanted to tell—beautifully. With the right instructor, writing creative nonfiction is a skill everyone can master and enjoy. ■

Welcome to Creative Nonfiction

Lecture 1

To write great creative nonfiction, a writer must tell a fact-based story in an imaginative way—not as easy a task as it sounds! Nonfiction writers must be dedicated to preserving the truth of their stories—the who, what, why, where, when, and how. The creativity enters through the use of perspective, which, like a camera lens, allows the writer to focus the reader's attention and engage his or her imagination.

The Elements of a Great (True) Story

- You have always wanted to write: Perhaps you have bought a book completing your novel in 90 days or breaking into publishing. Perhaps you have taken a creative writing class. Maybe you have a half-completed project in a desk drawer. Maybe you have started a family history, a biography, or a memoir.

- If you have ever wanted to write about a true event or your personal experience but wanted to do it with panache, then you have been thinking about writing **creative nonfiction**. To write creative nonfiction, you need to learn great storytelling.

- Great storytelling requires a strong central character, gripping dialogue, and a fabulous beginning. It needs paragraph after paragraph that keeps a reader wanting more, leading to a satisfying ending.

- There are tricks of the trade—things that published writers learn from struggling with the same challenges all writers face over and over, as well as from talking to each other about their struggles. And it is important to note, what works for a great nonfiction story works just as well for a great fictional story, too.

What Is Creative Nonfiction?

- Imagine you are trying to tell a story. That story will be about a main character, and it will take place in a setting, just as a play consists of an actor who performs on a stage.

- Because this story is nonfiction, it will consist primarily of facts. You will have facts about the setting—the "where" and "when" of the story. You will have facts about the main character—usually a "who," but possibly a "what."

- Based on just those few facts, you can write an opening paragraph. That paragraph should show the reader the who, where, and when, but in a way that raises as many questions as it answers to engage the reader's imagination.

- Opening paragraphs tease the reader by using the facts as they exist in the real world but delivering them from a certain perspective, or **point of view**, to make the reader start wondering about the character.

- The wonderful thing about creative nonfiction is that from the same facts, we can tell hundreds of different stories. Everyone has a different perspective; simply changing the focus on the imaginary lens changes the story.

- Learning to write creative nonfiction well is all about learning how to find your voice and your perspective on any story you want to write.

One Story—Two Perspectives

- Here is an example of how two versions of a single nonfiction story can be simultaneously true to the facts and yet completely different. In the first version, Professor Mazzeo enters The Great Courses studio, told with an air of mystery.

> The room was silent. As she walked to the oak podium, the carpet muffled the sound of her footsteps. Beyond the windows, there was only blue, and she remembered her own days as an undergraduate, days when she sat, pen in

The same scene can look very different when considered from different perspectives. The Great Courses set looks like a warm, cozy place...

> hand, far at the back of a room, filled with excitement. Now, she cleared her mind of the other things occupying her mind, things she couldn't tell anyone in this room about, things that shaped her own unwritten story. The problem that obsessed her receded to the end of a long and distant tunnel, and what she needed to do now was the only thing that came into focus. "Welcome to Writing Creative Nonfiction," she said. "I'm Tilar Mazzeo, and together we'll be exploring what it means to write a great story."

- Here is that same scene again, only this time, we consider the experience with a tone of tension and worry, as Professor Mazzeo lets us know what problem so obsesses her.

> The studio was oddly silent. She could see only the legs of the cameramen, hunched over the cameras, with their empty glass camera eyes staring back at her like space aliens. As she walked across the stage to the oak podium, the carpet muffled the sound of her footsteps, and the spotlight blinded

...but from the professors' point of view, it is bright, high-tech, and even a bit intimidating the first time they deliver a lecture.

> her for a moment. Beyond the false windows, there was only a blue panel, meant to suggest the sky, and she remembered her own days as an undergraduate. Her shoes hurt, and she wished she had chosen another pair this morning. But of course she couldn't say that. She put that to the back of her mind. "Welcome to Writing Creative Nonfiction," she said. "I'm Tilar Mazzeo, and together we'll be exploring what it means to write a great story."

- By shifting what facts you know, you see the character in a different context, and by changing that context, the way the story develops in the reader's mind changes. Notice, however, that in both cases, every piece of information was a fact.

The Importance of Facts

- Fiction, by definition, is a written work that is based on the writer's imagination. Fiction does not have to be true. Nonfiction, therefore, is the opposite. It is writing that is true to facts and history.

- On any given day, you might encounter many types of nonfiction: You might read the news in the morning; read a popular autobiography on your lunch break; and review e-mails, memos, and meeting minutes throughout your day at work.

- These are very different kinds of writing, but all of them are what we used to call, in a general way, good journalism—a "who, what, why, where, when, and how," fact-based approach to writing.

- Traditionally, university creative writing departments have been the place to learn fiction and poetry writing. Today, many schools are offering programs in creative nonfiction as well. It is the fastest growing part of the creative writing world—and the fastest growing part of the market for books too.

- Creative nonfiction gets a bit tricky because the "creative" part means the writer is using the techniques of fictional storytelling. Unless the writer has warned you, the reader, that he or she is indulging in some creativity, you have the right to assume everything in the story is true—and the right to get angry if it is not.

- Nonfiction writers have a sort of contract with readers: We are not allowed to make anything up. We must be rigorous reporters of lived experience. Our impulses must be documentary.

- Despite this, the opportunities for creativity in nonfiction writing are immense. When writing is done at the highest level of craftsmanship—when the way of telling the story is just as important as the story itself—we often call that literature.

- All the strategies for telling a great story are the same, whether you are writing a novel or a work of nonfiction: You must set a vivid scene that lets your reader see every detail. The difference is that details are historically accurate.

Mr. A and Ms. B—A Writing Exercise

- Here is your first writing exercise in creative nonfiction. First, read the following minutes of a conversation between two people—Mr. A and Ms. B:

> Mr. A expressed the desire to be given the envelope on the table immediately. "This is my history," he stated. Ms. B denied the request. Ms. B stated that his past actions were the source of her reluctance. Mr. A argued that his past actions had been misunderstood. Ms. B responded: "You are a big jerk!"

- The setting is an office. The characters sit on opposite sides of a long table, and there is another woman sitting at the end of the table, along with lots of empty chairs. There are fluorescent lights flickering.

- With so few facts, the real meaning of this scene is still up for debate, so here are some more: Mr. A and Ms. B are a couple. The other woman is a mediator. The envelope contains photos of their lives together. And once, years ago, Mr. A used their wedding photos as kindling for the fireplace by accident.

- The homework assignment is this: Using these and the other facts about the couple given in the lecture, write a paragraph describing what you see in that room. Tell a good story, but only using the facts. No making things up!

Important Terms

creative nonfiction: The art of bringing all the strategies of storytelling to the narration of factual events.

point of view: The perspective from which a story is told; may be first (*I*/*we*), second (*you*), or third person (*he*/*she*/*it*/*they*).

Suggested Reading

Lounsberry, *The Art of Fact*.

Ueland, *If You Want to Write*.

Questions to Consider

1. What are your goals as a writer? What projects are you interested in exploring?

2. What do you see as your strengths and weaknesses as a writer?

Welcome to Creative Nonfiction
Lecture 1—Transcript

Welcome to Writing Creative Nonfiction. I'm Tilar Mazzeo; together, we'll be exploring what it means to write a great story, especially a story that's based on true histories, and maybe even on your own experience. You've always wanted to write. Perhaps you've bought one of those books on the market telling you how to complete your novel in 90 days or break into the publishing marketplace. Perhaps you've taken a creative writing class or are in one now. Maybe you have a half-completed project somewhere in a desk drawer and are thinking you'd like to finish it. Maybe there's a family history you're working on; a biography of an amazing person; your own life story; the memories you might want to pass down to the next generation.

If you've ever wanted to write about a true event or about your personal experience but wanted to do it with panache, then you've been thinking about writing creative nonfiction. If you've ever been on an adventurous trip and thought about turning all those funny and dramatic events into a story you could share with others, that's creative nonfiction, too. In fact, if you want to write the truth about those experiences exactly because you believe that the real story is as great a tale as any invention, then what you're thinking about is what we're going to study here: creative nonfiction.

If you've tried to write creatively before, you've almost certainly learned that in order to write a great story, you need a strong character, gripping dialogue, a fabulous beginning. You need a satisfying ending and paragraph after paragraph that keeps a reader wanting more. You need to learn great storytelling. But what does all that really mean? How do you know if you've got a fabulous beginning? What really makes dialogue grab us and how do you work it into your story? What are the nuts and bolts of this craft of creative writing?

I'm an English professor and a writer myself, and I can tell you that there are tricks of the trade; things that published writers—the people whose books you've read and enjoyed and recommended to friends—learn from doing this over and over, from struggling with the same challenges all writers face, and from talking to each other. That's one thing we're going to learn in this course: how to write a great story. Many of the techniques that work for a great nonfiction story work just as well for a great fictional story, too. If it's a fabulous novel you want to write instead of a memoir, you'll learn some great skills here, too; so you're in the right place.

Since we're talking about you and about your story, in this course we're going to focus on one particular kind of storytelling: what is formally known in the world of college classrooms and professional writing as "creative nonfiction." But at its heart, it's the kind of writing that's all about telling personal stories. You can learn to write better, and I can help you do it; and we're going to start by showing you how you can do it immediately, right here in the first lesson.

What is creative nonfiction? What is it you're going to be learning how to write better? A good question; I gave you some hints when I mentioned memoir, biography, and travel writing. But how about I show you?

Let's imagine a story about the world we're going to share together during our time here. Here in the center of the stage, I'm going to be the main character of our story. This stage is going to be our setting. I want you to be the reader of this story right now; a real story; a story based on the facts that you can plainly see around you. Let's start with some facts—because, after all, this is nonfiction we're talking about—and we only need a few of them to start finding a story here.

Let's start with the setting; that's going to be this room around us. What do you notice? It's panel-lined. There's a writing desk, which I could sit behind for our time together. How about a few facts about characters? You have a professor. We have students in an audience; that's you, isn't it? And you've heard me introduce myself.

Based on just those few facts, we can write a great paragraph. How about something like this, written from the perspective of me, the professor:

> The room was silent. As she strode forward from the writing desk, the carpet muffled the sound of her footsteps. On the walls behind her were brightly colored posters and casement

windows, reminding her of her own days as an undergraduate; days when she had sat, pen in hand, far at the back of the room, filled with excitement. The secret, painful thought that had been nibbling at her all morning crept forward again, but she pushed it back with a heroic effort and smiled warmly. "Welcome to Writing Creative Nonfiction," she said. "I'm Tilar Mazzeo, and together we'll be exploring what it means to write a great story."

Now we've got you wondering, don't we? Who is this professor character? What's on her mind? Wow, there's got to be some story here, doesn't there?

It's true; what's on my mind, that's a secret. Like any of us, I have things that distract me from the work I'm doing; and I just told you the truth: that something was on my mind as I started my lecture. The rest of it's all true, too: Those panels do look like classroom posters. Those center frames have window casements. There's a desk and a pen right there. The room is silent. And you know that's how I began this lecture; after all, you were there, weren't you? That's exactly how I introduced myself.

Can you see yourself now, at the university in this course we're going to do together? Can you begin to feel yourself in this paneled room; imagine yourself way back there in the auditorium, taking notes, listening with rapt attention? Or maybe you're looking at those posters, wondering what you can learn from them. It evokes a classroom; and in your mind, can you see the ivy-clad brick walls and the quadrangle? If so, you're doing just what a reader should do in response to a piece of good nonfiction; a piece that's based on the facts but also telling a story.

This is an example of creative nonfiction. It's nonfiction because it's true, right? I didn't make up what this room looks like, after all. At the same time, I did try to engage your imagination. I gave you a paragraph that invited you to see yourself as the audience in an auditorium, but all I said was that the room was silent. I told you I had something on my mind that I was struggling to set aside at the moment the course began, but I didn't tell you what it was. I gave you a tease to capture your attention and your imagination. What did you think my secret was? Did the options run through your mind? It was meant to; but all I actually told you was that something was on my mind.

I never said that it was something big or dramatic; I let your imagination play in a role in shaping the story I was sharing with you. But I told you we were imagining together from the facts. I used facts and a certain perspective on them—a certain point of view for seeing this story—to make you start wondering about who this professor character is.

Here's the wonderful thing about creative nonfiction; about telling great stories based on facts and history: From the same facts, we can tell hundreds of different stories. Everyone has a different perspective on the facts; and if we just change the focus on our imaginary lens, those same facts change, and so does our story. That's also what creative nonfiction is all about: finding your voice and your perspective on telling a story; a story based on facts, but that captures a reader's imagination.

Not sure what I mean about why perspective is so important? Not sure how totally different stories can be simultaneously true, and yet different? Let me show you something else. I just told you a story about me, the professor; of a room that matches the facts you can see from your perspective. Every factual thing I wrote in that paragraph was something you could see and hear for yourself, wasn't it? That's part of the reason the parts you couldn't see or know—what happens in my head, my secret—become interesting. It's the thing you can't see, but want to discover.

But have you ever wondered what one of these courses looks like from the perspective of the professor? When I look at the facts of this room, I see something that tells a different story. Here, have a look at what it's like from the perspective of your professor; life behind the scenes of these great courses. Did you imagine this was a room in a university auditorium and that you were way back up there in the top seats? I tried to help you do that in my paragraph. But all I actually said was that the room was silent; and it was. That's because the only people in here are the camera operators.

What we have now is not the university classroom that I wanted to invite you to imagine, but something completely modern and up to date. We have a whole team of people working together to make sure you can enjoy this class from the privacy of your own home, on your schedule, at your own pace. We have set materials for other classes, by other professors, over here. Longtime customers of the Great Courses may fondly remember that ivy-covered wall from earlier sets. I did really remember my days as a college student when I came into the room this morning; I was thinking how, back then, nothing like this existed. But it's a different story in our minds now, isn't it? The facts, put in a different light, create a very different experience.

Do you know what? You've just learned one important thing about great storytelling already. Setting is one part of how we tell captivating stories; and setting is one element that helps creates character, too.

Here's what I also could've written. I could've started my paragraph in a different way; in this way:

> The studio was oddly silent. She could see only the legs of the camera operators, hunched over the cameras, with their empty glass camera eyes staring back at her like space aliens. As she walked across the stage in front of the desk, the carpet muffled the sound of her footsteps, and the spotlight blinded her for a moment. Her shoes hurt, and she wished she had chosen another pair this morning. But, of course, she couldn't say that; she put that to the back of her mind. "Welcome to Writing Creative Nonfiction," she said. "I'm Tilar Mazzeo, and together we'll be exploring what it means to write a great story."

I've shifted what facts you know and helped you to see the character in a different setting. In doing so, I've changed the story as it developed in your mind, haven't I? Now you know the first few tricks of the trade about storytelling—that setting creates character—and there are many more that we'll be talking about, too.

But here's the thing: It's creative nonfiction; so in neither of those stories did I make anything up at all. I never said this was a university in the first one; I just said it was a room, and helped you to imagine what room it might be through other kinds of hints. I never said what my secret was; and so I let you imagine it was a deep, dark one for the moment when it was really just my shoes pinching. The facts are the same, and all those different perspectives on this room are equally true. But the story is different, and that's because the frame through which we're seeing those facts has shifted. We're using the creative storytelling strategy of point of view to change your experience of events as a reader.

Let's think about this a bit more. How did I shift the perspective like that? How did I help you imagine one kind of room when what I was seeing was another, and still tell you just the facts to do it? I used creative nonfiction.

What, then, is creative nonfiction? Break down the two words in there. Start with the second word, "nonfiction." That's simple, right? After all, what is fiction? It's a work that's based on the imagination, obviously, isn't it? Fiction doesn't have to be true; that's the whole idea. Or at least it doesn't have to be true to any kind of real history. What matters to us is just that it's a great story. After all, we understand the contract between the reader and a fiction writer: Give me a great read and an imaginary world that I can believe in, we say, and in exchange I won't care at all if you made all this up.

If you think about it this way, you'll see where I'm going, won't you? Nonfiction: That's obviously going to be the opposite. Nonfiction is not-fiction. It's writing where what matters is that the story is true to a real, lived history. It's fact. It's a "true story."

When's the last time you read a piece of nonfiction? What was it? Think about it for a moment. If you picked up the newspaper this morning, you expected to read something that was reliable and accurate. Or maybe it was the autobiography of a talented businessperson who managed to make a staggering fortune and promises to let you in on all the secrets. Maybe you read the minutes of a meeting that you never quite got around to attending. All these things are what we used to call, in a general way, "good journalism"; a kind of "who, what, where, why, when, just the facts ma'am" reporting.

But while those are tried-and-true real life examples of creative nonfiction—our newspapers and meeting minutes—this is also where some of the most exciting new work in the world of writing is being done today. Truman Capote's 1966 book *In Cold Blood* is an early example of creative nonfiction, and David Sedaris's *Me Talk Pretty One Day* is a more recent one. I started my own career in creative nonfiction with travel writing and writing about the wines of California. My first book, *The Widow Clicquot*, was a biography of an early 19th-century French businesswoman who created one of the world's great champagnes. Since then, I've published a book on the history of Chanel No. 5 perfume, and I've just finished one on the Ritz Hotel in Paris.

Today, all around the world, creative writing departments—which have long focused on poetry and novel writing—have programs in creative nonfiction as well. It's the fastest growing part of the creative writing world, and the fastest growing part of the market for books, too. This is cutting edge stuff: a new genre emerging from old traditions and reshaping the books and essays and biographies and magazine articles you see around you in bookstores and libraries every day.

But can you already see where creative nonfiction is going to get a bit tricky? It's right there in the title, isn't it? "Creative": That means "story-telling," "using the imagination." "Nonfiction": That means that unless the writer has warned you that he or she is indulging in some imagination, you have the right to assume everything in the story is true, and the right to get angry if the writer breaks the unspoken deal with the reader, the deal that we call the "nonfiction contract."

What is the nonfiction contract? It sounds ominous, doesn't? But it's very easy to understand. Let me give you an example: Let's imagine you're reading your morning newspaper. You read there an article about something you're passionate about—politics, the economy, something happening in arts and culture, something about human rights or the planet's destiny—and because it's the newspaper, you assume that it's true and factual unless something in there tells you otherwise, right? How would you feel if it turned out that what you read in the newspaper was just invented? Unless it was April Fool's Day, you wouldn't be amused. You'd probably be pretty disappointed; in fact, you might even be angry. "I relied on you for accurate information," you might say to the author. "You misled me and abused my confidence. If you were going to make up the news, you needed to tell me what you were doing." There would be a lot of angry letters to the editor. You might cancel your subscription. I know I would.

Or think about the minutes of a meeting; take that example. Let's imagine you spoke out at the local school board, or at the town hall, or at a shareholder's meeting, and it was a topic that really stirred your passions. You made your point. You like to think you swayed your audience. Would it be okay if the secretary writing the minutes put into your mouth words you never said and that made you look foolish just because, hey, it makes for a better story? You'd be furious, wouldn't you?

We're going to look in this course at how to write great creative nonfiction, and the nonfiction part means that the contract we have with the reader is very simple: We aren't allowed to make up anything. Anything. We're going to be rigorous reporters of lived experience. We're documenting real history. Where is there any room in here for something creative? That's a good question; and the answer is that the possibilities for creativity are immense.

Let's think about it: What does it mean to write something creative? Is your grocery list creative? How about your tax return? Let's hope not. When you think about "creativity," what do you think? I'm betting you already know more about what makes for great storytelling than you might imagine. What happens in creative work; what engages your imagination?

You might say something like, "It means places and people I can really see in my mind and visualize and identify with." You'd be right; this is what a great novel does, isn't it? In fact, when it's done at the highest level of craftsmanship—when the way of telling the story is just as important as the story itself—we often call that "literature."

All the strategies for telling a great story are the same, whether you're writing a novel or a memoir or a biography. After all, what, there aren't people out there whose lives make amazing stories with exciting narratives, lots of drama, and rich character? Of course there are.

There are powerful ways to tell any story, even true ones, and the tools we use to do it as nonfiction writers are exactly the same ones used by fiction writers. You can set a vivid scene that your reader sees in every detail and creates a sense of maybe dark foreboding. As long as your details are historically accurate, you'd be crazy not to, in fact. But there's a catch in creative nonfiction dialogue: Your characters need really to have said the words you say they did. You can see pretty quickly that, in the lessons that follow, we're also going to have to think about where you might find that kind of interesting material.

Here's your first writing exercise in creative nonfiction, and we'll do it together. Remember what I said about those minutes of a meeting and how they were a record of the facts? Let me read you the minutes of a very short conversation between two people. We'll call them Mr. A and Ms. B. Here are the minutes:

> Mr. A asked to be given the envelope on the table immediately. "This is my history," he stated. Ms. B denied the request. Ms. B stated that his past actions were the source of her reluctance. Mr. A argued that his past actions had been misunderstood. Ms. B responded, "You're a big jerk!"

Want to see for yourself the difference between nonfiction and creative nonfiction? It's very easy. These are just the facts right now, right? Let's add in some more facts; facts we can use to see the story; facts that will help us understand who these characters are.

First, let me add in the setting. Did you have any ideas where this conversation was taking place? Maybe they're spies fighting over top-secret documents. Maybe one is blackmailing the other? But, in fact, here's the situation: These are two people in an office. They're at a long table, on opposite sides, and there's a yellow manila envelope. The office has lots of chairs along the side, and there's another woman sitting at the end of the table with them. There are fluorescent lights flickering.

Do you begin to see a story taking shape? There's something you still want to know, isn't there? Who are these people, and what's the source of the conflict between them? Why does Mr. A want the envelope? Why does Ms. B think he's a jerk? There's something going on here, and we need to know what it is, don't we? What do you think it might be? Are they competitors in a boardroom? Is one a police officer interrogating the other? Might be; but in this case, here's another fact: They're a couple, and in the envelope are photos of their lives together.

But why does Ms. B say that past actions are the reason that she won't give up the photographs, do you think? In order to understand their characters, we also need to understand their motivations and their history. Did Mr. A cheat on Ms. B and break her heart? Or it is just that once, years ago, Mr. A used the album of their wedding photos as kindling for the fireplace? In this case, it happens to be the latter.

Now we see the room; we know who the characters are; we know what's in the envelope, and why they're fighting over it. We know the setting: in a room, during a divorce, with a mediator. Of course we know that there are two pieces of dialogue we can use, but only two: "This is my history" and "You're a big jerk!"

Those two bits of dialogue are helpful, but if we're going to tell the story behind these minutes, we're going to need more than that to work with, aren't we? And we can't make up anything else they say. Think about it for a minute: What other information would be useful to you as a writer if you wanted to tell this story; if you wanted to make this into a scene worthy of the opening of your book? What's another way in which people say things about themselves besides their language? Body language, right? What new information about how they feel does that give you? Is someone clearly bored, frustrated, angry? Does it help if I tell you Mr. A is trying to fight back tears as he speaks; that Ms. B has angry, defensive body language? Or how about the fact that Ms. B is wearing a scarlet business suit and Mr. A is wearing his jogging gear? Or that she's 62 and he's 41, and that her name is actually Ms. Bernadice Bluster—what's in a name, right?—and his real name is Mr. Leslie Artbuckler?

All these facts are just concrete ways to think about some of the major components of all good storytelling: conflict and character motivation, setting the scene, finding a shape for your story, shaping voice, and crafting dialogue. This is what we're going to learn how to master along with lessons on how to honor the nonfiction contract by doing smart research; how to start your writing project and find the momentum to finish it; and how maybe to make your next step in the world of publishing because, after all, good stories deserve good readers.

Okay, are you ready for your homework? You now have some facts about Bernadice Bluster and Leslie Artbuckler. Go ahead; see if you can write a paragraph describing what you see in that room.

As you've already learned in this lesson, one of the first decisions you'll want to make is whose perspective to tell the story from. Remember what a difference the angle of vision made in our little paragraph about the professor? Will you present this scene from Bernadice's angry and indignant perspective? From Leslie's wounded and perhaps wounding soul? What about the divorce mediator, trying to sort this whole thing out; how does she view this scene? You might even go outside the room for a view on this story; perhaps from the perspective of one of Bernadice and Leslie's children, now grown up, looking back, trying to understand what went wrong and why. Whichever view you choose, it will change the facts that you want to highlight. Tell us a good story; but you can only use the facts I've given you. Remember: Keep the creative nonfiction contract.

In the next lesson, we'll start right off by looking at what you might have encountered as a stumbling block or two along the way; what you might have found worked well that you want to remember, and what you can learn from them both for next time. You can learn to write great stories. You already know more than you think, and teaching you new ways to think about writing is what we're going to do here together.

Finding the Story

Lecture 2

A story is not merely a series of events; it is a series of events with a compelling sense of momentum that carries the reader toward the conclusion. We call this momentum the narrative arc, and writers achieve it by having strong characters who experience challenges and conflicts and undergo changes as a result. In creative nonfiction writing, choosing the right character and the right conflict is an essential part of starting your story.

Choosing Your Characters

- Writers need to think about how to keep a narrative in motion. Some of the engines that move a narrative forward include subtext, stakes, tension, character conflict, scene, setting, good beginnings, and satisfying endings. Achieving any of these often requires revision.

- Returning to the exercise from the last lecture, were you able to find any of these narrative engines in the information you had? What did the minutes leave out that might have been helpful?

- Let us return to that same couple, but this time, we visit them at their first meeting, on a blind date. The first line of the minutes are as follows:

  > 12:05 p.m., Café Voisin. Present: girl, wearing heels, red lipstick, cute; guy, out of breath, foreign accent. Introductions. Girl orders double vodka. Guy orders espresso. Guy: "Sorry to be late, I was just…."

- What are the missing pieces of information in these minutes? We might wonder why the man is out of breath, or why the woman is drinking at noon, or why the date is so early in the day. Because we already know how this relationship works out, we are already looking for signs of impending doom, too.

- All of these questions are about character. We are looking for their investments and motivations. We can see the possibility of tension and miscommunication on the horizon. Once we start to see things on the horizon, we are thinking about **narrative arc**—where this story is going, what its forward momentum is.

- Another important question is what happened before this scene. One of the things we will talk a lot about later in the course is how something interesting has already happened before any really great story's beginning.

Teasing Out the Details

- If we were fiction writers, rewriting this story would be simple, because we could fill in the missing facts. In creative nonfiction, however, we cannot invent everything.

- If you already write fiction, you may be feeling hemmed in by the weight of fact. However, there is more than enough for a story in our scenario. Creative nonfiction stories also offer something fiction cannot: the power of true human experience.

- To keep the nonfiction contract with the reader, you will need to gather as many details as possible, because details are at the heart of character. In this case, facts can include nonverbal cues and logical inferences drawn from what we find in front of us.

- Think about the woman's red lipstick and the high heels, for example: What can you infer about her hopes or expectations for this meeting? How would you be confident in describing her, knowing nothing else about her? The same kinds of facts—such as his words, his accent, his observable demeanor—tell us about the man's character as well.

- Once you have tried revising these minutes to create a narrative scene, as you did with the argument in the boardroom in the last lecture, double check that you did not invent anything. Make sure you did not give in to the "it makes a better story this way" impulse.

Focusing the Lens

- When characters meet, something happens, but there is a difference between something happening and telling a good story. However, since you cannot change what happened in creative nonfiction, where does that leave you as a writer trying to craft a compelling narrative arc?

- You cannot invent dramatic moments, but you can choose the order in which you present the real moments to the reader and thus control the focus of the story.

  - If you begin the scene describing the woman's red lipstick, you invite the reader to think about romance and attraction.

  - If you begin with the phone conversation she had with her boss just before the man arrived—the one that drove her to order the vodka—you invite the reader to think about tension instead.

The Three Keys to a Story

- How do you decide what makes an interesting story? A good story must have at least three things:

  - It needs a narrative arc. Something has to happen. A series of events filled with dramatic tension must keep the reader wanting to reach the conclusion, even if he or she already knows what happens—as, say, when you are writing about a famous historical event.

  - It needs **dramatic conflict**, or tension. Again, even if we know the outcome of a historical event, a story is dull unless the main character faces some opposition and struggles in reaching his or her goals.

  - It needs a character to experience these events and conflict and, ultimately, to undergo a transformation. A lot of the time, your stories will be about conflicts between two characters with different goals.

- The things that make a character interesting are the same things that make people interesting in real life: complexity, uniqueness, internal conflict, passion, ambition, strength, and weakness. We can love or hate these characters, but the writer's job is to make us believe they are real and to make us care about what happens to them—even if we are hoping they meet a bad end.

The Liberation of Paris—A Writing Exercise

- For our next exercise, we will use a photograph taken during the Liberation of Paris at the end of the Second World War that once appeared on the cover of *LIFE* magazine. In the foreground, a French soldier runs, a rifle in his hand, past some old-fashioned cars and a streetlamp that immediately evoke Paris in the 1940s. Behind a car, a man on his knees takes aim at some distant target. Crouched at his feet is another soldier, half hidden from view. High on a window ledge of the building behind them, a civilian man stands, looking into the distance. Below him on the street are two other people, looking in the same direction.

Use this photograph from the Liberation of Paris during the Second World War as your jumping-off point for the writing exercise.

- If you were the journalist reporting on the streets of Paris that day, where would you find the story in this image? Where are the narrative arc, conflict, and character?

- There are at least nine possible characters to work from: The running soldier, the two crouching soldiers, and the three watching civilians—they make six. The crouching soldier's target is the seventh.

- The last two are trickier: First, there is the photographer. Second, you have yourself, looking at this image not from the streets of Paris but from some distant vantage point. The author can always be, in creative nonfiction, one of the characters.

- Each character has a different set of motivations and stakes in the events that are unfolding; each one offers a different narrative arc that shapes the story.

- Of course, this image captures a single moment, and without knowing more, you cannot write an entire nonfiction story yet. You cannot make up more details than you have, but if you wanted to, you could research them. We will talk more about research in future lectures.

- As an exercise in learning how to craft and shape storytelling, however, looking at photographs and listening in on bits of conversation are ways to think about what is powerful and interesting in a situation.

- You can practice this same exercise now on your own. The best place to look is an old family album because you do not need to do research. You know the characters and the narrative possibilities. Look for a photograph that has great dramatic tension.

Important Terms

dramatic conflict: Conflict, either internal or external, that characters experience that moves a narrative forward.

narrative arc: The idea that a story has a natural forward trajectory and that conflicts move toward complication and resolution.

Suggested Reading

Fandel, *Picture Yourself Writing Nonfiction.*

Zinsser, *On Writing Well.*

Questions to Consider

1. Creative nonfiction is about telling true stories. Think about the kind of truth photographs tell. Do you think photographs are a more objective form of history than creative nonfiction? Why or why not?

2. Look around you. How do the people you see reveal hints of character in their dress and external appearances? What can you learn about creating character from this?

Finding the Story

Lecture 2—Transcript

We talked in the last lesson about the particular kind of narrative that we're going to learn to master in this course: that new and exciting genre that's known as creative nonfiction; "creative" because it uses all the same strategies we see in fiction for telling a great story; "nonfiction" because nothing is invented. Currently, books in this genre are among the book world's biggest bestsellers. It's the form of a powerful biography or a gripping memoir. It's the history of interesting and fascinating people, told in the form of books or essays. Maybe not yet on the shelves of bookstores but someday, it's the story of your family or the story of your own unique experience. When we write it, what we're always negotiating is our promise to the reader that we'll tell a great yarn, but we'll tell it truthfully.

At the end of the last lesson, I suggested an exercise; and let's think about what you might have discovered trying it out. I asked you to write a paragraph or two describing Bernadice Bluster and Leslie Artbuckler's meeting and conversation; the encounter of Ms. B and Mr. A. Were you able to turn that scene into an interesting account; into the kind of narrative event with a story? Think back to what was running through your mind when you looked at those facts and started trying to imagine how you were going to give them a narrative; or maybe you got stuck thinking just about the question. Hopefully you got going again by thinking about the different ways you could use the facts to describe those characters' tensions. Did you find yourself thinking: Where do the facts leave us with interesting narrative openings? If so, that's the right strategy.

How about this: Let's try a similar exercise here again together and see if you can find the story in this exercise. How would you begin this narrative writing? Let's imagine we're listening in on two people at a café table, and let's imagine that I'm giving you the "just the facts" version of the events; the things you have to work your story with. Let's call them your factual "minutes." In the minutes, here are the essentials:

> It's 12:05 pm. It's Café Voisin. A busy street in a city. Our characters present: We have a girl. She's wearing very high

heels, red lipstick, and she's cute. She hangs up the cell phone furiously. There's a guy. He's out of breath, he has a foreign accent. Introductions are made. The girl orders a double vodka. The guy orders an espresso. The guy says, "Sorry to be late, I was just …" We stop here.

Of course, the conversation surely goes on; but think just about the very first moment and what we can start to do to make it into a story. What are the questions that are running through your head? What are the missing pieces of information? Why is the guy out of breath? Why is the girl ordering a double vodka at noon? What does it tell us about this encounter that they're meeting at noon anyhow instead of over dinner? Is it a blind date? Where's the guy from? Who's this girl wearing dramatic red lipstick? Who introduced these two and what in the world were they thinking? Because we already have an idea that if this love affair works out, it's going to be an odd kind of story.

All these questions are crucial elements of storytelling. When we ask ourselves these questions, we're looking to understand character. We're looking to understand their investments and motivations; we can see the possibility of tension and miscommunication on the horizon. Once we start to see things on the horizon, we're beginning to think about narrative arc: Where's this story going; what's its forward momentum? We want to know how the guy finishes that sentence and to see what his reason tells us about his personality and investment. What happened before this scene? Because one of the things we'll talk a lot about later in the course is how something interesting has always already happened before the beginning of any great story.

If we were fiction writers, rewriting this story would be simple, wouldn't it? We'd give the guy a name. He'd become maybe Edouard, an aging playboy still stuck in the 1970s from, how about Barcelona? And the girl, I'll name her Griselda. Maybe drinking at noon means she's an alcoholic, or maybe something very unusual has happened. Maybe she needs something from Edouard and is still gathering her courage. Maybe she's just witnessed something terrible. Maybe, maybe, maybe. In the world of fiction, those possibilities are endless.

In the world of creative nonfiction, though, we've made a deal with the reader: We aren't going to invent anything. He can't be Edouard from Barcelona, she can't be Griselda. Not unless during those introductions that's what you heard, that is; and that's not one of the facts I gave you.

Are you feeling hemmed in by the weight of fact here? For those of us used to fiction, that's understandable. But look again: There's more than enough for a story here. In fact, there's enough for several rich narratives. The thing about those narratives waiting to be opened up and told is that they have something fiction doesn't have: the power of true human experience behind them. Who cares about the romance of Edouard and Griselda? They're a figment of my imagination. But here at that café are two real, live people, perhaps beginning one of history's great love affairs. Or perhaps it will be one of history's great disasters. Or maybe it's not a date at all. After all, the facts don't make that clear either. Who knows what will happen? But whatever it is, it will happen to these two people in front of you, who will go on with their lives and their stories. Where there's character and narrative tension, there's always the possibility for powerful drama, and as a nonfiction writer you just need to learn how to look for it and how to shape it.

To transform this story of the couple at the café table into a scene worthy of a novel, while keeping that nonfiction contract that's part of the bargain, what are you going to have to do? The first thing you might have realized was that because you aren't going to be able to make anything up, you're going to need to think about how to get as much mileage out of those few details as possible, because details are at the heart of character. You're going to need to listen to the nuances of all of the smallest details; because if writers of creative nonfiction don't invent details, that means we need to collect as much information as possible.

Sticking to facts doesn't mean we aren't able to read nonverbal cues or draw logical inferences from what we find in front of us. Think about the red lipstick and the high heels in my example. What do those choices tell you, for example, about the ways in which you can confidently and accurately describe this woman, even without knowing her hopes or dreams or expectations? She's taken care with her appearance, but the dress is incongruous for the setting. She's pretty and has highlighted it by wearing vivid makeup. These are all facts, and facts alone, even these very public ones; they also tell us something about her private character. The same kinds of facts—his words, his accent, his observable demeanor—tell us also about the man's character.

The first thing we can take away from this is that the difference between a story and the reporting of the facts that I gave you is that stories show us character. We have an idea of who these people are, what they look like, what might have happened before they arrived in our stories, and how they might react based on it. We have an identity sketch, really. Have you ever seen one of those police dramas on television, where they bring in the artist to draw the portrait of a suspect based on a handful of facts that a witness remembers? That's a lot like what we are doing as writers of creative nonfiction. We gather up the facts and draw for our readers a portrait that's identifiable.

If you want, take a pause and try the exercise: See if, working with those "minutes" I gave you, you can use just to facts to find the story and to write a scene about these characters. Go ahead if you're feeling you want to try it.

If you did write the exercise, here's the thing you'd want to double check at the end of it: In your desire to turn these people into characters, did you invent anything? In fact, it's something to think about in the very beginning. Are there things that aren't actually facts, but your version of the "it makes a better story this way" kind of invention? If so, remember the nonfiction contract. We'll talk more about this later, too, because it's important.

For now, let's just think about those minutes and how you might have moved it into a story. The conversation provided you with some dialogue; the meeting gave you the basic structure of a possible narrative. But did you struggle with realizing that there's a difference between something happening and telling a good story? If you did, bravo; you've understood something essential about storytelling.

Since you can't change what happened in narrative nonfiction, can't invent dramatic moments unless that's what you witnessed, you really had one powerful tool at your disposal: You could choose where to begin—and ultimately end—the story, and that has huge storytelling potential. You could order the facts in the story and frame them in a way that revealed the stakes in this encounter.

What do I mean? Think about those minutes and this business about the power of beginnings. I could've written the scene beginning with a description of the woman sitting at the table, describing her red lipstick. It's a fact: I sat there; I saw her; I'm writing about it. I can begin anywhere, and I begin with her because she fascinates me. In doing so, I'd have started my scene by establishing her character. I don't have to say to my reader, "Look, a woman with red lipstick, and she is this or that kind of person as a result of it"; after all, in point of fact, I have pretty limited information about what kind of person she is. I have an impression. Reading about her, you're getting an impression, too. Maybe you're drawing some conclusions about this lady. We do this all the time in life, so why not in stories? But the key thing is: As the author, I've just given you factual details and invited you to engage your imagination. In fact, one of the other principles in storytelling that we'll talk about in this course—and maybe you've heard it before—is the principle that the best kind of writing happens when the author doesn't tell you these kinds of things but shows you, or lets you be the one to invent them.

The first facts that I give you are a powerful invitation indeed. It's not just your first impression of this woman; where I begin tells you what I'm inviting you to think this story is about also. After all, it's only important that the woman in my imagined café scenario is wearing red lipstick if I'm thinking of this as a narrative encounter about her and about romantic attraction, isn't it? The nonfiction contract with the reader doesn't mean that a writer is required to include every detail, and so what if she's wearing red lipstick? Perhaps, in the story that I watched unfold, that just wasn't part of what mattered.

Think about this: It's a different story if I begin my scene with the telephone conversation she's having before the man arrived, don't you think? What if it wasn't him? What if it were her boss, and what if she's a CIA agent? If I see this as a story of a romance, I leave that conversation out because I think of this as a narrative of two characters, a man and a woman, who are about to find out if they have a grand passion. But if I think that whatever happened in that telephone conversation has shaped this moment and this encounter in ways the guy, dashing up to the table late and breathless, can't imagine, then I'm inviting you to see a different kind of story; not a love story, but something else.

Or maybe it wasn't her boss the CIA agent. Maybe it was her AA sponsor, and this is really a story about that double vodka. Here, you see how where we choose to begin—and as nonfiction writers what facts we leave out and which ones we put in—have the power to set a narrative in motion and to create wonderful drama for our readers. I can't tell the reader the identity of the boss—after all, the facts don't describe it—but how I shape the details I do know gives the reader a suspicion about what's at the heart of the conflict and the characters.

Think back to your scene-writing exercise with Ms. B and Mr. A in our first lesson. Where did you begin it, and why? Looking at it now, what does it tell you about what you thought this narrative was about? What does it tell you about where this story unfolding in front of you seemed interesting and compelling? Who did you think these people were? What were their motivations and investments? The thing is: You had to begin somewhere, and when you did, you made a decision that launched a narrative arc in motion. What were you looking for when you decided, do you remember? Or let's put that another way: How do you decide what makes an interesting topic in general? You want to begin writing—your scene-setting exercise, the story of your life, the biography of some inspiring historical figure—how do you know what makes for a good story?

A good story must have at least three things: It has to have a narrative arc. Something has to happen, even if what happens is the story of someone experiencing abject boredom. Plot and a series of events filled with dramatic tension might drive the narrative arc and carry the reader along with a sense of momentum. "What will happen next?" the reader asks. "Will our heroine escape the burning building?" "Will the Allies win World War II?" "Will

Governor Ronald Reagan win the pivotal 1980 election?" "I want to keep reading," the reader thinks. "I want to enjoy the drama, even if I already know what happens."

A good story has to have some kind of conflict; some tension. "Will Governor Ronald Reagan win the pivotal 1980 election?" we ask in a presidential biography. It wouldn't be an interesting story unless there was a chance he wouldn't. He had to have some opposition. The heroine escaping the burning building is only a good story if she has to overcome obstacles. Love stories grab at our heartstrings when they have star-crossed lovers. As Shakespeare tells us in *Midsummer Night's Dream*, "for aught that I could ever read, Could ever hear by tale or history, The course of true love never did run smooth." Neither did any other story filled with great passion.

Someone has to experience this conflict and transformation, of course. All those events have to happen—unless we're writing a very experimental narrative indeed—to a person. So a great story needs character. It needs conflict between characters. Moments where they see the stakes differently; where they misunderstand each other, love or hate each other, question each other's motives, and maybe are blind to their own. What makes an interesting character? That same thing that makes for interesting people in life: complexity, uniqueness, internal conflict, passion, desires, ambition, strength, and weakness. We can love characters or we can hate characters, but the writer's job is to make us believe in their humanness and to make us care about what happens to them, even if we're hoping they meet a deservedly wicked end.

Three things in a good story: narrative arc, dramatic conflict, and interesting, believable characters. Did your scene-setting exercise start to include some of them? If so, then good work; and if not, now that you know what makes a good story, we'll try another exercise together.

Let's look at this photograph. It was taken in the summer of 1944 during the Liberation of Paris at the end of the Second World War. It's a shot of soldiers from General LeClerc's armed forces fighting for control of Paris, and it appears in the archives of *Life* magazine. What you know is that some editor chose it because it tells a powerful story. What if you were the journalist reporting on the streets of Paris that day? What if you were writing now your nonfiction account of the Liberation of Paris? Where would you find the story in this image? Remember, what we need to find are narrative arc, conflict, and character.

Take a minute and look at the photograph carefully. What kinds of ideas and observations occur to you? In the foreground, we see a French soldier, caught in midstride, his feet a blur of motion. He holds a rifle in his hand. There's one of those old-fashioned French cars and one of those evocative streetlights to immediately tell you this is Paris. Behind the car, a man on his knees takes aim at some distant roof or window. Look at that more closely: A man in a blazer, not a soldier, stands perched on a windowsill along the sidewalk. Below him on the street are two other heads, looking in the same direction. They're all watching something. Now we notice that crouched at the feet of the man shooting there's another soldier, half hidden.

What we have here is a historical photo, a documentary record of a small moment in the larger story of the Liberation of Paris and the final days of the Nazi occupation of France. It's a historical moment that's rich enough to sustain thousands of stories. In fact, it would be safe to say that the Second World War already has. As a writer, then, looking at this image and thinking about taking it as our topic, there are different things we need to be considering.

If we're professional writers—or if we aspire to be—and we want to write a book or an essay that's likely to get published, we need to think about the market. What were those other thousand books on the Second World War, and what would be fresh about our story? What is, as your new editor would call it, the hook of your story? That's the kind of decision that's going to involve some research, and we'll talk about how to find a new angle and how to find a marketable topic at the end of our course, in lesson 23. But all writers need to think about having a compelling angle, even if you aren't hoping to publish your project. An angle, after all, is just a way of coming at a topic. In fact, it's just another way of talking about finding our story. Let's remember—finding your story means finding about at least three things: character, narrative, and conflict, and how they come together.

In our photograph here, let's start by just exploring some of the options. Think about this image as the "minutes" version of our last exercise. Now we need to turn it into a story. What are the facts we have to work with; and especially, who are the possible characters? There are at least nine, aren't there? Did you get nine? If you didn't, pause for a moment and have a hard look. What are all of the possible perspectives on this story implied by the structure of this photograph?

There's the running soldier; the two soldiers crouching; the three civilians watching; and if you're doing that math in your head, you'll realize that's six. Who are those seventh and eighth and ninth characters? That's probably where you got stumped if you didn't come up with nine immediately. Think about it. Remember how in our last example we talked about how powerful thinking outside the immediate frame can be? Remember what we said about how the story changed if we started our scene during that blind date with the woman's telephone conversation with her boss instead? What are the other three perspectives just beyond the margins of this image?

One, our seventh, is the character of man who's the target of this gunfire; someone who history tells us is a faceless, nameless German sniper. The eighth character is the person who took the photograph, the photojournalist. If we wanted, we might even, with a bit of research, be able to find out his name or learn about his—or maybe her even—wartime experiences. The ninth person is you, the viewer. You can't tell the story from the first-hand perspective, because you weren't there to witness it; to imply that you were would be breaking the nonfiction contract. But you're witnessing it in the present; you're looking at this photograph, aren't you? You can write about that. The author can always be, in creative nonfiction, one of the characters.

The characters outside the immediate frame aren't always better. You could write a great scene that focused on that man standing on the window ledge, or one focused on the solider caught in mid-motion. But we want to keep in mind all our options, because what matters just as much as character is finding our narrative and the conflict. After all, the obvious conflict is the one between the man in the photograph who is shooting and—why else would all those soldiers be crouching and hiding?—his armed target.

But look at the image again. What are the other possible conflicts in this story? Or think of it another way: What are the different stakes that history tells us were in this singular moment present? What did you come up with?

Maybe you noticed that one of the men crouching is in fatigues and the man next to him is wearing formal military uniform. There's a difference here of rank and wartime experience. Surely the voyeuristic civilians have a different investment from the soldiers in the midst of combat. One civilian has climbed up on a window ledge that has a better view of the action. In fact, doesn't it make you wonder? Why does that civilian appear so confident that he's not the target? He's standing tall and looking out boldly. Or, wait; maybe he isn't a voyeur at all. Maybe he's a brave man who has recklessly offered to keep watch; an ordinary citizen drawn into duty in a dangerous national moment. Or how about the man running in the foreground of the photograph, what might be his story and his stake in the dramatic tension? Is it something he's running away from, or running toward?

What you'll see immediately is that if we have characters, and if we can find their motivations and their stakes in the events that are unfolding, the narrative arc begins to take shape in our minds.

This image captures just a single moment; and without knowing more, and doing some research, we can't write a nonfiction story yet. We don't have a sequence of actions yet, so we don't have an arc. We don't have dialogue. We'd need to know more about the setting and the characters to make a great piece of narrative, because in nonfiction, it's still the same thing: We can't make up any of the details. But if we wanted, we could go and find them. Maybe we could write an important book about it.

As an exercise in learning how to shape and craft storytelling, looking at photographs, listening in on bits of conversation, those are all fabulous ways to think about what's powerful and interesting. It can be an excellent place to start your research and to start your thinking.

Why don't you practice this same exercise now on your own? The best place to look is an old family album. After all, you don't need to do research. You know the characters; you know the narrative possibilities. But remember, you're looking for a photograph that has great dramatic tension. Learning to recognize narrative potential in a scene is actually the critical skill to master. Finding the right photograph might not come easily; it's maybe the hardest part of the assignment. But it's also a great way to make sure you really understood those three key principles from this lesson: the importance of character, narrative arc, and conflict in storytelling. In the lessons that follow, we're going to start building on them as our foundation. For now, find a photograph and keep thinking about where our stories begin, what's at stake in them, and all the different ways as a writer you can frame them.

Honoring the Nonfiction Contract

Lecture 3

Part of writing nonfiction means making a commitment to telling the truth. That can leave the novice wondering where exactly there is room for creativity. By looking at examples of creativity from two memoirists—Maxine Hong Kingston, who did it the right way, and James Frey, who infamously did it the wrong way—we can begin to see the shape of the nonfiction contract the author makes with the reader.

The Nonfiction Contract

- As your writing becomes more ambitious, you will likely want to take on larger and more complicated topics. That means you will need to do the kind of research that will let you put words into the mouths of your characters and maybe even write about their innermost feelings and motivations.

- This brings us back to the **nonfiction contract** and, in particular, the line between fact and interpretation. What do we do as writers when we really need to know something to move our story forward and we just cannot find it? How do we write about things beyond our experience and feel confident that we are doing it truthfully?

- One of the best ways to examine this issue is by looking at authors who got it wrong—who broke the nonfiction contract with their readers.

- Think about a moment in your life when you heard someone say something untrue or unfair about you. For most of us, the reaction is distress, pain, embarrassment, and anger.

- Because we write nonfiction, our characters are real people. If they are living people, we risk causing that same pain to others. Even if they are long dead, people may feel strongly about them or their reputations.

Why "Creative Nonfiction"?

- Until a decade or so ago, the term "creative nonfiction" did not exist, but narrative historical writing did. The roots of creative nonfiction actually lie in 20th-century literary journalism, the kind of work that someone like Ernest Hemingway wrote for a magazine like *Colliers*.

- Conventional, commercial journalism was cool, detached, and objective. It reported the facts and named names, but it did not try to bring the people in those stories to life as characters. Literary journalists like Hemingway and his colleagues—often struggling literary writers—took a different approach, reporting the news from a firsthand, personal perspective.

- These same techniques started appearing more and more, often in histories. In the 1970s especially, authors become interested in writing history from the perspectives of "average" people—people whose experiences were not covered in books about monarchs and presidents. Since the technique was being used outside journalism, the term "literary journalism" no longer fit.

- Another good reason for not using the term "literary journalism" any longer touches on ethical issues. For several decades now, television has been supplanting print journalism as the primary source of news, and more and more often, the television shows with the greatest number of viewers are those that blur the boundaries between reporting and satire or between journalism and commentary.

- Thus journalism does not always keep the nonfiction contract today, which is fine as long as the reader or viewer understands the nature of the bargain. Few viewers confuse satirical programming with factual reporting. In fact, getting the joke is part of the pleasure.

- The word "journalism" no longer automatically and reliably implies "I didn't make anything up," and it does not imply the same boundaries about commentary and interpretation.

- If writing creative nonfiction means having to walk such a fine line, why would an author want to write nonfiction instead of fiction? Because there is something powerful about reality. True stories teach us something about what it means to be human and what it means to struggle and triumph in life. True stories introduce us to amazing characters, characters who are all the more amazing for being real.

- Imagine you are writing a memoir about something terrible, criminal, or painful. As an author, you have an unquestionable right to write about your own experience. Yet people's perceptions of events change over the course of their lifetimes. You might think, "Why can't I decide what perception I want to have now? You know, the one that would make for a good story?"

- The answer is simple: You made a deal with your reader. If you want to alter your story, you do not have to call it nonfiction. You can write your life as a novel, and no one will make a peep about the changes you made.

The *Million Little Pieces* Scandal

- The only reasons to call a novel a piece of nonfiction are either to trick your readers or—more likely—to increase sales. The publishing world—and a whole lot of readers—tend to see this as fraud.

- One of the biggest scandals in the history of creative nonfiction involved the 2003 "memoir" by James Frey, *A Million Little Pieces*. He had tried to sell the manuscript as a novel, but it was rejected. When he billed it as a true story, it was published.

- The book tells the brutal story of his drug addiction and the people he met during his time in a rehab clinic. It was compelling human drama full of vivid characters, conflict, and tension.

- After Oprah Winfrey named it one of her Book Club selections, *A Million Little Pieces* became a national bestseller and made its author a great deal of money. His book was inspirational, especially for those struggling with addiction, and best of all, it was all true. Except, of course, it was not.

- Frey invented both character and narrative. The foundation of his work was always firmly in the world of fiction. When the press revealed the truth in 2006, Oprah Winfrey and many of Frey's readers were furious. There were lawsuits and refunds.

- Frey's excuse, found in the "Note to Readers" published in later editions of the book, tells us a lot about what writers know about storytelling: "I wanted the stories in the book to ebb and flow, to have dramatic arcs, to have the tension that all great stories require."

Doing It Right—*The Woman Warrior*

- The scandal raises some important questions about how writers of creative nonfiction manage telling stories when there are gaps in the information. The nonfiction contract does not mean the writer cannot speculate; it means you must be honest that that is what you are doing.

- You can even use what you do not know into a way to establish the author as a character. Memoirist Maxine Hong Kingston uses this technique in *The Woman Warrior*, a memoir of growing up in a Chinese American family.

- Hong Kingston's book returns again and again to the one thing she does not know about—and no one in her family will talk about—the story of her aunt, who committed suicide in China. It is a wonderful example of one way a writer can tell only what *can* be known.

- In her opening passage, Hong Kingston uses subtle word choices to acknowledge the limits of her information:

> You must not tell anyone, my mother said, what I am about to tell you. In China your father had a sister who killed herself. She jumped into the family well. … She *may have* gone to the pigsty as a last act of responsibility: … It was *probably* a girl; there is some hope of forgiveness for boys. [Emphasis added.]

- Since this is a work of nonfiction, the author had the option to leave the story of her aunt out. But this is a book about family secrets and what they do to us, so the secret is critical.

Hong Kingston's memoir recalls life in rural China—but not her own.

- Instead, the author uses the story her mother told her about the secret as her book's opening. This accomplishes several goals: It makes the aunt a compelling character; it makes the author a character and her quest to discover the secret a motivation, and it places the notion of secrets front and center in the book.

- We hear this history from the perspective of the other family members. The details change, but in every case, Hong Kingston keeps the contract with her reader and alerts us with her word choice. This book, she tells us, is historically accurate *unless* I give you the cue that I am imagining something.

The Liberation of Paris Revisited—A Writing Exercise

- Before the next lecture, think back to that photograph of the Liberation of Paris and choose one of the characters. Write a brief sketch in which you develop the character of one of the figures in—or outside—the frame of the story, using all the techniques you have learned about so far while honoring the nonfiction contract.

Important Term

nonfiction contract: The implied agreement between a reader and a writer that the author of creative nonfiction does not invent any facts in his or her storytelling.

Suggested Reading

Frey, *A Million Little Pieces*.

Hong Kingston, *The Woman Warrior*.

"James Frey and the Million Little Pieces Controversy."

Krakauer, *Three Cups of Deceit*.

Mortenson, *Three Cups of Tea*.

Questions to Consider

1. What does the creative nonfiction contract mean, and why is it important?

2. What do you think about the public controversies surrounding authors who have broken the creative nonfiction contract? Would you ask for your money back from a publisher if you were to learn that an author had knowingly presented fiction as fact?

Honoring the Nonfiction Contract

Lecture 3—Transcript

In our last lesson, we learned about the three foundational elements of storytelling—character, narrative arc, and conflict—and how to recognize them in an image or a conversation. But as your writing becomes more ambitious, you'll likely want to take on larger and more complicated topics. You'll learn to connect scenes to one another in an exciting narrative arc, and maybe you'll start to bring in some of your own historical research, the kind of research that will let you start putting words into the mouths of your historical characters and maybe even let you start writing about their innermost feelings and motivations. After all, you already know how important those tools are to a writer in building character. Maybe you'll want to bring your work to readers and try to get it published. That would be a fabulous goal for any writer.

Before you do any of this, though, let's take just a small step backward. Let's think with some greater subtlety about what we've already said was the nonfiction contract. In the introductory lecture, remember how I said that it was a controversial topic and a fascinating contemporary ethical issue? In the world of writing today, it's one of the most interesting and complicated. After all, what's the fine line between historical fact and interpretation? What are our responsibilities to our memories, even distant ones? And just on a practical level, what do we do as writers when we really need to know something in order to move our story forward and we just can't find it? How do we write about things beyond our experience and feel confident that we're doing it truthfully? One more thing: Let's think about the very idea of a contract with a reader. As writers, what is our relationship to our audience? What does the reader expect of us in any kind of story, and do we have to deliver?

Over the course of this class, we'll look at several examples of how some writers got it right and the craft-level techniques that we can learn from them. But first, let's think for a minute about the writers who got it wrong and what that also tells us about storytelling.

Here's a little exercise: Think for a moment about a time in your life when you heard someone say something untrue or unfair about you. Can you remember one? It happens to everybody. Maybe it was the kind of adolescent schoolyard gossip circulated by a mean-spirited classmate; maybe it was a workplace story fueled by a jealous colleague; maybe an ugly moment at the end of a love affair; maybe the kind of allegations made in one of life's emotional tangles; or maybe someone just misheard you, or misunderstood, or got carried away and exaggerated. But think of that moment: How did it feel? For most of us, the reaction is distress, pain, embarrassment, and often anger and those feelings are part of what a creative nonfiction writer always needs to remember; because if we can't invent things that means just one thing: Our characters are other people. When those people are distant historical figures, we're safe from their wrath. With living people, ones you know, the chances are much higher.

What's even more interesting is to think about this a bit philosophically: What are the ethical issues here, and why do we think about readers and writers having contracts? Remember in the beginning how I said creative nonfiction was a new, emergent, fourth genre? It makes you kind of wonder where it came from and why, doesn't it? It's currently the fastest growing genre in the book market, and it's the fastest growing part of many creative writing programs. In fact, until a decade or so ago, getting an MFA—that's a Masters of Fine Arts, the most popular graduate degree for creative writers—in creative nonfiction was almost impossible, and that's because the term hadn't yet been invented.

But just because the term "creative nonfiction" hadn't been invented, that doesn't mean that narrative historical writing didn't exist. Of course it did. Some people might argue that it's been around since the first history books were written. But, actually, the roots of creative nonfiction aren't in the history book as much as they're in the first newspapers. For much of the 20th century, people thought of this kind of writing as literary journalism, great gumshoe investigative journalism, the kind of work that someone like Ernest Hemingway published for a magazine like *Colliers*; the kind of riveting pieces of reporting that won someone a Pulitzer Prize.

Those in-depth pieces weren't like the mainstream kind of reporting. Conventional, commercial journalism was cool, detached, and objective. It reported the facts and named names, but it didn't try to bring those people to life as characters in stories. It didn't worry about having its own compelling narrative to engage the readers. If readers wanted drama, the facts of the event would have to provide them. No wonder scandalous stories were a popular favorite.

Outside this mainstream, though, was a cadre of journalists who took a different tack. These were the writers who wrote longer pieces for magazines like *Life* and *The New Yorker*, especially during the Second World War and the conflicts of the 1960s and 1970s. These were people—and often, no surprise, they were also struggling literary writers—who reported stories from a first-hand perspective. They turned journalism into a great narrative story. They also found their angle—and also their arcs and conflicts and characters—on assignment and told them as stories; and readers enjoyed it. Increasingly, it became a feature of mainstream journalism, and for a long time "literary journalism" was the word for what we now call creative nonfiction.

Why come up with that new term anyhow? First, a couple of reasons: These same techniques started appearing more and more in other historical books. In the 1970s especially, authors became interested in writing history from the perspective of average working people: women, immigrants, people whose experiences sometimes didn't get covered in books about the great politicians, kings and queens, and presidents. It was a new angle on the story, and that's what writers are always looking for. Because there were more of these "man-on-the-street" type subjects, the authors writing biography, history, and ultimately autobiography started drawing on those compelling journalistic ways of crafting more vivid and personal narratives.

Still, what was the need for a new term? It's very simple: Narrative nonfiction now wasn't just happening in journalism at all. We needed a broader category that could describe a whole range of different kinds of books that all used the same literary or creative strategies.

But there's another good reason for not using the term "literary journalism" any longer, too, and it's part of what's interesting about the nonfiction contract with a reader. It's part of the ethical controversy certain works in the creative nonfiction genre can sometimes generate also. Today, journalism is changing rapidly. Traditional print media like the newspaper are being replaced by digital formats. For several decades now, of course, many of us have used television and not the written word as our primary source of current information; and more and more often, the television shows with the greatest numbers of viewers and the highest rankings are those that blur the boundaries between reporting and satire, between journalism and commentary.

The trouble is journalism itself doesn't always keep the nonfiction contract today; and that's fine, as long as the reader or the viewer understands the nature of the bargain. Few viewers confuse satirical programming with factual reporting, and so few viewers get angry. In fact, getting the joke is part of the pleasure. The trouble for writers of creative nonfiction, though, is that the word "journalism" no longer automatically and reliably implies "I didn't make anything up when I'm telling you this story." It doesn't imply the same boundaries about commentary or interpretation either. Journalism won't work any longer to describe what really is a separate category; so although some people argue that we should now call it "literary nonfiction" or "the literature of fact," you should expect to see the term "creative nonfiction" stick around for a good while to come.

Of course, for creative nonfiction writers, things aren't always straightforward either. You already know the essential creative nonfiction contract. If it were a bumper sticker, it would read very simply "No Fair Inventing." But what's the line between logical historical inference and invention; and when does setting the scene or drawing character cross the line into imagining? This question of fairness—to whom does a writer have to be loyal anyhow?—what are we going to do with that? If writing the creative nonfiction contract means having to walk this fine line and having to promise not to make up any of the parts of your story, why would an author want to write creative nonfiction instead of fiction anyhow?

Actually, let's answer that last question first: Why not just write fiction? Let's think about it. Have you ever bought a book because you knew it was based on a true story? Have you ever watched a documentary or reality-based TV show or video? Why did you do that? There's something powerful about reality, isn't there? True stories teach us something about what it means to be human, what it means to struggle and triumph in life; true stories show us the characters of amazing or wonderful or terrifying people, people who we might actually have encountered, had place and time made it possible. The thing is, true stories have a different kind of power than fiction; and because of this, the market for people looking to read them is also larger in many cases. So why write nonfiction? Because it's uniquely powerful, and because the opportunities for publishing are much greater. Remember, if you want to write fiction, all the same strategies of storytelling apply to those genres, too.

If you do decide to write creative nonfiction, then, how do you answer those other questions? What's the line between historical inference and invention? When does setting scene or drawing characters cross the line into imagining? To whom does a writer have to be loyal? We know that how we represent other people has the power to wound; and when what's written isn't factually accurate, it's not a bad way for an author to find him or herself in an expensive lawsuit for libel, either. But the other party to whom an author owes loyalty is the reader. The creative nonfiction writer actually has more than one contract to manage.

Let's look at some famous examples of where authors found themselves on the wrong side of this line in one way or another. Imagine you're writing a memoir about something terrible or criminal or inevitably painful. As an author, you have an unquestionable right to write about your own experience. The only catch is that if you lead your readers to believe that what you are telling is a true story, you're still bound by the nonfiction contract. But it's my experience, you might think; why can't I make up the details of my life story? How is anyone ever going to know what I was really thinking at that moment? Geez, everyone knows that people can have completely different perceptions of an event over the course of living, why can't I just decide what perception I want to have now? You know, the one that would make for a good story.

The answer is simple: You made a deal with your reader. You don't have to call your story "nonfiction." You can write your life as a novel and no one will make a peep about it. You can write in the voice even of a first-person narrator who insists on the first page of every chapter "this story is true history," even if every word of it's invented. You just have to put a note at the front of your book that says to the reader, "Enjoy my story. It's actually fiction." And you can't write on the back of your book cover, "Amazing true story." Instead, up in that small print in the corner on the back of a book cover, where it tells you what this book takes as a genre, you need to print "Fiction."

The problem comes with this: The thing that most of us are most deeply compelled by is true stories. People's lives and the crazy things that happen in the world are fascinating; and books about real people living through real events often sell much better than books of fiction. Since the only reasons to call your novel a piece of nonfiction are either to trick your readers or—more likely—to increase sales, the world of publishing, and a whole lot of readers, tend to see this as a kind of fraud and crass betrayal. By publishing your book—some would say even by circulating it; by sharing it with even a single reader—you're entering into a contract that's essential.

This is what happened with one of the biggest scandals in the history of creative nonfiction as a genre. In 2003, an author named James Frey published a nonfiction memoir with the title *A Million Little Pieces*. He'd tried to sell it to his publisher as a novel and it was rejected. But when he billed it as a true story, it was published. In the memoir, he tells the brutal story of his drug addiction and the people that he met during his time in a rehab clinic.

It was a compelling human drama. There were vivid characters. There was plenty of conflict and tension. There were hair-raising moments on the narrative arc that went from abuse to recovery. When Oprah Winfrey read the book and named it one of her Book Club picks, it was because, for many people with addictions, it was a story of triumph and inspiration. *A Million Little Pieces* became a national bestseller, and it made its author a great deal of money. Best of all, it was all true, he told his readers. What an amazing life, and what an amazing story.

Except, of course, it wasn't: Frey had invented much of his life story; he had invented other characters; and, in a way, once you begin thinking about the nonfiction contract, you have a little bit of sympathy for him. Imagine how difficult it would be to write these kinds of terrible things about other people. Our right to tell our own story is one thing; but do we have the right to tell the stories of other people in their darkest moments, especially when we happen to meet them in rehabilitation? It's easy to understand the temptation to invent your characters; to make your inspiration unrecognizable. But it still broke the contract.

Frey didn't just invent characters; he invented the details of his own experience, too. He invented, in other words, both character and narrative. The foundation of his work was always firmly in the world of fiction. When the press revealed his secret betrayal of his reader, Oprah Winfrey and many of Frey's readers were furious. There were lawsuits and refunds; and Frey's response to the controversy tells us a lot about what writers know about storytelling. "I wanted," he explained, "the stories in the book to ebb and flow, to have dramatic arcs, to have the tension that all great stories require."

Think back to our exercise about the minutes of the hypothetical meeting between Mr. A and Ms. B. Did you have the temptation to make up facts because it made a better story? The problem: that nonfiction contract; "No Fair Inventing." But maybe now a little part of you feels some sympathy for Frey. It's hard working just with the available and sometimes limited facts when you want to tell a great story, right? You might have struggled with this feeling when you were doing our first two course exercises.

That scandal raises some important questions about how, as writers of creative nonfiction, we're going to manage telling stories when there are gaps in our information. The nonfiction contract doesn't mean the writer can't speculate; it just means that you have to be honest that that's what you're doing. In fact, you can turn what you don't know into a great way to establish the author as a character even. What do I mean? Let's look at an example of how a writer walks successfully the nonfiction line, shall we?

One of the best examples is the writing of the memoirist Maxine Hong Kingston in her book *The Woman Warrior*. It's the story of her family and the experience of growing up Chinese American; and there's one thing she doesn't know about, and no one will talk about it either: The story of her aunt, who committed suicide in China. She doesn't know anything about the life of this aunt beyond the barest details, and for one important reason: Everyone in the family refuses to talk about it. She's one of those great skeletons in the family closet.

Essentially, then, Hong Kingston as a writer is working with more or less the same kind of information you had in our exercise about the couple who went on their blind date in that café; or the same kind of information you had about what was really happening in that World War II photograph. That means—as you discovered yourself—she doesn't have very much information at all. Yet what she does with it is a wonderful example of one way a writer can tell a great story and tell only what can be known as well.

Let's listen to what she writes. As you're listening, I have a few hints for you: Listen for subtle changes in verb tenses. What is it this author does to acknowledge the limits of her information, and how does she turn that not into a problem of storytelling, but into an essential part of it?

Here's the passage:

> "You must not tell anyone," my mother said, "what I am about to tell you. In China your father had a sister who killed herself. She jumped into the family well. …
>
> "On the night the baby was to be born the villagers raided our house. …
>
> Their knives dripped with the blood of our animals. They smeared blood on the doors and walls. One woman swung a chicken, whose throat she had slit, splattering blood in red arcs about her. We stood together in the middle of our house, in the family hall with the pictures and tables of the ancestors around us, and looked straight ahead. …

> "Your aunt gave birth in the pigsty that night. The next morning when I went for water, I found her and the baby plugging up the family well. …"
>
> It was probably a girl; there is some hope of forgiveness for boys.

If you're like me, you found this story heartbreaking. You thought to yourself: This poor woman, driven to such a terrible act of desperation. The blackness of the sky, the brutal destruction of her family home are all so vivid; and that image of her walking to the well to drown herself and her baby as a last act of compassion for a child no one will love is awful to hear. What must she have felt, this nameless aunt whose name has been erased from this family's history.

When we have these questions about a character—what it must have been like for her, how she might have felt; so identification and compassion—that means the writer has done something important: She's brought a character to life. We identify with the experience; we're drawn into the story. We want to know more: What happened? That's what happens when we have in front of us a good story.

But for now, let's think about the problem Maxine Hong Kingston faced in telling her story. What she had was the problem of not having certain facts about a certain critical part of her family's history, wasn't it? Think about it: She knows almost nothing about her dead aunt. Her mother won't even speak her name. But the search for the story of this nameless aunt is part of what her book is all about.

Since this is a work of nonfiction, what are the author's options? She could leave the story of her aunt out. After all, she doesn't know the history, right? Except the thing is, this a book about family secrets and what they do to us. This secret is critical. On the one hand, what we've got here is a creative nonfiction writer, and the contract with the reader says that we can't make things up and represent them as factual history.

From a writer's perspective, Maxine Hong Kingston also has one huge technical dilemma: These are the first pages of her book. Think about all the things you know about writing a great story. You've probably heard that it's important to have a fabulous beginning so your reader will want to be hooked from the start and will keep reading. It's true, beginnings are crucial; and you can't start your story with a flat character, because that's just not interesting. That means the aunt has to come to life for us as a character. If you as a reader don't care about the story of this aunt, you won't care about Hong Kingston's memoir either. These are the first pages of her book. The fact of the matter is that most of us decide whether to continue reading a book within a few minutes of starting it. If we get bored at the beginning, are we really going to read on? How long are you going to give a writer to interest you? For most of us, it's not long at all, and that's why writers always tell you that if there's one thing that's essential it's a good beginning.

So what does Hong Kingston do? Something we talked about being an important possibility in that photograph of the Liberation of Paris: the fact that in creative nonfiction the writer can always be one of the characters. We'll talk a lot more about using this technique of the author-as-character in lesson 13 because it can bring with it some special problems and challenges, too; but what it lets Hong Kingston in her book do is invent a story for her aunt that makes her human as a character while keeping the nonfiction contract. "What you are saying?" you're thinking, "She's going to invent a character and call it nonfiction?" Well, yes. This is part of what writing from the first-person perspective in a memoir lets us do, as long as we're honest with the reader about the line between historical fact and our reaction to it.

Think back again to the Hong Kingston passage. In her story, she begins with the tale her mother told her about the secret; about what happened to the family's home. We hear this history from the perspective of the other family members. We learn that the aunt's story has been silenced. It's the one thing no one will talk about. Did you notice how Hong Kingston told us, "Hey, look, this part is all straight family history"? But when Hong Kingston turns to telling the story of what she imagines must've happened to her aunt, she tells her readers exactly that: "I'm going to imagine for a minute," she says. "I'm going to sketch out some of the possibilities for a moment."

What she does that's technically wonderful is she tells the reader how to read the passage and then just tells her story, leaving along the way subtle markers that remind us, "Hey, this bit is speculation." "She may have gone to the pigsty," she writes. "It was probably a girl." Those are the words that keep us honest, and the rest is just spectacular storytelling. She lets herself imagine for a moment as our first-person narrator that this book isn't fiction; it's a memoir about a real person, writing about another real person. Hong Kingston keeps the contract with her reader: "This book," she's telling us, "it's historically accurate unless I give you the cue that I'm imagining something." As writers, if we want to speculate about those gaps in our knowledge in a biography or memoir or any other nonfiction project, there's just one rule: We owe it to our readers to be honest about it. We need to use verbs like "must have" or "might have." We need to write "perhaps" or "maybe." We need to say to the reader, "Look, here's what I think this must have meant; how it must have been in that moment."

That's your exercise for the next lesson: Think back to that photograph taken on the streets of World-War-II-era Paris and choose one of the characters. Write a brief sketch in which you develop the character of one of the figures in or outside the frame of the story using all the techniques you've learned about so far and, above all, making sure you're also honoring the nonfiction contract.

Writing Great Beginnings

Lecture 4

Great beginnings need exactly what great stories as a whole need: character, conflict, and narrative arc. By examining great beginnings in both fiction and nonfiction, you will find that these three characteristics are interrelated: Interesting characters are conflicted; characters with conflict have come from somewhere and are going somewhere. Learning to write beginnings well involves choosing the moment when conflict drives the character to act and presenting it so that the reader wants to know what follows.

The Power of Secrets

- There are ways to keep the nonfiction contract with the reader and still leave room for speculation and interpretation. In fact, when there are things we cannot know about the past, it is sometimes our only option.

- One of the hardest parts of telling a story is beginning it. Once you commit to a beginning moment, from that moment certain things must follow. Any writer might find that daunting.

- It is actually pretty simple to find out whether you have a great beginning or not. Think back to Maxine Hong Kingston's example: "You must not tell anyone, my mother said, what I am about to tell you. In China your father had a sister who killed herself. She jumped into the family well."

- How do these sentences hook you? This particular story begins with a secret. Secrets are always tantalizing. Plus, the nature of the secret is highly dramatic, and human drama captures our attention as readers, too.

- In addition to the secret her family keeps from her, there is the secret Hong Kingston is (temporarily) keeping from us: Why did her aunt kill herself, and why does the family say it as if she had never been born? Who is this family, anyway?

Character—What Makes One Interesting

- Not every story can begin with a secret. But secrets are one example of what all great openings have. What a secret does is put two or more characters into some kind of conflict. Someone does not want someone else to know something.

- A secret also implies that something has happened before this story begins. It also implies where the story in part might be headed—the fight to keep or to learn the secret. That means what we have is a narrative arc, a story already in motion.

- In Lecture 2, we said every good story needs character, conflict, and narrative arc. A good opening needs to establish all three in the first few sentences, and a secret is one efficient way of doing that.

- There are many other ways to establish these elements in an opening, and it is a good idea to look for these in everything you read. We can look at a few examples from fiction as well.

- The opening line of C. S. Lewis's 1950 children's novel *The Voyage of the Dawn Treader* reads, "There was a boy called Eustace Clarence Scrubb, and he almost deserved it."

    - We have a character: a boy with an unfortunate name who *almost* deserves it. He must be a real challenge, but also sympathetic, or it would not be *almost*.

    - We have conflict: If Eustace were just rotten to the core, there would not be any tension to be resolved; the same applies if he were an angel. The fact that Eustace *almost* deserves such a terrible name makes things complicated.

    - We have narrative arc: Eustace has done something to *almost* deserve his name. Lewis has piqued our curiosity about that and about whether he will be a better boy or a worse one by the story's end.

- Here is the opening sentence to Sylvia Plath's novel *The Bell Jar*, from 1963: "It was a queer, sultry summer, the summer they electrocuted the Rosenbergs, and I didn't know what I was doing in New York."

- The clause "I didn't know what I was doing in New York" tells us we have an internally conflicted character. The connection between her story and a pair of infamous spies suggests conflict in the external atmosphere. Even the word "queer"—not a word typically applied to "summer"—heightens this sense of discomfort.

Conflict—What Motivates Characters … and Readers

- What conclusions can we draw from these two examples? First of all, we seem to have established that the core of an interesting character is some sort of conflict—be it internal (with the self) or external (with other people). In fact, conflict, as we will see, is the key to telling an interesting story in general.

- Conflict can be presented straightforwardly or subtly. Sylvia Plath's narrator tells us outright that she does not know what she is doing. Eustace, on the other hand, may not even be aware of his own conflict, even though the narrator sees his mixed good and bad qualities.

- These two characters are complex characters. The opposite of a complex character is a stock character. These are characters whose qualities are fixed and static. They never change; they have no real life or personality. They are not the characters to begin your story with, not if you want the reader to be interested.

- What makes a character interesting is the thing that does not seem to fit or does not meet our expectations about who this person appears to be. Perhaps it is a character who does not know his own motivations. Perhaps it is someone who is irritating yet somehow charming. Perhaps it is a character who is out of her depth.

Narrative Arc—Character in Motion

- What does the term "narrative arc" really mean in practice? Narrative arc is when action implies consequences. Something happens, and the reader knows something else must inevitably follow from that event. If there is an action from which nothing follows—if there are no consequences—then there is no story.

- Let's look at how character and conflict come together to create narrative arc by looking at the same story opening told two different ways:

  Example 1: Mrs. Maas was named the executor of the will of a friend who was a real estate developer. The letter arrived in the mail. Rich people often have complicated business affairs so it ended up being a little bit of work. There was a summer party on the afternoon the letter arrived.

  Example 2: One summer afternoon Mrs. Oedipa Maas came home from a Tupperware party whose hostess had put perhaps too much kirsch in the fondue to find that she, Oedipa, had been named executor, or she supposed executrix, of the estate of one Pierce Inverarity, a California real estate mogul who had once lost two million dollars in his spare time but still had assets numerous and tangled enough to make the job of sorting it all out more than honorary.

- In example one, we learn barely more than Mrs. Maas's last name. In the second example—which comes from Thomas Pynchon's novel *The Crying of Lot 49*—we have strange and symbolic names, a bit of suburban debauchery, and even some insight into both Inverarity's and Oedipa's personalities—his money troubles, her way with words. We know right off, this is going to be a strange story.

- How about conflict and narrative arc? In example one, there is very little. She is named executrix of a businessman's will, and it will be a bit of work. So what? Pychon's beginning, on the other hand, is rife with conflict. Inverarity has almost certainly left his business affairs in a muddle, and Oedipa has lost a friend and gained a complicated job she did not ask for.

The Three-Sentence Beginning—A Writing Exercise

- Now it is your turn to compose a great beginning for your story—whatever story you want to write. It is a very simple exercise, with just three steps.

    - Step one: Write a sentence where the reader wants to read the next sentence that is going to come after. In other words, write a sentence that has character, conflict, and narrative arc.

    - Step two: Write the sentence that comes after your first one. Make sure this one also leaves the reader wanting to read the next one.

    - Step three: write one more sentence after that.

- After you have written your three sentences, reread them and ask yourself the same questions we have been asking about good beginnings throughout this lecture. Do your sentences establish character, conflict, and narrative arc? If not, revise them until they do.

- If you are having trouble getting started, do not worry; that is normal. But it is important that you practice these skills. Here are some **story starters** to work with:

    - Think of a secret. It could be anything, mundane or important. Then, imagine you were not going to tell someone this secret but you wanted to drop a hint that there was a secret you are keeping from them. (Remember, when working with secrets, less is often more.)

- Imagine that two people are having a terrible phone conversation. It could be about absolutely anything, but it is an upsetting conversation. Now, imagine that you can only hear one side of it—the side of the person who is mostly doing the listening Describe what you see and what he or she says and does.

Important Term

story starter: The combination of character, conflict, and narrative that sets a story in motion—an essential element of a great beginning.

Suggested Reading

Ensign, *Great Beginnings*.

Lewis, *The Voyage of the Dawn Treader*.

Plath, *The Bell Jar*.

Pynchon, *The Crying of Lot 49*.

Questions to Consider

1. Think about the memorable characters you've encountered in your reading life. Why does your favorite character stay in your mind so vividly? Does he or she have the kind of internal conflict we have been talking about?

2. Thinking back over this lesson, what would you say to someone who suggested that, if you can't find a good way to start your narrative, you could just skip that for the moment and come back to it later? Would that work as a strategy? Why or why not?

Writing Great Beginnings

Lecture 4—Transcript

In the last lesson, we talked about the nonfiction contract and why it's sometimes tempting to cut corners when the truth—or when what we can't know about the truth—gets in the way of our telling a gripping story. Spicing things up is a real temptation, and sometimes protecting other people's feelings leads us to wish we could rewrite history. But if we want to write creative nonfiction, all of this is beyond the rules of the game. If we're inventing things, the only fair thing to do is call our book a wonderful new novel, a work of fiction.

But just because we aren't tricking our readers by calling something we've invented "true history," that doesn't mean we aren't using creative strategies. In fact, we're using all those same strategies of spinning a tale as a novelist, aren't we? There are ways to keep the nonfiction contract with the reader and still leave room for speculation and interpretation. In fact, when there are things we can't know about the past, it's sometimes our only option.

One of the hardest parts of telling that fabulous story is the beginning, isn't it? In writing, there's nothing harder. Until that moment you write your first sentence, everything is possible. Once you commit to a beginning, though, you've set a story in motion; and from that moment, certain things must follow. It's daunting isn't it? Have you ever thought, "I have a great story to tell, I just don't know how to begin it?" Want me to show you how? It's actually pretty simple to find out whether you have a great beginning or not. Sure, writing a great beginning is hard. I'm not going to tell you that's easy; writing isn't easy. But knowing when you have a great opening line is something you can learn to do just in the course of the next lesson.

Let's think back to that Hong Kingston example that we were talking about in lesson three. In particular, let's look at how she sets her story in motion. Remember how she wrote, " 'You must not tell anyone,' my mother said, 'what I am about to tell you. In China your father had a sister who killed herself. She jumped into the family well' "? Those are wonderful first sentences; and let's just look at them logically and see what lessons we can deduce from them about what a great beginning does. Let's read them again;

and this time, think about where these three sentences grab your interest as a reader. How do they hook you, and what conclusions can you draw from them about what a good beginning needs to do for a reader? Here they are again: " 'You must not tell anyone,' my mother said, 'what I am about to tell you. In China your father had a sister who killed herself. She jumped into the family well.' "

What did you notice? Maybe you noticed how the story begins with the idea of a secret. Secrets are always tantalizing. Maybe you were gripped by the idea of the aunt dying in such a dramatic and awful way. Human drama captures our attention as readers, too. Then, of course, there's this thing we can't quite understand: Why did she kill herself; why does the family say it's as if she'd never been born; and who is this family? There's a story here, and we want to know what it is. That's what makes this a great beginning.

But let's break it down a little bit more; after all, what is human drama? Does a good story always have to start, then, with a secret? Let's start with that last question, because it's one of the easiest ones: Of course every story can't begin with a secret; that would be limiting ourselves too much as writers. But think about what a secret does; it's part of something larger that all good beginnings do have. Secrets are interesting because they automatically imply two things: First, that we have here at least two characters, and that they're in some kind of conflict. Someone doesn't want someone else to do something. Someone has a motivation. As readers, we don't know something that we're now curious about. The second thing: A secret implies that something has come before. Learning the secret or keeping the secret might be what happens next; that's part of where this story is heading. But there's a back story here, isn't there? There's always a back story to secrets, in fact. There's always some reason why someone feels compelled to keep them, right? That's a story in itself.

That means that what we've got here is a narrative arc; we've got a story already in motion. Think back to what we said in lesson two about what every good story needs: character, conflict, and narrative arc. A good opening needs to establish all three in the first few sentences. Let me repeat that: What makes a great opening? It's a couple of sentences that do three things: They establish vivid character; they tell the reader that there's some kind of tension between characters, or perhaps some kind of internal conflict within a single character; and they set a story in motion. Often, they imply also that something has come before; that this dramatic tension between characters is the result of something that came before, something as readers we want to understand. We call that internal momentum narrative arc.

If you're thinking ahead, you're probably wondering, "Ok, great, but how do I establish vivid character? What does tension in a great beginning look like? What does a narrative arc really mean?" We're going to turn to all those great questions in future lessons. Here, let's just think today about what we need to know about them to get them to write a great opening; to get you started with your writing. To do that, let's just practice for a minute recognizing these elements in a great opening line.

How about this one from C. S. Lewis's book, *The Voyage of the Dawn Treader*, published in the early 1950s? Listen to it. I'm going to read you the opening line. As you listen to it, ask yourself, "Does this sentence establish character, tension, and story?" Here it is: "There was a boy called Eustace Clarence Scrubb, and he almost deserved it."

Did it get a laugh? Lewis has a wonderful dry wit in this sentence, doesn't he? But as an opening line, the work it does is serious. Listen to it again: "There was a boy called Eustace Clarence Scrubb, and he almost deserved it." Do we have character here? We do, don't we? We know that there's a boy with an unfortunate name, and we know that he almost deserves it. He must be a real challenge. But there must also be something sympathetic about him; otherwise it wouldn't be "almost," would it? If you're like me, you want to know more about this Eustace Clarence Scrubb and what he's done to deserve such a characterization. I'll bet it's going to be funny.

The thing is, we have tension, too, don't we? That comes from the very same thing. If Eustace were just a rotten boy, rotten to the core, there wouldn't be any conflict here. If he were an angel, there wouldn't be any story either, would there? It's the fact that Eustace almost deserves such a terrible name that makes him a complicated and conflicted character. It's what makes the narrator detest him and, at the same time, view him sympathetically. Where there's conflict, there's a story. That story: Has this sentence set the narrative in motion? It has. What you know is that we're next going to learn what Master Eustace has done to earn him this sentence. Who is he? What antics has he been up to? Lewis has piqued our curiosity and has made us interested in a character and his conflict, and that's a great beginning.

Okay, let's try another one. Here's the opening sentence to Sylvia Plath's novel *The Bell Jar* from the 1960s. Plath writes: "It was a queer, sultry summer, the summer they electrocuted the Rosenbergs, and I didn't know what I was doing in New York."

See how easy it really is to decide if something is a great beginning? We just have to ask ourselves, "Does it have character, conflict, and narrative all at once?" Once again, we do have conflict and character: "I didn't know what I was doing in New York," she writes. We have an internally conflicted character, don't we? What's this person doing in New York? Why doesn't she—and is it a she?—know what she's doing? What happened in her life that summer, and how did what happened in America to the Rosenbergs shape her story? That connection between her story and the Rosenbergs, that's another kind of conflict. The fact that it was a "queer" or unusual summer suggests more conflict. Conflict: That launches narrative. We know that there must've been some consequences, some connection, between the life of this confused and lost character and that "queer, sultry summer" when the Rosenbergs were executed. Something happened; we're going to learn what.

Do you feel like you're getting the hang of it? Great; and in a minute, I'll give you a little test to see if you're really to do it. But first, let's try to draw some conclusion out of these two examples about how you establish character and what narrative arc means.

What makes interesting character? We've already said it's conflict, right? That's the key to it. In fact, that's the key to story in general. But conflict in character can be a subtle thing. In the case of Sylvia Plath, it's straightforward. She tells us right up front that she has a character who doesn't know what she's doing. This character is internally conflicted, and that's interesting. But Eustace is internally conflicted, too, isn't he? Or at least, the narrator sees the conflict even if Eustace doesn't. Because what the narrator sees is that Eustace is a mixture of good and bad qualities; and what that means is that he's capable of change and of acting in ways that might surprise us, right? It means that he's a complex character.

The opposite of a complex character is what we call a stock character, and we're going to talk more about these kinds of characters in lesson 12. Stock characters are characters whose qualities are fixed and static. They're the bad guys who never change, and because they never change they have no real life or personality. Stock characters sometimes do have a role in the best stories, but they aren't the characters to begin your story with; not if you want the reader to be interested.

Here's a rule of thumb about character: It's the thing that doesn't seem to fit or doesn't meet our expectations about other people that make them interesting. It's characters who don't know their own motivations; characters who appear to be irritating but somehow capture our sympathy anyhow; characters whose situations are unexpected, who are placed in funny or impossible or challenging situations where they'll have to show us who they are in short order. Think about the people you meet in your own life every day: Who are the people who interest you? It's the people who manage to surprise us, isn't it? The button-down businessman whose tattoo we catch a glimpse of at the café table; the woman crying on the subway. Or think back to the photograph of the Liberation of Paris: It's that man standing there on the window ledge for reasons we can only imagine, isn't it? There's a story there. What these characters do and show us promises it.

How about narrative arc? What does that term really mean in practice? We'll talk later in detail about that, too. But here's the rule of thumb guide to narrative arc: Narrative arc is when action implies consequences. Something happens, and you know as a reader that something else must inevitably follow from that. That's a narrative, a story, set into forward motion, and that's momentum. Think about it this way: It's the old "If a tree falls in the forest and no one hears it, does it happen" philosophical riddle. Sure, a tree falling in the woods is an action, but there don't appear to be any consequences that are going to follow from it. Whether it exists or not we'll leave to the philosophers; but if it's an action from which nothing follows, if there are no consequences, then there's no story.

Ok, let's do a little test to see if you can tell the difference between a good beginning to a story and a boring beginning, shall we? Here are two examples. Remember, what you're looking for is simple: Do these sentences create character, conflict, and narrative arc?

Here's one example:

> Mrs. Maas was named the executor of the will of a friend who was a real estate developer. The letter arrived in the mail. Rich people often have complicated business affairs, so it ended up being a little bit of work. There was a summer party on the afternoon the letter arrived.

Think about it for a minute. Do you have a strong sense of character, conflict, and narrative?

Ok, let's try this one:

> One summer afternoon Mrs. Oedipa Maas came home from a Tupperware party whose hostess had put perhaps too much kirsch in the fondue to find that she, Oedipa, had been named executor, or she supposed executrix, of the estate of one Pierce Inverarity, a California real estate mogul who had once lost two million dollars in his spare time but still had assets numerous and tangled enough to make the job of sorting it all out more than honorary.

How about character, conflict, and narrative here?

Hopefully, you see that the second example is a stronger opening, right? In example one, do we learn anything about what makes Mrs. Maas tick? Not really; all we learn is her name, actually. How about her friend the real estate developer? Nothing. In the second example—which comes, by the way, from Thomas Pynchon's novel *The Crying of Lot 49*—we learn something more. She has the curious and symbolic name of Oedipa, as in oedipal complex. Her friend's name, Inverarity? We might get the hint that he's in-veracious or not-truthful. We learn that he loses money for sport. We learn that Oedipa is the kind of woman who goes to Tupperware parties where the ladies get tipsy on kirsch-laced fondue. We even get inside her head for a moment as she supposes that executrix is the female form of the word "executor." This is going to be a strange story alright, and we can guess that these crazy characters are going to be part of what makes it interesting.

How about conflict and narrative arc? In example one, do we have any? Not really, right? She's named executrix of a businessman's will. So what? That's nice. There was a summer party. Ho-hum. Letters usually do come in the mail, don't they? But in Pynchon's beginning, on the other hand, there's definite conflict. Inverarity has almost certainly left his business affairs in a muddle, we learn. Untangling his dealings is going to be a challenge. There are going to be some conflicts, too. Oedipa, she's got another conflict, doesn't she? After all, she didn't ask for this job, and here her friend is dead. In fact, it came as what we can guess might not have been an entirely welcome surprise.

Ok, how do you apply this to your own writing? Here's an exercise for the next lesson. How about you write the first three sentences of your story, whatever story it is you want to write? It's a very simple exercise, with just three steps. Step one: Write a sentence. Your goal in this sentence? Write a sentence where the reader wants to read the sentence that's going to come after. Write the most interesting and intriguing sentence ever written. Write a sentence that has character, conflict, and narrative arc. Step two: Write the sentence that comes after your first one; and your goal is the same: Write a sentence that leaves us wanting to read the next one. Step three: Write one more sentence after that. Simple.

After you've written your three sentences—your great beginning—go back and have a look to see how great they really are. Ask yourself the same question we've been asking about these other good beginnings throughout this lesson: Do your sentences establish character, tension, and narrative arc? If not, then you'll need to revise them. Are you thinking to yourself right now, "Oh no, I don't know where to start?" Don't worry. If you find yourself unsure of where to start and maybe a little bit frustrated at first, that's normal. We're still here at the beginning of the course; but it's important that you practice these skills. Before I send you on your way to complete your assignment, let's think about what you can do to get started if you can't think of a way to begin, shall we?

There's a reason beginning a story is the hardest part, isn't there? After all, I've just put a lot of pressure on you. I've just told you that in the first sentence, you need to grip your reader. You need to do several things all at once, maybe things you aren't yet sure about how to do at all. Don't worry. We're going to master all these parts of telling a great story, and many more, in this course together. But even after you learn the art of great storytelling, you know what? Beginning a story is still going to be hard. It's hard even for professional writers.

How do you come up with an idea for the beginning of a story? Here are a couple of different strategies you can use to generate ideas to get started. One of my favorite techniques is to work with what some writers call a story starter. What is a story starter? Have you ever made bread at home? If you have, you know that some recipes suggest beginning with some starter—a bit of yeast and sugar—to get that yeast robust and energetic before you add it to all the other ingredients. I like to think of the beginning of a story as a lot like that yeast starter: You're concentrating on making sure that the thing that will drive your story is really cooking before you go further.

One way to think of a story starter is to think about that idea of secrets. Think of a secret; it could be anything, mundane or important. Then imagine you weren't going to tell someone this secret, but that you wanted to drop a hint that there was a secret that you're keeping from that person. Let's say my secret is I've just hidden your car keys. Not a very interesting secret maybe; but it'll still drive you crazy, won't it, when I say, "Joe, take a hike" and I start giggling madly. If you're Joe, you're going to be wondering to yourself, "Why is she laughing?" The fact that I find something hysterically funny when you don't see the humor anywhere leads you to wonder two things, both story starters: Either I've just cracked and I'm having a nervous breakdown, or I know something you don't know, something that's probably really going to annoy you.

So here, I could begin my story: "I knew she'd finally cracked that morning. We'd all seen it coming for ages, but that it was so final, so spectacular, still surprised me." It's not a bad opening line. As a reader, you're left to wonder: What were the early signs? What made that crack so interesting? Who is this speaking and who has just lost it? Or I could begin that story by writing instead, "I suppose it would have ended differently if I hadn't done something that afternoon quite so childish. And I suppose if I hadn't laughed at Joe he might have coped better." The reader wants to know: How did Joe cope? What would've ended differently? "Fill us in," we say in our minds. We've launched a story.

Story starter number one: If you're stuck beginning this exercise, imagine a secret and then imagine you want someone else to want to know what it is; but you're not going to tell them, not yet anyhow. Let's try a first sentence or two together. What would be a good secret? Maybe I'm on a date and I haven't had the heart yet to tell my hunter beau that I'm vegetarian, and he's just cooked a romantic venison dinner. What would be a good way to open this story, and what would be a way that doesn't work so well either?

Here's one way you might start this story about our shy vegetarian; what do you think? Does this work effectively as a story opener yet or not? Here's my opener:

> Mary Jane hadn't told Buster that she didn't eat meat because she was worried about what he would think. Now he had cooked her a meal that he was proud of: venison steak from a deer he had shot himself last autumn. Buster presented it with a flourish. Mary Jane felt bad. It was little surprise that the date ended up a dud.

What do you think? Does it make you want to keep reading?

I haven't left you much to wonder about really, have I? Sure, you don't quite know how the date is going to go badly; you don't know exactly what Mary Jane and Buster are going to say to each other; but do you really care? After all, you have the hint that whatever goes wrong in this date, it isn't going to be dramatic.

Before you try writing your own opener, let's try this out together: How could we revise this story opener to put the mystery and idea of a dramatic secret about character conflict back in there? Why don't you go ahead and think about it for a minute. How would you rewrite this? What would your strategy be? Did you decide that we actually need to offer less information in this story opener? That we need to leave the outcome of the date in question?

How about this as a different way to tell the same story:

> Mary Jane looked up at the glassy-eyed deer's head mounted on the dining room wall. She looked down at Buster's homemade venison stew. She heard herself say the words. And then she had the strange sensation that the room was spinning.

Do you see how that story is a better opening? What is Mary Jane going to tell Buster? We have an idea that it's going to have something to do with that deer head and this stew, but we don't know that it's just going to be that Mary Jane's a vegetarian. We don't know what the relationship between her and Buster is. What did she say that had the room spinning, and why? This time, the opener has suspense and dramatic tension, doesn't it?

Ok, are you ready to try it yourself? Before you start, let me give you one more tip: If you're stuck on how to begin, here's another good idea for getting writing, your second story starter. If you get stuck with this first sentences assignment, how about this as another way of getting going: Imagine that two people are having a terrible phone conversation; it could be about absolutely anything, big or small, but it's an upsetting conversation. What is this conversation about? What makes it so terrible? Imagine the worst thing you can imagine. Now imagine that you can only hear one side of it: the side of the person who's mostly doing the listening, not the talking. Describe what you see and what he or she says. Do you see that, in a way, what I'm suggesting is the same thing as a secret story starter? What you're describing are the consequences on a character of a story that you can only see a piece of here at the beginning. That, in a nutshell, is at the heart of the start to any great story: consequences on a character of actions that are larger than the story at the moment we enter into it. The fact that there's more to know and understand, that's what grips us as readers, right from the beginning.

Ok, so you have your assignment; and if you get stuck here or along the way, you have two story prompts or starters. In the next lesson, we'll talk about how to bring those three sentences to life even more vividly by focusing on what writers talk about as the technique of showing versus telling. But for now, write those first three great sentences of your book, the one you've always imagined writing.

Show, Don't Tell

Lecture 5

You may already be familiar with the adage to "show, not tell" in your writing, but what does that mean? The three key elements of showing are using the active voice (that is, avoiding *to be* and *–ing* verb constructions); making precise, vivid word choices; and mastering the art of the metaphor.

Writing with Style—Active Verbs

- In your exercise for last time, you wrote three beginning sentences—sentences you tested to see if they created character, conflict, and narrative. Here is my example, which I kept light-hearted:

> Big Stan positioned the wailing infant under his right arm like a football and silently considered that perhaps everything at the corner Burger King that morning had not gone precisely as planned.

- We have a character, Big Stan, who carries babies in unusual ways, and he has conflict—witness the crying baby and the plans gone awry. We also have narrative arc because whatever has gone wrong has already happened, and now Stan must deal with the consequences. If this sentence made you curious, then I did my job correctly.

- There is more to writing a great beginning than establishing character, conflict, and narrative arc. You also need to do it with style.

- Have you ever asked yourself why some writing is vivid and other writing leaves you cold? For all that we discuss story*telling*, vivid writing is writing that shows, rather than tells. "Show, don't tell," is the mantra of creative writing teachers everywhere.

- The question is, how do we show when we write? Let's return to that sentence about Big Stan and look at two possible revisions. The first revision is telling and the second revision is showing.

  Revision 1: The little crying baby was under the arm of Big Stan, who carried it with him like a football that morning when he opened the door of the Burger King and walked out into sunlight, thinking about how everything hadn't gone precisely as planned.

  Revision 2: The door burst open as his shoulder struck it and, after a moment of shocked silence, the wail of the infant shattered the morning silence; as Big Stan positioned the squirming, shrieking bundle under his right arm like a wet football, he silently considered that perhaps everything there in the Burger King had not gone precisely as he had planned.

- If you look closely at these two sentences, the most important difference you will notice is the way the verbs are handled. Showing sentences use the active voice, and telling sentences use the passive voice, relying on what we might call "state of being" verbs.

- Let's compare three versions of one short sentence to see how this works. First, "The restaurant was being inundated by the sounds of street music." This is a passive construction because something is happening to the restaurant. And it takes three words—was being inundated—to express a single action.

- The second version—"The sounds of street music were inundating the restaurant"—is no longer passive because the music is doing something, but this sentence still has an *-ing* verb, which is often a warning sign of telling.

- The easiest way to change this sentence into a showing sentence would be to write "The sound of street music inundated the restaurant." Notice the verb is down to a single word.

Precision and Concision

- Of course, there is more to showing than verbs. Let's take another sentence and take the process even further. Here is the original: "By the end of the disastrous middle-school performance, the young ballerinas were all limping across the stage, with sweaty hair covering their once eager faces."

- We know first to get rid of those passive verb constructions, so our first attempt might read like this: "By the end of the disastrous middle-school performance, the young ballerinas *went awkwardly* across the stage, their once-eager faces *covered* with sweaty hair." Better, but still a little flat.

- Part of showing involves vivid imagery for your reader, and that means using detail. We do this through careful word choice. *Went* and *covered*, among others in that sentence, are both pretty generic words.

- Another clue that you have chosen a weak or a generic verb is the impulse to modify with an adverb. The reason *went* needs to be described with *awkwardly* is because *went* is not vivid at all. Adverbs are often used to cover up a weak verb choice.

- Strunk and White's *The Elements of Style* offers two guidelines to writing great prose: precision and concision. That means choosing the most precise words and using the fewest number of words possible.

- So how did our ballerinas cross the stage? Perhaps they limped, crawled, shuffled, or crept. Where else in the sentence can you get rid of vague terms?

- Here is my revision: "By the time the curtain fell over the sorry spectacle of the eighth-grade ballet recital, once-eager faces were plastered with sweaty hair and fourteen pairs of pink slippers limped across the stage."

- Instead of just *end*, we have *the curtain fell*—something you can see. I could even say whether it is a red velvet curtain or a crooked homemade curtain if I wanted to take this further.

- Instead of *the young ballerinas went awkwardly*, now *fourteen pairs of pink slippers limped.* You can visualize their struggle, and you even know how many of them there were.

- Taking this one step further, let's examine some sentences from the *New York Times* best-selling account of Thomas Jefferson's passion for French wines, Benjamin Wallace's *The Billionaire's Vinegar*:

> Now, as his horse-drawn carriage clattered along the post roads of France, he at last had a chance to see the most fabled vineyards in the world. … He passed through rich farmland planted with corn, rye, and beans. As soon as he ferried west across the Garonne … the picture changed. … As he rolled through the district of Sauternes and entered Bordeaux, he looked out through the glass windows of his carriage and saw nothing but grapevines.

- Because this is a work of nonfiction, all of the details in this description are true, but notice how Wallace presents the details. He does not say, "Jefferson traveled by carriage through the French wine country." His word choice is specific.

- Notice, too, that these details are not only visual. The carriage *clattered* along the road, letting us hear what Jefferson experienced. Although we call it showing, we are not limited to visual details.

- Jefferson also *ferried* across the Garonne. Wallace uses a verb that also encompasses a noun, getting extra efficiency out of his word choice.

Metaphors and Similes

- Wallace also makes particularly effective use of **metaphors**. Take two examples from this book: "The wail of the infant shattered the morning silence" and "Ocean-bound schooners heaped with barrels plied the broad waterway."

- Cries do not literally shatter things, of course, but Wallace's word choice implies a similarity between the auditory phenomenon to a physical one. In a sense, he puts two images in our heads at once. Similarly, he has schooners *ply* the river because the word evokes to us the twisting and twining of the strands of a rope.

- In addition to metaphors—these implied comparisons—writers can also use more direct comparisons called **similes**; these are comparisons that use "like" or "as."

- There is a role for both similes and metaphors in good writing. The difference is that a simile separates the two images (*A* is like *B*), while a metaphor yokes them (*A* is *B*). In that sense, metaphors show and similes tell.

- Mixed metaphors are comparisons that do not make sense. Sometimes these are used on purpose for comic effect, as in Tom Wolfe's *Bonfire of the Vanities*: "All at once he was alone in this noisy hive with no place to roost." But unless you are trying to be funny, steer clear of them.

Skilled writers like Tom Wolfe indulge in mixed metaphors for humorous effect.

- You may also run into just plain bad metaphors, when a comparison seems forced. A writer should never use a metaphor just for the sake of using a metaphor; their purpose is give the reader a deeper or more vivid experience.

Show, Don't Tell—A Writing Exercise

- Take a piece of writing you are already working on. See if you can find any telling errors and revise it to show more effectively. Alternatively, write a page or two of description—about anything you want—where you practice actively showing rather than telling.

Important Terms

metaphor: An implied comparison that allows readers to see things in a new light.

simile: An explicit comparison using the words "like" or "as" that allows readers to see things in a new light.

Suggested Reading

Strunk, White, and Angell, *The Elements of Style*.

Wallace, *The Billionaire's Vinegar*.

Wolfe, *The Bonfire of the Vanities*.

Questions to Consider

1. Do you think that our emphasis on showing rather than telling is part of the time-honored tradition of writing, going back centuries and across cultures, or do you think it has been influenced by the rise of mass media in the 20th and 21st centuries? What books would you use to make the case for your position?

2. When might an author deliberately choose to tell rather than show? What are the effects of telling, and are there moments where a writer might want to use deliberately "weaker" narrative techniques?

Show, Don't Tell

Lecture 5—Transcript

In the last lesson, we talked about how great opening lines in stories set in motion three things: complex character, dramatic tension, and narrative arc. We talked about how complex characters have internal contradictions, eccentricities, and make us believe in the possibility that they can change and, in doing so, surprise us. As with real people, we can only guess at what they might do—we can't be 100% certain—and that's what makes them fascinating. We also talked about how narrative arc and narrative tension begin the moment a story is launched. When we know that whatever the situation or action at hand something is going to happen as a result of it, these are actions with consequences.

In your exercise for last time, you wrote three beginning sentences; sentences you tested to see if they created character, conflict, and narrative. Did your first sentence look something like mine? Here's what I wrote; it's a light-hearted one: "Big Stan positioned the wailing infant under his right arm like a football and silently considered that perhaps everything at the corner Burger King that morning had not gone precisely as planned." Do you see the character, conflict, and narrative arc? We have Big Stan, who carries a baby like a football; that's a bit unusual. Who is the Stan person who carries babies that way? We know that it's strange for him to end up carrying an infant if that's how he does it; and we know something else: We know that something went wrong—here's our arc—and whatever has gone wrong, it's put Stan in his current unusual predicament. Do you want to know how Stan ended up with this baby and what went wrong at the Burger King? If you're curious, we've got the beginnings of a story.

What did you come up with? All that matters is this: that it was a sentence that kept the reader interested. This is how we write good stories, one sentence at a time. Every sentence should be moving one of those three elements of a story forward, and those crucial sentences at the beginning should set all three elements in motion simultaneously.

But there's more to writing a great beginning than just this, too, isn't there? You probably already suspect it; and maybe you're realizing that to establish character and narrative, it takes writing in a certain way, a certain style, too, doesn't it? Have you ever asked yourself why some writing is vivid—so vivid you feel like you can see the action in your mind's eye—and why some writing leaves you feeling just plain uninterested? That's what we're going to work on in this lesson: the technique that writers talk about as showing versus telling. "Show, don't tell" is the mantra of creative writing teachers everywhere, and we're going to learn today what that means and how to start using the technique to make your writing stronger. Along the way, we're going to talk about the role of word choice, and especially the role of adjectives, in strong writing, too.

"Show, don't tell," your writing teacher tells you; but what does this mean? Take a minute to think about it. What do you think showing rather than telling means? If I asked you to explain the difference, what would you say? Maybe you came up with the idea of writing in language that uses images. Right. Maybe you thought about something that puts the reader in the scene. You'd be right again. Those are both right at the heart of it. But the tricky thing is how, isn't it? The "how's" are always the hard part of great writing.

Let's go back and look at my example from the last exercise. I wrote: "Big Stan positioned the wailing infant under his right arm like a football and silently considered that perhaps everything at the corner Burger King that morning had not gone precisely as planned." This sentence does the three things we said a good beginning should do right at the start of a story, right? We've got character, tension, and narrative. But actually, when we start thinking about adding to a great beginning the technique of showing versus telling, this is just a so-so middle-of-the-road kind of sentence. Let's look at two ways we could revise this sentence and see what that might tell us about what showing looks like and what telling looks like.

Let's imagine I had written this sentence:

> The little crying baby was under the arm of Big Stan, who carried it with him like a football that morning when he opened the door of the Burger King and walked out into sunlight, thinking about how everything hadn't gone precisely as planned.

Think about it again for a moment and listen; would you say that this is showing language or telling language? Here it is one more time:

The little crying baby was under the arm of Big Stan, who carried it with him like a football that morning when he opened the door of the Burger King and walked out into sunlight, thinking about how everything hadn't gone precisely as planned.

Made up your mind about which it is? Ok, now listen to another version. Ask yourself the same question: Is this showing or telling? Also ask yourself: Which of these two versions do you think is the livelier and stronger writing?

Here's sentence two:

> The door burst open as his shoulder struck it and, after a moment of shocked silence, the wail of the infant shattered the morning silence; as Big Stan positioned the squirming, shrieking bundle under his right arm like a wet football, he silently considered that perhaps everything there in the Burger King had not gone precisely as he had planned.

How about this, showing or telling?

The first one is telling and the second example is showing, right? Did you see that? If so, well done. If you're able to see the difference, you'll have no trouble learning another important technique for how you can make your writing stronger and become a great storyteller. But how does it work at the level of the language? What makes one version a showing sentence and the other a telling sentence? The most important thing is the way we handle verbs. Showing pieces have active verbs and telling pieces have what we might call "state of being" verbs; and those active verbs in showing pieces go with active phrases.

What do I mean? Here are three short sentences again; let's look at the difference. Sentence one: "The restaurant was being inundated by the sounds of street music." Showing or telling? It's telling, right? Listen again to the verbs: "The restaurant was being inundated." It's a passive construction, isn't it? Something is happening to the restaurant. Look how many verbs it takes to make that happen: three, "was being inundated"; and "was being," that's a state of being verb isn't it? It's literally a verb that just means "was." Just existing isn't an interesting action; verbs should do something interesting. In fact, whenever you see an "-ing" verb, chances are we've got telling going on. There are two rules of thumb, then: Passive constructions and "-ing" verbs tend to appear in telling not showing passages.

Ok, how about sentence two? "The sounds of the street music were inundating the restaurant." Think about those two rules of thumb we just learned: Is this showing or telling, and how do you know? It's another example of an "-ing" verb, isn't it? Did you see that? If so, you're on track. In this case, we have an active construction—the music is doing something, right?—and in our first sentence, something was being done to the restaurant by the music. Now, the music is doing something to the restaurant. That's the difference between active and passive verbs. But this sentence still has the telling "-ing" state of being verb, doesn't it? "The sounds of the street music were inundating the restaurant."

Let's try again: What would it take to change this sentence to a showing sentence? Think about it for a minute. "The sounds of street music were inundating the restaurant." How do you get rid of that state of being verb? The easiest way is just to write: "The sound of street music inundated the restaurant," isn't it?

Let's try another example from the top. Can you turn this telling sentence into a sentence where the verb takes on a more active showing role? Here it is: "By the end of the disastrous middle-school performance, the young ballerinas were all limping across the stage, with sweaty hair covering their once eager faces." What does this look like as an active showing sentence? Did you come up with something that removed the passive constructions and the state of being verbs? How about this one: "By the end of the disastrous middle-school performance, the young ballerinas went awkwardly across the stage, their once-eager faces covered with sweaty hair."

Ok, so verb forms are one important part of how we show rather than tell in language; but let's look at some other ways we can make language more vivid, too. Verbs are crucially important to showing, but they aren't everything. Let's take our sentence and think about it some more. We wrote: "By the end of the disastrous middle-school performance, the young ballerinas went awkwardly across the stage, their once-eager faces covered with sweaty hair." The verb forms describe a direct action, but can you really see this image in front of you? Does it really come alive in your mind's eye? Probably not; after all, the details are a little skimpy, aren't they? We don't yet have an image to work with; and how do we create images in language? It's all about detail isn't it? Abstract ideas are abstract because they aren't specific; and concrete ideas, or images, are concrete because they're precise. So another one of the keys to showing is using detail, and we do this by thinking about word choice.

Listen again to the words in that sentence and as you hear it again, can you think of words that we might use instead that would be more precise and specific than the ones I've written? Here it is again: "By the end of the disastrous middle-school performance, the young ballerinas went awkwardly across the stage, their once-eager faces covered with sweaty hair." These are all pretty generic words. Where are we going to start with our revision? Here's one big hint: Beware of adverbs. Like "-ing" verbs, they often disguise telling words. We sometimes use adverbs to spice up something we know in the back of our minds isn't very interesting. There's a place for adverbs—it's not that we want to ban them from our prose—but we want to use them sparingly, and that means we want to ask ourselves: Are these covering up a weak verb choice? "The young ballerinas went awkwardly across the stage." "To go" is among the most basic verbs in the English language. It doesn't tell us anything about how the going went, does it? We use an adverb to spice it up a bit.

But there's another option: What if, instead of having to spice up our verbs, we chose a word from the outset that was more descriptive and more precise? After all, there are thousands of verbs in the English language. Hundreds of them describe just ways of going. If you remember that classic guide to well-written prose, Strunk and White's *The Elements of Style*, do you recall what their two essential pieces of advice were? If you want to write great prose, they suggested, two things be your guide: precision and concision. They were right. That's the principle here: We want to choose the most precise word possible, and that lets us be concise; lets us express ourselves in the fewest number of words. Precise words have another advantage, too: They are essential to writing prose that shows the reader rather than tells the reader something.

Think of our example about those young ballerinas. Can you think of a single verb that conveys the idea of "went awkwardly" and that gives us a great image of what that awkward going looks like? What did you come up with? How about, "The young ballerinas limped"? Maybe they crawled; maybe they shuffled or crept or trotted or galloped. Any of those words give us a better image, don't they? Creating images in the readers' minds, that's how we begin to show, not tell.

What about the other words in that sentence? I'll read it again, and this time take a minute to revise the entire sentence. Where can you get rid of vague and imageless telling words and replace them with words that show the reader this picture? Where can you add words that are precise? You can imagine this scene in any way you want during the revision, of course. Try to see this moment in your own head and to describe it in language that really captures that image. Here it is again: "By the end of the disastrous middle-school performance, the young ballerinas went awkwardly across the stage, their once-eager faces covered with sweaty hair."

What did you come up with? Here's my revision; does yours do something similar? I wrote: "By the time the curtain fell over the sorry spectacle of the eighth-grade ballet recital, sweaty hair plastered once-eager faces, and 14 pink slippers limped across the stage." Let's look at some of the words I added here to help show this passage. I replaced the "end" of the performance with "the curtain fell," for example. The end of a performance isn't something we can see, is it? But we can imagine a curtain falling. In fact, if I wanted to revise this passage further, I could describe in greater detail what that curtain looked like, couldn't I? There's a difference between, say, a red velvet curtain and a crooked homemade curtain, isn't there? Those details change the whole picture. How about the word phrase "middle-school performance"? It's not as specific as an "eighth-grade ballet recital," is it? When I say "ballet recital," the reader can begin to imagine who the performers are. Or, how about the difference between "the young ballerinas went awkwardly" and "14 pink slippers limped"? Do you see how it's easier to visualize seven limping girls in pink slippers than it is to know what going awkwardly looks like?

Now that you get the idea of showing and not telling, let's look at a few examples from the world of creative nonfiction. How about these sentences from the *New York Times* bestselling account of Thomas Jefferson's passion for French wines, Benjamin Wallace's *The Billionaire's Vinegar*, a nonfiction book that uses all those strategies of creative storytelling we've been learning about in our lessons. Here's a good passage to think about: Thomas Jefferson is traveling to through France in the late 18th century. See if you can visualize the image the author is describing, and see if you can pinpoint the words that help you to do it. Wallace writes:

> Now, as his horse-drawn carriage clattered along the post roads of France, he at last had a chance to see the most fabled vineyards in the world … he passed through rich farmland planted with corn, rye, and beans. As soon as he ferried west across the Garonne … the picture changed … as he rolled through the district of Sauternes and entered Bordeaux, he looked out through the glass windows of his carriage and saw nothing but grapevines.

Let's think about what Benjamin Wallace does here to make this a showing passage. As you listened to the passage, could you see the landscape rolling past Thomas Jefferson? Because this is a book of nonfiction, all the details in this description are true; but there are interesting ways to describe something factual, and uninteresting ways to describe the same thing. In creative nonfiction, our goal is to make those facts come alive through great storytelling.

Look at how Wallace describes the landscape. He could have said, "The landscape changed from agricultural to viticultural when he entered the city of Bordeaux." Or, "He traveled by carriage in the French wine country." But those are pretty boring descriptions aren't they? All the details, though, are effectively the same; it's just that this is telling. Showing language is the use of word and sound images. The carriage is "horse-drawn." We can see what kind of carriage it is, can't we? And the carriage didn't just "go" along the road, it "clattered," letting us imagine the kind of sound Jefferson experienced. This is an important point. Showing doesn't have to be visual images; it can be any image that asks the reader to use his or her senses of sight, sound, smell, or touch. How about when he writes that he "ferried west across the Garonne"? Here, we can imagine with that simple verb "ferried" how he travelled across this famous river to the French wine country, right?

Alright, you try an example now. Here's the last sentence from the Wallace example. Listen to it again, and see if you can turn it into an ineffective telling sentence. Remember, to do this, what kinds of writing errors are you looking to add back in? Passive constructions; "-ing" state-of-being verbs; and lots of vague words that don't let the readers use any of his or her five senses, right? Here it is: "as he rolled through the district of Sauternes and entered Bordeaux, he looked out through the glass windows of his carriage and saw nothing but grapevines."

What did you come up with? How about something like this: "Sauternes went by. Bordeaux was entered. All that could be seen from the carriage were grapevines." There's my passive construction, right? Something is being done to Saunternes and Bordeaux. Now, we don't know what the carriage looked like, and we don't know who is doing the seeing. That's much harder to see than the image of Thomas Jefferson looking out the glass windows on a passive landscape, isn't it?

Let's recap: So far, we've talked about creating sensory images, using precise and concrete word choices, writing in an active voice, and avoiding state of being verbs. Now you understand the essentials of showing and not telling language. Let's take it to the next level. Let me give you some examples of two even more powerful showing examples, also from Benjamin Wallace's book. Can you notice something unusual about the most powerful showing images in all of these examples? Let's listen to a few of them and see if you can observe something interesting here.

How about that sentence that describes the city of Bordeaux and its river trade: "Ocean-bound schooners heaped with barrels plied the broad waterway." Or here's one more: "The wail of the infant shattered the morning silence." There's something subtle going on here. When you imagine these phrases in your head, do you notice that you're bringing something else to the picture building that showing language lets the readers imagine?

The wail of the infant shattered the silence. Do cries literally shatter things? "To shatter," that's a verb that means "to break"; but it's something that breaks in a very specific way, isn't it? It's glass that shatters. So what this sentence tells us is, "Hey, reader, imagine it like this: The wail of the infant broke the silence like a glass splintering apart." It's a very graphic image, isn't it? It's a metaphor also. A metaphor is just the technical term for a comparison that's implied, and here it's the choice of the verb "shatter" that creates not just one but two images in our heads in this sentence. Two images: That's language that really shows, isn't it?

Or, how about schooners plying the riverway? What does the verb "to ply" really mean? We have three-ply rope out in the garage, right; or three-ply cashmere in our fancy sweaters? That's because "ply" means something that is woven or wrapped or twisted together. The boats twist and coil up and down the rope of the river, don't they? It's the same thing: not just one image but two. That's what a metaphor lets us do in writing.

I want to show you something else. Let's contrast two forms of the comparison. Remember how just a minute ago I said that the wail of the infant broke the silence like a glass splintering apart? That was another way of breaking down the metaphor I wrote when I said, "The wail of the infant shattered the silence." Both are ways of saying the same thing; but when we make a comparison using the words "like" or "as"—in other words, when we make the comparison explicit rather than implicit—that's a particular kind of comparison that we call a "simile." Two things are similar—a simile—and we don't mind saying so directly.

There's a role for both similes and metaphors in good writing; but let's think about the difference between the two. In a simile, we're separating the two images that we want to compare, aren't we? We are saying, "A is like B," or, "Just as B so is A." In a metaphor, on the other hand, the two images are firmly yoked together. It's more like saying, "A is also B." The silence is broken in the way a glass shatters, and the reader is invited to see both images at once; and we have to use our imagination to make the comparison. As writers, we want readers to use their imaginations, don't we? After all, it's when we use our imaginations most that we're deeply drawn into stories. That's the reason why there's another rule of thumb we might want to follow as writers: Metaphors show; similes tell.

Have you ever heard of a mixed metaphor and wondered what one is? Here we go: We just said that metaphors give us two images at once, right? That's powerful showing language indeed. But what if the second image a metaphor creates for us doesn't make any sense? What if it tries to do too many different things or goes in two different directions, and instead of helping the reader see something better, it just makes it all confusing? That doesn't help the reader see anything better, does it? What does a mixed metaphor look like? There's a great example from Tom Wolfe's novel about the 1980s, *The Bonfire of the Vanities.* Listen to this: "All at once he was alone in this noisy hive with no place to roost." This is an image that doesn't make sense, does it? We have a character who finds himself feeling alone in a room that's like the busy beehive of bumblebees, and he can't find any place to roost—in what?—in a beehive? That's crazy. We don't roost in beehives; we roost in chicken coops. Is that room like a beehive or is it like a chicken coop? It's got to be one or the other for the original comparison to work, and it doesn't work because it's all jumbled up; it's a mixed metaphor. Unless you mean to be funny by writing something that's bad on purpose, we want to steer clear of them.

Here's another kind of metaphor that doesn't really help us out as writers either. How about just plain bad metaphors? They definitely exist. Sometimes a comparison just doesn't make any sense and it seems forced; like the writer is writing a metaphor just for the sake of writing a metaphor, not because it helps the reader to see more clearly. Here's an example: The hot air balloon galloped into the air slowly. It's funny isn't it? What would a hot air balloon galloping look like exactly? Pity the poor riders aboard it is all I can say. Things don't gallop slowly either, do they? That's a contradiction. The result is a bad metaphor that's pretty much just nonsense. Once again, unless you're trying to be funny by writing something preposterous—the one great use of the bad metaphor—use this kind of showing language very carefully. Remember that old advice from Strunk and White again: concision and precision.

In this lesson, let's recap before you try showing rather than telling in an exercise of your own. We learned that to show and not tell we use active verbs. We learned to use concrete and precise word choices. We're going to remember that sometimes too many adverbs are a sign that we need stronger verbs. We learned that metaphors show things more effectively than similes, and that comparisons can be great ways of making things come alive for our readers. Above all, we learned that we want to find ways to show our readers what we're imagining in ways that engage their senses; because when we feel we're right there in a scene, that's when stories get really interesting.

For next time, why don't you try this out on your own? Maybe you already have a piece of writing that you've been working on. See if you can find any of these telling errors and revise it to show more effectively. Or, if you want to work on something new, that's great, too. Can you write a page or two of description—make it anything you want, maybe even something that's just happening in front of you—where you practice actively showing rather than telling? In the next lesson, we'll talk about some other ways of engaging your readers and beginning to handle creating a gripping narrative.

Launching a Narrative Arc

Lecture 6

We have seen how narrative arc applies to story beginnings, but to be a story and not just a group of events, a work of creative nonfiction must also have a narrative arc that carries the reader through the entire story. There are three broad categories of narrative arc: the linear narrative, the circular narrative, and the frame narrative. Each is appropriate for different kinds of stories, but the best choice is usually the simplest, most direct form of narrative that will get the job done.

Planning a Narrative Arc

- We have talked about how to set a story in motion, but what about that thorny problem of structuring the story as a whole? More writers may abandon their stories due to this problem than any other single issue.

- Plotting out the whole book's narrative arc can seem overwhelming to the most experienced authors, but if you understand a few basic principles, soon you will be able to plot stories with riveting dramatic tension. This will therefore be the focus of our next four lectures.

- Experienced writers will tell you that plotting a story in advance does not mean planning out every little detail before you set pen to paper or fingertips to keyboard. Sometimes stories and characters surprise us along the way, and the story takes on a life of its own. But you do need to ensure at the outset that you are telling a story and not simply listing a series of events and characters.

- Narrative structure is a craft problem that all writers have to negotiate. Certain narrative structures can only do certain things. Each structure has inherent advantages and disadvantages. Each creates expectations in a reader; the trick is finding the structure that will let you tell the story that is waiting to be told.

Narrative Arc in *The Widow Clicquot*

- Fulfilling reader expectations is important: If you are reading a mystery novel, you expect to learn whodunit by the end. Or recall the ancient theater maxim that a comedy ends in marriage and a tragedy ends with a death. Readers get irritated when writers do not deliver on narrative promises.

- When I was writing *The Widow Clicquot*, I ran into a dilemma. I was writing a biography, and a biography—unless it is about a living person—usually ends with the subject's death. Occasionally, they have experimental narrative structures; they may begin with the death, then proceed with a flashback, or events may be told out of order, but chronological order is the general rule.

***The Widow Cliquot* has two narrative arcs: the character's biography and the author's discovery of her subject.**

- There is a good reason for this: Experience creates character, and character is why we read biography. Therefore, if you are going to violate normal chronology, you need to have a very good reason for it.

- I had no compelling reason not to let the story unfold in historical time, from the beginning of Barbe Nicole Ponsardin's life to the end. The problem I encountered, however, was that all of the interesting events of her life—her childhood during the French Revolution; her encounter with Napoleon; her creation of one of the world's great champagnes—occurred in the first few decades of her life. She retired a very young woman and lived another 50-odd years. Those years were peaceful and happy, but they did not make for a compelling story.

- Clearly a straightforward narrative structure would leave us short of a great ending. One option was to try to make those last 50 years interesting, but readers are too smart for that.

- Another was to introduce secondary characters and let their stories carry the second half of the book—essentially creating a collective biography. The trouble with this technique is that each character would need his or her own narrative arc, which would end with each of their deaths … making the problem bigger, not smaller.

- In the end, I chose a third option. I introduced myself, the author, into the narrative as a secondary character. I told both the story of the Widow Clicquot's life and the story of my search to find out about her history. A big advantage of this approach was that I did not need to kill myself off at the end.

- Note that if I had not thought through my narrative arc before I started writing, I would have had a major problem halfway through the book, requiring a major revision.

Choosing Your Narrative Arc

- Generally, the best narrative structure to use is the simplest and most direct one that will do the job. Unless you are setting out to be the next great experimental writer, less is more.

- A narrative structure must do at least two things at once: It has to give the writer the space to tell the story, and it has to meet the reader's expectations. In a good narrative arc, the actions have consequences and everything that happens somehow contributes to the story.

- So, how to find the right narrative structure that will accomplish this, when there are many different ways of telling a story? It helps to think of narrative structures in three broad categories:

- A **linear narrative** has a **protagonist** with some sort of conflict. That conflict might be internal, but usually it comes in the form of another character—the antagonist—who thwarts the desire of the protagonist. Linear narratives consist of rising action, a crisis point, falling action, and a denouement, or resolution. It is about the tension and release of narrative desire, and a satisfying ending is vital. *Romeo and Juliet*, like many romances, follows a linear narrative structure.

- The hero's journey, or the **quest narrative**, is a **circular narrative**. The protagonist sets out to accomplish, discover, or resolve something. The obstacles and people he or she encounters along the way give the story its dramatic tension. Sometimes there is a turning point where the protagonist changes—or the protagonist's perspective on the problem or goal changes; other times, the climax is just a final obstacle. But in the end, the protagonist returns to the original desire or problem and finds some kind of resolution to it. Circular narratives are ideal for telling character-based stories, like family memoirs or travel narratives. Homer's *Odyssey* and James Joyce's modern retelling, *Ulysses*, are examples of circular narratives.

- The **frame narrative**, sometimes known as the Russian doll narrative, emphasizes the perspective of the narrator by letting characters become storytellers. Mary Shelley's *Frankenstein* is a frame narrative told through letters, but the most famous example in literary history is *1001 Nights*—in which a princess, threatened with death at dawn by her tyrannical husband, tells a series of tales-within-tales each night, so he has no choice but to let her live to hear the outcome. As wonderful as her individual stories are, she, the narrator, is the character we fall in love with.

Recognizing Narrative Structures—A Reading Exercise

- Before you move on to the next lecture, think back on your favorite books. Can you identify what kind of narrative structures they use?

Can you identify what effect the structure has on you as a reader? How would the story have to change if the author had chosen a different structure to tell that tale?

Important Terms

circular narrative: A narrative structure where the end and the beginning meet and where the story focuses on the transformation of the character during the experience of the events in it.

frame narrative: A narrative structure in which the essential story is bracketed at the beginning and end by a second perspective on it.

linear narrative: A narrative structure where events follow on events to build to a climax and resolution and where the plot is emphasized over the character who experiences it.

protagonist: The main character of a narrative, whose conflict is central to the story.

quest narrative: A narrative structure in which the main character goes on a journey in search of knowledge, experience, or some concrete object.

Suggested Reading

Arabian Nights: Tales from a Thousand and One Nights.

Homer, *The Odyssey.*

Joyce, *Ulysses.*

Pollack, *Creative Nonfiction.*

Shakespeare, *Romeo and Juliet.*

Shelley, *Frankenstein.*

Questions to Consider

1. If you were thinking about your life and memoirs, what narrative format do you think would be the most appropriate: circular, linear, or frame? Why?

2. One of the age-old truisms of journalism is "find the story." Thinking about what you have learned about narrative arc in this lecture, what do you think this means? Is it useful advice?

Launching a Narrative Arc

Lecture 6—Transcript

In the last lesson, we talked about ways a writer can make writing sizzle by learning to show rather than tell in storytelling; and you can see already how a great showing paragraph can create drama and tension to move a story along. We've talked especially about how to set a story in motion. How about that thorny problem of structuring the story as a whole, though? After all, who doesn't have the first few pages of the next great novel in his or her desk drawer? The question is: What do you do after you've got that great beginning? In fact, it's my guess that more stories don't get written because of this one thing than anything else. The trouble is figuring out where to go after those first few pages.

If you've ever started writing a book only to quit because you had the sense that you needed to figure out where this story was going before you wrote more, you had exactly the right intuition. A writer does need to have a good idea of where a story is heading before getting down to it. Plotting what writers call the "narrative arc" is part of the creative process that can seem overwhelming to even very experienced authors; but if you understand a few basic principles, soon you'll be able to plot stories with riveting dramatic tension. This is going to be our focus in the next four lessons.

In this lesson here, we're going to start by looking at the big picture. That's going to mean talking a bit right at the outset about what we mean by plotting a story in advance. Experienced writers will tell you this doesn't mean planning out every little detail before you set pen to paper (or these days, fingertip to keyboard). In fact, sometimes along the way, stories and characters surprise us, and the story we're telling takes on a life of its own. Instead, what we're talking about really is this narrative arc business, the idea that there's a story here and not just a series of events and characters. How do you decide where you're going to head with your story? Or, put another way, how are you going to figure out how to develop what those writers and editors call a narrative arc? How do you decide if you even have a story and not just things happening? It's actually not easy. But like everything else in the craft of writing, it's something you can learn to master; and once you do, you'll be well on your way to writing that memoir or biography that you've always imagined.

We've already talked a lot in several of the earlier lessons about this idea of the narrative arc. It's something like an arrow shot into space; an object in motion that has its own organic trajectory. We talked about how good beginnings launch narrative arcs and how character tension is one way of setting a story in motion. We talked about how what matters in storytelling are actions that have inevitable consequences. After all, those consequences are the shape of our story; and, in essence, asking whether a piece of work has a narrative arc is the same question as asking "Is there a story here?" Stories have narrative arcs; that's what makes them stories and not journal entries.

In this lesson, we're going to think about how to structure a story as a whole, and we're going to think about narrative structure as a craft problem that all writers have to negotiate. But why do I say it's a craft problem? Because here's an important take away from this lesson; are you ready? Here it is: Certain narrative structures can only do certain things. They have inherent advantages and disadvantages; inherent limits and expectations from a reader. What do I mean? At the simplest level, think about this: If you're reading a mystery novel, the expectation is that at the end of the book you're going to learn whodunit, right? It would be a pretty annoying mystery novel if we ended up not learning the answer to the riddle, wouldn't it? There's the old truism in the world of theater that a comedy ends in marriage and a tragedy ends in death. If writers start killing off their main characters at the end of a comedy, it isn't funny anymore; and readers tend to get irritated when writers willy-nilly don't deliver on narrative promises.

It's the same thing with other ways of telling stories. As a writer, the trick is finding the structure that will let you tell the story that's waiting to be told. Any old structure won't do. It has to be the right one; the one that gives you the room to navigate, but that's taut enough to give your readers a sense of fast-paced drama.

Let me give you an example. When I was writing *The Widow Clicquot*, I ran into a narrative arc dilemma. I was writing a biography, and the thing about writing a biography is it has to end with the subject dying, right? After all, it's the story of someone's life, and that's just how life stories end. So the reader expects the book to take us from the birth to death; that's the whole idea behind a biography, right? Sure, we could have an experimental narrative structure—we could start with the deathbed scene and have a flashback to the moment someone was born; we could, if we really wanted, tell some parts out of order—but sooner or later, you'd still end up having to tell the vast majority of the story in chronological order, wouldn't you? After all, what kind of biography would we have if it didn't follow the natural course of a person's life and lived experience? It's experience that creates our character, and any reader expects that to be true in a biography as well.

If you were going to have that clever flashback, you would have to have some very good reason for it, because it's a disruption of the natural order of how to tell the story of someone's life; it would have to bring something new to the story, something interesting and important enough to make up for the disruption. One of the tried and true rules of story structure to remember is this: Use the most direct narrative structure that your story will allow. Sometimes fancy narrative devices like flashbacks are absolutely necessary; they're the only way to solve a problem. But unless you need to use one, it's just flash and distraction.

The Widow Clicquot was a biography, and I didn't need to use flashbacks to begin my story. There was no compelling reason not to let the story unfold in historical time, from the beginning of her life to the end. Where I did run into a problem, however, was at the end of my story. Here's the thing about the life of Barbe Nicole Ponsardin, the Widow Clicquot, the first woman to run an international commercial empire: The first 40 years of her life are riveting and exciting. She lives through a childhood in the French Revolution and as a young woman she entertains Napoleon at home. She conquers the world of business. She creates one of the world's great champagnes. It's all great narrative: One thing leads to the next, and each event is more exciting and interesting than the last. Then, after her great triumph, she retires, still a very young woman, and she lives for another 50-odd years. She lives and lives and lives, and quietly: in a small castle and rural country houses; she does needlework and reads literature. It must have been a wonderful life, but it's not inherently a compelling story. Not enough happens for it to be a satisfying narrative, because one event doesn't really lead to the other. Her actions have no obvious consequences. This happened, and then this happened, and then this happened; it's what I said we wanted to avoid before: the journal entry that doesn't have an inherent story.

Think about the craft problem this creates for a writer. A biography is the story of a life, and the reader naturally wants to know how it ends. The life of the central character is one of the natural narrative arcs of the story as a matter of definition. It's not a very satisfying story, is it, if we have chapter after chapter of fascinating accomplishments, dizzy risks, tragedy and triumphs, and then end the book with one quickie chapter that says "Oh yeah, and by the way, and then she lived for another 50 years, a nice, quiet life and then she died, the end." The reader will feel cheated. It's a lame ending; and it's lame because if we imagine our narrative arc as an arrow gliding through space, the picture in our minds would have to be of an arrow plummeting straight to earth just as it reached its apex. Momentum, momentum, momentum, and then crash; it doesn't work.

So what are a writer's options? This is where figuring out the right narrative structure for the story you want to tell is critical, isn't it? Clearly, the straightforward narrative structure—the one where this is the story of a woman's life, told in the "she did this" third-person perspective—is going to leave us short of a great ending. So here, the writer has to think: How do I tell this so it's a great story from start to finish? Of course, one option would be to drag out the story of her last 50 years in detail and try to make them interesting. We could drag it out to make the story fit the narrative form. But it wouldn't really work; readers are too smart not to see that's what's happening, and to be annoyed.

Or a writer could take another tack: What if I introduce other characters into the story and let those characters carry some of the weight of the narrative in the second half of the book? That might do it. After all, if the people around our main character—people whose stories naturally intertwine—have fascinating lives, this would be one way to keep the arrow of our story moving forward. It becomes a collective biography maybe. The trouble here is that there's something else readers naturally expect: As readers, we want to know how stories end. We want to know what happens to characters, perhaps especially in nonfiction. So any character that gets introduced into this biography, we have to tell his or her life story as well; and at the end of the book, the author is going to have to tie up all the loose ends. To put it bluntly, in a biography, the writer needs to kill off all the key characters—and that can get very complicated if all these characters don't conveniently die in reasonable proximity to each other. After all, it doesn't solve a narrative problem to introduce at the end of a biography of one woman new characters whose lives we now have to narrate faithfully as well, and who live another 50 years themselves. We're going to end up telling two different stories in one biography, and we've created more problems than we've solved suddenly.

In the end, I chose a third option: I decided to introduce myself, the author, into the narrative as that secondary character. I told not just the story of the Widow Clicquot's life, but also the story of my search to find out about her history. Here's the useful thing about that: If the author is the other character whose story naturally intertwines, I'm also the one character I don't need to kill off at the end of the story. After all, the reader's expectation is that I'll still be around at the end of my own book.

We'll talk more in lesson 13 about how you can work with author-as-character as a specific strategy in your writing, especially in memoir and travel writing genres. For now, what we want to think about here is simply how strategic writers have to be when thinking about how to narrate your story. After all, imagine if I hadn't thought this through in the beginning. I'd have had a major problem halfway through the book requiring extensive revision.

Let's summarize a couple of rules—or maybe just general guidelines is a way to think about them—that we've already learned about narrative structure; then let me introduce you to a couple of new ones, and then we'll try an exercise together to see if you're beginning to understand the way a writer sets out to think about plotting a narrative structure.

First, we've learned that generally the best narrative structure is the simplest and the most direct one that will do the job. Sure, there are some exceptions; but unless you're setting out to be the next great experimental writer, less is more. We've also talked about the idea that a narrative structure has to simultaneously do at least two things: It has to give the writer the space to tell the story, and it has to meet the reader's expectations. Good stories don't just break off midstream. They don't rush their conclusions. Characters don't wake up and discover it was all just a dream. In a good narrative arc, the actions have consequences and everything that happens somehow contributes to the story.

When you set out to plot a narrative arc, you want to ask yourself two essential questions: First, what kind of story is this and what are the reader's expectations? Second, what way of telling this story will contain what I want to say so that the beginning and ending of my tale coincide with the beginning and ending of my narrative structure?

Ok, so let's go a bit deeper. Those are our guiding principles as writers; but what I still haven't told you is how to find the right narrative structure that will accomplish them, right? In fact, maybe you're wondering just how many different ways are there of telling a story. What are the different kinds of narrative structures available to me when I start writing? Let's take a closer look at the options.

In the world of traditional narrative, there are essentially three broad categories of storytelling structure. Many, many books—in fact, maybe most books—use different combinations of at least some of these three devices.

The first way to tell a story is linear. This is the kind of narrative structure most of us think of first. It's the story frame that comes to mind when we talk about narrative arc as an arrow shot into space, isn't it? A linear narrative has a protagonist—a main character—and the main character has some sort of conflict. That conflict might be internal, but usually that conflict comes in the form of another character: the antagonist, the character who somehow thwarts the desire of the protagonist.

Want an example? Let's imagine a love story. Juliet wants to marry Romeo. That's the arrow of desire shot into narrative space. They're in love, and that's an action with consequences. They're either going to be happy or unhappy together, aren't they? If Romeo and Juliet fell in love and got happily married and lived quietly ever after, it would be a terrific thing for our young lovers, who are also our protagonists. But it wouldn't make much of a story, would it? A good story also needs some conflict to keep it moving forward. So enter Romeo and Juliet's families, who are sworn enemies and who forbid their romance, our antagonists. Remember, one of the principles of narrative arc is that actions have consequences. Conflict is going to lead to action and tension; the tension mounts and mounts; and writers call this "rising action."

In fact, let's now say the action keeps rising. We're moving from a simmer to a boil in this story. Juliet's family fuels the flames by trying to force her to marry another man. Eventually, the tension results in some crisis or action. This—you probably know the term already—is the climax. Juliet loves Romeo. She doesn't want to marry this other guy, Paris. Her wedding day is coming. We're at the moment of crisis when whatever is going to happen has to happen now. Juliet comes up with a plan to bring the tension to a point of resolution. She won't marry Paris; she'll take a drug that for 42 hours will make her family believe she's dead to get out of this forced marriage. A messenger is sent to tell Romeo of her plan; the messenger, sadly, is unreliable.

From that set of circumstances, now a series of other events inevitably have to follow, don't they? At the moment of climax, characters are now going to have new responses and be moved to new actions. The climax has altered something essential in the direction of the story; that's its function really. From here on out, the story is going to narrate the consequences of this new and final set of circumstances.

What happens next is the fallout of that climactic action. Writers call it "falling action." Sometimes it's known as the "denouement," from a French word that describes the untying of a knot. The idea is that all the threads of a story come together at the climax, and they get unraveled and finished off by the end. In our love story, Juliet is put in a casket. In the crypt, the grief-stricken Romeo meets the grief-stricken Paris, and in a fight Romeo kills Paris. Good thinking on the author's part; after all, you have to get rid of Paris. Otherwise, Juliet is still going to have to marry him. Then Romeo kills himself with poison. Juliet awakes. She finds both lovers dead and so kills herself, too; and there's the end of our story. It was all the inevitable consequence of keeping passionate lovers apart in the very beginning.

You know the tale, of course; it's Shakespeare's Romeo and Juliet. Since all the main characters die in the end, it's clearly a tragedy. The central movement of the linear plot, then, is rising action, climax, falling action, and resolution. Or, put another way, it's about the tension and release of narrative desire. This building up of narrative desire in the reader is one of the reasons why a satisfying ending is so important in the linear narrative. After all, literary critics have noticed for a couple of centuries now that there's a reason this narrative structure tends to be used in romances: There's something perhaps inherently erotic in the journey the linear narrative takes its reader on. It's also a natural fit for stories with clear-cut life-and-death endings like a biography. After all, if there's one thing you know about the story of a great figure who lived 200 years ago and how it's going to end it's that surely you've got some good material for a deathbed scene.

But the traditional linear narrative isn't the only structure used in storytelling. In fact, there are other structures that are used just as often and just as effectively; and when you think about it you'll probably remember books you've read that use them. I said there were three very common structures, and now let's think about the second one: the hero's journey. This is sometimes called the quest narrative. But if you want to visualize it, it's not a linear narrative, it's a circular one. The protagonist—that's our main character—sets out at the beginning of the story to do or discover or resolve something. He or she encounters obstacles and other interesting characters along the way, and those experiences are what give this story its dramatic tension. Sometimes there's a turning point in the story; there's a moment where the protagonist changes, or something about his or her perspective on the problem or goal of the quest changes. Sometimes the climax is just a final obstacle that paves the way for success. But in the end, the protagonist returns to the original desire or problem that started the story and finds some kind of resolution to it.

Let's think of some examples from literature and test you to see: Can you tell the difference? How about the famous story in Homer's *Odyssey*? The hero Odysseus sets out from home to fight the Trojan War, and the *Odyssey* is the story of his homeward journey after those years of battle. Along the way, he encounters every obstacle imaginable. Time after time, he survives the challenges. At the end, he has to fight the hardest challenge of all: When he finally makes it back to Ithaca, he has to find out if his wife Penelope still loves him after all these years and he has to find a way to get rid of all the other guys who have lined up to marry her in his absence. What do you think? What kind of narrative is this, linear or circular?

You'd have been right if you had to think about it for a minute, actually. Odysseus, of course, succeeds; and, in a way, there's something linear about the plot: He sets out for home and he makes it. But essentially it's the story of a personal journey in which the idea of what home is becomes transformed for Odysseus. The climax isn't an event; the events in the *Odyssey*, one after another, are equally dramatic and difficult. The turning point instead is a change in the hero's perception; the way in which in resolving the obstacles that separate him from his goal he discovers something unexpected.

Or how about a more modern example, the Irish novelist James Joyce's masterpiece *Ulysses*? It's really just a modern retelling of the *Odyssey*, after all, but from a completely different perspective. The story there is set in Dublin, and the character is named Leopold Bloom and he leaves home and wanders the city. Along the way, all sorts of things happen to him, and he meets all kinds of interesting characters who shape his journey over the course of the day. But at the end of the story, he goes home and learns the answer to what he had wanted to know all along, the answer to the problem that launched his story: Does his wife Molly still love him?

Linear or circular? This one's another circular narrative, isn't it? It's another love story, but a completely different one from Romeo and Juliet. In Bloom's story—as in Odysseus's—the central conflict, despite all the fantastic events that happen along the way, is an internal one. Put another way: Circular narratives are ideal for telling character-based stories; stories in which the events in the plot lead to a transformation of a problem, goal, or perspective. What looks like an outward journey is really an inward one. It's a narrative structure great for telling stories about people and how events change them. It's great for writing a family memoir or a travel narrative.

Let's test you with another one. What kind of narrative is this story? Mary Shelley's 19th-century novel *Frankenstein*. Those of you who've only ever seen the old films are often surprised to learn how complicated and different the original novel is. In the book, the story begins and ends with a series of letters sent from a ship in the Arctic by the doctor Victor Frankenstein to his sister back in Europe. He's in the Arctic for the strangest possible reason: He's trying to hunt down and destroy his creature, the monster that all those movie versions mistakenly call "Frankenstein." In the end, he creates the creature and they destroy each other. In those letters home, Dr. Frankenstein tells the story of how he came to make this creature; how their relationship became one of cruelty, pain, and hatred; and how they finally set out to destroy each other. In other words, he tells, as a story within a story, the history of why he's up there in the Arctic. And as readers, he's the character we come to understand most intimately as the part of our literary experience. But Dr. Frankenstein never makes it home.

What kind of story is it? Did you say it was a linear narrative? If so, you were right, at least partly. This was a bit of a trick question, because there's also a third kind of narrative: the frame narrative. This is sometimes known as the Russian doll narrative because the idea is that its structure is to tell stories within stories; and if the other narratives emphasize plot (which is the case with the linear narrative) or character (which is the case with the circular narrative), the frame narrative emphasizes the perspective of the narrator. By placing stories inside frames, the writer structures his or her tale by letting characters become storytellers. That's what's happening here in *Frankenstein*, actually. It's a linear narrative told within a frame narrative, and that means we end up with a very particular perspective on the story being told.

The most famous example in literary history of a frame narrative is *1001 Nights* tales, in which the princess, threatened with death at dawn each morning by her tyrannical husband, survives and finally wins his heart by every night telling a new story, each with other stories inside of it. As entertaining and wonderful as her individual stories are, at the heart of the story is the princess herself, whose voice also charms the story's readers. It's the narrator we fall in love with, just as the sultan did after all those evenings.

Here's your exercise for next time: Thinking back on your favorite books, can you identify what kind of narrative structures they use? Can you identify what effect that decision has on you as a reader? How would the story have changed if the author used a different narrative arc to contain it? If you find yourself getting stuck for examples, think about some of those great classics of literature: The novels of Jane Austen. How about Toni Morrison's *Beloved*? A film like *The Wizard of Oz*, or one of the Harry Potter movies? *Alice in Wonderland*, *The Princess Bride*? Have a look at your bookshelf and see if you can decide which of the three narrative forms your favorites use. If you can, you're on your way to understanding the essentials of plotting a great story of your own.

Cliffhangers and Page Turners

Lecture 7

The secret to writing satisfying chapters is the same as the secret to writing satisfying books: strong narrative arcs. A good chapter begins with a sense of character and conflict and ends by giving the reader a reason to read on. This reason may be a cliffhanger—something withheld or interrupted—or a powerful emotional moment.

Chapters—Stories within a Story

- Many of the same rules that apply to the narrative arcs of books also apply to the narrative arcs of individual chapters. To write great chapters, we now need to deepen the way we think about structure and what writers call pacing.

- Have you ever stayed up too late reading a book? Every time you got to the end of a chapter and thought, *I should really turn off the light and get some sleep*, something happened that made you want to keep reading. The author achieved this with pacing, and it is not an easy thing to do.

© Stockbyte/Thinkstock.

How do you keep a reader reading well into the night? Chapter arcs!

Chapter Arcs—*The Da Vinci Code*

- One of the masters of pacing in contemporary fiction is Dan Brown. Let's look at how he manages the few chapters of *The Da Vinci Code*. The prologue opens thus:

Louvre Museum, Paris

10:46 P.M.

Renowned curator Jacques Saunière staggered through the vaulted archway of the museum's Grand Gallery. He lunged for the nearest painting he could see, a Carravagio. Grabbing the gilded frame, the seventy-three-year-old man heaved the masterpiece toward himself until it tore from the wall and Saunière collapsed backward in a heap beneath the canvas.

As he anticipated, a thundering iron gate fell nearby, barricading the entrance to the suite. The parquet floor shook. Far off, an alarm began to ring.

The curator lay a moment, gasping for breath, taking stock. *I am still alive*. He crawled out from under the canvas and scanned the cavernous space for someplace to hide.

A voice spoke, chillingly close. "Do not move."

On his hands and knees, the curator froze, turning his head slowly.

- From this brief introduction, the reader not only learns Saunière's age, occupation, and stature—admittedly, through telling—and quite a bit more through artful showing. We see his intelligence through his ability to act swiftly and effectively in a moment of crisis. We also know he is in mortal danger. Brown communicates all this through action.

- This passage also hint's at Saunière's conflict: He is a curator—someone dedicated to protecting art—and yet his situation is so dire he pulls a priceless painting from the wall. Whatever is going on here, the stakes must be enormous.

- The reader expects to find out by the end of the prologue whether Saunière escapes his stalker or not. Brown fulfills this expectation, but he also goes further:

  > Jacques Saunière was the only remaining link, the sole guardian of one of the most powerful secrets ever kept.
  >
  > Shivering, he pulled himself to his feet.
  >
  > I must find some way. …
  >
  > He was trapped inside the Grand Gallery, and there existed only one person on earth to whom he could pass the torch. Saunière gazed up at the walls of his opulent prison. A collection of the world's most famous paintings seemed to smile down on him like old friends.
  >
  > Wincing in pain, he summoned all of his faculties and strength. The desperate task before him, he knew, would require every remaining second of his life.

- We are told outright that Saunière has a secret; we are given hints of how that secret will be passed on to a new protagonist—just enough hints to tantalize—keeping the larger story moving forward. Those tantalizing hints are an instance of **foreshadowing**.

- This prologue also ends on a **cliffhanger**—a scene that is interrupted before its conclusion. This is another technique for building suspense and creating a page-turning pace.

- The prologue follows a circular narrative arc; it begins and ends with Saunière looking at paintings in the Louvre. It also begins with his thought *I am still alive* and ends with the final moments of his life, bringing that promise full circle as well.

Stringing Chapters Together

- As the prologue ends, the reader knows Saunière's death will have consequences. After all, if Saunière's secret dies with him, there is no story to tell.

- The next chapter introduces us to the book's protagonist, Robert Langdon. The Paris police come to his hotel and tell him Saunière is dead, then show him a photograph of the body. But Brown does not show the reader the photograph:

  > When Langdon saw the photo, his entire body went rigid.
  >
  > "This photo was taken less than an hour ago. Inside the Louvre."
  >
  > As Langdon stared at the bizarre image, his initial revulsion and shock gave way to a sudden upwelling of anger. … "I can't imagine who would do this to someone."
  >
  > The agent looked grim. "You don't understand, Mr. Langdon. What you see in this photograph. … " He paused. "Monsieur Saunière did that to himself."

- Brown uses the same pattern again: each chapter ends with a new cliffhanger, a new tease. Then the next chapter reestablishes a sense of place, character, and stakes. He uses this over and over again, throughout the entire novel.

- Perhaps Dan Brown's books are not subtle and literary. This is narrative at its most elemental—and most entertaining. That is the point of plot-driven, "popular" literature, as opposed to character-driven, "literary" works.

- To summarize, chapters—like books—contain complete narrative arcs. They tell a story that is part of a larger story; they begin with a conflict and end with either a resolution or a deepening of the conflict.

Foreshadowing, Cliffhangers, and Beyond—A Writing Exercise

- Chapters exist as little stories in their own right because of the way the novel developed in the 19th century. Like television shows today, a lot of novels were first published serially—in this case, in magazines. Each installment had to be satisfying in itself, as well as being part of a larger story.

- Foreshadowing and cliffhangers are two methods writers developed for this serial form. However, they are not the only ways to end chapters. Writers have more subtle options as well.

- Functionally, a chapter must do three things: Bring an episode to a conclusion of some sort; promise of new consequences from these actions; and draw the reader deeper into the story.

- A chapter can bring an emotional sense of resolution, even if an incident does not wind down at the end of a chapter. Making your reader laugh, cry, frightened, angry—really, making a reader anything but bored—will help keep a reader engaged in the story.

- As an exercise, return to your three-sentence beginning you wrote back in lecture 5 and write the ending of that chapter. It can be a cliffhanger, a heart breaker, a comic turn, or anything you want. Whatever you choose, it needs to make the reader want to keep reading.

Important Terms

cliffhanger: A strategy for building suspense and anticipation in a narrative by leaving the reader at a moment of crisis.

foreshadowing: A strategy for building suspense and anticipation in a narrative by giving the reader hints of things to come.

Suggested Reading

Brown, *The Da Vinci Code.*

Glass, *Americans in Paris.*

Janzen, *Mennonite in a Little Black Dress.*

Marquez, *A Hundred Years of Solitude.*

Questions to Consider

1. Is your own favorite book—whether fiction or nonfiction—a page turner, something that, once you pick it up, you have trouble putting down? Go read the first few chapters of your favorite book now. Do they have individual narrative arcs? Do they contain foreshadowing? Do they end on cliffhangers? Try not to get sucked into rereading the whole book!

2. *The Da Vinci Code* is a work of fiction—and very imaginative fiction at that! What is the difference, if any, between applying these techniques to a work of fiction and applying them to a work of creative nonfiction, given the nonfiction contract you must keep?

Cliffhangers and Page Turners

Lecture 7—Transcript

In the last lesson, we learned about some of the different possibilities for shaping the narrative arc (the story) of your writing; and when you went to look at some of your favorite books, did you see how the traditional forms we kept talking about kept coming up time and time again in great writing? When you thought about it, did you see that Jane Austen's *Pride and Prejudice* is a classic linear narrative? The shape of the book isn't so very different from the structure of *Romeo and Juliet*, except that it ends in marriage instead of a funeral. That's why we think of Austen's novels as a comedy of manners. How about *Beloved* or *The Wizard of Oz*? They're classic circular narratives, aren't they? After all, at the end of *The Wizard of Oz*, Dorothy and Toto make it home to Kansas, right where they started, don't they? *Alice in Wonderland* and *The Princess Bride*, meanwhile, are both frame narratives; stories within stories. But *Alice in Wonderland* has inside it a circular narrative, because Alice makes it home. The interior story in *The Princess Bride* is linear, though, isn't it? After all, it's a romance, and it ends happily with a wedding. If you were able to find examples of those classic narrative structures on your bookshelves, that's terrific; it means you understood an important lesson about narrative structure and how to plot your own stories.

In this lesson, we're going to think about chapters; and if you understood the idea of the last lesson, then you'll see quickly that all we're doing here is deepening the way we think about structure and what writers call narrative pacing. Because you need pacing in a great story, right? After all, it's not a great story if all the interesting parts of a tale get bunched together—say, at the beginning and the end of a book—and in the middle nothing happens; that gets boring. From a reader's perspective, we might say it was a book where the author didn't maintain the pace of the narrative. As the smaller units of a story, chapters are the building blocks we're going to be working with as writers when we think about how to tell a gripping story. After all, think about the last time you stayed up too late reading a book that you couldn't put down. Every time you got to the end of a chapter and thought to yourself, "I should really turn off the light and get some sleep, I have to go to work tomorrow," it turned out that something happened that made you want to keep on reading. "One more chapter," you promise yourself; and then another; and the next thing you know, there goes the alarm clock. We call books like this page turners, right? That's because the writer is telling us a story with great pacing. We're on the hook, and he or she keeps us there with fabulous chapter structuring.

That's what we want to teach you how to do in your writing, and it's not an easy thing to do. In order to master this skill, you're going to have to take all the different pieces of storytelling you've learned so far in this course and use them together at the same time. You're going to need to practice juggling three or four balls in the air, aren't you? Let's find out if you're ready.

How about we start out with an example of what an effective chapter—one that juggles all those balls at once—looks like. Ever wondered why Dan Brown's books are so often bestsellers? It's because he writes page turners. Let's look at how he manages the first chapter or two of *The Da Vinci Code*. Are you one of the million or so people who read it? If so, you'll remember how it begins; and if not, here's your introduction.

I'm going to read you the first few paragraphs of Dan Brown's prologue to the novel. Listen to how Brown launches his story. Remember what we learned about how a great beginning establishes character and conflict? Do you see evidence of it? How about establishing a narrative arc? What do you already know is going to happen in this story? As I read, see how many elements of good storytelling you can find. Here it is:

> LOUVRE MUSEUM, PARIS 10:46 P.M.
>
> Renowned curator Jacques Saunière staggered through the vaulted archway of the museum's Grand Gallery. He lunged for the nearest painting he could see, a Carravagio. Grabbing the gilded frame, the seventy-six-year-old man heaved the masterpiece toward himself until it tore from the wall and Saunière collapsed backward in a heap beneath the canvas.

> As he anticipated, a thundering iron gate fell nearby, barricading the entrance to the suite. The parquet floor shook. Far off, an alarm began to ring.
>
> The curator lay a moment, gasping for breath, taking stock. I am still alive. He crawled out from under the canvas and scanned the cavernous space for someplace to hide.
>
> A voice spoke, chillingly close. "Do not move."
>
> On his hands and knees, the curator froze, turning his head slowly.

What did you notice? Think about it for a moment. What do you know about the character of Jacques Saunière from this brief introduction? Quite a lot, don't you? We know how old he is. We know he's smart, because in a moment of crisis, he's able to think through pulling a painting from the wall to try to summon aid and to bring down the barrier. Look at how we learn this: Dan Brown does a nice job of communicating that information in the middle of action, doesn't he? Do you remember what we called this technique? It's classic showing not telling here, because we learn about the character by seeing what he does and not by being told about him.

How about the idea that it's tension or conflict that reveals character? We have that here, too. At the simplest level, we see how Saunière reacts in a moment of crisis. But great characterization goes deeper than that. What's unusual about his actions at this moment? It's the fact that he's a curator, someone dedicated to protecting art, and yet he pulls a priceless painting from the wall. We learn—we see, in fact—that whatever's going on here, the stakes must be enormous. Something extraordinary is happening when a curator starts damaging paintings in the Louvre, and Saunière has some serious internal conflict going on here.

If Jacques Saunière is our good guy—our protagonist—or at least for the moment, then we know that he's in conflict with our bad guy, this mysterious antagonist. We know what this story is going to be about already, don't we? There's a secret. Like the antagonist, we want to learn what it is. Discovering it, that's going to be our narrative. Dan Brown has created in a few short paragraphs narrative desire and launched his arc; and in the immediate term, we know where this chapter naturally has to go too, don't we? Either Saunière escapes his stalker, or he doesn't. That's the immediate conflict that we want to see resolved.

It's a great beginning. It establishes character and story, and it tells us what this episode is going to focus on. Now, let's look at how this chapter ends, because it will teach us a lot as well about what has to happen in the sections of a story in order to keep the reader hooked.

Jacques Saunière has a secret. The stranger—an albino man, it turns out—wants it. It's a secret Jacques Saunière has promised to keep, and it's dangerous in the hands of the wrong person. He refuses to tell, and is shot in the stomach and left to die slowly.

Now let's listen now to how the chapter ends:

> Jacques Saunière was the only remaining link, the sole guardian of one of the most powerful secrets ever kept. Shivering, he pulled himself to his feet.
>
> I must find some way…
>
> He was trapped inside the Grand Gallery, and there existed only one person on earth to whom he could pass the torch. Saunière gazed up at the walls of his opulent prison. A collection of the world's most famous paintings seemed to smile down on him like old friends.
>
> Wincing in pain, he summoned all of his faculties and strength. The desperate task before him, he knew, would require every remaining second of his life.

Dan Brown has kept the promise he made at the beginning of the chapter: We wanted to know how this episode between Saunière and his stalker would end. Now we do. There's a resolution to the immediate conflict, and that's what makes it a well-managed chapter. A chapter has to keep the larger story—the narrative arc of the book—moving forward, too. That arc, we know from the beginning, is going to have something to do with this very special secret. This chapter moves that story along, too, doesn't it?

Saunière is going to tell the secret; read on, and maybe you'll learn what it was the led to this grisly opening scene. We've already learned more about how important that secret is, which, of course, only makes us more interested in it. The end of the chapter teases us and makes us want to read more.

Think about that ending: Can you guess how Saunière is going to tell the secret? It's probably going to have something to do with those paintings he's looking at, isn't it? This hint is what writers call foreshadowing. It also serves to create tension for the reader. It's another secret in the story, and everyone wants to know secrets. Dan Brown pulls his reader into the story in one simple gesture by giving us a bit of information, but not the whole story. That's pacing: Learning how to give readers consistent parts of a story, so the experience of watching it unfold is part of the dramatic pleasure. After all, at the end of the chapter, we still don't know everything, even about Saunière's decision, do we? We know he's going to die, and we know he's looking for a way to pass along the secret; but how it all happens is still left for us to discover. In those last seconds of his life, he's going to do something important; something you can learn about if you keep reading. This chapter ends with a cliffhanger; you know, a moment like the ones you see in the movies where the scene is interrupted before it reaches its final conclusion. The car is about to drive over the edge of the cliff, the hero is about to perish, and then the scene cuts away to another moment in the story, leaving us hanging. It's all a way of building suspense. Remember, building suspense from one chapter to the next is the crucial element of narrative pacing. It's what keeps us reading.

Let's recap: We can learn a lot from just a few short paragraphs. We can see how to create character and how to balance the narrative arc of a chapter with the narrative arc of the larger story that it's a part of. We've learned how to use foreshadowing and cliffhanger endings to heighten the drama. We've learned that pacing is about learning to tell stories one piece at a time in order to make the telling a dramatic event. We've learned that chapters are stories within stories and use all the same strategies of storytelling as any narrative. If that's true, then we should be able to say what kind of narrative this is, right? Is it a linear or circular or frame narrative? Think about it for a minute: What's the narrative form of this chapter from *The Da Vinci Code*?

It begins and ends with Saunière looking at paintings in the Louvre, right? It's about how the character realizes something in the process of the events, isn't it? It's essentially a circular narrative; and just as is supposed to happen in a circular narrative, the main character is changed by the experience of the events. Saunière, now dying, realizes that his secret will die with him unless he does something drastic. He sees the paintings on the walls in front of him in a new light, capable of communicating something in a new way.

Look at how what was promised as the conflict in the opening sentences—when Saunière thinks to himself, "I'm still alive"—is resolved at the end of the chapter in a circular fashion, too, by his dying. We know from the beginning of this opening chapter where this story is going and what the central conflict is likely going to be. The chapter is the story of that conflict deepening, at the expense of our character's life.

At the end of the chapter, see how Dan Brown smoothly launches another narrative? We end this chapter knowing that the death of Saunière is also going to have consequences, don't we? If you remember back to our earlier lessons, we defined the plot of a narrative arc as a series of events that have consequences. It's not this happened, and then that happened, and so what; it's this happened, and something else happened as a result of it. That's what makes for story. If Saunière died on the floor of the Louvre and the secret died with him, there would be no story of the *Da Vinci Code.*

Want to see how Dan Brown does this again in the next chapter? It's no accident that this happens; it's what writers do in strong chapters. At the beginning of the following chapter, we're introduced to the main character—the protagonist—of the story, the symbology professor Robert Langdon. He gets a late night phone call and unannounced visitor in his hotel room at the Paris Ritz. It's a policeman who's come to tell him that Saunière is dead and to ask for help deciphering something strange. The policeman shows him a photograph of the dead body of Saunière. Look at how Dan Brown ends this chapter:

> When Langdon saw the photo, his entire body went rigid.
>
> "This photo was taken less than an hour ago. Inside the Louvre."
>
> As Langdon stared at the bizarre image, his initial revulsion and shock gave way to a sudden upwelling of anger. "Who would do this!"
>
> …
>
> Langdon nodded, feeling a chill as he looked up. "I can't imagine who would do this to someone."
>
> The agent looked grim. "You don't understand, Mr. Langdon. What you see in this photograph…" He paused. "Monsieur Saunière did that to himself."

See how it's a cliffhanger again? See how Dan Brown once again ends the chapter by launching a new step in his narrative and offering us another tease? Whatever is in the photograph is terrible. Robert Langdon sees it. We might get a look, too, if we keep reading; and we want to know what's so awful, don't we? Then, in the last line, there's another surprise for us. All along, we've been thinking something appalling was done to Saunière; some perverse crime there in the final moments of his life at the Louvre. Instead, we learn that he did it himself. We're reminded that we still don't know what the curator did there in the gallery before he died. We know it was something important; and we can already guess, can't we—more foreshadowing—that it's going to have to do with finding a way to share that powerful secret.

If you were to look at Dan Brown's book—all 500-odd pages of it—you'd see that he does this time and time again, chapter after chapter. Go ahead and take a look if you want. You can learn a lot from seeing how a writer of fast-paced thrillers manages chapters as mini-stories within a story.

In fact, let's try it out and see if you can write a cliffhanger to bridge two chapters yourself. Here's how Dan Brown ends one of the chapters that follow this one:

> Langdon held out his hand to shake. "Robert Langdon." Fache's enormous palm wrapped around Langdon's with crushing force. "I saw the photo," Langdon said. "Your agent said Jacques Saunière himself did—" "Mr. Langdon," Fache's ebony eyes locked on. "What you see in the photo is only the beginning of what Saunière did."

Once again, it's a good cliffhanger, isn't it? It's another great example of ending with the hint of some new tantalizing evidence; some secret we're going to learn the answer to, eventually. You know where we left the storyline earlier in the chapter, too: with the character Robert Langdon realizing that his friend Saunière had done something terrible to himself.

Ok, here's your exercise: Can you write a beginning to this chapter I've just given you the ending to? Let's think it through together, shall we? What information does a reader need to move our interest from one part of the story to the next stage in its development?

First, logically, we know this chapter has to get Robert Langdon out of bed and over to the scene of the crime, don't we? That's just good plotting. But how about that Robert Langdon: Aren't you wondering exactly why the police in Paris are calling up this professor in his hotel room? What's his expertise and his connection? Since he's clearly going to be our main character, I don't know about you, but I want to know more about him and what's happening inside his head as a character; his thoughts and feelings. I want to be able to see him. You know what, I want to know, too, what Saunière did to his body that's quite so horrifying! But we can't learn quite yet, because a good writer draws out the waiting and wondering to create suspense for readers.

Go ahead, and why don't you take a minute and try it. See if you can imagine the scene you might use to do all those things and to open the chapter. In fact, take a minute and write it down as a paragraph. Think about character development, scene, storyline, and helping the reader get ready for that next cliffhanger where the plot thickens.

What did you come up with? Hopefully it was something about Robert Langdon and his mission in Paris; his thoughts as he speeds over to the scene of the crime; something that helps us to see and hear him better. Are you wondering what Dan Brown wrote? Was it anything like yours? Here's how he crafted that chapter beginning:

> The crisp April air whipped through the open window of the Citroën ZX as it skimmed south past the Opera House and crossed Place Vendôme. In the passenger seat, Robert Langdon felt the city tear past him as he tried to clear his thoughts. … The frightening image of the curator's body remained locked in his mind.
>
> Jacques Saunière is dead.
>
> …
>
> Tonight's meeting had been one Langdon was very much looking forward to, and he was disappointed when the curator had not shown.
>
> … Again the image of the curator's body flashed in his mind. *Jacques Saunière did that to himself?* Langdon turned and looked out the window, forcing the picture from his mind.

Maybe Dan Brown's books aren't subtle and literary. This is narrative at its most elemental, and most entertaining. In a way, that's the point. Have you ever wondered: What is the difference between literary and popular books? It's really quite simple, at least in a general way. Most writers will tell you that literary books are character driven. In other words, they're about the people who inhabit and experience a story. Popular books are narrative driven. They're about what happens and the plot unfolding. True, we only get a glimpse into the mind of Jacques Saunière; just enough to establish him as a good character. True, in the course of the *Da Vinci Code* we're more interested in what Robert Langdon does in his interior life and how he feels about it, but mostly for how it helps us to understand and anticipate his actions and what's going to happen. In the lessons that follow, we'll learn a lot later on about how to develop complex, even literary, characters. But if you want to learn the essentials of plotting and how to write chapters and sketch characters that keep a story moving, Dan Brown is a contemporary master.

Let's summarize a few principles about chapters. We've seen that chapters, like books, have a complete narrative arc to them. They tell a story, which is part of a larger story, and they offer conflict and some kind of resolution or deepening of the problem. Ever wondered why chapters have this sort of independence; why they're little stories in their own right? It's because back in the 19th century, when the novel was being popularized as a form of mass entertainment, a lot like today's television soap operas, they were published serially in magazines. Each week, the readers read a new installment. That installment had to be satisfying in itself and had to be part of a larger story. Thus the idea of the self-contained but interlinked chapter was perfected.

We've seen that, like great beginnings of any story, chapters start by establishing character and launching narrative arc with the promise of tension, internal or external, and then the chapter complicates or resolves some part of that tension. Want another example of how that works? Think of the opening lines of Gabriel Garcia Marquez's novel *One Hundred Years of Solitude* maybe. There, Marquez writes: "Many years later, as he faced the firing squad, Colonel Aureliano Buendía was to remember that distant afternoon when his father took him to discover ice."

It's a great example of establishing both character and narrative arc in just one sentence. We know something about a firing squad is coming, and if we keep reading we'll learn why. We're curious; there's drama. We see that, in a moment of crisis, what the colonel remembers is an equally unlikely event from his childhood. There's a tension between where we started life and how he's going to end it; between being a colonel facing a firing squad and a small boy in rural South America. If you think about it, you guess what the shape of this narrative is going to be. This chapter is going to give us that flashback, isn't it? The author's made that promise, at least implicitly, and we know what to expect. Remember what we said in lesson 6: Much of good storytelling is creating—and fulfilling—your reader's expectations and desires.

Marquez is another example of a good beginning. Now, let's think a bit more about some good chapter endings.

We've seen that chapters end effectively when they have a promise of future conflict or resolution (a cliffhanger), or the promise of some future knowledge to be discovered (foreshadowing). But foreshadowing and cliffhangers aren't the only ways to end chapters. Let's look at some of the other perhaps subtler options you have as a writer, too.

Remember, at the end of a chapter—itself a mini-story within a story, an episode if you like—your goal as an author is to keep your reader interested. You want the reader to say, "I won't turn the light off after all, I'll read just this one last chapter." That means a chapter functionally has to do three things: It has to bring an episode to a conclusion of some sort; it has to make the promise of new consequences following from these actions or conflicts; and it has to draw the reader into the story. Hints and innuendo are one way to do it; that's foreshadowing. Endings that don't really give us all the conclusions are another; cliffhangers, right? Those stories of the sultana in *1001 Nights* are a classic example: If her reader isn't interested, he'll have her executed in the morning.

But a writer can also bring in the reader by playing on his or her emotions. A chapter can bring an emotional sense of relief and resolution, even if the story doesn't wind down at the end of a chapter. There's an old adage among screenwriters: At the end, make 'em laugh or make 'em cry. Comedy or tragedy. What's true of how to end a book or movie also works as another way of ending a chapter. But you can also draw on a wider range of emotions. You can also end a chapter by making your reader frightened—that's what a cliffhanger does, right?—or angry, or anything really except bored.

Are you ready to try a writing exercise on beginning and ending chapters yourself? You've learned everything you need to do to write a good one. Here's your assignment: Remember that great three-sentence beginning you wrote as an exercise back in lesson 4? What if you turned that into a chapter? What I want you to do now is write the ending of that story. You're going to want to make it a great ending, too—maybe a real cliffhanger; a heartbreaker; a piece of brilliant comedy; maybe a bit of foreshadowing—because no matter what, you want to end one chapter by making your reader hungry to read the next.

Building Dramatic Sentences

Lecture 8

Standard English sentences come in four structural varieties: simple, compound, complex, and compound-complex. Each of these has a different rhythm, and varying the types of sentences you use can give your writing emotional impact, whether by affecting pacing, creating character, or both. Varying sentence structure, along with careful word choice, can be the most powerful tool in a nonfiction writer's tool kit.

Subject-Verb-Object and Inversion

- Not only does the content of a sentence affect a reader; the rhythm of a sentence can alter the reader's sense of **pacing** and tension. Learning which sentence forms to use and what effects they create begins with knowing the different types of sentences.

- In English, the normal word order for a sentence is subject-verb-object: "Joe hit the ball." Listen to what happens when you scramble that up: "Hit the ball Joe did." This word order sounds eccentric and old fashioned (calling to mind, among other characters, Yoda from *Star Wars*).

- Inversion sounds old-fashioned because it reminds us of language that favors meter over form—that is, it reminds us of traditional poetry, where musicality was more important than sounding like natural speech. Inversion and playing tricks with word order is one of the simplest ways to change the tone of your writing and even establish character.

Four Sentence Types

- There are four kinds of sentences in English: simple sentences, compound sentences, complex sentences, and compound-complex sentences.

    - A simple sentence is one independent clause: "Joe hit the ball."

- A compound sentence is two independent clauses: "Joe hit the ball, and Martin caught it."

- A complex sentence is one independent clause and one dependent clause: "Joe hit the ball, which sailed over the outfielders' reaching arms."

- A compound complex sentence is two independent clauses and at least one dependent clause: "Joe hit the ball, and Martin threw his arms into the air, straining to catch it as it sailed just past the tip of his glove."

- Simple and compound sentences are **paratactic**. This means that each of the items in the clauses is given the same importance. Complex and compound complex sentences are **hypotactic**; some parts of the sentence are subordinate to the others.

- Paratactic structure makes a sentence sound simplistic. If you want to write in the voice of a character who is a child, for example, you can achieve that by using paratactic sentences and simple diction (or word choice), as in this example from *Winnie the Pooh*:

> They came round the corner, and there was Eeyore's house, looking comfy as anything.
>
> "There you are," said Piglet.
>
> "Inside as well as outside," said Pooh proudly.
>
> Eeyore went inside … and came out again.
>
> "It's a remarkable thing," he said. "It is my house, and I built it where I said I did, so the wind must have blown it here. And the wind blew it right over the wood, and blew it down here, and here it is as good as ever. In fact, better in places."

"Much better," said Pooh and Piglet together.

"It just shows what can be done by taking a little trouble," said Eeyore. "Do you see, Pooh? Do you see, Piglet? Brains first and then Hard Work. Look at it!! That's the way to build a house," said Eeyore proudly.

- Paratactic writing seems direct, spontaneous, and not necessarily disorganized but unorganized. If instead you want to sound (or want your character to sound) intellectual or literary, you would employ more hypotactic sentences.

Sentence Variation

- In most writing, you will want to employ a mixture of paratactic and hypotactic sentences. This **sentence variation** allows you to control the tempo and intensity of your writing.

- The late M. F. K. Fisher used this to excellent effect in her essay "Once a Tramp, Always"—a confession of her passion for Macadamia nuts. Listen to how the tension builds and releases in this paragraph:

> I have some of the same twinges of basic craving for those salty gnarled little nuts from Hawaii as the ones I keep ruthlessly at bay for the vulgar fried potatoes and the costly fish eggs. Just writing of my small steady passion for them makes my mouth water in a reassuringly controlled way, and I am glad there are dozens of jars of them in the local goodies shoppe, for me not to buy. I cannot remember when I first ate a Macadamia, but I was hooked from that moment. I think it was about thirty years ago. The Prince of Wales was said to have invested in a ranch in Hawaii which raised them in small quantities, so that the name stuck in my mind because he did, but I doubt that royal business cunning had much to do with my immediate delectation. The last time I ate one was about four months ago, in New York.

I surprised my *belle-soeur* and almost embarrassed myself by letting a small moan escape me when she put a bowl of them beside my chair; they were beautiful—so lumpy, Macadamian, salty, golden! And I ate one, to save face. One.

Appropriately crafted sentences can evoke high emotion about anything—even Macadamia nuts.

- Although there is nothing explicit or inappropriate in this paragraph, the tempo is a parody of erotica, thanks to the rhythm of her sentences. The first six sentences are compound or simple—writing in neutral. The seventh sentence is complex, and then each sentence gets shorter and shorter, punctuated with a climactic one-word sentence: "One."

- Fisher's first six sentences set up a pattern of expectation. As a reader, you settle into the prose. Then, using sentence variation, Fisher breaks the pattern for dramatic (in this case, comically dramatic) effect.

- Fisher speeds up the end of her paragraph to create intensity; a writer could alternately slow down the end of a paragraph to create a dreamy effect. The possibilities of sentence variation are almost endless.

- Learning this skill is crucial for a nonfiction writer. Remember, you cannot invent any facts, but you can always play with your story's pacing.

Creating Voice through Rhythm—A Writing Exercise

- This exercise is tricky because you need to do several things at once: You need to write one great paragraph that is the exact opposite of the *Winnie the Pooh* paragraphs, namely, a paragraph in the voice of a professor ruminating on the meaning of life.

- You need to convey that this character is male, 80 years old, British, and highly educated without actually saying any of these things—in other words, by showing, not telling.

- Two of the skills we talked about in this lecture will be among the most powerful in your tool kit for accomplishing this: Sentence variation and word choice. A professor would speak in hypotactic sentences and sophisticated language. But you will also need to build his emotional distress to a climax in this paragraph.

- How does your paragraph compare to the one I wrote for the professor, shown below? This paragraph begins with long, hypotactic sentences and ends with short, simple ones, a bit like Fisher's Macadamia nut piece:

  > In our passage through the days of our lives, thoughts come to me, unbidden, and I cannot help but reflect on the challenges and complications attendant upon it. There have been so many years, so many days, so many long and sleepless nights, if I am truthful, when I have contemplated the futility of my grand work, my vast intellectual project, and nearly thrown myself upon the bosom of those waves as letter after letter from publisher, one fool after another, turned aside my tome and cast me into despair. The cruelty, cruelty of this wicked world of publishing, I rant, I rail, I spit upon the wretched men who bring a brother to this precipice; to be so reviled by such fools upon the face of this vast planet. No, it cannot be! Gasping my last, refuse it.

- Now try just the opposite. Write a paragraph in the voice of a shy teenage girl who has no date for her junior prom and is writing about it in her diary. Use sentence structure and sentence variation to create plenty of high-school drama and end with a climax.

- After you have written your paragraph, ask someone who is not taking this course to guess who the character in your paragraph is. If your listener guesses correctly, you will know you have done a great job.

Important Terms

hypotactic: A sentence structure characterized by subordination.

pacing: The writer's ability to influence the reader's experience of a story's drama by speeding up or slowing down the narrative.

paratactic: Sentence structures characterized by a lack of subordination.

sentence variation: A strategy of mixing sentence types to influence the reader's experience of the narrative pacing, drama, and intensity; an element of strong writing.

Suggested Reading

Fish, *How to Write a Sentence.*

Fisher, "Once a Tramp, Always."

Hacker, *A Writer's Reference.*

Questions to Consider

1. We talked about sentence structure and word choice, but how important do you think grammar is in establishing character? Do you ever evaluate people based their grammatical quirks?

2. Have you ever read a piece where you felt the author overused any of these techniques—where the style distracted from, rather than added to, the substance? As a writer, how do you know when you have crossed the line?

Building Dramatic Sentences

Lecture 8—Transcript

In our last lesson, we learned how to structure a chapter, and you practiced writing the end of a chapter that left your reader wanting more. We said that pacing and narrative tension were some of the ways that writers can create drama and interest for readers. Maybe your paragraph was a cliffhanger. Maybe you used foreshadowing to hook your reader's interest. But as you were writing your paragraph, did you think about the way that the kind of sentences you chose could add to the mounting drama or heartbreaking pathos of that final paragraph? Did you think about how the rhythm of a sentence itself can create a kind of climactic moment that signals to a reader that one scene is ending and a new aspect of the story is beginning? This is something that great writers know is also part of how we shape the reader's experience in storytelling.

Learning which sentence form to use and what it can do to create pacing and tension means that we have to know what the different types of sentences are, don't we? This means that we're going to have a short grammar lesson. What we're going to learn in this chapter are some of the most powerful skills a writer can use; but this is also the most technical lesson of our entire course, too. We'll go slowly, and you'll want to pay close attention; but it will all be worth it.

Do you remember those lessons you had back in middle school where you learned how to diagram sentences? Or maybe you never had those lessons at all. But if you did have them, you probably remember something very important: that in English, the normal word order is subject, followed by verb, followed in many cases by an object. But listen to what happens if we turn the normal word order around. What if "Joe hit the ball" becomes "Hit the ball Joe did"? It starts sounding pretty unusual, doesn't it? In fact, it sounds a lot like that character of Yoda in the *Star Wars* films; and the screenwriters created that distinctive Yoda-speak by using a technique called "inversion": when you invert or turn around the normal word order in English. The result is Yoda speaks in a way that sounds old-fashioned and eccentric and wise, isn't it? It's a great way to establish character tacitly.

And are you wondering why inversion sounds old-fashioned and eccentric and wise? It's easy: It's because, until relatively recently, most poetry in the English language was written in meter, a pattern of very rigid accented and unaccented syllables that created a kind of musicality. There's a reason why a line like Keats's "already with thee tender is the night" from "Ode to a Nightingale" sounds beautiful and poetic. It's written in iambic meter—"tender is the night"—and it's inversion, too, do you see that? It should be "the night is tender with you"; that would be subject-verb-object. "Tender is the night," however, because it's not the daily pattern of speech, sounds more formal and more old-fashioned and somehow to the ear just more poetic, doesn't it? Here's our first take away from this lesson: Inversion can change the tone of your writing and can be a great way to establish a certain kind of voice and a certain kind of character.

There's another way to do this, too. If word order can change the voice of our writing, so can other ways of putting sentences together, especially what we do with those different kinds of sentences. There are four kinds of sentences in English: simple sentences, compound sentences, complex sentences, and compound-complex sentences. If you don't remember the distinctions, it's simple: A simple sentence is one independent clause. A compound sentence is two independent clauses. A complex sentence is one independent clause and one dependent clause. That means, of course, that a compound-complex sentence has both two independent clauses and at least one dependent clause, right?

You know all this; but here's why all this matters to a writer when it comes to writing great sentences: Some of those sentence types use what prose stylists call "paratactic structures." All that means, really, is that each of the items in the clauses is given the same importance. Some other sentences use what we call "hypotactic structure," and in hypotactic structure, not all the clauses are emphasized equally; some are subordinate to the others.

In a minute, we're going to look at some examples and explore what you can do with sentence structure and variation as a writer. But first, here's why it matters to you: Paratactic structures sound simplistic; so if you want to write in the voice of a character who's a child, you're going to want to use a lot of simple sentences or paratactic sentences. If you wanted to write in the voice of a very stuffy professor, you would want to use a lot of hypotactic sentences.

Here, look at what I mean. Here's an example from that classic of children's literature, *Winnie the Pooh*. Listen to this dialogue, where Eeyore has lost his house:

> They came round the corner, and there was Eeyore's house, looking comfy as anything.
>
> "There you are," said Piglet.
>
> "Inside as well as outside," said Pooh proudly.
>
> Eeyore went inside … and came out again.
>
> "It's a remarkable thing," he said. "It is my house, and I built it where I said I did, so the wind must have blown it here. And the wind blew it right over the wood, and blew it down here, and here it is as good as ever. In fact, better in places."
>
> "Much better," said Pooh and Piglet together.
>
> "It just shows what can be done by taking a little trouble," said Eeyore. "Do you see, Pooh?
>
> Do you see, Piglet? Brains first and then Hard Work. Look at it!! That's the way to build a house," said Eeyore proudly.

From a writer's perspective, what makes this section effective as children's voices is all that paratactic syntax combined with the simple diction: the simple word choices; the kind of words kids might know. In the short sentences, this is easy to see. "There you are"; a simple sentence.

Take another look at even the longer sentences, though. It's the same thing. "It is my house, and I built it where I said I did, so the wind must have blown it here." Technically, what we have there is three independent clauses in a row, right? The thing is, all of them are weighted equally. The effect is a writer's voice that says this and then this and then this.

That sentence is three independent clauses in a row, strung together with a conjunction. It's classic paratactic syntax, and it sounds like the voice of a child. Used in the mouth of another character, it might also sound breathless and hurried. It might sound like stream of consciousness. It might even sound bored and mechanical. It would all depend on the character you're creating; but paratactic writing has a very particular set of effects based around thoughts that seem direct, spontaneous, and not necessarily disorganized, but unorganized. On the other hand, if you really want to sound highfalutin and intellectual, or very literary, or if you want your character to, you'd want to write very complicated and maybe even convoluted sentences.

Are you beginning to see how you can use sentence structure to create character and voice and, because that's what we're going to look at next, climax and tension in your writing? If you write in a dramatic, simple way, you can get a childlike voice. If you write in a dramatic, complicated way, you can create a very educated voice. If you use inversion, your character can sound old-fashioned or alien.

But most of the time in writing, what we really want to do with these sentence forms is to mix them up and to use them in such a way that the changes in tempo and intensity that they can help create help us with the drama. If you want a cliffhanging chapter ending, for example, you want to have a paragraph that ends with fast pacing and not slow pacing, right? This is what's called sentence variation, and what it means is that the writer changes up the different sentence types in a way designed to create pacing.

I'm going to give you an example of this. Here's a paragraph from an essay written by the wonderful food writer, the late M. F. K. Fisher. She's writing about her passion for, that's right, macadamia nuts; and she's being tongue-in-cheek here and joking a bit by making it sound like these nuts are one of her great life's passions. It's an ironic paragraph but, of course, she's also serious about how much she really, really, really likes macadamia nuts. Here's something else you probably want to know: The title of this essay is "Once a Tramp, Always." It's another ironic joke. What's a tramp? It's a hobo, right?

That's part of the joke: She's borrowing a title from Mark Twain's piece and she's writing about how she traveled the world indulging in her love of food. But a tramp is also something else, isn't it? It's a woman who's maybe a bit too free with her favors. It's the kind of woman who throws herself into love affairs. Maybe even the kind of woman who fantasizes about macadamia nuts with shameless abandon. I'm going to read you this passage and as you listen to it, think: Where does this paragraph reach its climax? Then we're going to look at how M. F. K. Fisher technically achieves this.

Here we go; Fisher writes:

> I have some of the same twinges of basic craving for those salty gnarled little nuts from Hawaii as the ones I keep ruthlessly at bay for the vulgar fried potatoes and the costly fish eggs. Just writing of my small steady passion for them makes my mouth water in a reassuringly controlled way, and I am glad there are dozens of jars of them in the local goodies shoppe, for me not to buy. I cannot remember when I first ate a Macadamia, but I was hooked from that moment. I think it was about thirty years ago. The Prince of Wales was said to have invested in a ranch in Hawaii which raised them in small quantities, so that the name stuck in my mind because he did, but I doubt that royal business cunning had much to do with my immediate delectation. The last time I ate one was about four months ago, in New York. I surprised my belle-soeur [that's her sister in law] and almost embarrassed myself by letting a small moan escape me when she put a bowl of them beside my chair; they were beautiful—so lumpy, Macadamian, salty, golden! And I ate one, to save face. One.

Where's the climax? It's right there at the ending, isn't it? It's meant to be a bit funny. Did you laugh out loud at the overwrought drama of her enjoyment? Without being too risqué, let's just say it: It's meant to be mildly erotic, this climax in her writing.

But how does Fisher achieve that? After all, there's nothing explicit or inappropriate in this paragraph, is there? It's entirely G-rated. She ate a macadamia nut. She moaned. If we start reading into the metaphors—the possible double meanings—okay, sure, we get a hint that she's teasing us and making fun of the intensity of her own passion for this delicacy. But the way this paragraph builds up to its climactic ending—the reason it's funny and melodramatic—is because Fisher is doing, as a master writer, something important with sentence variation.

The first six sentences are basic compound or simple sentences. Perfectly good writing; and it's writing in neutral. Simple, compound, compound, simple, compound, simple. But let's pick up again with that last simple sentence. Listen to the end of this paragraph again, and what I want you to do is see if you can figure of what kinds of sentences Fisher is using and in what variation.

Here it is again:

> The last time I ate one was about four months ago, in New York. I surprised my belle-soeur and almost embarrassed myself by letting a small moan escape me when she put a bowl of them beside my chair; they were beautiful—so lumpy, Macadamian, salty, golden! And I ate one, to save face. One.

"The last time I ate one was about four months ago, in New York"; it's simple, right? "I surprised my belle-soeur and almost embarrassed myself by letting a small moan escape me when she put a bowl of them beside my chair." There's one subject, "I," and there are two verbs, "I surprised my belle-soeur and almost embarrassed myself." We could rewrite that as "I surprised my belle-soeur, and I almost embarrassed myself"; that would be two independent clauses. But what we have here instead is one independent and one dependent; so it's a complex sentence, did you see that?

How about "they were beautiful—so lumpy, Macadamian, salty, golden!" It's simple. "And I ate one, to save face." Simple; and more than that, simple, and each sentence is getting shorter, which is something else to notice. The last sentence: "One." It's definitely simple. In fact, it's so simple it's not even a sentence, it's a fragment; and sometimes good writers do break grammar rules to make a point. Fisher definitely is here.

What we have here is something interesting: A paragraph that begins with a series of simple and compound sentences where each of the independent clauses is more or less the same length. Listen to the tempo that creates: 1-2-3, 1-2-3, 1-2-3. It lulls us into a pattern of quiet expectation. Then, suddenly, we get one unusual complex sentence, and it slows the pace of the entire paragraph down midstream. Do you see what I mean? Think about it just literally: That long complex sentence actually takes longer to read, and because it's hypotactic—that word—it's a series of clauses that are all tangled up with each other instead of independent and easy. It's a languid sentence, maybe even a sensual one. After all, it's the sentence where Fisher confesses that she has a secret passion and lets out this little moan.

Then, suddenly, the paragraph starts accelerating. A short, simple sentence at the end of a complex one: "they were beautiful—so lumpy, Macadamian, salty, golden!" In fact, it's a sentence punctuated with a dash rather than a comma, and that also makes the pace faster. "I ate one, to save face." Simple, and even faster and even shorter. It's drama and pacing here. "One."

This is a great example of how a writer can use sentence variation and sentence length to control pacing and create drama. Remember how I said a few moments ago that the first six sentences or so of Fisher's paragraph were writing in neutral? What I meant was that they were part of the setting up of a pattern of expectation. They weren't part of the breaking. After the first sentences as a reader, you settled into the prose. You started just reading along happily. Then, using sentence variation, Fisher breaks the pattern. First she slows us down with one long sentence; and she does that because what she really wants to do is to start this paragraph racing, and she knows that if she slows it down a bit, maybe without your quite noticing, once those sentences start racing the effect is going to be even more dramatic. You could do the opposite as well. You could create a dreamy ending of a paragraph, and a chapter, by slowing the writing down in the end. In fact, the possibilities for what you can do with sentence variation are endless; as endless as writing itself. It's one of the tricks of the trade that all professional writers know.

As a creative nonfiction writer, especially, this is a crucial skill. Fisher is writing memoir here; and that means, under the terms of the nonfiction contract we have with our readers, she can't invent what happened when she ate that Macadamia nut. She had to really be in New York. She had to eat the nut offered by her sister. But the craft of creative nonfiction writing is to take what really happened and find great ways to tell the story, and pacing is a technique you can always use as a writer.

Are you getting the idea? Let's have you give it a try yourself. Let's do it together and see if you're getting the hang of it. It's a tricky exercise, because I'm going to ask you to do several things all at the same time to see if you've mastered these skills. Great writers are always using a whole range of techniques all at once, and now you're going to write one great paragraph. Are you ready? Here's the exercise: Let's write a paragraph, in the voice of, let's say, your favorite tweedy professor, ruminating on the meaning of life. Let's use sentence variation and appropriate word choice to build to a crescendo at the end. In your mind, before we start writing, create a mental image of precisely who you imagine this person to be: age, gender, education, anything we can imagine about the character.

What do you think? Let's make our tweedy professor a man. How old should we make him now? After all, he could be 40 or he could be 80. Let's go with the more extreme age and make him 80. He's a professor, so we know he's going to be very well educated. What else? Does he have an accent? Let's make it a bit of an extra challenge and make him British.

At the minimum, our goal is to convey the voice of an educated and articulate person who is feeling a bit philosophical without anywhere in that paragraph saying anything in the content about the age or gender or nationality of our character. That's the challenge; do you see what I mean? How do we reveal character by the words we give someone to use? How do we do it with sentence structures and something as subtle, but powerful, as his command of grammar? Sentence structure and variation are going to do all the work of creating character and tension here.

Ok, so let's give it a whirl. Let's set out a scene: Tweedy professor, standing on a beach at the edge of the ocean, reflecting on his life and its meaning. What would he say? Would his first sentence be, "Man, life is hard and messy"? Or would it be, "In our passage through the days of our lives, thoughts come to me, unbidden, and I cannot help but reflect on the challenges and complications attendant upon it"? If you were a tweedy professor, what would you say? Sentence two, right? Why? It's the sound of it all, right? But look at how that's created. Sentence one is a simple sentence with simple diction; and "man," that's a casual idiom that sounds much younger than 80, right? Sentence two, meanwhile, is a compound-complex sentence, and it uses words that demonstrate what we call "high"—you might say "highfalutin"—diction.

If we want to build to a climax here, what do we need to do? We need to make those sentences get longer and longer, building structural emphasis. Then we need a final simple sentence—something really powerful—that brings our poor professor crashing back to earth in a climax. How about this for a next sentence?

> There have been so many years, so many days, so many long and sleepless nights, if I am truthful, when I have contemplated the vast futility of my grand work, my vast intellectual project, and nearly thrown myself upon the bosom of those waves as letter after letter from publishers, one fool after another, turned aside my tome and cast me into despair.

Our professor is upset. He writes in such wordy sentences we can't tell what he means, so don't you feel for his editor? But even if the sentences are pretty wordy, from their pattern and length you can hear the professor's anguish actually, can't you? Here's a man who's worked up over his disappointment. He's thinking about throwing himself in the ocean because no one appreciates the brilliance of his latest—and we're sure very long—academic study.

Let's make our professor even more frantic, what do you say? Here's a third sentence:

> The cruelty, cruelty of this wicked world of publishing! I rant, I rail, I spit upon the wretched men who bring a brother to this precipice; to be so reviled by such fools upon the face of this vast planet.

What we have here so far are three long, complicated sentences, each increasingly feverish; do you hear it? How have we created that effect as writers? You can hear a lot of strategic repetition in there, can't you? We're going to talk a lot more about that and how we can control patterns of repetition in lesson 9. We also have complicated and hypotactic sentences, right? Sentences with one dependent clause after another; the kind that it takes sophistication to control, not something a child would be capable of managing. We have diction—word choice—that matches that sentence structure. Those things here together tell us: Here, this person is educated. How about the gender of the speaker? How do you know it's a man? I slipped in the reference to another brother, did you catch that? How about age? Have you heard many young people you know going around talking like this? I'm betting you haven't.

Now, we need to bring our paragraph to a climax; to a kind of natural resolution like a balloon bursting. Something has to happen to our tweedy professor. Let's finish him off, want to? Here we go, from the top one last time, our climax. What do you think? Is it going to be a long or short sentence that punctuates this paragraph? Wait and see.

> In our passage through the days of our lives, thoughts come to me, unbidden, and I cannot help but reflect on the challenges and complications attendant upon it. There have been so many years, so many days, so many long and sleepless nights, if I am truthful, when I have contemplated the futility of my grand work, my vast intellectual project, and nearly thrown myself upon the bosom of those waves as letter after letter from publisher, one fool after another, turned aside my tome and cast me into despair. The cruelty, cruelty of this wicked world of publishing, I rant, I rail, I spit upon the wretched men who bring a brother to this precipice; to be so reviled by such fools upon the face of this vast planet. No, it cannot be! Gasping my last, I refuse it.

It had to be a short sentence, didn't it? We wanted a big contrast. We wanted a sense of urgency as those all those long words ran out, and finally even our professor was propelled into action. In fact, even if you didn't have any words in those sentences, we still had the structure of a climax. If you heard that paragraph or a paragraph with the same structural patterns of length and variation in ancient Greek or Turkish or any unfamiliar language, it would still convey to you drama and climax. That's because, in writing, structure carries a tempo and its own silent kind of meaning, and great writers learn to work with the structure of their language from the beginning.

Now you're on your way to doing just that, and, of course, becoming a great writer. Are you ready for a final exercise where you can see how much you've learned? Great; let's have you try exactly the opposite. Write a paragraph this time in the voice of a young person, maybe a shy young lady who hasn't got a date for her junior prom and is writing about it in her diary. Can you use sentence structure and sentence variation to create plenty of high school drama and a climax? After you've written your paragraph, then I want you to do one more thing: Ask someone who isn't taking our course to guess who the character in your paragraph is. If your listener guesses correctly, you'll know you've done a great job.

Rhetorical Devices and Emotional Impact

Lecture 9

Sentence variation works at the whole-paragraph level to create emotional impact. Rhetorical devices do this work at the level of sentences, clauses, phrases, words, and even individual sounds. Rhetorical devices can be broadly divided into structural devices and sound-based devices. Both types are aimed at fine-tuning the reader's experience.

What Is Rhetoric?

- If you understood the last lesson, you're well on your way to writing stories that keep your reader hooked. These are techniques that you can use to end chapters, to control the tempo of your dialogue, and to reveal the emotional states of characters—all indirectly.

- The tools writers use to affect the reader indirectly are called rhetorical devices. These devices can be traced to the great orators of the ancient Greek and Roman worlds. For this reason, they have Greek names.

- Keeping in mind that content is direct and rhetoric is indirect, let's return to a line from Fisher's *Once a Tramp, Always*. As she speeds up her paragraph by using sentence variation, she also uses another technique, called **asyndeton**.

- Asyndeton—meaning "without connectors"—is a device where a writer deliberately chooses to leave out the expected conjunctions. Fisher writes: "They were beautiful—so lumpy, Macadamian, salty, golden!" Not "salty and golden!" It creates a sense of urgency.

- The opposite of asyndeton is **polysyndeton**, or adding more conjunctions. The purpose of polysnydeton is also to create intensity and importance and drama—as I just did in that sentence.

- Look at the paragraph you wrote for the exercise in the previous lecture. Did you happen to use either polysyndeton or asyndeton without thinking about it? If not, can you see a place you could add one of these devices?

- Characters and narrators need unique voices, and rhetorical devices are key to creating them. Rhetorical devices work by creating reader expectations and then breaking or highlighting those expectations in different ways for emphasis.

- This is exactly what we learned to do with sentence structure in the previous lecture; the difference is that with rhetorical devices, you are doing it on the level of the word or phrase, rather than the entire sentence.

- There are basically two categories of rhetorical devices: Those that work on the level of structure, and those that work on the level of sound.

Structural Rhetorical Devices

- Good writing uses **parallelism**. That means that we communicate similar ideas with similar structures.

- Here are two versions of a sentence, the first with faulty parallelism and the second with strong parallelism. Notice the verb forms:

  BAD: The life of a pastry chef involves getting up early in the morning, working in a hot kitchen, and delicate procedures are used to make a great croissant."

  GOOD: The life of a pastry chef involves getting up early in the morning, working in a hot kitchen, and using delicate procedures to make a great croissant.

- Parallelism can be used in very dramatic ways. In fact, this is what made John F. Kennedy's inaugural address one of the great political speeches in American history. Here is one of its most famous sentences:

  > Now the trumpet summons us again—not as a call to bear arms, though arms we need—not as a call to battle, though embattled we are—but a call to bear the burden of a long twilight struggle, year in and year out, "rejoicing in hope, patient in tribulation"—a struggle against the common enemies of man: tyranny, poverty, disease, and war itself.

- When Kennedy says "not as a call to bear arms, though arms we need," the repetition of "arms" is an example of **antimetabole**, when the word at the end of one clause is repeated at the beginning of the next clause. It creates a rousing emphasis and a call to action.

- The structure "not as a call to bear arms, though arms we need—not as a call to battle, though embattled we are" is another type of repetition called **anaphora**, where the same word or phrase is repeated at the start of successive clauses. This is often used to create a sense of urgency and climax.

- Where Kennedy says "not as a call to battle, though embattled we are," he is using a **polyptoton**, repetition of words with the same root. This is also an example of that poetic, elevated inversion we noted in Lecture 8.

- Notice how each of the four repetitious clauses are of the same relative length: "not as a call to bear arms, though arms we need—not as a call to battle, though embattled we are." This is called **isocolon**; it lulls a reader into a pattern of expectation, so that when you break it, it delivers a powerful rhetorical punch.

- The effective use of rhetoric, therefore, explains part of the power of the most famous sentence from Kennedy's speech: "And so, my fellow Americans: ask not what your country can do for you—ask what you can do for your country." It contains both antimetabole and poetic inversion.

- Antithesis is parallelism taken to the opposite extreme, presenting contrasting ideas in similar structures to accentuate the contrast between them. Here is an example from John McCain, speaking at the 2008 Republican National Convention: "We were elected to change Washington, and we let Washington change us."

- In **epanalepsis**, the writer repeats at the end of a clause the word or words used at the beginning. One of the best examples comes from Kennedy again, from an address to the United Nations in 1961: "Mankind must put an end to war—or war will put an end to mankind." The effect is to contain a thought neatly, like a sound bite.

- **Epistrophe** is the opposite of anaphora; here, a word is repeated at the end of two or more clauses in a row. Once again, we turn to Kennedy, speaking at Wittenberg College in 1960: "For no government is better than the men who compose it, and I want the best, and we need the best, and we deserve the best." It conveys closure and control. This particular example also includes polyptoton and isocolon.

- **Anadiplosis** means repeating the word at the end of a clause at the beginning of the next clause. Here is a famous biblical example: "In the beginning was the Word, and the Word was with God, and the Word was God." It is a rhetorical construction that lets the writer intensify and redefine an idea.

Sound-Based Rhetorical Devices

- **Alliteration** is the repetition of any sound at the beginning of successive words. We usually think of this as a poetic device, but fiction and nonfiction writers can use it, too.

- **Consonance** is a pattern of consonant sounds being repeated, whether at the beginning of words—a type of alliteration—or anywhere else in a word. The repetition of vowel sounds anywhere in a word is called **assonance**.

- Repeating sounds heightens their emotional effect. Some sounds sound harsh and grating—K, P, C. Some are soothing and quiet—M, S, O. Some are fast and vigorous—I, T, D. A writer's choice and use of sound can shape how a reader responds to the writing.

Using Rhetorical Devices—A Revision Exercise

- The number of rhetorical devices discussed in this lecture may seem overwhelming. You should not feel that you need to use all of them at once to be an effective writer, and you do not need to memorize their names by any means. The chart below should help you to learn them as you go.

- To get yourself started, return to the paragraph you wrote at the end of the previous lecture, and try revising it by adding one or two of these rhetorical devices.

- You might also want to start keeping a notebook with a page for each kind of rhetorical device where you can collect examples from your own reading and maybe your own writing, too.

Figure of Speech	Description	Example
alliteration	The repetition of the same sound at the beginning of successive words.	The soul selects her own society.
anadiplosis	The repetition of the final word of one clause at the beginning of the next clause.	For Lycidas is dead, dead ere his prime.
anaphora	The repetition of the same phrase at the beginning of two or more successive clauses.	With malice toward none, with charity for all, with firmness in the right.

Figure of Speech	Description	Example
antimetabole	The repetition of phrases in successive clauses in which the order in the first clause is reversed in the second clause.	I know what I like, and I like what I know.
antithesis	The expression of opposing ideas in parallel grammatical structures or clauses.	Many are called, but few are chosen.
assonance	The repetition of the same vowel sound in successive words.	The cool blue moon.
asyndeton	Omitting normally used conjunctions.	He's a genius, a wild man, a star.
consonance	The repetition of the same consonant sound in successive words.	He struck a streak of rotten luck.
epanalepsis	The repetition of the same word or group of words at the beginning and end of the same clause or sentence.	Nothing comes of nothing.
epistrophe	The repetition of the same word or group of words at the end of successive clauses.	When I was a child, I spoke as a child, I understood as a child, I thought as a child.
inversion	Reversing the normal subject-verb-object order of expression in English.	Blessed are the pure in heart.
isocolon	Successive clauses of a similar length.	I came, I saw, I conquered.
metaphor	An implied comparison that allows readers to see things in a new light.	Life is a voyage into the unknown.
metonymy	A kind of metaphor in which one object is described by reference to another object somehow associated with it.	"Suits" to mean "executives": "There go the suits."
parallelism	Expressing parallel or antithetical ideas in similar sentence structures.	Government of the people, by the people, for the people.
polyptoton	Repetition of words of the same root in successive clauses or sentences.	Not as a call to battle, though embattled we are.

Figure of Speech	Description	Example
polysyndeton	Using more conjunctions than one would normally expect.	Neither rain, nor sleet, nor snow.
simile	An explicit comparison using the words "like" or "as" that allows readers to see things in a new light.	My love is like a red, red rose.
synecdoche	A kind of metaphor in which the part of an object represents the whole.	All hands on deck!

Suggested Reading

Corbett and Connors, *Style and Statement.*

Zinsser, *On Writing Well.*

Questions to Consider

1. How do you think the sounds, rhythms, and musicality of language affect us? Can you find examples of how rhetoric subtly communicates and persuades in your daily experience?

2. Apart from rhetorical devices and sentence variation, what other strategies have you learned for building excitement in your writing?

Rhetorical Devices and Emotional Impact

Lecture 9—Transcript

In our last lesson, we delved into some of the very detailed ways that grammar and the kinds of sentences we use can create voice, character, and tempo in our prose. How did your assignment go? Was your listener able to guess that you were practicing writing in the voice of a teenager? Were you happy with how you were able to use different kinds of sentences both to create voice—because you probably worked with paratactic syntax, didn't you?—and to create drama building to a climax.

If you understood the last lesson, you're well on your way to writing stories that will keep your reader hooked, and these are techniques that you can use to end chapters, to control the tempo of your dialogue, and to reveal the emotional states of characters, all without directly saying anything.

In fact, this idea of affecting the reader's response to our writing indirectly is very important. There's a very important set of tools that writers call "rhetorical devices." You see them most often in speechwriting, actually; but they're an essential part of learning to control the craft of writing in any context. These devices go back to ancient Greece and Rome, and to the great orators like Demosthenes and Cicero, and for this reason they have complicated Greek names. But the idea behind them is very simple: The idea of rhetoric is the idea that writing and speech can persuade us or move us indirectly. Content—the "what" we say—that's direct. If I tell you, "Hey, the end of Romeo and Juliet, it's sad; the young lovers die," maybe you're a real softy and that will get you crying. But what rhetoric lets a writer do is control the indirect—the emotional—elements of writing to help you feel sad during the final scene.

In this lesson, we're going to do two things: We're going to take one last look here at some of these rhetorical devices and think about how you can also use these as a writer to control pacing, build tempo, and reveal character in your prose.

Let's have another look at that Fisher paragraph from *Once a Tramp Always.* In the last lesson, we saw how she used sentence variation to create a kind of ironic climax in her paragraph, right? But let me show you one other way Fisher makes that paragraph start working faster; one other way she creates momentum and tension for a climactic ending.

Fisher is doing something else to speed up those sentences at the end of her paragraph: She's also using an important rhetorical device, called—here we go with the Greek—"asyndeton." This is a device where a writer deliberately chooses to leave out conjunctions that would normally be there. In other words, having conjunctions would be neutral; leaving them out on purpose is in order to create a certain effect. Here's the sentence I'm thinking of: Fisher writes, "they were beautiful—so lumpy, Macademian, salty, golden!"

Listen to that sentence again; what's missing in it? "They were beautiful—so lumpy, Macademian, salty, golden!" Do you hear it? It should be "so lumpy, Macademian, salty, and golden," shouldn't it? There should be a conjunction between the last two items in a series. That's one of those very basic grammar rules in English; so why is Fisher leaving it out here in her climactic paragraph? Because the function of asyndeton—which just means "without connectors"—is to increase the pacing of writing; to create urgency and intensity and pulse-racing drama.

Want to see what the opposite is? Listen to my last sentence again; the one I was using to try to convince you that asyndeton was something you should be excited about. I said, "The function of asyndeton is to increase the pacing of writing; to create urgency and intensity and pulse-racing drama." "Urgency and intensity and pulse-racing drama"? It should be "Urgency, intensity, and drama," shouldn't it? I'm adding in more conjunctions there than is normal, and that is a rhetorical device called "polysyndeton," "poly" meaning "many"; "many connectors." The purpose of polysyndeton is also to create urgency and a sense of importance and drama, but this time by making things seem intense rather than hurried.

How about that paragraph you wrote for your last exercise? Look at it carefully. Even without knowing about these rhetorical devices, did you happen to use either polysyndeton or asyndeton naturally? If you did, that's really terrific, and it means you have a great ear. If you didn't, that's no trouble either. You've probably never heard of these devices before. But go back and take a quick look at your paragraph now. Can you see a place you could add in one of these devices to accentuate the pace of your writing even more dramatically? That would be a great example of how a writer can keep revising a work to make it better and better.

In this lesson, we're going to learn about a couple of other rhetorical devices you can use in your writing. Up until now in this course, we've covered narrative arc and the structure of storytelling. The next several lessons are going to focus on character, so maybe you already see where this is heading. Remember how stories need narrative arc? Characters and narrators need voice, and rhetorical devices are key to creating it. You've learned about how inversion—when we turn around the natural order to words in English—can make a character sounds old-fashioned or wise or just plain funny.

Wait, did you hear that? What did I say? "Inversion can make a character sound old-fashioned or wise or just plain funny." What device did I just use to make that pronouncement sound more important; did you catch it? That's right, it's polysyndeton. You already know some others, too. You've already learned about the difference between metaphor and simile, and in your last assignment you learned how to use climax to create a successful sense of an ending and drama. Those are all rhetorical devices, and you can already use them successfully.

But since we're already looking at how grammar shapes voice anyhow, and since you've come this far with rhetoric, how about we learn some other techniques writers can use to tell stories and convey character without actually telling us anything.

Do you want to know the secret to understanding all these rhetorical devices? They all have complicated Greek names, and it can sometimes make your head spin. But here's the one thing they all have in common: These rhetorical devices are about creating patterns of expectation and then breaking or highlighting those patterns in different ways in order to control what we're emphasizing. You already knew this, right? After all, that's exactly what we learned Fisher was doing in the last lesson, wasn't it? To create climax, she lulled us into a pattern of sentences that were all pretty similar and then, suddenly, she started writing sentences that got faster and faster and faster and that was her climax. It was all about the element of surprise. When I tell you dramatically that those sentences got faster and faster and faster, I'm using repetition to be dramatic, aren't I? It's really the same thing with all good writing. There are basically two kinds of rhetorical repetition in writing: We can repeat or change the structure of clauses or sentences, or we can repeat words and sounds. Structure or sound; those are the two options. Let's start with structure.

You've already learned about using sentence variation, so we've already practiced using whole sentences in order to build climax in a paragraph. But in this lesson, I also want to show you how you can use variation in the clauses of sentences to do the same thing. How you arrange sentences one after another is sentence variation. Now we're going to think about how you connect and pattern things within a sentence. Here is the most important thing to learn in this lesson: Good writing uses parallelism.

What is parallelism? It's easy: It's the idea that in writing we communicate similar ideas in similar patterns. Here, see if you can spot the difference. Let me give you an example of a sentence with faulty, or bad, parallelism. Can you hear how we would make it parallel? Here's our sentence; and again, listen for what isn't in the same form as the other clauses, and take a minute to see if you know how to fix it: "The life of a pastry chef involves getting up early in the morning, working in a hot kitchen, and delicate procedures are used to make a great croissant."

What was the part that didn't fit the pattern? It was that last clause, wasn't it? The simplest way to have corrected it would be to write instead: "The life of a pastry chef involves getting up early in the morning, working in a hot kitchen, and using delicate procedures to make a great croissant." "Getting," "working," and "using"; the verb forms are parallel, aren't they?

Here's another example of faulty parallelism. Can you do it quickly? How do we fix this one? "The book covered everything I wanted to know about becoming a pastry chef by explaining the technique of kneading, going through baking temperatures, and by reminding us to watch the time carefully." Did you hear it? "By explaining," "by reminding," and "going through?" That's not parallel. A better sentence would be: "The book covered everything I wanted to know about becoming a pastry chef by explaining the technique of kneading, by reviewing baking temperatures, and by reminding us to watch the time carefully."

One last example; how about this one: "When I was teaching my sister to bake croissants, I explained every step slowly, patiently, and with a lot of care." "Slowly, "patiently," "and with a lot of care"? What's the parallel choice? It's "carefully," isn't it? Do you get the idea? Great; because this is important for what comes next. What I'm going to show you are some ways that you can not only use parallelism, but use it in very dramatic ways.

Let's start this way: Have you ever read—or heard, perhaps—John F. Kennedy's inaugural speech, one of the great political speeches in American history? Have you ever wondered why it's one of history's great speeches really? We can easily analyze it for all the many things it can teach us about rhetorical devices and parallelism; and if you're looking for an additional exercise, having a look at it sentence by sentence is a great way to test your understanding. This speech is packed with parallelism and rhetorical devices. What if you could use those same techniques in your creative nonfiction project, to tell the life of a great historical figure, the story of your family history, or the memoir you've always thought would capture the imagination and hearts of your readers? That would be something.

Actually, you can learn to do this by seeing how Kennedy's speechwriters managed it. Let's look at just a few of the most famous sentences in that speech. Maybe you even remember some of them. Here's one that really captures my attention:

> Now the trumpet summons us again—not as a call to bear arms, though arms we need—not as a call to battle, though embattled we are—but a call to bear the burden of a long twilight struggle, year in and year out, "rejoicing in hope, patient in tribulation"—a struggle against the common enemies of man: tyranny, poverty, disease, and war itself.

It's one of the things that define this sentence from a writer's perspective: the fabulous and complex parallelism. Here's one example of it in there:

Kennedy says, "a struggle against the common enemies of man: tyranny, poverty, disease, and war." Want to hear what it would be like if I messed up the parallelism on purpose? How about this: "a struggle against the common enemies of man, tyranny, poverty, the problems of illness, and war itself." There's nothing eloquent about that. But did you hear other patterns of repetition in there? If you did, you should congratulate yourself; that means you're on track to already understanding rhetorical devices.

How about this part of the sentence, because it's all one long sentence: "not as a call to bear arms, though arms we need—not as a call to battle, though embattled we are." It sounds great doesn't it? In fact, it sounds so good that there's a fancy Greek word for just this rhetorical device. This is an example of a technique called antimetabole. Basically, all that means is that this is when the word at the end of one clause of a sentence is repeated at the beginning of the next clause, like in the example "not as a call to bear arms, though arms we need." What's the effect? You can hear it, can't you? It creates a rousing emphasis and a call to action. It's writing that stirs up the emotions of the readers, and the tone is a bit formal.

Here's an antimetabole quiz for you: Let's say you have the sentence "When the going gets tough, that's when resolute people recommit themselves." It's a perfectly fine sentence, right? But what's the phrase that's on the tip of your tongue; the one that's a lot more memorable? Or put it another way: Can you turn this into antimetabole? What did you get? If you did it right, inverting the clauses, you came up with, "When the going gets tough, the tough get going." It's inspiring, noble, serious; and that changes when you might use this device, doesn't it? If you have a character who's a military general convincing his troops to head off into battle, now you know one of the devices you want to pepper his dialogue with. But you probably aren't going to use something this formal if you're writing about a playground squabble, no matter how persuasive one of those children is trying to be.

But you know what, that's just the tip of the parallelism iceberg in this sentence, because there's another repetition in here. Listen to it again: "not as a call to bear arms, though arms we need—not as a call to battle, though embattled we are." Here, Kennedy's speech also repeats two times in a row the beginnings of clauses, doesn't it? The word for that technique is "anaphora," and very often it's used to create a sense of urgency and climax in writing. After all, can you hear how each time it's repeated it seems more important? Because here those repeated clauses are in the negative—"not as"—this effect is only intensified. After all, we know that sooner or later we're going to learn what it is a call to do, and it's going to be dramatic and important.

How about this anaphora quiz: What would it take to turn this one into anaphora? It's a line from a famous movie (almost): "Of all the gin joints anywhere in the world, she walks into mine." Make it anaphora; what do you get? Humphrey Bogart in *Casablanca* said it much better, didn't he, when he quipped: "Of all the gin joints in all the towns in all the world, she walks into mine"? There's a reason the original line is so memorable. That's rhetoric in action.

You know what, there's still another kind of parallelism in that speech by President Kennedy. How about where Kennedy says, "not as a call to battle, though embattled we are." Think about that for a minute. What do you think it is? It's antimetabole again, isn't it? At least sort of: "battle" and "embattled." They aren't quite the same word, but they are the same root of a word; and when we repeat words with the same root in successive clauses, even if we don't reverse the order and use antimetabole, it's called "polyptoton." The effect of polyptoton is to emphasize things while also livening them up. It's a way of avoiding singsong repetition and dull writing by making the reader think of the same thing, but in different contexts. Did you notice, too, the inversion again: "embattled we are"? Remember, inversion is a rhetorical device that sounds formal, thoughtful, and elevated.

How about a couple of other things going on in this same phrase, because we're still not done? Let's listen to that sentence again: "not as a call to bear arms, though arms we need—not as a call to battle, though embattled we are." Notice how each of the four clauses are of the same relative length? That's a device called isocolon, and if you remember from the Fisher essay, where she also used clauses of similar length, it lulls a reader into a pattern of expectation so that when you make a change and give the reader something longer or shorter, then you can deliver a powerful rhetorical punch just by making a simple change in sentence length. After all, that was how Fisher created climax, wasn't it?

How about another famous sentence from the Kennedy speech? Remember the one where he says, "And so, my fellow Americans: Ask not what your country can do for you—ask what you can do for your country"? One of the sentences you remember, maybe? If so, you had a good reason for choosing it: It's a famous political quote. It's also an example of … Wait, you tell me. What rhetorical device is it an example of? Let's listen to it again: "And so, my fellow Americans: Ask not what your country can do for you—ask what you can do for your country." Think about it for a minute.

Did you come up with antimetabole? If so, good work. After all, it's a clause in one order, and then the words repeated in reverse in the next clause, right? There isn't anything old-fashioned about politicians using this device, either; it's a modern favorite of stump speeches. Winston Churchill once said, "Let us preach what we practice—let us practice what we preach." John McCain told the 2008 Republican National Convention, "We were elected to change Washington, and we let Washington change us." President Bill Clinton once said, "People the world over have always been more impressed by the power of our example than by the example of our power." It's antimetabole everywhere in the world of politics, and that's because it does what you want to do in your own writing, too: It moves people; inspires them; riles them up; convinces them of the power and persuasiveness of whatever you're saying.

Antimetabole creates a sharp contrast between two clauses, doesn't it? For that reason, there's no surprise that these kinds of sentences also often use other rhetorical devices, too: antithesis. Antithesis is parallelism taken to the opposite extreme. Here, contrasting ideas are presented in similar structures in order to accentuate the contrast between them. That John McCain quote is a perfect example: "We were elected to change Washington, and we let Washington change us." It's one thing and its opposite, tied together in their language and form in order to emphasize the irony of the contrast. That was the senator's point, wasn't it? You get the point.

There are just a couple of other rhetorical devices we'll add to this list, so you have a full sense of the range of possibilities. There's epanalepsis, and one of the best examples is another Kennedy speech, this one from an address to the United Nations in 1961 where he told the audience, "Mankind must put an end to war—or war will put an end to mankind." In epanalepsis, the writer repeats at the end of a clause the word or words used at the beginning. The effect is, to put it bluntly, to create a great sound bite. It sounds like an aphorism, and it's a way of creating a memorable line that no reader or listener is going to forget quickly.

Then there's epistrophe, which is just the opposite of anaphora. Remember how anaphora is repeating the same word at the beginning of two clauses in a row? Epistrophe is repeating the same word at the end of two clauses in a row. Here's another Kennedy example: "For no government is better than the men who compose it, and I want the best, and we need the best, and we deserve the best." It creates a graceful way of reassuring listeners. In this rhetorical construction, everything is under control. The repetition of "better" and "best," think about that for a moment; what's that also an example of? That's right, polyptoton. Did you hear the isocolon? "I want the best, we need the best, we deserve the best." Isocolon: clauses of the same length.

OK, just one more. Anadiplosis: when you repeat the word at the end of a clause at the beginning of the next one. Here's a famous Biblical example: "In the beginning was the Word, and the Word was with God, and the Word was God." It's a rhetorical construction that lets us intensify and redefine an idea.

One more deep breath; hang in there another few minutes; because we still need to cover the repetition of sounds. What we've just covered is the repetition of structures, right? This part is easy. There are four more important devices.

Alliteration: the repetition of any sound at the beginning of successive words. We usually think of this as a device of poetry, but fiction and nonfiction writers can use it, too, to create rhythm. Listen to this famous passage from the Biblical book of Ecclesiastes, which was beautifully translated into rhetorical and poetic language in the King James Version. We read, "All streams flow into the sea, yet the sea is never full. To the place the streams come from, there they return again." "Streams flow into the sea," "there they"; do you hear the repeated "s" and "th" sounds at the beginning of the words? That's alliteration.

But did you hear something else in this passage? Those "s" and "t" sounds aren't just at the beginning of the words, either: "Yet there they return." Since "s" and "t" are both consonants—which is anything in English except "a," "e," "i," "o," "u," and sometimes "y"—what we have here is a pattern of consonant sounds being repeated sometimes at the beginning of words (which is alliteration) and sometimes anywhere in a word. The term for that—the repetition of consonants anywhere in the words—is "consonance."

What would the opposite of consonance be? The repetition of vowel sounds anywhere in words, right? "Streams," "sea," "there," "they"; do you hear the repeated "e" sounds as well? It's not just in the Bible and poetry that we get this repetition of sounds. Rap artists use it in their music on a regular basis, too. Take the rapper Eminem's lyrics to the song "Backstabber," for example. He sings in the opening lines: "Attention all units, attention all units / We have an All Points Bulletin out on a man with green hair I repeat, we have an APB on a man with green hair." It's the same thing, isn't it? "Attention all," it's alliteration. "Man," "green," consonance. "Out on," assonance. There's a reason the song lyrics are catchy.

What's the effect of all of this repetition of sounds? Some sounds sound harsh and grating; "p," and "k," and "c," for example. Some sound soothing and quiet, things like "m," and "s," and "o." Some sound fast and vigorous, like "i," "t," and "d." That's what good writers also know: By controlling the way sounds feel to us, we can control how readers feel when they read it. As with all these rhetorical devices, it's about shaping how a reader responds to our writing—feeling quiet or rushed, anxious or calm, full of tension or winding down to a conclusion—just through the sounds and structure of our language alone. What those politicians know and the ancient orators know is that this is an important means of tacit persuasion.

All this is a lot of information, and you don't need to memorize this. Like the last lesson, it's been pretty technical, and we can now move on to some of the larger issues about character and diction and shaping our readers' responses in storytelling. If you don't feel like you have all this down quite yet, don't worry. You can look at the chart in your guidebook for the course, and you can find all the information any time you need it; and it's easy to see visually when you think about it. It's really just a simple matter of changing around the many different positions where you have had repetition occur in a sentence and using fancy Greek names to describe them.

But while you don't need to memorize these rhetorical devices, what they do for us as writers is absolutely critical. The key thing is that these different patterns of parallelism can powerfully shape the persuasive power of our writing. It can create memorable passages. It can make a reader laugh or cry; make them worry about our characters; make then turn the page to read our next chapter, even though it's past bedtime. It's essential to writing a page-turner creative nonfiction book.

Your exercise for next time: Remember that climactic paragraph you wrote at the end of our last lesson? How about you do a thorough revision? This time, see if you can add to the mix in your prose some of these new devices from this lesson in order to make the sense of character and the sense of climax even more powerful. I would also suggest that you might want to start keeping a notebook with a page for each kind of rhetorical device with a definition underneath it. You can invent an example of each device of your own, or you can collect examples from your reading and maybe your own writing, too.

Putting It All Together

Lecture 10

Now that you have an entire tool kit full of craft skills, it is time to put them all to work at once. In this lecture, we will use some badly written prose as a springboard for thinking about how to write—and revise—well. Sometimes, that means recognizing that a story must be revised in its entirety, starting with the narrative arc.

The World's Worst Narrative?

- The past few lessons have focused mostly on the "how" of writing instead of the "what"—the form rather than the content. Great writing is about matching form and content. Without form—without craft—even the best story will fall flat.

- Before we turn our attention to content for the second half of this course, let's take moment to see how well you have really mastered the skills of craft. In this lecture, you will have a chance to test yourself on everything we have covered so far by learning what bad writing can teach us about how to write better.

- One of the most important lessons we have learned is that **revision** is part of any writer's process—even the most experienced professional writer. Therefore, you are going to get a chance to practice some revision on what I think might be the world's worst short narrative, a mystery story I wrote that breaks all the rules we have spent the course learning:

  > The Airbus plane had an engine that was whining like a broken washing machine, and our flight had taken off from Boston four hours ago. Sodas were being brought to people by the flight attendant, and she was grumpy, which probably wasn't too surprising, since it was long, boring flight. I was going to Oakland, and since my husband was

diabetic I noticed when the man and the woman in front of me in the seats started talking about her blood sugar.

They were probably in their 60s, and they both seemed confused. I think she was confused because of her blood sugar, and I benignly assumed that he was just not sure about her new medical condition. So I watched them for a while, blundering around like they didn't know what to do, and then I leaned forward in my seat.

"Is your wife diabetic?"

"Yes, she is," he told me.

"Oh."

Then after a minute, I said to the man, "Hey, you know I think she's got low blood sugar." He was pulling out a needle to give her an injection of insulin, and what I was telling him was that this wasn't a good idea. If she had low blood sugar and he gave her more insulin then that could kill her. So I tried to give him a hint.

"Mind your own business," he snapped at me.

That was pretty rude, I thought. And then he gave her a shot of insulin. Ten minutes later, she passed out. I wasn't sure what to do. I was trying to decide whether to tell the flight attendants, but it wasn't really my business, and anyhow eventually he pushed the call button.

The announcement came on the loudspeaker: "Is there a doctor on board?" And there was. So they put the lady on the floor and gave her CPR. I'd never seen anyone get CPR before, and it was awful. You could hear her ribs cracking, and her feet kept jumping up and hitting the floor again, ker-thunk. And did you know that your mother was right:

you should always wear cute underwear? Because this poor lady, in order to get a pulse in her leg they had to cut her pant legs open, and she had yellow old-lady underwear on. I am sure she would have been embarrassed if she knew we all saw it there on the plane.

They gave her CPR for 40 minutes, then we had an emergency landing in Denver. They never told us if she died or not, but obviously she must have because if you give someone CPR for 40 minutes without her recovering that's a really bad sign. I thought to myself: "How sad for that poor man, he will have to live with the idea that he killed his wife by accident for the rest of his life."

When I told my husband the story, he said to me, "Do you think it's possible he killed her on purpose, and you witnessed a murder?" It would be the perfect murder, if you think about it. But I guess we'll never know.

- This *could* be a great little story—full of tension, drama, character, and suspense. But it is not working effectively. We need to tell it differently. Take a few moments and jot down the suggestions that come to mind immediately before going on.

Fixing a Bad Beginning

- We know a great beginning should launch a narrative arc by presenting us with character and tension. Like all good writing, it should show rather than tell. How does this beginning stand up?

    - The first sentence—"The Airbus plane had an engine that was whining like a broken washing machine, and our flight had taken off from Boston four hours ago."—describes a humdrum moment on a plane with no character or tension by using a broken metaphor.

    - The second sentence—"Sodas were being brought to people by the flight attendant, and she was grumpy, which probably wasn't too surprising, since it was long, boring flight."—is almost as nondescript, with little character and no tension, and it throws in the sin of passive voice. So far, almost every detail we have read is unnecessary to the story's conflict.

- Sentence three—"I was going to Oakland, and since my husband was diabetic I noticed when the man and the woman in front of me in the seats started talking about her blood sugar."—gives us some plot-relevant information about our narrator, but it is not vivid characterization, and she is not personally invested in the action.

- What we have here is the beginning of a story in search of character, in search of tension, in search of narrative arc—and written in a resolutely passive, abstract, and telling kind of language, with the occasional bad metaphor thrown in to make it all more confusing and ineffective.

- The second paragraph also consists of three sentences. Note that two are basic compound sentences, and the third adds a dependent clause, but not a well-constructed one. The phrase "blundering around like they didn't know what to do" is redundant: blundering around *means* acting like you don't know what to do. This is just wordy writing.

- These sentences are also rife with telling phrases like "They seemed confused." Showing would be giving readers a picture of what they were doing that shows their confusion.

- The dialogue—"Is your wife diabetic?" "Yes, she is," he told me. "Oh."—is also flat. If this is nonfiction, we are stuck with the words as spoken, but you can use more interesting dialogue tags to convey how the words were said: "Is your wife diabetic," I asked, my voice wavering.

© Ingram Publishing/Thinkstock.

Revisions can mean everything from changing a single word to changing the entire framework of your story.

- If we were to look at this entire story, we would want to ask the same questions at each step: Are there wordy passages? Passive, telling constructions? Missed opportunities to build character? Events that do not have any consequences? Lackluster dialogue?

From the Ground Up—A Revision Exercise

- Sometimes, the most important revisions are not the little ones. Sometimes you need to reimagine the entire frame of your story.

- Where is the real story in this incident? What is the proper shape of its narrative arc? This story does not have to start with a character sitting on a plane. It could start with the character's husband asking her, "Do you think you saw a murder?" It could start with the moment the man injects his wife with insulin. It could start with the tense dialogue. It could be told from another character's perspective—maybe even the alleged murderer's. We could even shorten the story's time frame to the 10 minutes between the injection and the wife passing out.

- All great writers revise—sometimes radically. Because writing is hard work, we all get invested in the sentences we have put down on paper. But hanging onto sentences, paragraphs, or even chapters that are not the right ones for the story is not the way to write a fabulous narrative.

- A narrative arc is something like a path that guides us through a labyrinth. There are moments when a writer might make the wrong turn. The real wisdom lies in quickly recognizing that we need to go back and try a different direction.

- Settle in to do a revision of my story, and as you do so, see if you can bring everything you have learned so far into action. Start by thinking about the big picture.

- You have complete freedom to revise and retell this story. For the moment, do not worry about the nonfiction contract.

Important Term

revision: The process of reworking a piece of writing to strengthen the finished product.

Suggested Reading

Miller and Paola, *Tell It Slant*.

Perl and Schwartz, *Writing True*.

Questions to Consider

1. Think about how you would prioritize the various skills we have discussed in this lecture. As you set out to work on a writing project, what are the three most important things to pay attention to?

2. At the start of this course, I asked you to think about your strengths and weaknesses as a writer. Now, as we approach the mid-point, have you discovered strengths you did not know you had? Have you discovered skills you particularly want to work on going forward?

Putting It All Together

Lecture 10—Transcript

In the last lesson, we focused on some micro-level writing issues and on the rhetorical devices that can help you control pacing and a reader's emotional response to your writing. In fact, the last few lessons have focused mostly on the how of writing instead of on the what; the form rather than the content. This is critical. Hopefully you understand by now what I mean when I say writing is about matching form and content. That form can be the right narrative structure to contain your story, like we talked about a few lessons ago. It can be the way you use sentence variation and rhetorical devices to create a climax in any paragraph, as we just saw. It can be the form of a chapter and understanding the reader's expectations before he or she ever begins reading, regardless of what the story you want to tell is. Of course, form is about crafting great sentences; ones that keep the reader wanting to turn the page, ones that show rather than tell.

Form is one half of what every writer needs to master. In fact, without form—without the craft part of the writing process—even the best story will fall flat. You know this already, don't you? Some people can make a silly incident seem like the funniest story you've ever heard and entertain a room of people at a party. Other people can't tell even a simple joke and get a laugh to save their lives. The difference between them is how good they are at the form of storytelling.

The other part of writing great stories, of course, is content; and in the second half of this course, that's what we're going to turn our attention to. We're going to think about developing characters, creating dialogue and voice, working with perspective. We're going to think about the role of humor and how to master the fine art of timing in storytelling. Above all, in this course on creative nonfiction, we're going to come back to the important question of how to do all this—to tell great stories—while still keeping the nonfiction contract with our reader to only use real content. We'll think about creative research skills; what to do when you don't know something and still need to write about it; how to get into good writerly habits; how to revise your work and take constructive criticism gracefully; and how to launch your career maybe as a professional writer.

That's all ahead of us in the next part of the course; the nuts and bolts of the "what" side of storytelling. Of course, the "what" all depends on the "how," doesn't it? We're going to be relying on the skills you've already learned now moving forward; which means this might be a good moment for see how well you've really mastered those skills so far, doesn't it? In this lesson, we're going to do a review and give you a chance to test yourself on what we've learned so far, and we're going to do this by learning what bad writing can teach us about how to write better.

But first, let's think back to what we've already covered. Does lesson one seem a long time ago now? In fact, you've been building on the skills from our first lessons all along in this course, and I think you'll be surprised at just how much you've learned so far. In our first lessons, we talked about that nonfiction contract, didn't we? If you think about it, we've actually talked a lot in a whole series of different ways about how part of writing is understanding and satisfying a reader's expectations. There's the reader's expectation that in nonfiction we aren't making things up. There's the reader's expectation that in a mystery novel, we're going to learn whodunit, and that in a circular narrative the main character is going to undergo a change. In a linear narrative, there's going to be a climax, and at the end of each chapter there's going to be a hook that keeps us wanting to read more. Readers expect actions to have consequences in good stories, and they expect characters to experience conflict and tension. They expect good pacing and for the story to continue right up until the end of the book they're reading.

Then there are some other things we learned along the way that readers enjoy; maybe not part of the contract every writer makes with a reader, but things a reader would be happy to discover in a story. Things, in other words, which make the difference between a so-so story and a great one; things that make the difference between ho-hum writing and prose that captures the imagination; things that make a reader say, "Wow, this is a great book." There, what readers want most is a story that starts out interesting, gets more interesting, and comes to a satisfying conclusion. As readers, we like to be shown rather than told things, because showing is a way of bringing us into the story isn't it? That means we like active and concrete verbs in sentences. We like smart metaphors that help us see things in new ways. We like tense pacing, writing that moves us, characters speaking in voices that convince us, and chapters that move the story along gracefully.

We also learned that revision is part of any writer's process, even the most experienced professional one. In this lesson, you're going to get a chance to practice some revision, because what I'm going to share with you now is what I think might be the world's worst short narrative. I wrote it just for you, and luckily for me I wrote it just as an exercise. In it, I'm breaking all the rules that we've spent the course learning about. Here's your chance to test yourself by seeing how many of the common mistakes of storytelling you can spot in this short chapter. So sit back, and listen to the beginning of my story. See if you can tell me all the things I'm going to need to do to revise it. In fact, get out a pen and some paper if you like. Keep a list of them, because you know I'm going to ask you to practice the skills we've learned by making some of those revisions together after.

Here's my story; it's a mystery:

> The Airbus plane had an engine that was whining like a broken washing machine, and our flight had taken off from Boston four hours ago. Sodas were being brought to people by the flight attendant, and she was grumpy, which probably wasn't too surprising, since it was long, boring flight. I was going to Oakland, and since my husband was diabetic I noticed when the man and woman in front of me in the seats started talking about her blood sugar.
>
> They were probably in their 60s, and they both seemed confused. I think she was confused because of her blood sugar, and I benignly assumed that he was just not sure about her new medical condition. So I watched them for a while, blundering around like they didn't know what to do, and then I leaned forward in my seat.
>
> "Is your wife diabetic?"

"Yes, she is," he told me.

"Oh."

Then after a minute, I said to the man, "Hey, you know I think she's got low blood sugar." He was pulling out a needle to give her an injection of insulin, and what I was telling him was that this wasn't a good idea. If she had low blood sugar and he gave her more insulin that could kill her. So I tried to give him a hint.

"Mind your own business," he snapped at me.

"That was pretty rude," I thought. And then he gave her a shot of insulin. Ten minutes later, she passed out. I wasn't sure what to do. I was trying to decide whether to tell the flight attendants, but it wasn't really my business, and anyhow eventually he pushed the call button.

The announcement came on the loudspeaker: "Is there a doctor on board?" And there was. So they put the lady on the floor and gave her CPR. I'd never seen anyone get CPR before, and it was awful. You could hear her ribs cracking, and her feet kept jumping up and hitting the floor again, ker-thunk. And did you know that your mother was right: you should always wear cute underwear? Because this poor lady, in order to get a pulse in her leg they had to cut her pants open, and she had yellow old-lady underwear on. I am sure she would have been embarrassed if she knew we all saw it there on the plane.

They gave her CPR for 40 minutes, then we had an emergency landing in Denver. They never told us if she died or not, but obviously she must have because if you give somebody CPR for 40 minutes without her recovering that's a really bad sign. I thought to myself: "How sad for that poor man, he will have to live with the idea that he killed his wife by accident for the rest of his life."

When I told my husband the story, he said to me, "Do you think it's possible he killed her on purpose, and you witnessed a murder?" It would be the perfect murder, if you think about it. But I guess we'll never know.

This could be a great little story, full of tension, drama, character, suspense. But it's not working as effectively as it could be yet, is it? If we could just tell it differently as a writer using the strategies of effective storytelling, it has huge potential. Luckily, that's where you're going to come in. In this lesson, we're going to work together to transform this sorry little tale into a good story. Think about it for a minute.

First, let's focus on some of the things I've done wrong in this story. It's your chance to review what you've learned in the class so far. Do you have a list of a few things you'd suggest by way of a revision? Great; where are we going to start, at the beginning? What do you think of that beginning? I wrote:

> The Airbus plane had an engine that was whining like a broken washing machine, and our flight had taken off from Boston four hours ago. Sodas were being brought to people by the flight attendant, and she was grumpy, which probably wasn't too surprising, since it was long, boring flight. I was going to Oakland, and since my husband was diabetic I noticed when the man and the woman in front of me in the seats started talking about her blood sugar.

Let's think back to the things we know a great beginning should do. Like all writing, it should show rather than tell, right? It launches a narrative arc and immediately captures our attention with vivid character and tension. That gives us the idea as readers that something important is going to happen here and makes us want to keep reading. It should frame the story so we start off with a narrative form that's going to be interesting right up to the end of our story. Remember our exercise back at the beginning about the story of the man and the woman at the café, and how big a difference it made where we chose to enter the story? We're going to think about that, too. Of course, we want tense pacing, concrete images, and great metaphors.

What do you think about it; do we have any of that here? No, we definitely don't. Listen to that first sentence again: "The Airbus had an engine that was whining like a broken washing machine, and our flight had taken off from Boston four hours ago." Does that metaphor there make sense to start with? Did you notice that? It really doesn't. Maybe an engine whines. Okay, there's a metaphor; in fact, it's personification. That's the technical term for the kind of metaphor where we give inanimate objects the qualities of living creatures. So, fine, our engine whines. But there's also a simile in there: "like a broken washing machine," and this is just confusing now. Washing machines don't whine naturally, either. This is officially a bad metaphor. That's our first problem.

But what did you think about it as a beginning otherwise? Did that first sentence make you think, "Wow, I'm just dying to read the next one and see where this story goes?" Probably not. "So what," you were asking yourself, "So the airplane is an Airbus. Not exactly a revelation. So the engine whines. That's what engines do. It left from Boston. So what?" What we want in a great story beginning are actions that are going to have inevitable consequences. But what's the consequence of Boston? Nothing, right? This sentence might be interesting if it sounded like this plane was about to crash, but so far this is all just life as usual on an airplane. Ho-hum; not exactly filled with tension.

How about character? Is there a character here anywhere? All we know so far is that this is going to be narrated in the first person; the narrator says "we." But that's all we know about this person at the heart of our story, and it's not enough to be interesting. This is officially a boring first sentence.

What about the second sentence now? Here is it; listen to it again and take a minute to think about what you think might be the problems here: "Sodas were being brought to people by the flight attendant, and she was grumpy, which probably wasn't too surprising, since it was long, boring flight." What did you come up with? Did you ask yourself those same questions again? If so, that's the right approach. Is there character here? Not really. There's some anonymous female flight attendant on an airplane; not very surprising. She's handing out sodas. She's grumpy. It's a long flight. All run of the mill. Do any of these actions promise consequences? Do they generate tension?

No again. In fact, so far, everything in this story is completely irrelevant. If the flight attendant were happy, would that change the direction of this story in any way? It really wouldn't. If she were handling out pretzels instead, would that matter? In short, is there a narrative arc? Not that I can see.

Did you notice that I did something that made that sentence even less effective? Listen to this again: "Sodas were being brought to people." Did you catch that it was also a passive construction? It's one of those telltale "-ing" verbs here, isn't it? Do you remember what passive constructions and "-ing" verbs can alert us to in writing? Do you remember? It's a sign of telling, not showing. After all, can you really visualize this scene clearly? Ok, you've been on a plane before, and they all look alike; but do you know what the flight attendant looks like? Could you tell us anything about her character? We still don't know anything about our faceless narrator either.

So far, I've written a pretty weak story, though it has a lot of potential. Let's have a look now at sentence three. Again, listen and see if you can point out the problems? Here it is: "I was going to Oakland, and since my husband was diabetic I noticed when the man and the woman in front of me in the seats started talking about her blood sugar." At least we have some information about our narrator now, don't we? But not much. We know she's a woman and married and that her husband has diabetes; that she's going to Oakland. Ok, that's something; it's better than the nothing we've had so far at least. But it's still not exactly vivid characterization here, is it? After all, remember how we learned that tension and conflict is one of the most effective ways to establish character? This character doesn't seem to have any motive or any conflict, does she? She's just sitting there on this flight like a passive lump, just as passive a lump as that last passive sentence we read. She might as well be going to Kansas. Did you hear again those telling "-ing" verbs, "started talking"? What we've got here is the beginning of a story in search of character, in search of tension, in search of a narrative arc, and written in a resolutely passive, abstract, telling kind of language with the occasional bad metaphor thrown in to make it all the more confusing and ineffective.

Now you try the second paragraph. In fact, this time, why don't you listen and see: Is there any sentence variation here? Are there are patterns established and then significantly broken to create drama or pacing? Here it is:

> They were probably in their 60s, and they both seemed confused. I think she was confused because of her blood sugar, and I benignly assumed that he was just not sure about her new medical condition. So I watched them for a while, blundering around like they didn't know what to do, and then I leaned forward in my seat.

Three sentences; and what kinds of sentences were they, did you stop to figure that out? They're pretty much just basic compound sentences: independent clause, conjunction, independent clause, repeat. The only exception is that last sentence, which has a short little dependant clause tucked in there. That clause doesn't really help the situation; it's that phrase where I describe the couple as "blundering around like they didn't know what to do." "Blundering around" means action like you don't know what to do; so that's like saying "the dog barked like a dog." It's worse than an ineffective simile; notice the comparison using the "like" there. It's just wordy writing.

We don't have sentence variation. But these sentences don't zing for another reason, too. Think back: If we want to make sentences come alive for our readers, what's one technique we can use? Do you remember? We can show and not tell; that's the easiest remedy. Listen to all that showing language in there: They "seemed confused"; that's telling. Showing would we giving readers a picture of what they were doing that shows their confusion. Did the man's hand tremble? Did the woman keep asking the same question? They blundered around; what did that look like? If we were revising this story for showing, we would give our reader a picture of what we were seeing, wouldn't we?

Then, how about that dialogue? "Is your wife diabetic?" "Yes, she is," he told me. "Oh." That's a pretty dull conversation; but even without changing the words that were spoken—after all, in the nonfiction contract, we can't change things, if that's what's really happened—we can spice up the dialogue. We can help the reader understand how these words were said. "Is your wife diabetic," I asked, my voice wavering. "Is your wife diabetic," I asked firmly. "Yes, she is," he said with a shy glance. "Yes, she is," and his voice said, "Mind your own darned business, lady." In other words, we can give the reader a sense of how to read and interpret the words being spoken, and we can start to build our characters in the process. Because so far, that's a lot of the problem here, isn't it? Can you see these characters in your mind? Do you have a sense of their motivations and the tension between them? If you do, it's because you have a good imagination, not because I've written a wonderful story.

You get the idea, don't you? If we were to look at this entire story, we would want to ask at each step of the way the same questions: Are there wordy passages? Passive and telling constructions? Missed opportunities to build character? Events that are thrown in there but don't seem to have any consequences or real bearing on the direction of the story? Is there lackluster dialogue? We already know there's a weak beginning. How about that ending? Is it satisfying? "It would be the perfect murder, if you think about it. But I guess we'll never know." I don't know about you, but an ending like that—one that leaves us hanging and seems to undermine the importance of the entire story we've just heard—that's just plain annoying.

Can you guess what your assignment is going to be at the end of this lesson? That's right, your job is going to be to listen again to this story and to settle in to see not only if you can identify these common errors, but to see if you can revise—maybe even rewrite—this story to fix those common missteps. It's a story that actually has a lot of natural drama and human interest, but it needs a serious revision.

But let's talk for a minute here about revision generally, in fact. Here's something that every great writer knows: Sometimes the most important revisions aren't the little ones; sometimes what you need to do is reimagine the frame of the story first. Before you settle in to think about how to improve the content of the story—how to make the language more active, how to build character, how to describe scenes, how to show; before you do all that great work—stop to think for a moment about all these issues of form we've learned about so far in our time together. Think back again to the exercise we did at the very beginning, when we thought about where to begin the story of the strange couple at the café. Think back to our exercise about all the different possible perspectives we could tell the story of the World War II photograph from and how radically each different perspective could reshape the narrative arc that was set into motion. Think about how

Dan Brown begins and ends his chapters, and what we learned about writing sentences at the outset that establish character, tension, and narrative arc. Think about how *Romeo and Juliet* would be a different story entirely if it were told as a circular narrative rather than a linear one.

Before you settle down, then, to revise this story I've told you here, what I want you to do is think: Where's the story here? What's the shape of its narrative arc? How can I take the elements I've got to work with here and rearrange them to tell this story in a more dramatic and effective way? In other words, before you start with the little revisions, see if you don't want to make some major ones; and that means thinking especially about those larger issues of framing the story and giving it a structure that lets it all come alive.

Beginnings are crucial, aren't they? You learned that already. You know that where a story starts determines a good part of the outcome. We don't have to start this story with a character sitting on a plane. We can start this story with the character's husband asking her, "Do you think you saw a murder?" That would certainly be an opening that would catch the reader's attention.

Or, we could start this story with the moment the man injects his wife with insulin. We can start with that bit of tense dialogue. In fact, we could even tell it from the man's perspective: What if he is a murderer and that fact came out later? What must be going through his head as this meddlesome lady in the seat behind him starts to ask questions? That would be a whole different take on this story, and a potentially riveting one.

Or, here's another idea: What if the narrative frame of the story is that 10-minute period between the moment he injects his wife and the moment she passes out? We could compress the frame of the story, focusing on the most important period of the action. Then we could tell the story from the perspective of what the three people all might be thinking at that moment. It would be a chance to work with different kinds of interior monologue and perspective. After all, you know the perspective of the narrator. You can imagine the perspective of the man maybe. But what must that woman have been thinking?

Or, what else can you come up with? What other narrative shapes are there that might let us expand or contract this story in ways that would make the telling of it better? There are dozens of fabulous ways to rewrite this little story, but the key thing is you need to find your angle; then, you need to find the structure that lets you tell it.

Settle in to do a revision of my story idea here; and as you do it, see if you can bring everything you've learned so far into action. Start by thinking about the big picture. You have complete freedom here to revise and retell this story. For the moment, don't worry about the nonfiction contract. In the lessons that are coming up, we'll talk a good deal about how to work around the limitations of reality and how you can use voice and perspective to do that. For now, take the opportunity to look back and put what you've learned into action. See if you can use all the skills we've talked about so far in the course in your writing. Then, we'll move on to some of the finer techniques you can use as a writer to develop character and shape story.

Revealing Character in Words and Actions

Lecture 11

Sometimes, character attributes make sense, and it is the detail that fits to a T that will become a source of tension for the character. At other times, it is the quirky, unexpected detail that reveals a character's hidden conflicts. When writing creative nonfiction, an author must learn to sift out these details from among the many facts gathered during the research process, whether the subject reveals them through words or actions.

Capturing Details of Character

- We have thus far examined the how of great writing; over the next few lectures, we will turn our focus onto the whats: character, dialogue, perspective, and scene.

- We have already talked about the formal aspects of character. Character is about tension and conflict. Sometimes characters are in conflict with each other—a protagonist and an antagonist. Sometimes characters are struggling against a situation instead. Sometimes characters are in conflict with themselves. What matters is that conflict reveals character.

© Goodshoot/Thinkstock.

Conflict, whether internal or external, helps you reveal your characters.

- Many things reveal character. In your mind's eye, picture someone you know well, then make a list of things you know about this person. What makes him or her different from anyone else in the room?

- Review your list. What are the most interesting details you came up with? They are probably those details that seem unexpected or out of character, or they are the things that seem to perfectly capture the essence of character. Small details stand in for larger elements of character.

- These kinds of details are also about introducing tension into a story. Things that are out of character suggest that a person is more complicated that he or she appears—internal conflict. A detail that fits a character to a T creates narrative suspense; some element of the plot will force this person to act against character.

Where Do We Find the Details?

- In creative nonfiction, discovering these kinds of details is particularly important precisely because we cannot invent things. The little details that tell the story of character are a large part of bringing a character to life.

- When I was writing *The Widow Clicquot*, one of my biggest challenges was how few personal details I could find about Barbe-Nicole Clicquot. Few letters by or about her have survived. What I did know was that a 27-year-old, upper-middle-class woman with a small child and no business experience, in an era when women did not have careers, convinced her father-in-law to loan her the equivalent of a million dollars and to let her rebuild and run her husband's failed wine business.

- This information alone told me a lot about Madame Clicquot and her father in law. She must have been an amazing woman, and he must have been astute to recognize this and do the unthinkable.

Three Character Sketches

- You can find some of the most fabulous efforts at character sketches in the modern world in dating advertisements. When a person writes one, he or she is essentially inviting a reader into a narrative about a romance. Let's start with this example:

SWEET LADY, mother and now grandmother. Interesting and interested in the world. Scientist, birdwatcher, intrigued by beautiful art and smart people. Still loves fast cars. Active mind. Decent soul. Hopes to meet accomplished, responsible, sensitive, hopelessly handsome man for good laughs and much merriment.

- Not only does this ad contain lots of detail and some interesting internal tensions (a speed-demon granny?), it makes you wonder who will respond to this ad. When you can start projecting a story out from a character description, that is good writing.

- Let's try another personal ad:

ECCENTRIC EUROPEAN ADVENTURER, 72, former revolutionary, award-winning artist, trim, brilliant, lives part-time in Africa, part-time in France, married, seeks permanent mistress or second wife in complete agreement with first. Requirements: 30–40, sensual, talented, open-minded.

- There is a lot to digest here! This character could be the protagonist of a very interesting story. And the word choice is important, too: What kind of person has "requirements" in a mate? And what sort of woman in her 30s would respond to this?

- Here is one last example, which is quite different:

Sexy lady needs one decent guy: witty, responsible, available. So we can dream about all the things we once believed in and make love again like teenagers. In my mind, I will be young and beautiful. If you close your eyes, you will be too. We will dream together and you will read children's stories and *The Economist* to me. All night, we will touch fingers and dream of soaring. Me, late 40s. You, as young as you wish to be.

- This piece is quite sad and lyrical and tells us a lot about her internal conflict and motivations. Another thing that makes this advertisement particularly effective is its point of view: She uses *I* and *you* to create a sense of intimacy.

Character and Point of View

- The **first-person** point of view lets readers get into the head of a character. This is the point of view of experience and internal perspective.

- The *I* voice in a story can be reliable or unreliable. The *I* can be someone we suspect is a liar, deluded, or an exaggerator. Likewise, the *I* voice can be omniscient; it can know everything that we know. Or it can be limited; we can know some things that the *I* does not get to see.

- The **third-person**—the *he*, *she*, or *they* perspective—seems all-knowing and objective. It is more distanced, cooler, and more detached. It has the advantage of making the character *in* the story more important than the character *telling* the story.

- Of the three personal ads above, the former revolutionary seems the most distanced in terms of our insight into the mind of the author. Notice, there is no *I* in there at all. There are hardly any verbs and no pronouns. It is possible that the gentleman did not write the ad himself; perhaps it was a third party—even his wife! This fact could change our narrative arc completely.

- Among the three ads, the aging lady lamenting her lost youth is the most intimate. Part of the reason is that the content is inherently more private, but it is also the use of the first-person perspective, both singular (*I*) and plural (*we*) and the **second person** (*you*). It is a point of view that invites the reader to think of himself or herself as part of the story.

Personal Ads—A Writing Exercise

- It is time to try your hand at writing a personal advertisement for yourself—but yourself reimagined as a character. You can use any voice that you like. Just remember, character is identity that implies action. Make this an advertisement for a fabulous character—the kind of person someone else wants to be in a story with.

Important Terms

first-person narrative: A narrative that uses an *I* or *we* point of view.

second-person narrative: A narrative that uses the *you* point of view.

third-person narrative: A narrative that uses a *he*, *she*, *it*, or *they* point of view.

Suggested Reading

Rilke, *Letters to a Young Poet.*

Zinsser, *On Writing Well.*

Questions to Consider

1. You will sometimes hear people comment on the ways in which modern technology, abbreviated communication styles, and the speed of the Internet are making us a culture of careless writers. Do you think this is true? Which format do you think best reveals true character, in a book or in life: a well-polished letter or a hasty e-mail communication? Why?

2. Why do you think we are often more interested in characters who are unusual and even quirky than in characters who are average? What can you deduce about the art of storytelling from that?

Revealing Character in Words and Actions

Lecture 11—Transcript

In our last lesson, we reviewed what you've learned so far in this course, and you practiced revising a story that was falling flat because the author—that was me—made a series of storytelling missteps. As you looked at the original and started doing your revision of it, did you see how much you've already learned about effective ways of shaping a great narrative? That's great. Remember what I said in the last lesson: We wanted to do a major review and revision exercise at this point in the course because we're about to shift gears a bit. So far, we've been spending a lot of time looking at form issues of storytelling; the "how's," if you like. We talked about the different structures a story can have, how to write a great beginning and ending, how to write paragraphs that use rhetorical devices and pacing, that show and don't tell; and those are all skills we want to keep using. Great writing is like being like a master juggler: We want to keep all sorts of balls in the air at once.

In the next few lessons, we're going to take a different tack and spend some time looking into the "what's" of great writing, and that means focusing on character, dialogue, perspective, and scene. Then, toward the end of the course, we'll come back to this business about the nonfiction contract and I'll show you how you can also use all these new skills to write a great memoir or biography or to shape your research and writing process to maximize your creative potential.

Character: What does that really mean? We've already talked a bit about the formal aspects of character, haven't we? Remember, so far we've said that what a great beginning does is establish character, and that character is about tension and conflict. Sometimes we have characters who are in conflict with each other, a protagonist and an antagonist. Sometimes we have characters who are trapped in a situation that they need to struggle to negotiate. That's another kind of tension. Sometimes there are characters who are in conflict with themselves, an internal tension. Maybe it's a character torn between the devil and the angel on each shoulder; maybe it's a character torn between desire and duty; or maybe it's something different entirely. What matters is that conflict reveals character.

But other things reveal character, too. Think about it for a moment: In your mind's eye, picture someone you know well. Maybe your spouse or partner; maybe your best friend or your worst enemy; your mom and dad, one of your kids; that really annoying guy at work; anyone will do. Make a list of the things that you know about this person; ways that you would describe or visualize who this person is and what makes him or her different from anyone else in the room. In fact, take a minute and complete this exercise by making a list on a piece of paper if you like.

What did you come up with? Maybe you wrote down something about your mother's favorite perfume; about that whiny, grating voice of the pipsqueak at work. The way your irritating brother-in-law always wears white tube socks with dress pants? Maybe it was someone's nervous ticks; the way that someone serious always cracks up over the stupidest puns; the way your clueless friend somehow always manages to find the perfect birthday present, leading you to suspect that there's something going on behind the surface that most people don't see.

These are all things that fall into one of two categories if we think about it. They are either details about a person that are wonderful because they seem unexpected and out of character, or they are things that seem to perfectly capture the essence of character. Do you see what I mean? The fact that the clueless friend is actually paying close attention to the little things we say: Ah, things are not as they appear; how interesting. The things that seem out of character are precisely what define character here. Your annoying brother-in-law wearing the white tube socks: Wow, that stands in for a whole set of small, socially inappropriate things that guy does that just drive you crazy every time you see him. He's just that kind of guy, isn't he? He would wear the wrong socks; that's him to a "T." Small details here stand in for larger elements of character.

In fact, on your list, take a minute and have a look. Can you categorize the details you wrote down into one of those two slots? If you can, you chose good details; details that are going to help you learn to sketch character effectively in your writing.

If you think about it, these kinds of details are also about introducing tension into a story, aren't they? After all, things being out of character and still defining character suggests that this person is more complicated than it appears. It suggests that behind the scenes there's some internal conflict; some discrepancy between what is and what appears to be. As readers, we're interested, aren't we? We want to understand why the uptight businessman in a suit and bowtie is wearing pink thong underwear. We want to know why that sloppy woman at the gym, with sweatpants covered in condiments, has the neatest house you've ever seen. We want to know why Jack Sprat married his Rubenesque wife. There's a story here; that's what this kind of detail tells us about character. When a character has a story, that's narrative arc in a nutshell, isn't it?

The same is the case, actually, with the detail that fits a character to a "T" as well; because when all the details make too much sense—when a writer tells us, "Hey, this is just this kind of person who you can expect to do that"—that creates a narrative tension, too, doesn't it? After all, if I tell you Joe Schmoe always was a bow tie and a suit and you can count on him to act accordingly, what I've just given you is great narrative suspense. You know that if I'm a good storyteller, Joe Schmoe is going to find himself in a set of circumstances where he's going a have to act differently; to act out of character; and, in the course of those events, reveal who he really is.

In creative nonfiction, being on the lookout for these kinds of details is particularly important precisely because we can't invent things, right? We can only work with what history gives us. But if we learn to look for all the little ways in which details tell the story of character, this is part of what we're going to need to bring a character to life. Let me give you an example from when I was writing *The Widow Clicquot*. One of the tricky things about that book, you'll remember my telling you, was how few personal details there were about Barbe-Nicole Clicquot. All those letters she wrote describing her personal life, they didn't survive; and neither did a lot of the letters written about her. But facts tell stories, too. Think about this: What you have there is a story of a 27-year-old upper-middle-class woman with a small child and no business experience. She has no business education, either. She lives at a moment in time when women don't have careers. Her husband has just tried to launch a wine business, and it has been a financial disaster. His father told him it would be.

What happens next? She asks her father-in-law, "Will you let me try running the business, and will you loan me a million dollars?" You know what? He says, "Yes." Wow, now that tells us something about character. A stuffy businessman like her father-in-law gives a young woman with no experience a million bucks? That's out of character; the kind of out of character detail that defines him. Why does he do this? It must also tell us something about Barbe-Nicole Clicquot, mustn't it? She must have been an amazing woman for her father-in-law to recognize something in her that would make him do the absolutely unexpected, even the unthinkable. This is about some rare talent and ambition that he recognized in her, and that's a story. That's also how character can tell story; do you see what I mean?

What we know so far, let's summarize: First, we know that character is about tension, internal or external. Second, we know that details reveal character. If you think about it, that's really just another version of something else you've already learned: Character is about showing and not telling, isn't it? Because details are a way of showing, of revealing, character. Joe Schmoe wore his usual Brooks Brother's suit to work, but what those on the number six train saw when he leaned over to pick up his briefcase that morning was the flash of hot pink leather underwear. That's a better way to tell us who Joe Schmoe is than to say, "Joe Schmoe is a boring respectable guy who sometimes cuts loose in private." See what I mean?

Want to know where I think we can find some of the most fabulous efforts at character sketches in the modern world? In dating advertisements. After all, those are essentially our best efforts at character sketches, aren't they? What we're doing when we write them is inviting our readers into a narrative with us. The whole point of the dating advertisement is to say, in a 100 words, "This is who I am and why you and I, we should make history together." It's the ultimate narrative invitation, and a great example of how character can launch a narrative arc.

Let me show you what I mean, and let's see what we can learn about crafting character in narrative writing from them as well. Here's a personal ad:

> SWEET LADY, mother and now grandmother. Interesting and interested in the world. Scientist, birdwatcher, intrigued by beautiful art and smart people. Still loves fast cars. Active mind. Decent soul. Hopes to meet accomplished, responsible, sensitive, hopelessly handsome man for good laughs and much merriment.

Come on, you kind of want to meet this wonderful grandmother, don't you? Don't you want to know her story? "Still loves fast cars"; that's something pretty unexpected. Remember what we said earlier about how it's the unexpected that can define character. Even more interesting, this lady tells us that this is part of her youthful past, not the present. Now she drives carefully. But you have to know that, at heart, she still has a racecar driver's soul, and that time is the only obstacle. It's a great image. Internal character tension, there it is, too. She's given us an insight into some interesting character conflict, and I'll bet there's a story there. This grandmother, she's funny too, isn't she? She doesn't want just a good looking nice guy; nah, this cool lady is looking for someone hopelessly handsome. If she knows someone that someone handsome is impossible, and yet she's still placing a personal ad, there's some conflict and narrative tension right there for you.

In fact, this isn't a bad beginning to a story, is it? After all, it makes you wonder: Who is the man who's going to respond to this ad? How are they going to meet? You can already guess where a dapper gentleman is going to propose they meet on a first date, can't you? When you can start projecting a story out from a character description, that's what character is supposed to do. That's good writing.

Let's have a look at another personal ad. There's a real story here, too. Here it is:

> ECCENTRIC EUROPEAN, Adventurer, 72, former revolutionary, award-winning artist, trim, brilliant, lives part-time in Africa, part-time in France, married, seeks permanent mistress or second wife in complete agreement with first. Requirements: 30–40, sensual, talented, open-minded.

What?! Admit it, that was your first reaction, wasn't it? It's not the fact that this man is looking for a mistress or a second wife that's the interesting part of the story; for me, what really defines character is the fact that this man just threw in there, along with a string of other pretty run-of-the-mill details about his character, the phrase "former revolutionary." A former revolutionary? This person could also be the protagonist of a very interesting story—maybe your first novel, maybe a nonfiction biography—because, admit it, you're inclined to see if you can find him on Google just out of sheer curiosity, aren't you? The fact that he uses the word "requirements"; do you see how that suggests character, too? Only a certain kind of man uses a word like that in a dating advertisement. It's a great example of how word choice can reveal character.

You sort of have to wonder what 30-year-old independent, adventurous, witty young lady would be interested in being the second wife of a 72-year-old former revolutionary, too, don't you? But the fact that we have to wonder means that the narrative arc this advertisement sets into motion is a particularly interesting one. In fact, if you're looking for a writing exercise, trying to sketch out her character wouldn't be a bad one. You might even want to stop for a moment and try it if you're looking for a quick writing exercise to see if you're getting the hang of all this character development. Who do you think she would be? How would they meet? What do you think is the personal advertisement she would write about herself? More importantly, what would be the moment when the three of them meet? It would have to be an interesting moment, wouldn't it? There's a story just waiting to be told somewhere in this personal advertisement. In its way, it's a great advertisement. The fact that we can begin to imagine it so readily, that's a sign that we have a sense of this person's character from his sketch of himself.

Let's look at one more example and see if you get the idea about how detail shows character and how it launches story, too. Because, remember, a character sketch has to answer two questions: The first is, "Who is this person?" and the second is, "What motivates him or her in a situation that has tension or conflict?" Character is identity that implies action. Remember how, in a good narrative, the things that happen have consequences? It's the same with character: Good character in a story is identity that leads to action or expectation.

> How about this one? Sexy lady needs one decent guy: witty, responsible, available. So we can dream about all the things we once believed in and make love again like teenagers. In my mind, I will be young and beautiful. If you close your eyes, you will be too. We will dream together and you will read children's stories and The Economist. All night, we will touch fingers and dream of soaring. Me, late 40s. You as young as you wish to be.

Wow, does this establish character. "You will read children's stories and *The Economist*"? That jumps out as one of those unique elements of this woman's character, doesn't it? Those are two things I totally don't expect to go together. It's quite a sad and lyrical advertisement: the idea that this woman knows she's no longer beautiful and young, but wants to close her eyes and one more time imagine. In fact, it's a great personal ad. This is someone who really invites us into her world and makes us feel that we really know her, or that we would want to. That's exactly the point of the advertisement she's placing. We know a lot about one part of her internal conflict and her motivations, don't we? If character is identity that implies action—action that has consequences—this advertisement captures it perfectly.

Let's look at one other thing that makes this advertisement particularly effective; it's something technical. All these advertisements are written in what writers call the first-person voice, the perspective where a story is told from the "I" or "we" point of view. A writer can also write from the second-person perspective, the "you" point of view; or the third person, the "he or she" point of view. Remember when we talked about how different narrative structures—linear, circular, or framing narratives—how they all had different advantages and disadvantages? The same is true of the perspective a writer uses. The first-person point of view, when the writer speaks as "I," what that gives us is the power to create intimacy. What the first-person point of view lets us do as readers is get into the head of someone; someone who is sharing the events of the story with us from his or her unique—and admittedly subjective and personal—perspective. This isn't the point of view of fact necessarily; this is the point of view of experience and internal perspective.

There are lots of different modes to the first-person perspective. The "I" voice in a story can be reliable or unreliable. In other words, the "I" can either tell us what we believe is the truth or the "I" can be someone we suspect is a liar, or deluded, or an exaggerator. Likewise, the "I" voice can be omniscient: It can know everything that we know in the story. Or it can be limited: We can know some things in the story that the "I" doesn't get to see. We'll come back to all those modes—and learn a few more modes we can use as writers, too—in the next lesson. But for the moment, let's just think about those three simple points of view.

The first-person "I"; what it gets us is intimacy, and so it makes sense that a personal ad is written in the first-person, doesn't it? After all, what the author is trying to do is invite someone—you, the reader—into an intimate relationship. That's the whole point of a dating advertisement.

The third-person, the "he or she" perspective, what this has is the advantage of seeming all-knowing and objective. It's more distanced; it's a cooler, more detached way of writing; and it has the advantage of making the character in the story more important than the character telling the story. This can sometimes be tricky: What we want to remember is that even when there doesn't seem to be a narrator telling a story, there always is. There's always a point of view, and a point of view is a kind of consciousness; and if we have consciousness, we have character. With the third-person "he or she" point of view, the identity of the narrator is more remote. Sometimes, it's so remote that it seems to disappear or be the same as the author. But stories are always told from the perspective of some consciousness; that's something important to remember.

Third-person "he or she" means greater detachment and objectivity; less insight into the narrator's consciousness. Think about it for a moment: Which of the three advertisements I've read you—the grandmother with the penchant for fast cars, the radical artist looking for a young mistress, or the lady looking to close her eyes and dream herself young again—which of these is the most distanced in terms of our insight into the mind of the author? It's the radical revolutionary, isn't it? There's a reason why. Listen to that ad again:

> Adventurer, 72, former revolutionary, award-winning artist and professor, trim, brilliant, lives part-time in Africa, part-time in France, married, seeks permanent mistress or second wife in complete agreement with first. Requirements: 30–40, sensual, talented, open-minded.

There's no "I" used in there at all, is there? That's something about it that makes it a bit distant as a personal advertisement. In fact, it's hard to tell, now that we think about this: Is this written from the first-person or the third-person point of view even? The only verb in that advertisement is "seeks," and that's a pretty remote verb. In fact, we think "he seeks" must be the perspective implied. If the author had written "seeking," then we could imagine an "I" grammatically, "I am seeking." But there are hardly any verbs, and there are no pronouns; not once does this gentleman write "I". Actually, think about it: What if this advertisement wasn't written and published by the gentleman at all? What if his first wife is the one who wrote it? That would be a twist. Suddenly, the character in the story, and the narrative arc being launched into motion, change entirely, don't they?

What's great about this absent and objective voice in this advertisement is something else: the way that voice matches a certain kind of character silently. This kind of writing, in the distanced and cool space between first-person and third-person, this is exactly how an academic perhaps is supposed to write. It's the style of an objective and unemotional commentator. It's the voice I might expect from someone whose persona is so cool-handed and unsentimental; so it's perfect for our revolutionary to write in such a professorial, artistic style. Something we learn about the character of the person who wrote this is the way he or she writes; and we learn, in fact, as much about who this person might be through what he or she doesn't say ("I") as through what's written. This is what I mean when I say that even when it doesn't appear that there's a narrator, there always is, really.

Among our three ads, which is the most intimate? It's the last one—the one written about the aging lady lamenting her youth—isn't it? Part of the reason why is the content—what she shares with us—is inherently more private, isn't it? She talks about her dreams and her wishes rather than her requirements. But there's something else she does that creates additional intimacy. Listen to the advertisement again. What are the points of view being used here?

> Sexy lady needs one decent guy: witty, responsible, available. So we can dream about all the things we once believed in and make love again like teenagers. In my mind, I will be young and beautiful. If you close your eyes, you will be too. We will dream together and you will read children's stories and The Economist to me. All night, we will touch fingers and dream of soaring. Me, late 40s. You as young as you wish to be.

There's the first-person, of course, right? "I will be young and beautiful." But there's also a first-person plural point of view: "We can dream about all the things we once believed in." "We will dream together." This is an even more intimate and inclusive form of the first-person perspective, because here the "we" isn't two "I's." She's not talking about herself and her current husband and saying "We" are looking for another member of our ménage a trios; she's saying "I" plus "you," that's the "we" she's imagining. It's a point of view that invites the reader to think of himself—and it's clearly himself in this case—as part of the experience she's describing. It pulls the reader into her story, and her life, and makes us part of the story in just reading it. In fact, she even uses the second-person "you" point of view, too, doesn't she? "You will read fairy tales." "You, as young as you wish to be."

What we see about the second-person point of view is that its advantages are precisely this: It's an invitation to the reader to think of him or herself as part of the story. It's another way of establishing intimacy. In this case, it's intimacy with what seems to be an awfully nice lady. But remember, you can also use this voice as a writer to create intimacy with readers even when the characters are completely unsavory.

Alright, so that's our introduction to character and to point of view. We're going to work more on this in detail in the next few lessons. But your exercise at the end of this lesson? Here's what I want you to do: Write your own personal advertisement. Imagine that you need to describe yourself in less than 250 words, and you need to do it in a way that captures the truth of who you are, but also functions, like any personals advertisement should, as the beginning of a good story. After all, that's what we're always doing in this genre: inviting other people to become part of our story. You can use any voice you like. Just remember, character is identity that implies action; and great beginnings are about conflict and tension and drama. Make this an advertisement for a fabulous character, the kind of person someone else wants to be in a story with.

Creating Compelling Characters
Lecture 12

A book's antagonist is the character who opposes the main character, or protagonist, but a protagonist may also be a negative character, someone who is unpleasant to be around in real life. Whether nice or nasty, a main character must be compelling to engage the reader and avoid becoming a stock character. Complexity and inner conflict are the keys to creating engaging characters.

Antagonists versus Negative Characters

- In personal ads, we are all the heroes of our own tale, and what you wrote for the previous exercise was the character description for a protagonist—a main character whose experiences and struggles could shape the narrative arc of a story. In this lecture, we will explore the other characters in a narrative—minor characters and **antagonists**.

- It is important not to confuse an antagonist with a flawed protagonist. Sometimes a bad guy or gal—a **negative character**—can be the main character in a story. This is more common than you might think, from rogue cops to serial killers. A well-crafted negative character is one whose flaws we recognize and somehow find compelling.

- Among English professors, the ultimate example of the negative protagonist is Satan in John Milton's epic poem *Paradise Lost*. While Satan is the ultimate bad guy in Christian culture, as a character, Satan is still incredibly compelling because he is complicated, internally conflicted, and multifaceted.

***Paradise Lost*'s Satan is the classic well-crafted negative character.**

- In comparison, Adam—who is solidly good, without any emotional complexity—comes off as a **stock character**. A stock character is a character whose identity can be reduced to a single attribute or two.

The Flawed Protagonist and Richardson's *Clarissa*

- The longest novel in the English language—also one of the most brilliant—is the 18th-century epistolary novel *Clarissa*, by Samuel Richardson. The titular Clarissa is being forced by her family to marry a man she despises; Lord Lovelace offers to rescue her. When she flees with him, he imprisons and rapes her.

- All this happens in the first few hundred pages. For another thousand or so pages, the emotional implications of these events unfold. The reason for this narrative arc is that *Clarissa* is not a novel about plot; it is a novel about character.

- Clarissa is not the character who compels readers. She is not the protagonist. As the story goes on, Clarissa becomes more and more irritatingly pious. Her world is black and white, and her observations ignorant and trite, and she becomes a kind of stock character.

- Instead, Lovelace—who is by any standards a wretched and evil man—becomes so richly human and so tensely conflicted, that the reader begins to feel more and more sympathy for him. He is the emotional engine of the narrative.

- What we want to learn is how to craft characters who can compel readers like this—whether they are good guys or bad guys. We also want to know what the effect is of introducing a stock character into a narrative.

- Stock characters essentially do one thing: They turn readers off. While they can have important functions in a narrative, stock characters are risky choices and need to be used with care.

- One of the best uses of a stock character is as a means to reveal something about the main characters. For example, if your protagonist is going to experience a midlife crisis on page 200, having him pay a bit too much attention to the clichéd one-dimensional bombshell at the bar on page 5 foreshadows that event.

- The bombshell is a stock character because she does not matter as a character. She only serves to reveal something about the main character's internal conflict.

Developing Multifaceted Characters

- In the previous lecture, you made a list of the attributes of a person you knew well. This time, think about the most interesting person you know and make a list of the things that make that person fascinating.

- When you review your list, certain items are likely to stand out. Interesting people are often interesting because they are unique, because they defy expectations, or because they rise above internal conflicts or external barriers.

- Fascinating people have depths. They have interior lives that are complicated and sometimes contradictory. They struggle with their own decisions. This is true of interesting characters, too.

- Interesting characters can be nasty or nice, generous or narcissistic. They can be brave or weak. They can be self-reflective or self-deluded. They do not have to be perfect people; they just have to be complicated human beings whose lives speak to the truth of human experience in some way.

- Writing about negative characters can be a challenging proposition. The reader needs to be able to relate to every non-stock character in the story, even the terrible ones. You do not want your negative characters to be pure and simply evil; such characters are stock characters.

- Negative characters, whether they are protagonists or antagonists, must have some kind of internal conflict or private motivation. That is not the same as saying monsters must be sympathetic. They do not have to be nice deep down inside, nor must they have redeeming characteristics. But readers must be able to understand why they are the way they are, even if they despise or fear them.

- As a rule of thumb, the more terrible and wicked a character is, the more important it is that the reader understands his or her complexity. Likewise, the more pure and angelic a character is, the more important it is that he or she has some internal conflict.

- In other words, the closer a character is to either one-dimensional extreme of good or evil, the more crucial it is to make that character complex and multifaceted.

The Life of Coco Chanel—A Prewriting Exercise

- One of the difficulties of being a writer is that you know more than you can tell. Part of the pleasure of reading a story is watching it unfold. If the writer gives away everything in the beginning, then the narrative holds no suspense. Foreshadowing works because it lets readers guess what direction the story might take but leaves room for wonder and surprise.

- Professional writers often use prewriting exercises to develop characters precisely because knowing more than you tell is so important in crafting a great story. Many novelists develop character sketches for their main characters—brief life histories that might include where they were born, their middle names, their greatest childhood fear, their first jobs, the cars they drive, and so forth—even if none of it will ever make its way into the narrative. Other novelists will write the resume for their characters or answer a character questionnaire.

- If you are writing a novel, you are at liberty to make things up about a character. Nonfiction writers must search out telling details—or perhaps we should call them showing details—that suggest something about our characters. To know which details are important, we need to make lists of everything we have to work with.

- In writing nonfiction, we start with research, and part of research is actively seeking out facts that will 1) move a narrative arc forward and/or 2) reveal complex character and internal conflicts.

- Below, you will find 12 facts from the life of Coco Chanel. Imagine you were writing a biography of her, starting with only this information, and try to answer the following two questions: What would be the best narrative arc to use—linear, circular, or frame? What do those facts tell us about her internal conflict and motivations?

    - She grew up in poverty in a strict convent in the southwest of France and was abandoned as a child by her peasant father.

    - She was an illegitimate child at a time when that was socially unacceptable.

    - She left the convent to become the mistress of a series of rich and fickle men.

    - The men that she fell in love with all refused to marry her because of her origins.

    - Those same men helped her get a start in the fashion industry, but she resented their trying to undermine her becoming an independent businesswoman.

    - She eventually did become a famous and rich designer, celebrated around the world.

    - When Chanel No. 5 perfume was invented, she finally agreed to bring some rich men into her business to help her.

- She resented those rich business partners, and the result was decades of lawsuits about money and respect.

- She complained about being taxed under French law as a spinster, even though she never married.

- She did terrible things in the process of these lawsuits, including using the laws of Nazi-occupied France against her partners, who were Jewish.

- In her final settlement with her last remaining male business partner after the war, he agreed to pay her taxes, to pay all her bills forever, anything she wanted.

- In the final settlement with her business partner Coco Chanel agreed to give up the rights to her name and let him take it.

Important Terms

antagonist: The character who is in central conflict with the main character of a narrative.

negative character: A character—not necessarily the antagonist—with unpleasant or off-putting traits.

stock character: A character who represents a familiar type of person, rather than an individual.

Suggested Reading

Faulkner, *Sanctuary*.

Richardson, *Clarissa*.

Questions to Consider

1. If you had to define what makes for a great character in a book, what elements would you consider essential?

2. What would you do if you wanted to turn Coco Chanel into a stock character? What elements of her story would you need to omit to turn her into a stereotype?

Creating Compelling Characters

Lecture 12—Transcript

In our last lesson, we talked about the three main points of view that a writer can use—the first-, second-, and third-person perspectives—and the different effects they can have in writing. We also talked about how showing details are an effective way of establishing character, which we defined as identity that implies action. For your exercise, you sketched yourself as a character—seriously or ironically—working in the frame of a personal advertisement. But even if you were a bit ironic in your personal advertisement, I'll bet that you didn't present yourself as a negative character, did you? In a personal advertisement, we're all the heroes of our own tale, and what you wrote was the character description of a protagonist; a main character whose experiences and struggles are going to shape the narrative arc of a story.

In this lesson, we're going to explore working with characters who don't play a starring role in a narrative—the so-called "minor characters"—and we'll talk about working, too, with negative characters, antagonists; the kind of characters no one likes to deal with in real life. Minor characters and negative characters, it's very important to remember, sometimes don't come together. Sometimes a bad guy—or a gal—can be the main character in a story. Either way, we'll explore the particular challenge of creating flawed characters who are still believable and capable of moving the narrative along; because remember, that's what characters help to do: launch narrative.

Let's start off by thinking about what it might mean to write a story in which the main character is also the bad guy of the story; in other words, a story in which our protagonist is actually a negative character. Think about it for a minute. Have you ever read a story that was told from the perspective of the killer, or the liar, or the cheater? Or have you read a book in which that killer, liar, or cheater, even if his or her perspective wasn't the point of view, was still in a way the hero of the story? It's not as uncommon as you would think; in fact, in thrillers it happens pretty often. It lets us get inside the head of the psycho, which sometimes only makes things more frightening and dramatic for us as readers. If you've ever seen, for example, the old Dirty Harry films with Clint Eastwood, you're familiar with one version of the flawed character as protagonist. After all, as cool and sexy as Clint Eastwood makes Dirty Harry seem, he is, after all, dirty; he's a rogue cop and a killer. Dirty Harry is a great example of what we want to work with here, because even though he's rogue, we end up rooting for him and even sympathizing with his sense of vigilante justice, don't we? That's the sign of a well-crafted negative character: one whose flaws we recognize but who somehow, with his or her humanness, compels us to the story anyhow.

Dirty Harry is one example. Want one more highbrow and literary? Among English professors, there's an old saying about John Milton's great epic poem *Paradise Lost*. We quip about *Paradise Lost* that Satan is the hero of the poem. Satan is pretty clearly the ultimate bad guy in Christian culture, isn't he? What does it mean that he's the hero of Milton's epic? It means that, as a character, Satan—despite being negative—is still incredibly compelling. He's complicated; he's internally conflicted; he's multi-faceted. Darn it, he's so essentially human that we're drawn to his experience and to his story. In fact, we even sympathize with him because, you know, being Satan isn't as straightforward and easy as it sounds in Milton's version of the Biblical story. In comparison, Adam—who's just good, good, good, without any emotional complexity—seems like something else we're going to talk about in this lesson: a stock character.

That's a character who's one-sided, and whose identity can be reduced to a single attribute or two. They are stock in the sense that, hey, if you need a good guy, whose only function in the story is to be good, stick in Adam; or stick in the cowboy in the white hat, or stick in a Ken doll. Stock characters are characters who are caricatures of themselves. We're going to come back to the idea of character and caricature again in a bit when we're thinking about how to craft characters.

Let me give you one more example of a famous main character who's also negative. The longest novel in the English language—also one of the most brilliant—is the 18th-century epistolary novel (that means it's written in the form of letters) by Samuel Richardson, called *Clarissa.* I can save you hundreds of hours of time if you've never read *Clarissa*. Want the plot of the story? Here it is: A rich girl named Clarissa is being forced by her evil family to marry a man she despises. An aristocrat named Lord Lovelace offers to help her escape her family. While he pretends he wants to save her, what he really wants to do is rob her of her virtue, because he's a libertine and a rake. Clarissa flees; Lovelace imprisons and rapes her; and all this happens in the first couple of hundred pages of the novel. Then, for a thousand pages, the emotional implications of this event unfold for the characters.

The real story—the narrative arc—of Clarissa is all in those last thousand pages or so; and the way I'm telling the story, I make it sound pretty dull. Actually, it's wonderful. The reason is that *Clarissa* is not a novel about plot; it's a novel about character. As one critic once wittily said about the novel, "If you were to read Clarissa for its plot, you would hang yourself. But you must read it for the sentiment." In other words, it's the feelings—the emotional complexity of the character—that makes it one of English literature's greatest novels. The thing is, it's not the character of Clarissa that compels us. In fact, Clarissa becomes, as the story goes on, more and more irritatingly pious. For her, everything is so simple. Things are black and white and the words she writes are so unobservant and trite that—and this is the psychological brilliance of Richardson's novel—as the book goes on, she becomes a kind of stock character. As the story goes on, Lovelace—who's by any standards a wretched and evil man—becomes so richly human and so tensely conflicted that the reader begins to feel more and more sympathy for him. We identify with him because he's where the story lies; or, to put it in the terms of our lesson about character in the last lecture, Lovelace is the figure whose identity propels action. He's the emotional engine of the narrative.

It's not an accident that we come to feel this way about Lovelace; come to feel that he's the hero of the novel. The author, Richardson, has set up the story precisely so this will happen. When we enter the world of a writer, a writer can shape our feelings, and our sympathies, and our responses. In the case of *Clarissa*, the writer can mess with our heads a bit and create a novel that's about the complexities of evil and the psychology of passive participation in horrors.

What we want to learn to do is craft characters who can compel readers like this, whether they are good guys or bad guys, right? We want to know what the effect of introducing a stock character into a narrative is as well; because stock characters essentially do one thing: They turn readers off. In the example of *Clarissa*, Richardson wants to turn us off from his heroine, and he uses her growing one-dimensionality as a technical way of distancing us as readers from her experience. In other cases—cases where writers aren't using stock characters well or for clear narrative purposes—a stock character just turns a reader off without any reason. We encounter a stock character and we think, "Who cares? This character isn't believable. This character isn't interesting. This character is a cardboard cutout of a character. I think I'll go watch the grass grow instead of reading this story," and that is something, as writers, we want to avoid. So a cautionary note: Stock characters, while they can have important functions in a narrative if used very carefully, are risky choices. Writers need to use stock characters surgically.

There is one thing that stock characters can sometimes usefully do in a story, though: They can serve as shorthand means of creating foreshadowing. If your protagonist is about the experience a midlife crisis on page 200 of your book, having him pay a bit too much attention to the clichéd, one-dimensional bombshell at the bar on page 5 sends the reader a message: Pay attention to this; our hero, he's vulnerable. But what we also understand as readers is that foreshadowing the weakness of our midlife gentleman is the only purpose of this lady. When the time comes, she's not going to be the reason he strays. She's a stock character because she doesn't matter as a character. In fact, we're pretty sure she's a character we're never going to see again. She serves only the narrative function of revealing something about the main character's internal conflicts or temptations. Because remember, strong character is identity that implies action, and what this bombshell lets us see through foreshadowing—through implying the future—is that there's something in the character of our protagonist that's going to lead to his downfall. This stock character reveals his fatal flaw; and so she serves to move the narrative arc forward, even though she's nothing more than a stereotype.

But what exactly is a stock character? Or, more importantly, how do we make sure that we're crafting the opposite, giving our readers a fully developed and multifaceted character? Stock characters are essentially the clip art of the writing world. You know on your computer how there's that file of preloaded clip art, generic images you can use to illustrate the school report, family holiday letter, or office banner? That's a lot like what a stock character does for a writer. Another way to think about a stock character is that a stock character is a stereotype: our bombshell along the bar; the mean and pretty cheerleader; the sleazy used car salesman; the pompous professor with a tweed jacket; the greedy lawyer. In fact, if you think about it, most off-color jokes about broad categories of people, you'll see those depend on stock characters. Sometimes, stock characters can be used in our writing as a joke: when we want to call attention to the way we're knowingly, and ironically, using stereotypes.

But using stock characters without this sense of irony comes with some high stakes. In the best-case scenario, a stock character simply leaves the reader unengaged; but in a worst-case scenario, stock characters can be offensive. Blondes often don't think dumb blonde jokes are very funny. Lawyers rarely find negative stereotypes of lawyers very witty. A smart reader recognizes that when a writer uses a stock character naively, it's either a sign of ineffective storytelling and a lack of imagination or it better be a joke.

Let's think a bit about what it takes to develop a complex character. Take a minute and try this: Think about the most interesting person you know. Stop for a minute and really make a list here. The most interesting person you know, what is it that makes this individual fascinating? Because here's the thing: What makes people interesting is the same thing that makes characters interesting. So go ahead and make a list.

Now take a minute to look at the things you came up with. What kind of things did you find intriguing? Did you come up with something about how this person is just very unique? Fascinating individuals are just that—individuals—aren't they? There's the opposite of a stock character right there. Stock characters are generic, by definition. What kinds of things make a person, or a character, unique? Did you maybe write down something about how this person isn't what people expect him or her to be? Does this person defy expectations? Maybe it's your friend who survived a cancer diagnosis courageously and beat impossible odds; the mom or dad who, even though there were huge stresses at work, always came home and played with you kids; the celebrity who turned out to be a real person when that was the last thing you would have expected; the hardnosed boss who you all discovered one year has quietly been doing important charity work for years? Interesting people surprise us, and they don't do what they're supposed to do. They do something else; something born out of their character.

Or maybe you noted that your most fascinating person is someone who was faced with a difficult situation, even an irresolvable one, and was able to rise above those internal conflicts. Maybe it's the person who was torn between desire and duty and never let on how difficult that private choice was. Maybe it's the recovering alcoholic you know who battled private demons. For me, when I was writing *The Widow Clicquot*, I was struck by how this young woman was such a jumble of opposite impulses. She paved the path for women in the world of business, but she refused to let her own daughter play any role but a rich man's idle wife. She presented a gruff and forbidding exterior, but at moments she revealed by accident what a softie she really was, which made you realize that all the little slights and insults must have wounded her more than she ever let on. Fascinating people have depths. They have interior lives that are complicated and sometimes contradictory. They struggle with their own decisions. That's true of interesting character, too.

What have we learned about interesting character, then? We know that interesting characters surprise us. They don't fit the stereotypes. They strike us as unique individuals. They have complex interior lives, which are sometimes out of synch with how other people perceive them. They have private struggles and often contradictions. They defy easy expectations with the depth of their experiences. They have desires and wishes and dreams, and they don't always get exactly what they want; because, remember, character is also about conflict. They can be nasty or nice, generous or narcissistic. They can be brave or weak. They can be self-reflective or self-deluded. They don't have to be perfect people; they just have to be complicated human beings whose lives speak to the truth of human experience in some way.

Writing about negative characters can be a challenging proposition. Think about the worst character you can imagine. For me, I always think of this example: I once met a woman who was writing a memoir about some horrific childhood experiences. She had a long-term incestuous relationship with her father that began—rather unusually—in her 20s. For years, she'd suspected—although couldn't prove it—that her mother had coolly murdered him when she discovered it. That father, I have always thought, what an awful character he must have been. But, in fact, this is a pretty compelling story, too, isn't it? The reason it's compelling is because the interpersonal dynamics of the whole situation are so obviously complicated. The father isn't a run-of-the mill pedophile; the daughter's a grown woman. The mother; the poor mother, really: Do you have any difficulty imagining her internal conflict? Yes, she's also perhaps a murderer.

The trouble is, if we were to write the story of this event and simply portray the father as a bad man, evil in every way, whose psychology is so perverted as to be unimaginable, we destroy what's true about the story, don't we? In order to tell a great narrative, the reader needs to be able to relate to all the characters in the story, even the terrible ones. Otherwise, a complex negative character can end up seeming like a stock figure by accident. After all, one-dimensional people are purely and simply evil, right? If they only have one character trait, they're by definition one-dimensional. To write a story with a persuasive and truly terrifying negative character, that character also has to be complicated and nuanced; and that often means that this character has to have some kind of internal conflict or some kind of private motivation.

That's not the same thing as saying we have to make our monsters sympathetic. They don't have to be really nice guys deep down somewhere, and we don't have to portray them as having redeeming characteristics. What we do have to explain to our readers is what motivates them to be so bad, and we have to give our readers enough of a picture that they can understand the character even if they despise or fear him.

Let's think about a classic example of this from literature. One of the most disturbing novels I know is William Faulkner's book *Sanctuary.* It's the story of a deeply evil and perverse older man named Popeye who stalks and ultimately rapes the young college student Temple Drake in a barn at a drunken party. What's brilliant about Faulkner's novel is the atmosphere of suspense and foreboding he creates. For pages and pages, the reader knows something terrible is going to happen. Even after the crime occurs, it takes the reader pages and pages more to understand that this violation of Temple Drake was uniquely and particularly brutal. It's a perfect example of how a negative character can be used along with foreshadowing to create taut narrative tension and pacing. If there's a character in literature more disturbing than Popeye, I've yet to see it. But part of the reason he's so memorable and compelling as a character is because Faulkner also lets his readers understand Popeye's own twisted, emotional need and motivations. Popeye, it turns out, is impotent. He's a man consumed by his rage. The reader can understand his complexity as a character, and that's what makes him so terribly real and what makes *Sanctuary* an amazing narrative.

If you think about it, the same thing happens with Lovelace in Richardson's novel *Clarissa*, doesn't it? What those thousands of pages of letters do is let us get inside of that criminal as well. What Lovelace does to Clarissa is indefensible; but at the same time, the essentially human quality of his flaws and crimes makes the story powerful. Here's a rule of thumb for you: The more terrible and wicked a character is, the more important it is that the reader understands the complexity of the human drama. Likewise, the more pure and angelic a character is, the more important that he or she have some internal conflict. In other words, the closer a character is to either one-dimensional extreme of good versus evil, the more crucial it is to our storytelling to make them complex and multifaceted in our presentation of them. Otherwise, they risk becoming stock characters without our ever meaning it.

How do we translate this into our actual writing? The difficulty of being a writer is that you have to know more than you tell. After all, part of the pleasure of reading a story is watching it unfold, isn't it? If, as a writer, you give away everything at the beginning, then what kind of suspense or mystery is there left for us to enjoy? Foreshadowing works because it lets us guess as readers what the direction might be, but it leaves room for wonder and surprise in case we're reading too much into something. Remember what I said earlier: Writing a story is like going on a road trip with your characters. You're the one driving; it's a good idea to have a map. But these should be real people on that trip with you, not cardboard cutout figures. That would make for a boring trip, and a boring story, for all of us.

Professional writers often use a series of pre-writing exercises to help them in developing character precisely because knowing more than you tell is so important in crafting a great story. Crafting character in creative nonfiction has especial challenges, too. After all, if you're writing your novel, you're at liberty to make things up about a character when the story demands it. In nonfiction, writers don't have this option. Instead, what we need to do is search out what I'm going to call "telling details, except that we really should call them "showing details," shouldn't we? These are details that suggest something great about the character, or internal conflict, or foreshadowed action. In order to know which details are important, we need to make a list of everything we have to work with.

Fiction writers are familiar with these pre-writing exercises, too. Many novelists write character sketches of their protagonists. That means you take the time to write down in a working notebook a kind of life history of the character—where she was born, her middle name, her greatest childhood fear, her first job in high school, the car she drives, her worst break up ever—and you imagine all of this, even if none of it will ever make its way into your narrative, so that you're conveying to readers the sense that this is a fully-developed character. Otherwise, other novelists will write the resume of their character or do a character questionnaire, a kind of mock pop-psychology quiz for an imaginary character. In fact, sometimes when I'm in the middle of writing and I find myself in a dentist's waiting room, I play a little mental exercise with those "What kind of communicator" quizzes you find in the back of glossy women's magazines: I imagine that one character or another is taking it. What's useful about that exercise is that if you find yourself getting stumped and realizing you don't know how a character would answer the quiz, you know you need to go back and do some more thinking and research.

These are great tried and true methods used by fiction writers to imagine character before writing. But what about nonfiction, where you can't make things up? With creative nonfiction, what we need to do is make a list of what we do know; and, more importantly, what those facts logically or emotionally might suggest about character.

Let's do an exercise together so you can see what I mean about how as a nonfiction writer you can start to use factual details to sketch fully rounded characters. This is an actual exercise I used when I was writing the history of Chanel No. 5 perfume recently, and I was thinking about how to understand the character of Coco Chanel. In your course guidebook, there's list of 12 facts that you have to start with, and I'm going to ask you to try it with her character.

But first, let's try a short version of this exercise together to make sure you know how to get started. Are you ready? Let's imagine together that we have a set of facts about a person. Let's imagine it's someone who's done something terrible. Let's say it's one of the most famous Nazis, someone perhaps like Hermann Goring, who was Hitler's second-in-command. It's easy to make a Nazi into a stock character, isn't it? After all, he's someone guilt of terrible crimes against humanity, someone no one would want to defend morally. If you look at Hollywood films of the Nazi period, this is always one of the dangers: The Nazis are always turning into stock characters. One of my favorite films from when I was younger is the Indiana Jones series; and if you remember those films, you'll remember how the Nazis are the bad guys, bad without any complication. They only function in the story as foils to showcase the brilliance of Indiana Jones and his daring adventures.

But what would it take to write a story in which Hermann Goring's character wasn't a stock character? It would mean finding some character conflict; and, in his case, likely something internal. You can see why people tend not to do it. But what if you knew—a historical fact here—that Goring had a fetish for expensive jewels that he used to handle obsessively to calm himself down when he got anxious? There was something, those who witnessed it always said, sort of sadly childish about it. Do you see how this is an entry into developing character? It's something that suggests an internal conflict or complication.

In writing nonfiction, we start, of course, with research of just that kind. In fact, at the end of the course, in our final few lessons, we're going to talk a lot more about that and how to do it well for the project you want to write maybe. Part of what you want to go into your research knowing is that you're looking actively for facts that will help you do two things: move a narrative arc forward with a great story, and reveal complex character and internal conflicts.

Out of those facts, as a writer, one has to do two things: Find the narrative arc of a story and, in the assignment I'm going to give you, find the character of Coco Chanel. That's your assignment here at the end of this lesson. Have a look at those dozen facts listed in the course guidebook. What is the narrative here? Is it going to be linear, circular, or a frame narrative? There's one option that should jump out at you immediately as a strong first possibility. What kind of story is there here? What is the character of Coco Chanel? She also does some terrible things, and some terrible things happen to her; those are the facts. But we want to figure out something else: What do those facts tell us about her interior struggles? What was her conflict? What did she want that she couldn't have? What do you think were her motivations? For next time, see if you can answer those questions, and we'll begin the next lesson by seeing if you can get the hang of writing great nonfiction character.

Character Psychology

Lecture 13

Building a nonfiction character from researched facts involves not just knowing what a person said about him or herself or what was said about that person; you must also understand the inner life a person's behavior reveals and be able to present that to a reader through effective use of detail. Writers often use metonymy and synecdoche—two special types of metaphor—to achieve this effect, as well as making careful choices about direct and indirect discourse.

Behavior as a Simile

- The exercise at the end of the previous lecture was about learning how to look at the facts you gather about another person reading them for the character they reveal. From that list of a dozen facts about Coco Chanel, it is obvious that she is a naturally complicated character.

- A linear narrative would be the easiest narrative structure in which to tell Coco Chanel's story. Plenty of things happen to keep the story in motion without any tricks of timing. This is also a case where actions reveal character, which is also a good fit for a linear, plot-driven narrative.

- On another level, this also happens to be a love story; it is about men hurting Coco Chanel, or Coco Chanel hurting them right back. Love stories are also well suited to linear narratives.

- As to Chanel's motives, why do you think in the end she agreed to give up her name in exchange for being economically cared for by one man? To me, writing her story, it suggested that she wanted an entrepreneurial marriage. All of her actions stemmed from her internal conflict about marriage and money.

- As a nonfiction writer, I cannot state as fact "Coco Chanel's final business deal satisfied her longing to get married" unless somewhere Coco Chanel said so. What I can say is, "Coco Chanel's final business deal *looked* a lot like an entrepreneurial marriage." This distinction is crucial.

- I can say her earlier failed love affairs hurt her because Coco Chanel did say that in letters and in interviews. I can connect those facts to my interpretation of them to reveal her character and to move the story forward. Ultimately, what I am building is a simile: The business deal is *like* a marriage.

The Conscious versus the Unconscious

- The actions of real human beings reveal not only our conscious desires but our unconscious ones. In a way, we all have an internal conflict between our conscious and unconscious wishes. One way to develop a multifaceted character, therefore, is to show how a character acts in ways that are both self-aware and not self-aware.

- In real life, we make associations between objects. We let something stand in for something it is not. We take a little piece of our experience and make it stand in for the whole. Sigmund Freud called this **displacement**.

- There are two main types of displacement. In **metonymy**, something associated with an object is used to represent it, as when someone wears a crucifix to show that they are Christian. In **synecdoche**, a part of something represents the whole, as when you call a business executive "a suit."

Choosing Your Narrative Voice

- A character is essentially a set of consistent attributes, qualities that stand in for their entire identities. We give our characters certain recognizable speech patterns—knowing that a reader can extrapolate from dialogue a whole wealth of things about class, education, and cultural background. We dress our characters in certain ways, knowing that readers will make assumptions based on this information.

- We have talked a bit already about how word choice—diction—can reveal a lot about who a character is. That is the easy part of using dialogue and voice to create characters. The trick to speech synecdoche, in fact, is not learning how to do it; it is learning how to not overdo it. If dialogue becomes stereotypical, then we can accidentally create a stock character.

- The interesting—and harder—aspect of creating character through voice involves choosing point of view. The usual advice to new writers is, unless you have some compelling reason to choose the first or second person, the third person, *he/she/they* perspective is the safest bet. Why is this?

- The normal way to write a biography about George Washington is to say he did this and then he did that. However, writing in the third person is not as simple as it seems at first. There are more ways to write in the third person that you probably imagine.

- Sometimes the third person needs to draw in the first person—for example, when you want to quote George Washington's own words

- Within any point of view, there are different modes we can use as writers: direct discourse, indirect discourse, and free indirect discourse. Each mode makes a different kind of truth claim. Each implies a different relationship to history and our ability to know it.

- **Direct discourse** is another name for direct quoted speech, for example:

    George Washington's mother was a woman he admired greatly.

    "What did you think of your mother," a friend asked George.

"I attribute all my success in life to the moral, intellectual and physical education I received from her," George said.

- The advantage of direct discourse is that it is, of course, very direct, but it is also neutral and objective to the point of distant. We do not get inside George's head or build a sense of George's inner self.

© iStockphoto/Thinkstock.

We cannot put words in the mouths of historical figures.

- **Indirect discourse** is information attributed to a character, but it is not placed in quotation marks. For example:

  George's friend was impressed with the president's admiration for his mother and asked him about it. George told him that he attributed all his success to the education in morality, scholarship, and athletics that he received from her.

- Here, we do not have the exact words that George used, but we know the substance of the exchange, and that substance is presented to us as a fact. Once again, it is cool, detached, and objective. It is the way we often write history when we know what happened in a general way but not specifically. The trouble is, indirect discourse is a bit clunky.

- In the next lecture, we will look at a third option, free indirect discourse. It's one of the nonfiction writer's most important storytelling tools.

Direct versus Indirect Discourse—A Writing Exercise

- Let's make sure you have mastered the distinction between direct discourse and indirect discourse. Write a paragraph or two in which you do two things: 1) develop a character—historical or imaginary—who you reveal to the reader using either metonymy or synecdoche, and 2) write this paragraph using both indirect discourse and direct discourse.

Important Terms

direct discourse: Quoted speech in a narrative that is attributed to a speaker.

displacement: A kind of metaphoric thinking in which one idea is substituted for another. *See* **metonymy**.

indirect discourse: Speech in a narrative that is attributed to a specific speaker but is not directly quoted.

metonymy: A kind of metaphor in which one object is described by reference to another object somehow associated with it.

synecdoche: A kind of metaphor in which a part of an object represents the whole.

Suggested Reading

Fish, *How to Write a Sentence*.

Hood, *Creating Character Emotions*.

Questions to Consider

1. What is speech synecdoche, and how does it help us to write effective dialogue?

2. If you listen to the conversations around you, what do you notice people use more commonly when quoting others, direct or indirect discourse? What does this tell you about the art of writing dialogue?

Character Psychology

Lecture 13—Transcript

In our last lesson, we learned about the role that negative characters can play in great storytelling, and we talked especially about avoiding one-dimensional, stock characters in favor of rounded and believable characters. We thought about what makes up character, and how fiction writers think about the process of inventing characters. Then we reminded ourselves that as creative nonfiction writers, we have to try something a bit different. After all, we can't make things up; we can't invent our characters at all. We need to find them; we need to discover them; and that means doing our research carefully, of course. But it also means learning how to look at the facts we've gathered about another person and seeing how to read those facts for the character they reveal.

At the end of the last lesson, I asked you to think about a nonfiction exercise that I used when I was writing *The Secret of Chanel No. 5* to try to understand the character of Coco Chanel. Remember how I gave you the example of how even someone has reprehensible as a Nazi like Hermann Goring can be turned into a fully developed historical character in a story? Finding the character of customarily stock figures can be controversial, but without it, it's hard to develop a real story.

I gave you in the guidebook a list of a dozen facts in the final exercise; facts about someone entirely different, the fashion designer Coco Chanel. In that exercise, I asked you to try your hand at doing two things; things that will synthesize what we've learned so far not just about character, but also about finding narrative arc: I asked you to decide what kind of narrative this story falls into naturally, and I asked you to see if you could figure out what Coco Chanel's motivations and private conflicts might be that would account for these actions and help us to sketch her character in ways that are historically sound. In short, I asked you to read back from the facts to the character behind them because this is crucial to how we find character in memoirs, biography, and other nonfiction forms of storytelling.

What did you come up with? Let's look at those facts that I gave you again in your course guidebook. She grew up in poverty in a strict convent in the southwest of France and was abandoned as a child by her peasant father. She was an illegitimate child at a time when that was socially unacceptable. She left the convent to become the mistress of a series of rich and fickle men. The men that she fell in love with all refused to marry her because of her origins. Those same men helped her get a start in the fashion industry, but she resented their trying to undermine her becoming an independent businesswoman. She eventually did become a famous and rich designer, celebrated around the world. When Chanel No. 5 perfume was invented, she finally agreed to bring some rich men into her business to help her. She resented those rich business partners, and the result was decades of lawsuits about money and respect. She even complained about being taxed under French law as a spinster, though she never married. She did terrible things in the process of these lawsuits, including using the laws of Nazi-occupied France against her partners, who were Jewish. In her final settlement with the last remaining business partner after the war, he agreed to pay her taxes, to pay all her bills forever, anything she wanted. In the final settlement with her business partner, Coco Chanel agreed to give up the rights to her name and let him take it.

There are some peculiar and disturbing details in there, aren't there? There are some obvious moments where, as readers, we feel sympathy for Coco Chanel; and there are some moments when it's harder to see her as the heroine. Using the laws of Nazi-occupied France against your Jewish business partners? That's not so admirable. But having the men you loved refuse to marry you because you were born poor, despite everything you managed to achieve? That's not so nice, either. The good news is we've got from the start a naturally complicated character. We know that Coco Chanel—who is neither all bad nor all good—isn't in danger of becoming a stock character, as long as we just represent the complexity of her true experience.

What kind of story is this inherently? You can tell a story, as we've seen, in many different ways; and remember what we said about how finding the right narrative structure for the natural arc of the story was the first key step in writing any great narrative. This one here: What's the heart of the story? Is it going to be a linear narrative; that old standby of love stories and tragedies? Is it going to be a circular narrative, where the character undergoes a voyage and a transformation of self-knowledge? Or is it going to be a frame narrative, where we learn about the character and the subjectivity of the narrator rather than emphasizing the plot.

Well? Did you say linear narrative? If so, good job; you spotted the easiest narrative structure to work with here. After all, plenty of things happen, right? So this can stand up to being a plot-driven narrative. Here's a case where we've already said it's actions revealing character; that's also a good fit for a linear narrative that focuses on those actions. After all, what I haven't listed here is a series of diary entries from Coco Chanel reflecting on her life and private experience, have I? If my facts in my research were a series of personal comments, then I might very well have decided on a circular or a frame narrative, depending on how much she evolved as a character in the course of her journey, or depending on how much I wanted to emphasize a narrator in the story. For all those reasons, the linear story is a good choice. Did you see that this also happens to be at heart a love story? It's about men not marrying Coco Chanel; about being a chaste and unhappy girl in a convent; about being the mistress of rich men; about doing business with rich men and not wanting them to get the better of her. The story here is Coco Chanel, money, and men.

When you thought about character and motive, did you also see the story trying to peek out here? Let's think about her motives for a minute: Why do you think in Coco Chanel's lawsuits with her business partners that it was agreeing to give up her name and have all her expenses paid for the rest of her life that made her happy? Why didn't she just ask for that settlement instead of millions and millions of dollars to do anything she wants with? What that action says about her character is that she wanted a kind of entrepreneurial marriage, doesn't it? She enters into an agreement with a man; she gives up her name; he takes care of her. Really, how different is that from the economic relationships she had had with men all her life? The only difference is she signs a contract that involves, at last, giving up her name. What the facts on the page suggest to me, as a writer of nonfiction, is that Coco Chanel's motives as a character—why these actions are on the page of her life and not other ones—stem from her internal conflict about marriage and money.

Do you see how this works? As a nonfiction writer, I can't make up any facts. I can't say "Coco Chanel's final business deal satisfied her longing to get married." I can't say that unless somewhere Coco Chanel says so. But what I can say is, "Coco Chanel's final business deal looked a lot like a kind of entrepreneurial marriage. Those earlier failed love affairs—all the men who wouldn't marry her—had hurt her deeply." I can say that because, to me, it does look a lot like this; this business deal and a traditional marriage. I can say those earlier failed love affairs hurt her because Coco Chanel did say that in letters and in interviews. I can connect facts to my interpretation of them in order to use events to reveal character and to move the story forward. This is the real art of writing in nonfiction genres: finding the story and the character in facts and treading that fine line between history and story.

When I write, then, "Coco Chanel's final business deal looked a lot like a kind of entrepreneurial marriage. Those failed love affairs—all the men who wouldn't marry her—had hurt her deeply," it's a kind of statement of narrative facts that each happened, and it's signaled to the reader as an interpretation: the way that I see them connected. In fact, do you see that what I'm suggesting is finally a kind of metaphor? The business deal is like an entrepreneurial marriage. If I put it that directly, it's a simile, isn't it?

This idea of character and metaphor is an important one. If we want to create complex characters, it's not just that their actions reveal their motives and desires, is it? Sometimes part of how real human beings are complicated is that our actions reveal not our conscious desires, but our unconscious ones. In a way, we all have an internal conflict between our conscious and unconscious wishes. One way to develop a multifaceted character in a narrative is also to show the reader how this character acts in ways that are both knowing and unknowing. Giving our characters an unconscious implies a very rich consciousness indeed, doesn't it? Writing characters successfully is about making them come alive on the page; making them become characters our readers can believe, and invest their imaginative and emotional energies in.

Giving the character an unconscious gives us rich character and immediately implies internal conflict, both of which are qualities of a strong character in a narrative. But what's this got to do with metaphor? Think about how our unconscious actions operate in real life. We associate one thing with another. We let something stand in for something it's not and we conveniently forget the connection. We take a little piece of our experience and make it stand in for the whole, because the whole is something too big for us to deal with. According to the psychoanalyst Sigmund Freud, there are two basic ways that we deal in our conscious minds with unconscious desires or traumas. One is through displacement. That's where we associate some thing with another. Someone is having marital difficulties because her husband is too focused on his career. But instead of getting angry with her husband, the woman takes it out on her career-focused girlfriend, criticizing the friend's decisions and destroying a friendship she never meant to ruin. This woman, she doesn't quite know why she can't stop herself from criticizing her friend. After all, she's really quite proud of her friend's brilliant career. What she doesn't realize for herself is that she's displacing her fears and anger toward her husband and her crumbling marriage on her girlfriend; and this displacement is a kind of metaphor.

Or let's imagine another character. This one is a man, and he's been accused of a strange crime: breaking into high-end boutiques and destroying boxes and boxes of expensive shoes. When the police look into his background, it all becomes clear. He had fallen hopelessly in love with a glamorous and beautiful woman. He was crazy in love with her, and he'd have done anything. In fact, it was his first romantic experience. He thought that they would be together in love, forever. She dressed sumptuously, and she always wore sexy high-heeled shoes. Then, one night, he came to the apartment to surprise her and instead saw her get into a car with another man; a man with whom she's clearly amorous. He's devastated. His crimes against the shoes are the way he expresses his fury. The shoes come to stand in for the woman; they represent her in his mind.

In both cases, the character is struggling with the tension between conscious and unconscious desires by using displacement. In fact, in both cases, what we have here is a kind of metaphor that's technically called "metonymy." That's a comparison where something associated with an object is used to represent it. When someone wears a crucifix to show they're Christian, for example, that's metonymy. One communicates the message "I believe in Jesus" by wearing a cross; and why? Because a cross is associated with Jesus; the cross stands in for him metaphorically.

That's one way that metaphors operate in psychology, and how you can use them to build believable character. But Freud said that there was also another metaphor that people use in the same way. This one is technically called "synecdoche," and all that means is that it's a kind of comparison—because that's, after all, what a metaphor is, is a comparison—in which the part represents the whole. The classic example is when a drowning man cast adrift in the ocean sees a boat that will save him on the horizon and calls out to his companion, "A sail, a sail!" He doesn't really mean a sail is coming, of course, he means a boat is; a boat is coming to save them. But a sail is part of a boat, and the part is standing in for the whole. It's the same thing if I say to you "Give me a hand." I mean, "Lend me the strength of your body," and your hand here represents it; it's a synecdoche.

Here's an example of how that works in building character. Let's go back to our situation with the woman who finds that she keeps attacking her successful career-oriented friend, without understanding why her friend makes her so angry. Let's say in a mean-spirited moment she calls her friend "Ms. Career." What she's doing is reducing her friend's entire life experience into something that's really only a part of it, isn't she? Even if her friend is dedicated to her career, she still has other parts of her life. She's someone's daughter; she has friends. She likes to go to aerobics classes and cook Italian food. She takes long cruising vacations at the holidays. But her angry friend, she's letting the part—her friend's career—represent the whole; and that's because the angry friend has an internal conflict that her fixation on her friend's career reveals, isn't it?

What or who a character associates with—the way a character selects what to focus on and what to ignore—is a powerful clue to the reader as to what's going on behind the scenes in a character's mind. It's a way of showing the depth of a character's psychology, and it's a powerful tool for a writer.

There's another way writers can use synecdoche as well. We can do the same thing the angry friend in our example just did. Think about how a writer reveals character. Character is essentially a set of consistent attributes. What do I mean? If I tell you that the character is blonde and plump and left-handed, then you're going to get pretty confused if, halfway through my story, I suddenly talk about her brown hair, aren't you? It's the same with other qualities of a character. What we're trying to do as writers is, in a kind of shorthand, tell our reader who a character is, what motivates him or her, and what actions we can anticipate being the result of that identity.

What we do is give characters qualities that stand in for their entire identities. We give our characters certain recognizable speech patterns, knowing that a reader can extrapolate from dialogue a whole wealth of things about class, education, and cultural background. We dress our characters in certain ways, knowing that readers will make assumptions based on this information about unspoken parts of a character's life. One of my favorite mystery novelists, Cara Black, writes a series of mysteries set in Paris, and her character is repeatedly described as a woman who owns just one fancy dress suit, but it's couture. That fact—that the heroine is the kind of woman who owns just one good piece of clothing, but makes sure it's superb—is a great character sketching device. Or think back to those personal ads. Those are also perfect examples of how writers build character through metonymy or synecdoche.

What about using dialogue and voice to create character? I just said a minute ago that this was also a rich device writers can use. Are you curious about that? We've talked a bit already about how word choice, or diction, can reveal a lot about who a character is. If we want to sound like a child, we use simple words. If we want to sound like the professor, we use complicated ones. If we want to sound uneducated, we make grammatical errors. If we want to sound like someone whose thoughts are racing, we would run all of our sentences together madly. If we want to sound like a teenager, we use current youth culture slang.

That's the easy part of using dialogue and voice to create characters. The trick here, in fact, isn't learning how to do it; it's learning how to not overdo it. After all, if we overdo it and our dialogue becomes stereotypical, then we can fall into creating a stock character by accident here, too, can't we? No teenager really uses "like" in every sentence; it just seems like it. No professor—take my word for this—actually uses five-syllable words over the breakfast table. Using dialogue and what we can call "speech synecdoche" is something that requires a very light touch.

Are you seeing that I say this pretty often, this business about things requiring a light touch in writing? That might be the most important thing of all to remember: Your readers are smart enough to get your hint after you make it once or twice. You don't need to beat them over the head with repetition. In fact, overdoing it undermines the pleasure for readers, and it undermines the sense that our characters, in particular, are authentic people rather than cardboard cutout figures. If word choice and speech patterns are the easy part of creating character through voice, though, are you wondering what the hard part is? If you knew there had to be a hard part, you did a great job picking up on my narrative foreshadowing there, didn't you?

Here's the interesting, and harder, aspect of how as writers we can create character through voice. In fact, as creative nonfiction writers, some of these strategies are absolutely essential. This gets a bit technical, so are you ready? Let's think about using the third-person voice in writing. The rule of thumb advice to new writers is: Unless you have some clear reason why you're writing in the first- or second-person voices—the "I" or "we" and the "you" points of view—the third-person "he or she" perspective is the safest bet. It's essentially neutral, or it can be.

Of course, if you're writing a memoir, that's a case where using the first-person is obvious; and if you're writing a letter to someone, using the second-person will come naturally. But if you're writing, let's say, a biography, do you see how you could theoretically do it from any of these perspectives? You could write the biography of George Washington from the first-person, as though this were Washington's own memoirs or autobiography. You could; but it would be a bit experimental, wouldn't it? If we were claiming that it was nonfiction that would get dicey. Even if all the details were true and all the words that we put in his mouth were accurate, we'd still be creating a sort of misrepresentation to the reader that could get complicated. You could write this biography of George Washington theoretically in the second-person. You could say, "You, George Washington, you did that and you did that." It would be possible, but it would be pretty unusual, wouldn't it? It would essentially make the narrator—the person speaking to George

Washington—the main character of somebody else's biography. That's a little weird. But technically, it would be possible to write a biography from the first- or second-person.

The "he or she" third-person makes a lot more sense, doesn't it? The normal way to write a biography about George Washington is to say, "He did this and then he did that. On this day in 1776, he got on his horse and went about his business." The thing is, however, writing in the third-person isn't a simple matter. There are more ways to write in the third-person than you've probably ever imagined. Sometimes third-person needs to draw in the first-person; for example when, in our biography, we might want to quote some of George Washington's own words in order to build his character, right? When we tell the story of George's feelings for his mother, where he famously says, "I attribute all my success in life to the moral, intellectual and physical education I received from her," we want him to be able to say "I attribute my success" directly. We don't want to have to write "He attributed all his success." There are third-person ways of using the first-person.

What was that? Did I just say that there are third-person ways of using the first-person? I did. Hang in there and I'll explain what that means, and why, as a nonfiction writer, you really want to know about this.

Let's start at the beginning: Third-person is the "he, she, or it" point of view; but within any point of view, there are different modes we can use as writers. In the next few minutes, we're going to look at the difference between direct discourse, indirect discourse, and free indirect discourse. What's important about each mode here is that they make different kinds of truth claims. In other words, they imply different relationship to history and our ability to know it. You can see immediately that that's going to be important for us as nonfiction writers, can't you?

Let's start with the simplest one: direct discourse. This is another way of saying we have direct quoted speech. Here's an example:

> George Washington's mother was a woman he greatly admired. "What did you think of your mother," a friend asked George.

> "I attribute all my success in life to the moral, intellectual and physical education I received from her," said George.

"I attribute all my success" is presented to readers as a direct quote, and the source of it is attributed directly: "said George." We know who said it, and we are being told as readers this is a fact; this is exactly what George really said. It's a plain fact. As nonfiction writers, if we have a source that says George Washington really said this, that's great. We can use direct discourse. The advantage of direct discourse is that it's very direct. It's also a very neutral and objective—even distant—way of telling a story isn't it? That can be either an advantage or a disadvantage. But there's no getting inside George's head here; it's "just the facts, ma'am" reporting. There's no first-person perspective. What it's hard to do sometimes with direct speech is to build a sense of a character's inner self, unless the things they say in those direct quotes are themselves sufficiently introspective and revealing.

There's also a way of telling a third-person story called indirect discourse. This is when we don't use quotation marks but what we said is still attributed. In other words, we know who's saying or thinking something, even without the quotation marks. If we rewrote that same example in indirect discourse, we would read:

> George's friend was impressed with the president's admiration for his mother and asked him about it. George told him that he attributed all his success to the education in morality, scholarship, and athletics he had received from her.

Do you see the difference? There are no quotes, but we know at each moment who said what. We don't know the exact words that George used; but we know the substance of the exchange, and that substance is presented to us as a fact. Once again, it's cool, detached, and objective. It's the way we often write history when we know what happened in a general way but not in a specific sense. When we're writing biography, very often this is the kind of information we have: information that something happened, but not an exact record of the dialogue between the people involved. The trouble is, indirect discourse is a bit clunky, isn't it? Writing a whole biography—or even the overwhelming majority of it—in indirect discourse sounds very academic.

As you can maybe begin to see, it's going to be hard to build great character using it, isn't it? How do we ever get inside a character's head? How do we show rather than tell, because this is strong telling language? How do we create dramatic tension or communicate a character's internal conflict? In short, how are we going to tell a great story using just indirect discourse?

The answer is: We're not. In our next lesson, we're going to learn about something called free indirect discourse, and it's one of the nonfiction writer's most important storytelling tools. But as an exercise at the end of this lesson, let's make sure you've mastered direct discourse and indirect discourse before we build on those skills. Here's your exercise. Write a paragraph or two in which you do two things: One, develop a character, historical or imaginary, who you reveal to the reader using either metonymy or synecdoche; and two, write this paragraph using both indirect discourse and direct discourse. You'll start to get a feel for what each technique allows a writer to do, and you'll get practice at quickly sketching believable characters.

Getting Inside the Heads of Your Characters
Lecture 14

Free indirect discourse is an invaluable tool in the creative nonfiction writer's tool kit. It allows the author to suggest how a character may have felt or thought based on a reasonable interpretation of the evidence, but without having to use the character's exact words, or what we might call "hard" evidence. It gently blurs the line between the author and the character in a way that does not violate the nonfiction contract.

What Is Free Indirect Discourse?

- Direct discourse and indirect discourse have one thing in common: They attribute thoughts and expressions to a speaker, thinker, or character. **Free indirect discourse** is another third-person perspective that lets a writer bring in the first-person voice.

- Unlike direct discourse, free indirect discourse does not use quotation marks. In fact, it does not require the writer to attribute remarks at all. Because remarks can be unattributed, a writer is also free to use a bit more imaginative room—even in nonfiction.

- Free indirect discourse offers something very precious to nonfiction writers: Because the remarks are unattributed, they do not have to be based on historical facts. The remarks *could* be our own as authors. They could be interpretation. The writer can use this technique to get inside a character's head in a speculative manner without breaking the nonfiction contract.

- Let's look at the George Washington example again. If we rewrite it in free indirect discourse, we could say something like this:

> George Washington was asked why he so much admired his mother. How could one explain what a mother gave a child? What words were there to encompass it? It was a beautiful thing. He knew that he owed everything to her education.

George told his friend that his mother was the reason for all his success in his life.

- The first and last sentences are simple indirect discourse, but in between, who is speaking? The discourse here is free *and* unattributed. Maybe it is the author or narrator asking a rhetorical question, or maybe it is George Washington thinking this to himself.

- The writer might be inviting the reader to think of this as the private thoughts of George Washington; after all, he probably *did* think something like this. But here is the critical distinction: the author does not say that George Washington had these thoughts.

- There is nothing here that is historically untrue. There has been no breach of the nonfiction contract. Writers can play with the ambiguity of free indirect discourse to help a reader imagine what is going on inside the character's head.

Free Indirect Discourse in Fiction

- Jane Austen is widely regarded as the most accomplished practitioner of free indirect discourse in English literary history. She uses it to give readers a glimpse into the minds of her characters while maintaining the narrator's third-person point of view.

© Photos.com/Thinkstock.

Jane Austen was one of the masters of free indirect discourse.

- Here is a famous example of free indirect discourse from *Northanger Abbey*—Austen's comic Gothic novel about a naïve young girl named Catherine who goes to stay at an ancient country estate. She begins to imagine ghosts and terrible crimes everywhere around her, based on her reading of trashy horror novels. She even begins to imagine that her host, General Tilney, murdered his late wife, Mrs. Tilney.

> This apartment, to which she had given a date so ancient, a position so awful, proved to be one end of what the general's father had built. There were two other doors in the chamber, leading probably into dressing-closets; but she had no inclination to open either. Would the veil in which Mrs. Tilney had last walked, or the volume in which she had last read, remain to tell what nothing else was allowed to whisper? No: whatever might have been the general's crimes, he had certainly too much wit to let them sue for detection.

- We assume that these are Catherine's thoughts, since Catherine is the "she" being described in the third-person narration at the beginning of the paragraph. But Austen never actually says that Catherine is thinking these thoughts. It could be the narrator voicing these opinions.

- Another novelist who uses this technique beautifully is Virginia Woolf, in her book *Mrs. Dalloway*. It is the story of a middle-aged woman named Clarissa Dalloway preparing for a dinner party, thinking about her friends and neighbors and the complicated relationships among them. Here is a sample:

> Times without number, Clarissa had visited Evelyn Whitbread in the nursing home. Was Evelyn sick again? Evelyn was a good deal out of sorts, said Hugh, intimating by a kind of pout or swell of his very well-covered manly extremely handsome upholstered body … that his wife had some internal ailment, nothing serious, which as an old friend, Clarissa Dalloway would quite understand without requiring him to specify. Ah yes, she did of course; what a nuisance; and felt very sisterly and oddly conscious at the same time of her hat. Not the right hat for the early morning, was that it? For Hugh always made her feel, as he bustled on … that she might be a girl of eighteen.

- There are no quotation marks here, although there is discourse. Some of it is attributed to Hugh; much of it is not. It could be Clarissa's thoughts, or it could be the narrator's.

Claims of Fact versus Narrator Speculation

- If Clarissa Dalloway were a historical figure, what in this passage would we have to have researched sources for, and what claims could we make without sources while still keeping the nonfiction contract?

    - "Times without number, Clarissa had visited Evelyn Whitbread in the nursing home" is a claim of fact that would need to have historical evidence, such as letters, diary entries, the nursing home visitor book, and so forth.

    - "Was Evelyn sick again?" is free indirect discourse that does not require a source.

    - "Evelyn was a good deal out of sorts, said Hugh, intimating by a kind of pout or swell of his very well-covered manly extremely handsome upholstered body … that his wife has some internal ailment, nothing serious, which as an old friend, Clarissa Dalloway would quite understand without requiring him to specify." This needs several types of proof: First, that Hugh said Evelyn was ill in some way during this encounter, although not his exact words; second, that Clarissa thought Hugh was manly and extremely handsome; and finally, that either he tried to communicate a nonverbal message about his wife's health to Clarissa or that Clarissa thought he did. Again, this would require some sort of personal records kept by one or both parties.

- Obviously, writing creative nonfiction involves a huge amount of research. The writer needs an enormous amount of information about the smallest details because the more details the writer has, the more freedom he or she has to shape a story like a fiction writer within the boundaries of the nonfiction contract.

- Free indirect discourse allows a writer to float an idea. It is an invitation to the reader to attribute the thoughts of the writer to the thoughts of the character. The reader can accept or reject the invitation, but the writer has been truthful by not making claims of fact without evidence.

Ten Facts—A Research Exercise and a Writing Exercise

- This exercise is aimed at developing creative ideas for researching your own creative nonfiction project. Imagine that you had to prove the "facts" in *Mrs. Dalloway*. Make a list of 10 places that you would go to start looking for this factual information to support this passage.

- Next, return to your own story idea and make a list of 10 facts that you could build a story on. Using those 10 facts, try writing a paragraph or two, using free indirect discourse to work at the boundaries of what you know to really get inside the head of your character.

Important Term

free indirect discourse: Speech in a narrative that is not quoted and is not attributed to a specific speaker.

Suggested Reading

Austen, *Northanger Abbey*.

MacKay, *The Cambridge Introduction to the Novel*.

Woolf, *Mrs. Dalloway*.

Questions to Consider

1. In this lesson, we are learning about the ways in which a writer can use the voice—and character—of a sometimes "invisible" narrator to shape the atmosphere of a story. If you are the narrator of your stories, what

kind of character would you like to be? How would you like readers to perceive you?

2. Many of the techniques we are studying in this course apply to fiction as well as nonfiction, but some help us meet particular challenges in nonfiction writing. Can you name two that are especially useful for creative nonfiction writers?

Getting Inside the Heads of Your Characters

Lecture 14—Transcript

In the last lesson, we explored the psychological motivations of characters in our writing and the role metaphor plays in creating characters with complex personalities. We talked especially about how using metaphor to develop character is especially important for writers of creative nonfiction because they let the writer suggest connections and motivations while respecting the nonfiction contract. We also learned that with the third-person point of voice, there are a whole range of different modes a writer can use to narrate discourse and a character's thoughts. One of the things that we discovered is that direct discourse and indirect discourse have one thing in common: They both rely on thoughts and expressions being attributed to a speaker, or a thinker, or a character. The difference between them is that in direct discourse, we use quotation marks around speech or thoughts; in indirect discourse, we don't use quotation marks, but summary.

But remember how I said there was a third option? It's hugely important, and for the nonfiction writer incredibly useful for one reason: It doesn't require attribution of speech or thought. It's a more complicated but often tricky last mode of writing in the third-person called free indirect discourse.

Are you ready for another craft lesson? Here we go. First, let's recap direct discourse and indirect discourse again very quickly. Direct discourse: It's when the discourse, what somebody says, is attributed directly, right? The way that we attribute directly what someone says is by putting those words in quotation marks; so direct discourse is when I write: "I see it's a beautiful day out there," Mary said cheerfully. Indirect discourse; it's actually obvious, isn't it? It's when the discourse is only attributed indirectly. That means we don't use quotations, but we do still know who said it. It's indirect attribution, but it's still attributed. There I might write: Mary said cheerfully that she could see that it was a beautiful day out there.

Free indirect discourse, what is that? Like direct discourse, it's a third-person perspective that lets a writer bring in the first person voice. After all, in direct discourse, with quotations marks around speech, we can incorporate the "I" voice when, for example, in George Washington we read something like:

“ ‘I attribute all my success in life to the moral, intellectual and physical education I received from her,’ he said.” It’s direct discourse. George Washington’s words are in quotes. It’s attributed; we know who said it. George Washington did. After all, I wrote, “he said.” Like indirect discourse, however, free indirect discourse also doesn’t use quotation marks. After all, that’s what “indirect” discourse means, right? It meant we didn’t use quotations but instead said something like, “George Washington said that he attributed to his mother all the success he had achieved in life.” We don’t know the exact words he used, but we know that it’s being stated as a fact that he did say something very much like that, and we know that he’s the one who said it. No quotes; but a fact and attributable.

The question is: What does “free” mean? If you think about it, maybe you can guess that it’s going to have something to do with that issue of attribution. Basically, free indirect discourse is indirect discourse—so no quotation marks—but with one other element; and unlike both direct and indirect discourse, it doesn’t require the writer to attribute the remarks at all. For this reason, because the remarks are technically unattributed, we call them “free”; free from a speaker or a thinker. Because they can be unattributed, a writer is also free to use a bit more imaginative room, even in nonfiction.

Free indirect discourse; did you get all of that? Here it is again: Free indirect discourse is when we don’t use direct quotes, but we also don’t have to directly attribute the remarks either. We could attribute the remarks, but because we don’t have to, that means something very important for nonfiction writers: We don’t have to rely on historical facts. That’s the key thing to remember here. The remarks could be our own as authors. They could be, for example, interpretation.

Is your head spinning a bit? Don’t worry, I’ll explain, and I’m going to show you plenty of examples, so hang in there. But for now, remember this: What free indirect discourse lets us do as nonfiction writers is to get inside the character’s head in a speculative manner that doesn’t break the nonfiction contract. That means that this technique is critical.

All of this is pretty abstract, I know. Let's look again at the George Washington example. If we rewrite it in free indirect discourse, we could say:

> George Washington was asked why he so much admired his other. How could one explain what a mother gave a child? What words were there to encompass it? It was a beautiful thing. But he knew that he owed everything to her education. George told his friend that his mother was the reason for all his success in his life.

The first sentence is written in simple indirect discourse. But how about those other sentences there in the middle? "How could one explain what a mother gave a child? What words were there to encompass it?" Who is it that's speaking there? We don't know, do we? The discourse here is free; it's unattributed. Maybe it's the author or narrator here, asking a rhetorical question. But maybe it's George Washington thinking this to himself, too, isn't it? Because it's not attributed, we aren't saying one way or the other; a reader can read it either way. Ok, we might even be inviting the reader to think of this as the private thoughts of George Washington. After all, he probably did think something like this. The author is proposing it. But here's the critical thing: The author doesn't actually say that George Washington had these thoughts. There's nothing here that's historically untrue, and there's been no breach of the nonfiction contract.

As a writer, we can use free indirect discourse to play with this ambiguity about attribution to help a reader imagine him or herself into the character's head without actually saying, "This is what George Washington thought." In fact, do you see that if had written instead, " 'What had his mother given him,' George asked himself," we'd have direct discourse rather than free indirect discourse? In that case, we would have to have a historical source where we knew for a fact that George had had that thought and had reported it in those exact words. If we don't have his exact words, we'd have to write it in indirect discourse: "George asked himself what his mother had given him."

Questions of this sort are one way of using free indirect discourse; but statements—even whole passages of thought—can be in free indirect discourse as well. In that example, I wrote: "It was a beautiful thing." That's not a question; it's a statement. But once again, who's saying this? It's free speech, so it's unattributed. Maybe, again, it's me, the author or narrator, saying this. But maybe it's what George Washington was thinking, too. The language suggests it might have been George, and if we can get inside the head of a character to understand what he or she is thinking or feeling, we can help write a great story that will grip our readers. But we cannot tell a lie; that's the nonfiction contract. That's why free indirect discourse is one of the most powerful tools in our writerly repertoire.

Do you think you're beginning to get the idea here? I warned you, it's a bit technical; so don't worry if you're still a little hazy. We're going to look at some examples from other works of writing to give you a clear idea of how this works, and then, of course, I'll give you an exercise that will help you practice this mode of writing in your own work. By the end, you'll have a new tool you can use in crafting your work of nonfiction.

Have you ever wondered why Jane Austen's novels manage, despite what are very largely conventional romance plots, to create such masterful characters? There's a good reason: Jane Austen is widely regarded as the most accomplished practitioner of free indirect discourse in English literary history. It's one of the things she's technically famous for, actually. She uses it—as you can, too—to give readers a glimpse into the mind of her characters while keeping her own third-person point of view as the narrator. That classic Jane Austen gentle irony? It's the result of that subtle ambiguity; the contrast between what we learn goes on in subjectively the minds of her characters and how the third-person narrative perspective reveals them to us objectively.

Here's a famous example of Austen's use of free indirect discourse from *Northanger Abbey*, her comic Gothic novel about a naïve young girl named Catherine who goes to stay at an ancient—but thoroughly modernized—country estate. She begins to imagine ghosts and terrible crimes everywhere around her based on her reading of trashy horror novels. She even begins to imagine that her host, General Tilney, perhaps murdered his late wife, Mrs. Tilney. She is, of course, comically wrong. Austen writes:

> This apartment, to which she had given a date so ancient, a position so awful, proved to be one end of what the general's father had built. There were two other doors in the chamber, leading probably into dressing-closets; but she had no inclination to open either. Would the veil in which Mrs. Tilney had last walked, or the volume in which she had last read, remain to tell what nothing else was allowed to whisper? No: Whatever might have been the general's crimes, he had certainly too much wit to let them sue for detection.

I've said it's written in free indirect discourse, haven't I? But think about this for a moment; can you explain why? In fact, do you want to be really sure you understand the difference? The best way to be sure you understand something is to try to teach it. See if you can explain to someone who's not taking this course what free indirect discourse is, and see if you can explain it using this as an example. If you want to test yourself for a minute, pause the course and see what you can come up with.

What are you going to say? You're probably going to start with the fact that we assume that these are Catherine's thoughts, don't we? Catherine is the "she" being described in the third-person narration at the beginning of the paragraph. She's the one who's been given this apartment, so it's fair to assume that she's the person having these thoughts. But does Jane Austen actually say anywhere that these are Catherine's thoughts here? Does she ever say, "Catherine thought to herself," or "Catherine wondered"? She doesn't, does she? In fact, it could be the narrator asking that question, "Would the veil in which Mrs. Tilney had last walked remain?" It could be the narrator; and it could be the narrator voicing the opinion that if the general had committed these crimes, he was too cunning to leave a trace of them. Because the thoughts aren't directly attributed—because there are no quotation marks, which would make it direct discourse; no she said/I thought identifiers, which would make it indirect discourse—we have language that's free. Free; and because there are no quotations marks, free and indirect.

Is that what you came up with? If so, that's great. You're getting the hang of a difficult, but important, technique. It's a technique novelists like Jane Austen can use to tell a great story. But because of the freedom to switch from the perspective of the author to the perspective of the character without actually attributing the thoughts to either one, for nonfiction storytelling it's crucial.

If you're not sure you get it quite yet, don't worry; let's try another and see if you can start to get the hang of it. Another novelist who uses this technique beautifully is the writer Virginia Woolf in her novel *Mrs. Dalloway*. This is the story of a middle-aged woman named Clarissa Dalloway, and she's spending the day prepping for a dinner party, thinking about her friends and neighbors and the complicated human relationships among them. Are you ready? I'm going to give you a passage from the novel. As you're listening, can you identify the moments when the writing slips into free indirect discourse? Can you also find moments of indirect discourse? There are both forms of indirect narration in the passage, and here's a great chance to see if you can spot the difference. Here we go:

> Times without number, Clarissa had visited Evelyn Whitbread in the nursing home. Was Evelyn sick again? Evelyn was a good deal out of sorts, said Hugh, intimating by a kind of pout or swell of his very well-covered manly extremely handsome upholstered body … that his wife had some internal ailment, nothing serious, which as an old friend, Clarissa Dalloway would quite understand without requiring him to specify. Ah yes, she did of course; what a nuisance; and felt very sisterly and oddly conscious at the same time of her hat. Not the right hat for the early morning, was that it? For Hugh always made her feel, as he bustled on … that she might be a girl of 18.

What did you come up with? Let's go through this one sentence by sentence so you can be sure you've mastered the technique. "Times without number, Clarissa had visited Evelyn Whitbread in the nursing home." That's just straight third-person narration, right? There's no discourse here, indirect, direct, or otherwise.

Here's the next one: "Was Evelyn sick again?" In the text, there are no quotations around this, and that's the entire sentence. There's discourse here; something is being said or thought. So no quotes means indirect discourse. Is it attributed? Does Woolf say, "Clarissa wondered"? No, she doesn't; so it has to be free indirect discourse, doesn't it? If you caught that, that's fabulous.

Here's the third sentence:

> Evelyn was a good deal out of sorts, said Hugh, intimating by a kind of pout or swell of his very well-covered manly extremely handsome upholstered body … that his wife had some internal ailment, nothing serious, which as an old friend, Clarissa Dalloway would quite understand without requiring him to specify.

Is there discourse here? There is, right? Evelyn, Clarissa is told, is "a good deal out of sorts." Who tells her this? "Said Hugh"; so the speech is attributed. Because Hugh doesn't say, "Evelyn is out of sorts," but is made to say without quotations that "Evelyn was out of sorts," it's not direct discourse. This is classic indirect discourse in this sentence, but it's not free, because there's that tag "said Hugh."

Here's the next sentence: "Ah yes, she did of course; what a nuisance; and felt very sisterly and oddly conscious at the same time of her hat." Is there discourse here? There is, isn't there? There's something here that Clarissa is thinking to herself: that she understands Evelyn's unspoken illness; that she has received Hugh's nonverbal message. In fact, Clarissa thinks to herself, "What a nuisance." Or, at least that's what we assume is going on, don't we? After all, Virginia Woolf doesn't say that Clarissa is thinking this at all. But as readers, we're meant to assume that she's thinking this. A character's private interior train of thought is given here without attribution. You got it: It's free indirect discourse.

One more: "Not the right hat for the early morning, was that it?" Is it discourse? Yes. Is it attributed? No. Free indirect discourse again.

Here's the last sentence: "For Hugh always made her feel, as he bustled on … that she might be a girl of 18." Is it discourse? That's not totally clear, actually. It could be more of Clarissa's interior train of thought. In that case, it's also unattributed and so would be free and indirect. On the other hand, it could just be Virginia Woolf making an elegant transition back out of the head of her heroine into objective third-person narration, couldn't it? It could be the narrator telling us this about Clarissa Dalloway. Or, it might be Clarissa Dalloway thinking this about herself. It's that wonderful ambiguity nonfiction authors want to learn to use to their fullest advantage in working with free indirect discourse.

Let's just reiterate what we mean by that: the special advantages of free indirect discourse for nonfiction writers. Let's imagine for a moment that Clarissa Dalloway was a historical figure, and that we're writing the nonfiction biography of her life. What in this passage from Virginia Woolf would we have to have sources for, and what kinds of sources would we have to have? For what claims would we not need sources, while still keeping the nonfiction contract?

I'm going to read you the passage again, and this time, for each sentence, make a note: Does this claim need a historical fact to back it up? In other words, does the writing make a truth claim; does it say, "This is what happened?" If so, here's another thing I want you to jot down: What's that piece of evidence you need to support your claim going to look like? What exactly is it going to have to say? What are the truth claims you'll need verified? Remember: With free indirect discourse, sometimes sentences don't actually make truth claims at all. Sometimes they pose possibilities; and possibilities don't need historical documentation in the world of nonfiction as long as we don't tell our readers they're something more than possibilities.

Here we go again with Virginia Woolf's passage:

> Times without number, Clarissa had visited Evelyn Whitbread in the nursing home. Was Evelyn sick again? Evelyn was a good deal out of sorts, said Hugh, intimating by a kind of pout or swell of his very well-covered manly extremely handsome

> upholstered body … that his wife had some internal ailment, nothing serious, which as an old friend, Clarissa Dalloway would quite understand without requiring him to specify. Ah yes, she did of course; what a nuisance; and felt very sisterly and oddly conscious at the same time of her hat. Not the right hat for the early morning, was that it? For Hugh always made her feel, as he bustled on. … that she might be a girl of 18.

Let's have a look at what you came up with listening to this. Sentence one again: "Times without number, Clarissa had visited Evelyn Whitbread in the nursing home." What's the piece of historical evidence you must have here? In a work on nonfiction, you're going to need some document that shows that Clarissa Dalloway visited Evelyn Whitbread in her nursing home on many occasions, aren't you? After all, this sentence makes a very direct truth claim. It tells us this is a fact, and facts need evidence to verify them in nonfiction. It's not that you need to make a footnote or tell your reader what the source is; you can just go ahead and tell your story. But the silent contract you make with the reader is: If I say this is true, then you can trust me. Out there, this fact exists. If I had to, I could show you a document—a letter, another biography, a set of photographs, whatever—to prove it.

How about the sentence "Was Evelyn sick again?" What do you think? You don't need any evidence, do you? After all, it's free indirect discourse. That means you aren't saying, as a writer, that anyone said this. The speech is free from attribution. It might just be a rhetorical question. That's not what we're invited to think; we're invited to think that Clarissa Dalloway thought this to herself. But we haven't said that, have we? If we haven't said it, we haven't made a truth claim at all. If we had written " 'Was Evelyn sick again,' Clarissa asked," and if we had put that question into quotation marks, then what we're saying is "Clarissa said this, and she said exactly this." In that case, we would need a source where we could show that Clarissa said those very words in this context. We would need a letter, a diary entry, or a document where another person reported hearing this said at the time. On the other hand, if we had written, "Clarissa wondered if Evelyn was sick again," does that make a truth claim? Think about it carefully. What's this sentence proposing is true? It's making a truth claim, isn't it? It's claiming that Clarissa wondered this. It's claiming that she had this thought. If we're making a truth claim, then in nonfiction writing we need to be able to produce a source. What kind of evidence do we need here? That's right; we need a source that proves that Clarissa had that thought, either because she said she did or because she told someone else that she did, and that person reported the conversation. This is where it gets tricky for nonfiction writers; are you beginning to see that? Are you beginning to see why free indirect discourse is so liberating?

In fact, you're probably beginning to see that this writing creative nonfiction—using the techniques of a creative writer to write about historical materials—is going to involve a huge amount of research, isn't it? You're probably realizing that you're going to have to have a lot more information about the smallest details than you ever imagined. If you're realizing this, you're exactly right. You need to become a scavenger of lost details. You need to find the facts that you can use in the smallest passages, because you want the complete freedom to shape a story like a fiction writer; but what you're bound by, always, is the nonfiction contract. That contract says: If I represent to you that something happened, you can rely on the fact that I'm telling you the truth. What free indirect discourse lets a writer do sometimes is float an idea. It's an invitation to the reader to attribute the thoughts of the writer to the thoughts of the character. The reader can accept or reject the invitation; but the writer has been truthful about not making claims of fact.

Thinking back to this passage from *Mrs. Dalloway*, here's your end of the lesson exercise on working in that gap between fact and speculation that free indirect discourse gives a creative nonfiction writer. We're going to use it to gear up for thinking about some creative ways you can get down to doing some interesting research for your creative nonfiction project. If this really were nonfiction and you had to prove the facts in *Mrs. Dalloway*, see if you can make a list of 10 places that you'd go to start looking for this factual information. The first 5 or 6 places are going to be easy; in fact, I've already given you hints about some of the places nonfiction writers turn for details. It's the last couple of places that might stump you; and that means, like a nonfiction writer, the first place you're going to have to get creative is in thinking about your research. As you'll see here in the last part of our course, creative research is absolutely essential. We'll look at your list and talk more about research and dealing with things you don't know or can't discover in lesson 15.

After you've thought through some of the places you could go looking for materials, how about this for the end of the lesson exercise? See if you can make a list of 10 facts that you could build a story on; after all, you already know how to shape a great one. Using those 10 facts, try writing a paragraph or two and using free indirect discourse as a way of working at the boundaries of what you know to really get inside the head of your character.

Using Narrative Perspective

Lecture 15

Perspective, or point of view, is not as simple as choosing to write from in the first-person, third-person, or rarely used second-person voice. Not only does each of these choices have a dramatic effect on your reader's perceptions, each of these voices has different modes. Each mode, in turn, allows the real author to create an implied author who shapes the story in different ways by choosing what to reveal to the reader.

Choosing First, Second, or Third Person

- Writers use the third person more often than any other perspective in storytelling. They can do all sorts of interesting and unique things with that perspective and can make it anything other than boring, but it is also as neutral a perspective as we have in English. It can seem objective, as though there is no narrator. But there is always a narrator.

- The most unusual narrative perspective is the second person—the *you* form, in which a story is told from the perspective of the reader. It implies the presence of an *I*, who might be also used (that would be mixed-perspective narrative) or who might remain only implied (a strict second-person narrative).

- By using the second person, the writer is inviting you to see yourself in this story. In fact, the writer is insisting on it. The reader is not an objective voyeur—someone who can watch the story from a safe distance—but someone who has also been made a character in a story.

Who Is the Implied Author?

- All stories have an **implied author**, a perspective from which the story is told and a consciousness directing the narrative. Sometimes this implied author can look like the historical author—that is, the person whose name is on the book—while sometimes they are clearly different.

- In fact, the implied author and the historical author are *never* precisely the same. Even when a writer says, "I am Tilar Mazzeo, and I am telling you this story," there is a distance between me the person and me the narrator, because a narrator is also a character in the story.

- When you read a story about "John's" life being in danger, it is a different experience from reading about "my" life or "your" life being in danger. The third person makes us think not about who the narrator is but about who the character is. The author's identity is hard to grasp.

- Third-person writing seems like an objective statement of facts. It tricks us into believing that the author is invisible, irrelevant, or nonexistent. But even the most objective story has a narrative structure. Your experience is shaped by the writer's choices from the moment you set eyes on the page.

- Having a strong implied author—as you do in a second-person narrative—is no more or less powerful than an invisible implied author. It is simply different.

- A first-person narrative has a strong implied author. The reader thinks, whoever this *I* is, he or she is telling us the story directly.

- The implied author is the person whose point of view is controlling the narrative perspective in that particular moment. It is not the same as the historical or "real" author—the person who is *really* controlling the entire narrative perspective.

- It is easier to understand the difference if you look at stories with more than one implied author.

- Boccaccio's *Decameron* is a Renaissance classic where a group of people at a house party in Italy during the bubonic plague take turns telling each other stories.

- A modern example comes from William Faulkner's *The Sound and the Fury*, in which four siblings each tell the story of their childhood from different perspectives.

- In both cases, there is an implied author controlling all of these perspectives, who is still different from the historical people Boccaccio and Faulkner.

- Readers are conditioned to assume that first-person narrators are implied authors. However, writers can work with layers of implied authors, each of whom knows more or less than the others.

- Implied authors are not the same as historical or "real" authors—even when we try to get you to believe that. Implied authors—even the invisible ones—are always characters in the story. They are developed according to the same rules of character you have already learned. They move narratives forward. They have motives and conflicts.

- If the *I* says "I, Tilar Mazzeo, am in a dark room, and the rising smell of gasoline is making my pulse begin to race," I am creating the impression that the historical author and the first person narrator are the same.

- All I have actually done is create a character within my story who I want you to believe is me, the author. But it's not me. You are not getting the totality of my experience. I am not really in that room; I am actually typing at my computer. Even if this is a work of nonfiction, that experience is in my past, and I am re-creating it from a carefully constructed perspective.

- What you are getting is a limited part of a consciousness—a narrative perspective—that I want you to think is radically nonfictional. Even though it is, like anything in creative nonfiction, a creative construction.

- Just because I do not break the nonfiction contract, that does not mean that I am not shaping your experience of this story by what I tell, what I do not tell, and how I tell it. That is the whole point of creative nonfiction.

Third Person Modes

- Just as different structures silently emphasize different things in a story, so do different narrative perspectives. They also can create multiple levels of implied authors through controlling who knows what information.

- Writers have terms to describe what any particular narrator knows in a story. What a narrator knows is sometimes the same—and sometimes different—from what a reader knows at that same moment.

- Traditionally, we talk about three modes of the third-person perspective. Each creates a different kind of implied author—and a different kind of story.

    - The first is the **omniscient mode**. In this mode, we get to see the story from the perspective of both the character(s) and the implied author. We get direct reporting of events that are not part of the consciousness of any characters. It is omniscient because we have access to everything.

    - The second mode is the **objective mode**. In this mode, we get only the perspective of the implied author, who is more or less invisible to the reader even though it is entirely the implied author's perspective the reader is getting. Objective third-person narrative looks like straightforward factual reportage; the reader loses the interior perspective of the characters.

- The third mode is the **subjective mode**. In this mode, we are limited to the experiences of the characters in the narrative. We have no access to the implied author and no objective narration. We experience the lives of the characters more intimately, and the narrator is almost invisible—yet the implied author is, in fact, controlling our perspective much more forcefully.

- Each of these devices can be used powerfully in different circumstances. A subjective third-person narrative from the point of view of a serial killer, for example, can make an exceptionally frightening thriller. A third-person objective story is great for an old-fashioned country-house whodunit.

- A writer can also use all these perspectives in different combinations. A story does not have to have one perspective all the way through, although shifting perspectives is a high-level skill and something that beginning writers want to experiment with carefully.

- Both narrators and implied authors can be more or less reliable. People can tell us lies. They can withhold the truth or misdirect our attention. The unreliable narrator can be an effective tool, particularly in first-person narrative as the reader realizes, often slowly and dramatically, that the implied author is not to be trusted.

Choosing Your Mode—A Writing Exercise

- For your assignment, write the end of a chapter—something with a real cliffhanger, without thinking too hard about how you are writing it. After you have written it, ask yourself, What perspective did I write this from? Why did I choose this? What were the advantages and limitations? Could I have chosen better?

- If you are feeling ambitious, rewrite that paragraph in whichever modes you did not use before. Try to use at least the first person and each of the third-person modes.

Important Terms

implied author: The personality of the author that the reader gleans from the narrative, as distinct from the narrator's or point-of-view character's personality.

objective mode: A mode of writing that purports to report the facts unemotionally.

omniscient mode: A mode of writing in which the narrator is assumed to have complete knowledge of all events.

subjective mode: A mode of writing in which the narration is presumed to be filtered through the subjective opinions and experiences of a particular consciousness or character.

Suggested Reading

Calvino, *If on a Winter's Night a Traveler.*

Raisley, *The Power of Point of View.*

Questions to Consider

1. In the story you want to write, what kind of narrator do you want readers to perceive you to be? What new strategies have you learned that would let you shape that voice?

2. The second-person point of view is rarely used. What particular circumstances can you imagine in which it would be ideal? Why?

Using Narrative Perspective
Lecture 15—Transcript

In our last lesson, we looked at some of the complicated and subtle ways a writer can control point of view to have important effects, and we looked especially at how free indirect discourse has unique advantages for writers of creative nonfiction. That's because free indirect discourse hovers on the line between the thoughts and words of a character and the thoughts and words of an author or narrator. It's a productive kind of ambiguity. It's language where we can express interior thoughts without having to nail down their attribution.

Before we move on, are you wondering why I use the term "author or narrator" here and why I did in the last lesson? It's a bit curious, isn't it? But don't worry, before the end of the course, we're going to spend plenty of time talking about how you can work with turning the author into a character in a narrative, and I'm going to explain that. But for now, here's the key idea to keep in mind: Remember, all narratives have some perspective. All narratives have a narrator, to put it very simply. The most invisible narrator is one that looks like the same thing as the author. Looks; but isn't. I'll explain in more detail soon. For now, we'll just talk about the author or narrator, or, in the lesson here, I'll use the more general term for this: the implied author.

In this lesson, we're going to learn more about narrative point of view and the different kinds of perspectives a writer can use to frame a story and a reader's point of entry into the world we create in a book. We've covered already so far the basic elements of perspective in narrative, haven't we? Let's recap them quickly once again to review.

We have the first-person perspective; that's the perspective when the story is told from the "I" point of view. It's something we see pretty often in stories, but it's more tricky to use successfully than the neutral third-person perspective. For that reason, beginning writers might be wise to avoid using the first-person perspective in a story unless there's a good and important reason that you can explain clearly why you need to use it. It's not that you should avoid it; it's just that you shouldn't use it unless you know why you're doing that.

More often, writers use the third-person; the "he, she, or it" point of view in a story. Writers can do all sorts of interesting and unique things with that perspective and can make it anything other than boring. But it's also as neutral a perspective as we have in English. It's the perspective that can seem objective, as though there's no narrator, which, of course, you already know there is. That's something we're going to talk more about here.

The most unusual narrative perspective is the second-person—the "you" form—in which a story is told structurally from the perspective of the reader. It implies the presence of an "I," who might also be used (that would be a mixed perspective narrative) or who might remain only implied (a strict second-person narrative). What would that mean? You can see immediately, can't you, it's going to be unusual. It means something like this—I would start a story by saying:

> You are in a small dark room, and the rising smell of gasoline is making your pulse begin to race. There is a flicker of a match in the distance. Your heart sinks. It can only be minutes before the flames and the gasoline meet. You think, "This is the end."

Let's think about this for a moment. How does a second-person narrative affect you as a reader? Think about it for a minute. If you aren't sure, think about this: What would it be like if instead of writing, "You are in a dark room, and the rising smell of gasoline is making your pulse begin to race," I had written, "John was in a dark room, and the rising smell of gasoline was making his pulse begin to race"? How is that a different experience for the reader?

Your relationship to the story is materially different, isn't it? In the second-person version, what the writer is doing is inviting you to see yourself in this story; in fact, the writer's insisting on it. But when someone says "you," someone has to be saying it, right? We've put the reader into the story, and we have the presence of an unidentified speaking "I" who any reader is pretty soon going to start getting curious about. They're in some kind of very unique relationship. The reader isn't an objective voyeur, someone who can just watch a story from a safe distance, but someone who's also been made a character in a story; because as readers, we have to assume that the unspoken "I"—the person who's calling us "you"—must be the author, right? All stories have an implied author, a perspective from which the story is told, and a consciousness directing the narrative we're reading. It's very important to remember that while sometimes this implied author can look a lot like the historical author—the person whose name is on the book—and while sometimes they're clearly different, the implied author and the historical author are never precisely the same. Even when a writer says, "I'm Tilar Mazzeo, and I'm telling you this story"; even then, there's always a distance between me the person and me the narrator, because the narrator is always also a character in a story.

Is your head spinning again? It's complicated, isn't it? Don't worry; hang in there with me, and this will all become more clear as we go forward. It's complicated because it's the kind of thing we aren't used to seeing in stories; and we aren't used to seeing it because it's meant to be invisible. That's part of the trick of how it works so beautifully.

Meanwhile, if you want a fabulous example of a novel that uses this second-person perspective brilliantly, I recommend to you the novel *If on a winter's night a traveler* by the Italian writer Italo Calvino. It's a story about a reader reading a book and how he gets tangled up in the life of the author and the characters.

Let's recap: The second-person perspective makes the reader a character and implies that there's some first-person "I" out there who's describing us in this odd fashion. There's a strong implied author whose identity is a mystery, at least for the moment.

When I write about these same events happening to "John," it's different, isn't it? As a reader, we can sit back in safety. Even if John gets blown up, our lives aren't in any jeopardy. "Poor John," we think. In fact, that's it exactly: The third-person makes us think not about who the narrator is, but about who the character is. Who's John, and what the devil did he do to get himself into this predicament? Who's the author? It's hard to see in this example that there is one, isn't it? You might say to me, "Yes, of course there must be an author. I mean, this is a sentence, so someone must've written it," but this is objective. It's just a statement of facts; a reporting of what happened and how John felt. You'd be right: That's what third-person perspectives help us to believe, that the author is invisible, or irrelevant, or nonexistent. The author is a name on the cover of the book, and this is a story that lets us see the narrative as though it isn't filtered through anyone's mind but our own.

But do you see the catch? Think of everything you've learned so far about how an author shapes a story. It's impossible, isn't it? Even the most objective story has a narrative structure. Someone else decided on it. Even the most objective story either has simple sentences or compound complex sentences. Someone else wrote them. Your reading is being shaped by the writer's choices from the first minute you set eyes on the page, and there's always an implied author; always a perspective we're seeing this from; especially when that perspective is one that's meant to look so neutral and so normal that we forget it's there. If this happens to you as a reader, think of how powerful a tool it's going to be for you as a writer. Remember, having a strong implied author—like in the second-person example—isn't any more or less powerful than an invisible one; it's just different.

Now, how about the first-person? Can you answer that question before we even talk about it? What kind of an implied author will there be in a first-person narrative, strong or weak? That's right: strong. First-person narratives give us the implied author right up front. If we wrote that sentence, "I am in a small dark room, and the rising smell of gasoline is making my pulse begin to race," you start to wonder about who "I," the narrator, am, don't you? You think, "Whoever this 'I' is, she's telling us her story directly. She's the implied author."

Something very important: The implied author is the person whose point of view is controlling the narrative. It's not the same as the historical or real author, the person who's really controlling the entire narrative perspective. Let me repeat that: There's a gap between the author who writes a book—you in real life—and the implied author, the person who the reader experiences as controlling the story. If it's a small gap, it's the difference between the real "you" and the "you" you're presenting to a reader. After all, there's a difference for all of us, every day in life, between who we are and the face we present to the world, isn't there? But that gap in storytelling can also be much wider.

What do we mean? Think of it this way: Can you imagine a book in which I could write a story where I'm a writer and I'm telling a story in which my characters get to tell their own stories, too? Of course you can; that would just be a normal frame narrative, the kind we talked about back in our lesson on structure. That's the idea of a famous literary classic like Boccaccio's *Decameron*, where a group of people at a house party in Italy during the bubonic plague take turns telling each other stories.

Another example: Can you imagine a book in which different characters take turns telling their stories in the first-person, but there isn't a stated "I" who's clearly in charge of the story? This book would be one first-person narrative after another, without someone having to explain to us how they're related. It's the idea of William Faulkner's wonderful novel *The Sound and the Fury*, where four siblings each tell the story of their childhood from a different perspective. That's easy to imagine, isn't it? John can tell the story of his frightening experience with gasoline; and after John has met his untimely end, his daughter Mary can tell the story of what happened after "The day I heard my father, John, died in a terrible blaze and I was giving birth to my sixteenth baby." That means there are multiple first-person narrators, each of whom is the implied author of his or her narrative moment.

But who's in charge of all these multiple perspectives? There must be another implied author who's controlling them, right? So far, we've seen how implied authors must be there but can be made to seem invisible. Here's what we've learned: Readers are conditioned to assume that first-person narrators are implied authors. However, writers can work with layers of implied authors, each of whom knows more or less than the others. But any narrative must have at least one implied author who's in control of the entire vision of the story; whose consciousness structures the perspective from which we are seeing everything; and who knows what the writer's tool is for crafting perspective, as we're going to see in a minute.

One last thing: Implied authors, again, aren't the same as historical or real authors, even when we try to get you to believe that. There's always that gap I was telling you about; always.

One last thing on top of that: Implied authors, even the invisible ones, are also always characters in a story. They're developed according to the same rules of character that you've already learned about in this course. They move narratives forward; they have motives and conflicts. What do I mean? Think about this: If the "I" says "I, Tilar Mazzeo, am in a dark room, and the rising smell of gasoline is making my pulse begin to race," I'm creating the impression that the historical author—that's me—and the first-person narrative that's creating an implied author are the same, aren't I? You see my name on the book jacket. You see that I say "I, Tilar Mazzeo, am telling you this story." But all I have done is create a persona, a character within my story, who I want you to believe is the same as me, the author, who in my office wrote this book. But it's not me. You're not getting the totality of my experience. I'm not including in my book how I got up and took a coffee break; or how typing made my back ache; or how on a lovely summer day I played hooky from writing at all.

No, what you're getting is the "I" that I want you to see; the "I" who I believe helps me to tell this story better, who has a role to play in moving the narrative along, in creating tension and drama, in making you feel closer to the story and more identified with it. What you're getting is a limited part of a consciousness—a narrative perspective—that I want you to think is radically nonfictional, even though it is, like anything in creative nonfiction, a creative construction. I won't lie to you, and I won't break the nonfiction contract. If I tell you I'm writing this book in the Alps, then you know that I must really have written it there in the mountains. But just because I don't break the nonfiction contract, that doesn't mean that I'm not shaping your experience of this story powerfully by what I tell, what I don't tell, and how I tell it. That's the whole point of creative nonfiction.

Remember how when we were talking about finding the right structure for your narrative—about whether it would be linear, or circular, or something else—we said that different structures silently emphasize different things in a story? Remember how linear structures highlight plot; circular structures are great for character-driven stories? It's the same thing with choosing a narrative perspective, isn't it? The choices we make as writers, especially the invisible choices we make about structure, have as much effect on how a story affects our readers as the content of our book does. Without a great structure—the right one for the story you want to tell—there can't be amazing storytelling.

I said a minute ago that who knows what information is key to creating multiple layers of implied authors. That's why writers have a set of precise terms to describe what any particular narrator knows in a story; and what a narrator knows is sometimes the same, and sometimes different, from what a reader knows at the same moment.

So far, you've learned about the three perspectives we can use as writers. Traditionally in storytelling, we also talk about three modes that come up especially if we're using the third-person perspective; that one where our implied author can be made to seem invisible. These three modes are ways in which a writer can limit the information we get as readers in order to put us in the heads of some characters and to keep us out of the heads of others. Each creates a different kind of implied author, and a different kind of story.

The first is the omniscient mode. We have a third-person narrative. We're reading about John's perils in the dark room with the gasoline and matches. Let's imagine that John's would-be killer, Jack, the man with the matches, is now part of our story, too. The question is: How much do we get to know as readers about what's going on in Jack's and John's heads? Do we get to see things happening that John can't see? Do we get to see things both characters can't see? In the omniscient mode, we essentially get to see the story from the perspective of both the character and the implied author. We know what John and Jack are feeling; we know what Jack is about to do to John that John doesn't yet have a clue is going to happen; but we're also allowed to know things the villain Jack doesn't know yet, too.

Here's how our story might go in the omniscient mode:

> John was in a dark room, and the rising smell of gasoline was making his pulse begin to race. He looked at the chains on his feet. How the devil had he ended up here? He couldn't remember. He slumped unconscious against the wall.

> The harsh grating of a match on stone filled the room. The world was cast into shadows. Jack was enjoying this. He could smell John's fear. His old enemy deserved it. What Jack didn't see, as he tossed the flame lightly in John's direction, was that he, too, was standing in a puddle of oil.

We know what's going on it John's head, but our perspective isn't limited to it. We know what's going on in Jack's head, but we aren't limited to that either. We get direct reporting of events that aren't part of the consciousness of either of our characters. "The world was cast into shadow." That's objective narration, just a kind of neutral reporting. We know something that neither Jack nor John know, too: that Jack was standing in a puddle of oil also. The fact that we know something that someone sees—and lets us see—in a story, too, means that we're getting the perspective of the invisible implied author as well as the characters. It's omniscient because we have access to everything.

The second mode is objective narration. This is when, in a third-person story, we get only the perspective of the implied author. Since, in a third-person perspective, the author won't ever introduce him or herself as "I"—because that would be first-person—the implied author in a third-person narrative will always be more or less invisible to us as readers, even though it's entirely the implied author's perspective that we're getting. What the objective third-person narrative looks like is straightforward factual reportage. Here's how we might write John's story:

> John was in a dark room, and the rising smell of gasoline was making his pulse begin to race. John looked at the chains on his feet. He didn't remember how he had ended up there. Dazed, he slumped unconscious against the wall.
>
> The harsh grating of a match on stone filled the room. The world was cast into shadows. Jack was enjoying this. He could smell John's fear. What Jack didn't see, as he tossed the flame lightly in John's direction, was that he, too, was standing in a puddle of oil.

What we've lost in this more objective narration is the interior perspective of the characters: what's going on in their heads as they experience the events of our story. What we aren't allowed to know, for example, is Jack's revengeful thought that his old enemy deserved what was coming to him.

The third mode, as you can perhaps guess, is the subjective mode, and it's precisely the opposite: It's a story where we're limited only to the experiences of the characters in the narrative. We have no access to the implied author and no objective narration; everything is subjective. This is the mode that makes the implied author the most powerfully invisible of all. Here's John's story again:

> John was in a dark room, and the rising smell of gasoline was making his pulse begin to race. He looked at the chains on his feet. How the devil had he ended up here? He couldn't remember. He let himself slump against the wall.
>
> The harsh grating of a match on stone filled the room. The world was cast into shadows. Jack was enjoying this. He could smell John's fear. His old enemy deserved it. As he tossed the flame lightly in John's direction, he felt the cool dampness that he knew suddenly must be the oil creeping along his pant leg.

Here, everything we know is mediated by the consciousness of the two characters, isn't it? John, for example, can't logically know that he's unconscious, so we can't write that in this subjective narrative. When Jack learns he's standing in oil, we have to learn it with him; we can't know something he doesn't know, too. Because we're so in the minds of the characters and learning things with them, it means that our implied author is choosing to limit our perspective dramatically. She isn't telling us things she already knows. We experience the lives of the characters more intimately, but we have an implied author who is, in fact, controlling our perspective much more forcefully.

Hopefully you can see that each of these devices can be used powerfully in different circumstances. A subjective third-person narrative form in the point of a view of a serial killer, for example, is a whole different kind of frightening thriller. A third-person objective story is great for creating an old-fashioned country-house whodunit. A third-person omniscient whodunit—where we knew the character's private thoughts and motivations—that's going to be a whole lot harder, isn't it? After all, it's hard to keep alive the mystery of what happened and to enjoy the pleasure of watching the riddle unfold when we're already inside the head of someone who knows how it ends and hides from us nothing.

Of course, a writer can use all these perspectives in different combinations. A story doesn't have to have one perspective all the way through it; though shifting perspectives is a high-level skill and something that beginning writers want to experiment with carefully. It requires a deft touch to pull off successfully for the simple reason that if you change too abruptly or too often, you end up with too many different kinds of implied authors, don't you? You'll probably remember that this idea of using the fewest and simplest number of techniques to tell your story is a good piece of advice if you're a beginning writer. Shifting perspectives takes the same light touch as writing in the second-person. Unless you have a very good reason—a reason that's organic to and necessary for your story—the percentage play is to find one perspective and to work to master its storytelling potential.

Remember how I said the implied author is always a character? Characters can change in the course of stories, but they can't be so schizophrenic from one moment to the next that we can't recognize this as one character either, can they? That's the risk that comes with too many shifting perspectives. Character in narrative is a function of consistency punctuated by eccentricity, not—at least not normally—by the complete psychic collapse of identity.

This brings us to one last point about perspective: Both narrators and implied authors can also be more or less reliable. After all, people can tell us lies, can't they? They can withhold the truth from us or subtly try to divert our attention. When there's a gap between the different kinds of implied authors—between characters narrating in the first-person and an implied author beyond that, especially—the unreliable narrator can be very effective as a tool. The reader realizes, often slowly and dramatically, that what the implied author of the first-person narrative says maybe isn't a reliable picture of what the overarching implied author of the entire story is telling us is true. Likewise, overarching implied authors can evade us.

These are very advanced writing skills and require a lot of practice to accomplish successfully, so don't worry if you aren't sure how to use them. They're the kind of thing you would expect to learn about in a graduate-level course in creative nonfiction or in creative writing. They're also the sort of thing that, as you become more and more experienced as a writer, and as you come to see how your stories find their natural best structures, that you'll start to pick up on without even knowing it. The best way to learn writing, after all, is to do it.

But here, you've already learned some of the advanced tricks that writers know and that, by now, I think you're ready to start working with in your writing. For your assignment, let's have a try; it's your turn. This time, let's have you write the end of a chapter, something with a real cliffhanger. It'll be a chance to review what we learned about writing cliffhangers and creating narrative tension earlier in the course. If you don't remember, it's a good moment now to review. Remember, a cliffhanger is one way to end a chapter that both offers a satisfying conclusion and opens the door to a new step in the narrative arc, the development of tension, and the deepening of character.

Go ahead, write a short paragraph. You can write about anything. After you've written it, first decide: What perspective did you write it from, and why? What were the advantages? What were the limitations? Then, if you're feeling really ambitious, what you can do is rewrite that paragraph, just as we did here with the sad story of John and Jack, in the first-person and in each of the third-person modes.

Shaping Your Voice

Lecture 16

Understanding the difference between the writer, or historical author, and the implied author gives you the freedom to shape the implied author into a character. That character should have conflicts and motivations that drive the story along, just like any other character. The implied author will also have a distinctive voice, and choosing the right voice is crucial for engaging your readers.

Choosing a Voice

- Writers of creative nonfiction need to think especially carefully about narrative perspective. Think for a moment about the project you most hope to write some day, or the project you are already working on. What point of view do you imagine that story being told from, and why?

- If you want to write a memoir, the obvious choice would be first person; for a biography, some version of third person is more appropriate, but as we saw in the previous lecture, choosing third person requires you to make a series of other decisions.

Any story can be told from multiple perspectives. It is important to choose one carefully at the outset.

- Just as you need to decide about your narrative arc before you get too far into your writing project, you need to decide on your perspective early on as well. The perspective a writer uses is part of the structure of a story.

- Whatever perspective you choose, you will have to negotiate one important question: Who is the implied author, and what is his or her role in the story? All stories have a consciousness that organizes them and that communicates with the reader. In essence, the implied author is another character.

The Narrator as Character

- You will be able to use perspective and mode much more effectively if you think of the implied author as a character. What matters is that this implied author has a distinct and reliable set of traits and moves the narrative forward rather than hindering your storytelling. For this reason, we sometimes call the implied author the author-narrator.

- I used the technique of blending first-person and third-person narration, turning myself as author-narrator into a character, in *The Widow Clicquot*. I used the story of my quest to tell this story to bridge the gap in the historical evidence.

- I introduced my implied author as a first-person tour guide through history in the opening pages of the book. I needed this character to be someone the reader trusted and cared about right from the outset. I could not drop this character into what seemed like a normal historical biography without warning.

- I also could not simply use this *I* persona as a frame, at the beginning and the end. I needed this implied author to develop as a character all the way through the story and to show up regularly enough for the readers to be comfortable with her insights.

- Because I, as author-narrator, was a character, I needed tension and conflict, too, that drove what happened next in the story. In the end, I wove the circular quest narrative of Tilar Mazzeo's research throughout the linear biographical narrative of the Widow Clicquot.

The Third-Person and Purple Prose

- Let's look at how altering the implied author's voice affects the reader's response through an example of a family history. We will see how the objective third-person perspective can have a real personality of his or her own without ever resorting to the first person to describe him or herself or being described by another character.

- The narrator in these examples is Mary, the great-great-granddaughter of Philippe the Pirate. Mary the writer's task is to develop Mary the implied author as a character in the story without description or direct self-revelation. Here is her first try:

  > In August of 1685, Philippe left France for the Windward Islands aboard a ship named *Providence*, and unknown to the captain of the vessel he was part of a gang of young men who had already decided to take control of the ship. There was a predetermined signal that the young men had agreed upon in Marseilles, involving a secret handshake at the first watch.

- This is a rather dull paragraph. The implied author is boring, if precise and neutral. In her next revision, Mary goes in the opposite direction:

  > In August of the year 1685, the venerable Philippe left the shores of France for the far-flung Windward Islands aboard a vessel named *Providence*, and unbeknownst to her captain, Philippe had conspired with some of his young compatriots to seize control of the schooner. There would be a secret handshake upon the first watch, a predetermined signal that the momentous moment of revolution was upon them.

- This implied author is considerably more pompous. Our invisible narrator is a bit more visible that we want her to be. Thus, as a writer, you can draw a reader into a story—or make a reader want to back away from it—all through subtle choices in perspective.

- In the second example, Mary has indulged in **purple prose**. This is what writers call prose that is ornate and overwritten. It is language that calls attention to itself as language. The reader sees a writer who is more interested in the writing than in the story.

- Sometimes, in great literature, purple prose can sweep a reader away with emotion and enthusiasm. In theory, it could serve a narrative function, especially if the writer is trying to be ironic or funny, but most of the time, purple prose does not do anything useful.

- Even an experienced writer can fall into prose that has a bit of a bluish tint from time to time. It is always a danger when writers try to use language to shape the rhetorical and emotional reactions of our readers. Like sentence variation, language is a tool that must be used carefully to be used well.

- The risk of purple prose is that an author overwrites a passage to the point of unintentional comedy. It's essentially the same thing as turning the implied author into a stock character. It means that you have created—probably unintentionally—an unreliable narrator. After all, what reader is going to rely on a narrator who cannot write good prose?

- The words we choose and the way we put those words together create the voice of the implied author. That voice does not have to be *your* voice. In fact, because it is a character construct, because it has to be the right voice for the particular story you want to tell, it will never be exactly your voice.

- Writers learn to write in many different voices, all of which are ours—and yet not ourselves. Writers inhabit the minds and lives and perspectives of other people—some real, some imaginary—to tell their stories and our stories at the same time.

Philippe the Pirate—A Writing Exercise

- Rewrite the story of Philippe the Pirate from that imaginary family history in the voice of an implied author who is wry, witty, smart, and funny. Have a friend read your revision. How does your friend describe the voice of your implied author? Does it match the person you wanted to portray? If not, try another revision.

Important Term

purple prose: Writing that is overwrought or self-consciously written and calls attention to itself and away from the narrative; generally seen as negative.

Suggested Reading

Mazzeo, "The Author as Character in Narrative Nonfiction."

———, *The Widow Clicquot*.

Questions to Consider

1. In the project you imagine writing, who will the implied author be? What role will that character play in your story?

2. What would a story without any implied author at all look like? What would you have to do to write one? Could you still have a story?

Shaping Your Voice

Lecture 16—Transcript

In our last lesson, we learned about the different kinds of narrative perspective that a writer can use to shape the structure of a story and to shape the experience of the reader in powerful ways. Those techniques we learned in the last lesson apply to all kinds of writing, whether you're crafting a novel, or your memoir, or even a biography. In this lesson, let's think a bit more about how we can use these different narrative perspectives—these different ways of telling a story—in creative nonfiction especially. To prepare ourselves for talking about how to write great dialogue in lesson 18, we're also going to talk a bit here about what makes up voice in writing and about the common error that beginning writers sometimes run into—what's called "purple prose"—and why it undermines a great story.

Let's start today by thinking about why a writer of creative nonfiction might want to think especially carefully about narrative perspective. Think for a moment about the project that you most hope to write someday, or maybe the project that you're working on now even. What point of view do you imagine that story being told from; and maybe more importantly, why did you choose that perspective? Think about it for a minute.

If you want to write a memoir, the answer was probably pretty obvious, wasn't it? The whole idea of a memoir is that it's written in the first-person. It's the story of what you personally experienced, and how you want to share that story with your interested readers.

How about if you wanted to write biography? That's a little trickier. After all, we probably expect a biography to be written in the third-person. But, as we've seen, the third-person is actually one of the more complicated perspectives a writer can use for the simple reason that you now have to make a series of other decisions, don't you? Are you going to let readers into the minds of your characters as a biographer and use a limited subjective mode, or are you going to go with the classic bird's-eye view of history and use the objective mode? If you don't let your readers in the minds of your characters, what other techniques are you going to use to create strong character? After all, you don't want to write an academic term paper; you want to write gripping narrative nonfiction, the kind of writing that tells a great true story. Or maybe you want the omniscient mode where you can do both; and then you have to think about how to switch between two modes gracefully, don't you? Or you might have a story that switches between first- and third-person perspectives, even. That happens very often in biography and narrative history, especially.

Don't worry, it's actually not as hard as it sounds; you'll be an old hand at this in no time. But these are important decisions to make before you get too far along in your writing. Just like how we launch the narrative arc at the beginning of a story shapes how a tale can end, the perspective a writer uses is part of the structure of the story; the imaginary box that our story must fit comfortably and even naturally into.

Whatever perspective you choose as a writer, there's always one question that an author has to negotiate in any story: Who's the implied author and what's his or her role in the story? Is there more than one implied author in a story? Because, as we've seen in our discussion of the nuances of the third-person modes in our last lesson, the fact is that all stories have an "I" in them, at least implicitly. That's because all stories have a consciousness that organizes them and that communicates with us. The writer is always part of the story a reader experiences in some way or another. So who is that implied author going to be? How much like the historical author do we want this persona to appear to be? What narrative function will he or she perform?

Do you want to know the easy answer to that last question? There is one. The answer is this: The implied author functions as a character in your story. What kind of character is up to you and depends on the story you're telling, of course; but the implied author is always there as a character, and you'll be able to use perspective and mode—and ultimately voice—much more effectively if you think of this imaginary persona as a character. Maybe it's a cool, detached, invisible character of whom you leave hardly any traces and you're working with a strict third-person objective mode; just a distant, omniscient consciousness organizing a tale for our enjoyment. Maybe you want a wry and funny voice in your writing of your family history, and so you want a third-person objective mode that hints at a perspective beyond the events in your story. Maybe you want a narrator who sometimes steps into the story and acts as a tour guide at crucial moments, so you're blending first- and third-person narration. Maybe you want a narrator who looks just like you; or nothing like you at all. Anything is possible. What matters is that this implied author has a distinct and reliable set of traits and moves that narrative forward, rather than hinders your story telling. After all, that's what any developed character does, right?

Are you wondering what I really mean by all of this? Let me show you an example: the example of what writers sometimes call the author-narrator. It's a very clear and simple example of how a writer turns the implied author into a character; and it's especially clear because it's usually used in cases where a writer is blending third-person and first-person narration. Let's say I'm writing a biography; in fact, let's take the example again from the Widow Clicquot, which was one place where I personally used this technique.

Remember how I said back in lesson 6 that one of the problems I encountered in writing that story was that there was uneven historical evidence; a lot of material from the beginning of the Widow Clicquot's life and a fair bit at the end, but a couple of longish and vexing gaps, especially toward the conclusion? Turning the author into a character is one way of bridging that gap, because if I let the writer into the story as a character, I have another way of keeping the arc of the narrative going forward, don't I? I have someone who can say to the reader, "What a quest history is! What a search for the past we're on! Come with me on a hunt to uncover the story of this fabulous woman's life. When there are gaps, we can think together about how capricious history itself can sometimes be."

As a result, I introduce my implied author—a first-person voice that I identify as me, the author, but that you already know is still a character—and I introduce my implied author, your first-person tour guide through history, in the opening pages of the book. Because, after all, if this is going to be one of the two most important characters in the book—the other is the subject whose life story I'm searching for—I can't have this narrator pop up just at the middle of the book where things are getting complicated. I need to have this character be someone the reader learns to trust and care about right from the outset. I can't start my book in an objective third-person voice and suddenly drop in a first-person perspective without any warning, really. Because, after all, a reader is going to assume that my objective third-person historian voice and the first-person "I" voice are both the implied author, isn't she? If they aren't the same, after all, what's this "I-the-author-as-character" doing in this biography, anyhow? It would be very strange to have this odd character running around in my story for no good reason.

I can't just introduce my author-narrator at the beginning and the end, either. I need to have this persona—this implied author—developing as a character all the way through the story. I need to have the "I" voice showing up regularly enough for readers to be comfortable with the idea that the "I" is a more personal insight into the normal third-person implied author who's telling them this history. For that, I can't just have the "I" show up randomly here or there; I need to have it develop as a character in the way all characters do.

Think about it for a minute: What does that mean? It means I need tension and conflict, doesn't? That conflict either needs to be internal or external. It needs to be a conflict that somehow drives what happens next in the story; a story that also has to be—because this is a biography, after all—more or less chronologically structured. In my case, I used the classic quest narrative: The "I" is on a journey and is seeking something; something that will change his or her perspective at the end of the story. The first-person author-narrator in the book is part of a circular structure. The third-person objective narration is part of a linear and chronological structure. Their stories begin and end at the same moments, and how one impacts the other is part of the narrative tension I was working with structurally.

Here's an example of how we might think about the implied author as a character, and as a character who's fully developed and serves a narrative function; in this case, getting us over the gaps in a narrative arc and adding both dramatic tension and a sense of intimacy for the reader. Do you want to try it for yourself? Let's try an exercise together so you get the hang of this in a hands-on fashion. Let's take that example I gave you a few minutes ago of a family history; it's a kind of collective biography in a way, isn't it? I said we might want to have a family history in which we used the objective third-person narrative—the one where we only see events in the story from the perspective of the implied author but don't get into the heads of the characters—but we want one where that implied author also has a real personality of his or her own.

The question is: How are we technically going to do that? How do we create the character of an implied author who's a person who's never going to use the first-person to describe him or herself and who's never going to be described to us either? After all, if we're using a third-person objective, the narrator can't just say, "Hello, I'm Mary the narrator, the great-great granddaughter of Philippe the family's famous pirate." That would be using the first-person. There can't be anyone else who says that the narrator is Mary, because then there would be another narrator. So Mary can't say anything about herself; but Mary also needs to be a developed character in our story, just as any implied author always is. How are we going to get an idea of who Mary is, this Mary who's telling our story? This is really another way of asking: How do we create character if we can't use description or direct self-revelation?

You already know one approach to this. After all, you've already learned about how diction, rhetoric, and sentence variation can all reveal character. You already know about how the things we don't say can tell a story. This is just an extension of the same principle. What about this in a new instance? How do we also silently reveal the character of an implied author in a story? Let's see if we can figure this out by looking at three different examples of how we might write that short paragraph on Philippe the family pirate and how we might develop an implied author. Both are going to be written in the third-person objective perspective. Let me give you the first example:

> In August of 1685, Philippe left France for the Windward Islands aboard a ship named *Providence*, and unknown to the captain of the vessel he was part of a gang of young men who had already decided to take control of the ship. There was a predetermined signal that the young men had agreed upon in Marseilles, involving a secret handshake at the first watch.

It's a rather dull paragraph; an experienced writer might say that there simply isn't anything lively in this prose. It's a kind of very staid third-person description. Do you have any idea of who the implied author is? Actually, you do, don't you? What you know is that this implied author is a very boring person who wants to tell a story with absolute precision and neutrality. Sure, the narrator is invisible—shielded behind the objective perspective—but that doesn't mean we can't see his or her character if we look for it.

Here's my next revision of that same paragraph. As you listen to it, here's the question for you: How have I changed your impression of who the implied author is? What's his or her character? Here we go:

> In August of the year 1685, this venerable Philippe left the shores of France for the far-flung Windward Islands aboard a vessel named *Providence*, and unbeknownst to her captain, Philippe had conspired with some of his young compatriots to seize control of the schooner. There would be a secret handshake upon the first watch, a pre-determined signal that the momentous moment of revolution was upon them.

Technically, this is still written in the objective third-person narrative, so nothing has really changed at all. Yet everything has, hasn't it? It gives us a completely different perspective as a reader. What's your impression of who this invisible implied author is? He or she is a pompous git, no? Who writes like this? Only someone who's a ridiculous, self-impressed snob; someone who still isn't telling that interesting a story, but is completely impressed with him or herself. Our invisible narrator is a bit more visible that we actually want him or her to be.

Let's think about it again. What if I wrote: "In August of the year 1685, the venerable ancestor Philippe left the shores of France for the far-flung Windward Islands aboard a vessel named *Providence*?" Now I've made the presence of the implied author even stronger, haven't I? But I'm still using the same third-person objective perspective. Now, within that point of view, you're starting to have a clearer and clearer sense of who this implied author character is, aren't you? It's perhaps not a useful character; in fact, it's probably someone who is turning you off from the story I'm writing here. That's because there's something essentially exclusive about starting a story that tells the readers, "Hey, there's an inner circle, and you're not part of it." That's what the idea of a "the venerable ancestor"—my ancestor, but probably not yours—conveys. In fact, it's a little bit annoying. That's the key point in this lesson: As a writer, you can draw a reader into the story or you can make a reader want to back away from it, all through subtle choices in perspective. The important thing is that, as a writer, precisely because those choices are subtle but the effects are larger, you need to be in control of the perspective that you're shaping. Imagine writing a story with an invisible implied author who pushes a reader away from your story without even meaning to do it. That would be a real problem for us as writers.

That's precisely what purple prose does in a narrative. What is purple prose? It's the term writers use to talk about writing that's ornate and over-written; or it can sometimes be almost parodic. What do I mean here? It means that purple prose is language that calls attention to itself as language. It's consciously fancy or poetic. It's a moment where what the reader sees is a writer who's more interested in the writing than in the story he or she is telling. Sometimes, in great literature, purple prose can sweep a reader away with emotion and enthusiasm. In theory, it could serve a narrative function, especially if one's trying to be ironic; then it could be quite brilliant. But most of the time, purple prose doesn't do anything useful; it's just bad and a bit embarrassing.

One of the places we see it most often is in those romance novels known as "bodice-rippers"; you know, the love scenes in inexpensive romance novels where everything is described in adjectives like "sweeping," "dazzling," and "throbbing." It's when something becomes so overwritten that it becomes ridiculous in its badness, whatever the genre. Even if you aren't trying to write a melodramatic love scene in a romance novel, it's actually an easy mistake to make if you get carried away with ill-considered metaphors and too many adjectives.

Want to have an example of what purple prose looks like? Here's the story of Philippe the pirate as a purple passage. As you're listening, ask yourself, "What's the impression I have of the implied author?"

> When the sultry sirens of the August winds sang to men and the summer of the year 1685 was at its intemperate apex, our venerable ancestor flung himself from the shores of his beloved

> homeland, France, like an autumn leaf cast upon the winds of chance. His eyes looked toward the far-flung Windward Isles, aboard a ship called not by chance alone *Providence*. With his young compatriots, passions running riot in their leonine breasts, Philippe had set his resolve upon the plan of seizing from the captain the control of that ship of destiny. With a secret handshake upon the first watch, this band of brothers would signal each to each that the moment of their revolution like the sun upon the setting sea had come to a final moment of blazing glory.

That, I believe, surely must qualify as the worst paragraph I've ever written in my adult life. It's pure and simply awful writing; truly terrible. That's purple prose at its worst, and I've exaggerated it here appallingly. The trouble is that when our language gets away from us, even in subtler ways, even an experienced writer can fall into prose that has a bit of a bluish tint from time to time. It's always a danger when we're trying to use language—as any good story teller has to—to shape the rhetorical and emotional reactions of our readers. You'll remember from our lessons on sentence pacing, and variation, and creating dramatic tension that we have to use those tools to tell a gripping tale; but if we overuse them, or don't use our tools wisely, purple prose is one of the dangers, a moment where the writing itself hinders the telling of our story by calling attention to itself.

As I was reading that passage to you, what did you think of the implied author who's writing it? Did you laugh? Who were you laughing at? You were laughing at this terrible, terrible writer who's telling this badly written story, weren't you? In fact, it's easy to draw some very quick conclusions about who this author is. He or she's an idiot; someone pompous, flowery, and melodramatic; someone who's completely full of himself; someone with no sense of audience or timing; someone who doesn't understand metaphor; someone who can't tell a story; someone who is, in short, ridiculous.

Do you know who I had in mind when I was creating this voice in that passage? Can you think of a famous character in literature who talks like this? I was thinking of the character of Mr. Collins in Jane Austen's *Pride and Prejudice*. He was the pompous cousin who wanted to marry the witty and clever Elizabeth Bennett, a woman whose greatest strength in that book is her very keen sense of audience and restraint. Remember that great line when he wants to ask Elizabeth to marry him and he says to her mother, Mrs. Bennett, in his pompous way, "May I hope, Madam, for your interest with your fair daughter Elizabeth, when I solicit for the honour of a private audience with her in the course of this morning?" It's ridiculous. Mr. Collins is an example of how purple prose in the mouth of a character can be used to great comic effect; and her deft command of it is what makes Jane Austen a master of character development. In one simple stroke, she manages to tell us everything we ever need to know about the "drivelish" Mr. Collins and why Elizabeth is lucky to have escaped a life with him.

Purple prose is one thing in the mouth of a silly character; it's something entirely different when the character it calls attention to is the implied author. The risk of purple prose is that an author overwrites a passage to the point of unintentional comedy. It's essentially the same thing as turning the implied author into a stock character. It's not a good stock character; it's the stock character of the bad writer.

Think about what that means if something's written in purple prose, especially if it's laughably bad. It means that you've just created—probably unintentionally—an unreliable narrator. After all, what reader's going to rely on a narrator of a story who can't even write good prose? What kind of narrator is that? Unless you mean for the character of your implied author to be "A Bad Writer," then you suddenly have a big problem. If you mean for your implied author to appear invisible—say, you're choosing to use a third-person subjective perspective for strong storytelling reasons; the perspective in which the reader gets what's only in the head of the characters and not the narrator—what you've just done is shot yourself in the foot. You wanted to disguise an implied author to get the readers closer to a character and, instead, what the reader is aware of is a comic difference between what the character says—which might be perfectly good dialogue—and how the story's being told, which is in the voice of an implied author who isn't in control of his or her own writing. The point is that purple prose isn't a problem just because it's weak writing—though it is that—but it's a problem because it has the ability to undermine the essential foundations on which any great story is built: structure.

Have you noticed how I've twice now used the word "voice" to talk about how we create the character of the implied author? That's what we're really talking about here in this lesson, isn't it? We've said that we want to think here about how in the third-person perspective—when the narrator can't say anything about him or herself directly—we can reveal character. The answer is that it's the words we choose as writers and the way we put those words together that creates the voice of the implied author. That implied author doesn't have to be our voice; in fact, because it's a character construct, because it has to be the right voice for this particular story at this particular moment, it's never going to really be our voice. After all, in another story, in another way, we'll have to tell that tale differently, in different words, and looking to create different effects for our readers. What we learn as writers is to become comfortable with a kind of imaginary schizophrenia. We learn to write in many different voices, all of which are ours, and not us. What writers do is inhabit the minds, lives, and perspectives of other people—some real, some imaginary—in order to tell their stories and our stories at the same time. Do you see? To do this, we have many tools available to us. But one of the most silently powerful is how we structure the consciousness who tells our story: what he or she sees; who he or she is; how he or she speaks, and thinks, and perceives the world that the implied author is inviting us to inhabit.

In this lesson, I've given you a negative and comic example of how we can use voice in the third-person objective perspective to create a comic and foolish implied author. In our next lesson, we're going to talk about how you can create character and dramatic tension by working with other kinds of silences and gaps in narrative perspectives. But first, are you ready for an end of the lesson exercise? How about this one? Go back and rewrite the story of Philippe the pirate and that imaginary family history; and this time, your goal is to craft the voice of an implied author who is wry, witty, smart, and funny. Here's the text we started with again:

> In August of 1685, Philippe left France for the Windward Islands aboard a ship named *Providence*, and unknown to the captain of the vessel he was part of a gang of young men who had already decided to take control of the ship. There was a

> pre-determined signal that the young men had agreed upon in Marseilles, involving a secret handshake at the first watch.

After you've done your revision, have a friend read it and test yourself. How does your friend describe the voice of your implied author? If your friend can imagine who the person telling the story is, who appears in his or her mind, and what the words are that created that impression, then you've learned how to control voice. In our next lesson on crafting good dialogue, that will be crucially important to storytelling.

Writing the Gutter—How to Not Tell a Story

Lecture 17

Sometimes, the parts of a story a writer chooses not to show the readers are as important as the parts he or she chooses to show. Using the metaphor of the gutter—the spaces between the panels of a comic strip—as our guide, we will look at how not giving readers every detail of a story makes them more active participants in storytelling by engaging their imaginations.

Pregnant Pauses

- Up until now, we have been talking about the ways a writer can hone descriptions to make them work most effectively—how to make what we say as effective as it can be. Counterintuitively, sometimes in writing not saying something is a storyteller's most powerful tool.

- Silence has an important role to play in storytelling. It can create drama and suspense. Think about a writing mystery: If you give too many hints, the reader figures it out on page 15, ruining the fun.

- When I am trying to decide what to leave out of a story, I like to use the idea of the pregnant pause. This is a quiet moment that seems like a gestation, where the story promises something important is about to happen. In our daily interactions, a pregnant pause occurs when we ask an important question and the response is a telling silence, a delay, or a hesitation.

- We want to learn to use that kind of unspoken drama and tension in our writing, and we want to use it as a way of showing, not telling our stories.

Writing the Gutter

- If any group of writers depends on showing as a way of telling a story, it would be graphic novelists. These writers compose what

Writing the Gutter. Notice how much of the story is "missing" in the spaces between the panels of a comic strip. This is no barrier to the reader; in fact, it can be an asset. The space asks the reader to engage his or her imagination.

many of us still think of as comics—the illustrated stories of our childhoods and the newspaper funnies—but today these stories have grown up, and graphic novels are a serious adult literary genre.

- In a graphic novel or comic strip, there is a series of panels with a line or a space between each. Space is limited; there simply is no room for part of the story, only a few images and a line or two of dialogue with each. A graphic novelist must master the art of the implied narrative.

- The space between two panels is what graphic artists call the gutter. We are going to borrow the idea of the gutter as a metaphor for our own work. What happens in the gutter—in the spaces between the panels—are the parts of the story that the author does not tell but that the reader fills in with his or her own imagination. Thus, writing two moments of a story can imply an entire narrative.

Part of the power of the sentences in *The Woman Warrior* is how like a snapshot—or comic panel—each sentence is. Each moment stands on its own, a vivid individual image in the reader's mind.

- The gutter is part of any good storytelling. The gutter is about silence—about how to tell a story by not telling certain parts of it. Writers do not need to illustrate every event in a sequence. In fact, telling us too much makes a story less interesting. The best writers show what the reader needs to know and demand the reader's participation.

Writing the Gutter in *The Woman Warrior*

- Maxine Hong Kingston's *The Woman Warrior* uses the gutter to great effect in its opening passages. As we saw earlier, the memoir opens with Hong Kingston's mother telling the story of the night her aunt drowned herself. Notice what the mother does and does not say:

> On the night the baby was to be born the villagers raided our house. The villagers broke in the front and the back doors at the same time, even though we had not locked the doors against them. Their knives dripped with the blood of

> our animals. They smeared blood on the doors and walls. One woman swung a chicken, whose throat she had slit, splattering blood in red arcs about her. We stood together in the middle of our house, in the family hall with the pictures and tables of the ancestors around us, and looked straight ahead. ... We swept up the rice and sewed it back up into sacks….Your aunt gave birth in the pigsty that night…I found her and the baby plugging up the family well.

- With these powerful images, Hong Kingston is obviously showing, using vivid language and a lot of action. But this passage is also effective because of how she uses the gutter. It is a series of individual images, rather than a string of continuous action, each of which could stand like a panel in a graphic novel.

- The spaces in between are what allow Hong Kingston to tell a moving story with such economy. The spaces in between leave things to the readers' imagination. As our minds move from the gory and active image of the chicken swung in a bloody arc to the family standing motionless among the pictures, we cannot help but think "What must they have felt?"

How Wide Is the Gutter?

- How much information should a writer leave out? Imagine three frames on a piece of paper. In the first frame, a man and a woman stand by a river, and the woman asks coyly, "Do you like my hat?" The second frame shows the man responding, "I hate how you're always thinking about your clothes." The third frame shows the hat floating down the river.

- What would make this story use the gutter more effectively? The story here is not about the hat itself; it is about the tension in between these two characters. If we only had the first frame with the question and the final frame of the floating hat, we would know everything we needed to know, and we would be drawn in by imagining the connection between the two moments.

The gutter in this comic is wide, but could it be wider? Is the second panel necessary to tell the story?

- The first thing to remember is that if you are telling a dramatic story, you need to think about not overnarrating. The gutter works because it gives the reader two pieces of information and trusts him or her to transform them into a single storyline. Engaging the reader's imagination makes the reader an active participant rather than a passive recipient.

- As a writer, consider what is essential for a reader to know. Our instinct is to tell the reader everything, but if we tell everything, there is no room for the reader's imagination. The writer's craft is in giving what is essential and using the silence of the gutter to connect the dots of the narrative.

- It is all about balancing precision and concision: marrying the most vivid way of telling a story with an economy of language. It is about trusting our readers enough to let them have a role in the story we are telling.

Writing the Gutter as a Style Choice

- You might argue that people did not write the gutter 100 years ago. After all, comics—and film, which also uses this technique—were not part of the way people encountered great stories, and to some extent that is true.

- Writing styles change with time, and today what we value the most is writing that balances precision—using the right words to capture an image, character, or tension—and concision—using the most efficient language possible. That was not what readers of, say, the 19th century valued most, but you will certainly find examples of writing the gutter in the great 19th-century novels.

Ways to Write the Gutter

- There are many ways the gutter can work into great writing. Several examples can be found in the diaries of Hélène Berr, a young Jewish woman who lived in Paris during the Second World War. Berr tells her story with silence as well as words. Here is one dramatic example:

> On Boulevard de la Gare, there are currently two hundred people, men and women, living together in one room, with one sink between them. There is no privacy at all; men and women are being stripped of modesty with exquisite refinement. That's where Monsieur Kohn is. … They are all suffering, it's just that for people who are intensely sensitive like M. Kohn it must be even worse. Went to Neuilly, waste of time. To Saint-Denis at 11:30. Wept after dinner.

- What Berr is expressing in those final sentences is that she and her family went looking for their friends and did not find them. This is a bit more subtle than the Hong Kingston example, but by not saying what she saw at Neuilly and Saint-Denis, telling us only that she wept, she invites us to imagine.

- In another example, Berr writes:

> At Boulevard de la Gare there are aisles for every sort of thing, furniture, sewing kits, haberdashery, jewelry. Entirely made up of things stolen from the dwellings of people who have been taken and deported, which are packed and crated by the internees themselves. The crates are sent to Germany right away.

- The image of the street, filled with luxuries, is juxtaposed with the image of the internees packing crates and the third image of the crates on trains to Germany. What is not shown is the internees' pain at packing. We are also, perhaps, imagining what else (or rather, who else) these trains are used to transport.

- Joan Didion's essay "Goodbye to All That" contains a particularly subtle example. It is the story of how, as a young woman, she moved to New York City from California and how she finally decided to go home. She writes:

  > All I ever did to that apartment was hang fifty yards of yellow theatrical silk across the bedroom windows, because I had some idea that the gold light would make me feel better, but I did not bother to weight the curtains correctly and all that summer the long panels of transparent golden silk would blow out the windows and get tangled and drenched in afternoon thunderstorms. That was the year, my twenty-eighth?, when I was discovering that not all of the promises would be kept, that some things are in fact irrevocable and that it had counted after all, every evasion and ever procrastination, every word, all of it.

- In this image of the bare apartment with the single gold curtain, getting wet in the thunderstorms, the gold fabric is a metaphor for the golden sunlight of California, but in the last sentence, the reader is invited to make a connection between that image and the emotional fallout of her time in New York. As readers, we must struggle with meaning, just as she struggled with this time in her life.

Thinking in Panels—An Imagination Exercise

- If you are working on a project right now, can you begin to imagine a key moment as a series of graphic scenes? What does the reader have to know in this scene, and what could remain implied?

Important Term

writing the gutter: Using juxtaposition and untold aspects of a story to heighten a reader's drama and interest.

Suggested Reading

Berr, *The Journal of Hélène Berr*.

Didion, "Goodbye to All That."

Hong Kingston, *The Woman Warrior*.

Questions to Consider

1. Can you think of a time when you told a story, and leaving information out was part of what made that tale effective?

2. Do you think your favorite films or television shows use the gutter, or are films and books fundamentally different in their strategies?

Writing the Gutter—How to Not Tell a Story

Lecture 17—Transcript

So far, we've learned that showing and not telling is one of the essential maxims of effective storytelling in creative nonfiction, or in any prose genre for that matter. We've talked about how a savvy writer can use a whole range of narrative techniques, from quickly sketching a character in a single bold stroke to working with historical detail, in order to give the reader the experience of witnessing an event instead of just hearing about one. But what we've been talking about up until now are the ways a writer can hone his or her descriptions to make them work most effectively. What we've been talking about is how to make what we say be as effective as it possibly can be. We've talked about how overwriting can lead to purple prose and can turn the author-narrator into a comic stock character; not what we're looking for in most cases.

In this lesson, we're going to take a different tack entirely. As the old adage goes, silence is golden. The smartest writers know when not to tell something; and it's counterintuitive, but sometimes in writing, learning when to keep quiet is the storyteller's most powerful tool. Silence has an important role to play in storytelling; it can create drama and suspense especially. Think about a mystery writer: If I tell you the answer to the mystery too soon, I spoil all the fun, don't I? If you give too many hints so you the reader figures it out on page 15, it's even worse; that's just maddening.

When I'm trying to decide what to leave out of a story, there's one metaphor I like particularly: the idea of the pregnant pause. It's the quiet moment in a text when silence seems like a kind of gestation; where the story promises something important is about to happen. It's very apt for thinking about one of our literary examples of great writing today; but we can just start by thinking about what we mean by the pregnant pause in our daily interactions. We've all experienced it: an occasion when we ask something important—do you love me; will you marry me; will you loan me a thousand dollars; are you happy; am I fired?—and the response is a telling silence, a delay, or hesitation. In that moment, silence speaks. That's the kind of unspoken drama and tension we want to learn today to use in our telling of nonfiction stories. We want to use silence as a way of showing and not telling especially. There's a lot going on here, so you can see that this is going to get tricky.

But if one group of writers depends more than any other on showing as a way of telling a story, it would certainly have to be what today we call "graphic novelists." These are writers composing what many of us still think of as comics; the illustrated stories of our childhoods and the newspaper funnies. But today, they've grown up, and graphic novels are a serious literary adult genre.

Think about what a comic book writer needs to do; you've seen it over and over in the newspaper funnies. There's a strip of boxes. Between each of those frames, there's a line or maybe a space. In just a couple of boxes and with very few words, the comic artist needs to sketch out for us a whole story. There's not room to tell everything. There's room, in fact, for only a few lines of dialogue. We're working here with the art of the implied narrative.

Let me show you what I mean by looking at a comic by Scott McCloud. In fact, in just a few simple frames, we can tell a pretty dramatic story. Let's imagine we have several boxes. In the first box, there's an image of a waitress in a diner with a coffee pot and a patron. The patron says, "Hey, that lady forgot her purse." In the next image, a hand reaches for a purse and a voice says, "Oh geez, I'll be right back." In the next frame, the waitress yells out, "Leslie, you forgot your purse." Nothing here is very subtle; we get the idea immediately. It's just a good sequence of action. Now we turn to the last frame. It's a view of Leslie gasping, and the sound effects of screech and crash.

What can we learn here about storytelling? Here's the thing: The space between the panels is what graphic artists would call the "gutter." We're going to borrow this idea of the gutter from our comic book artist colleagues, but instead of the space between the panels, we could also think of it as the line between the frames in any comic strip. What happens in the gutter? According to the author of our comic strip, Scott McCloud, it's this: In the space between the frames, in that space where something is unspoken but that the reader can fill in imaginatively, the parts of the narrative are brought together as a single story idea.

The gutter is also part of any kind of good storytelling, actually; and the idea of the gutter is that in writing two single moments in a story can imply an entire narrative. We can fill in the gaps between the moments. After all, between the image of the woman rushing out with the purse, and Leslie's horrified reaction, and the screech and the crash in the distant background, we can fill in what happened. This is the key idea: As readers, we fill it in; we bridge the gap that separates one part of the story from the other. The gutter is about silence, about how to tell a story by not telling certain parts of it. When we come to this last frame, in which we see the waitress dead in the street with a gory little picture in the middle of traffic, we aren't at all surprised, are we? We already knew what was coming; we could see it. We don't need the writer to illustrate every event in a sequence. In fact, telling us too much makes it all less interesting. The best writers show us what we need to know and demand our participation. By leaving something out, the writer relies on the reader's imagination to make the connections. Once we've engaged the reader's imagination in our writing, we're well on the way to telling a great story.

Let's look at an example of how one successful writer uses this to create a story with suspense and drama. After all, I'm showing you what comic book writers do for a reason: We can use this same strategy in writing creative nonfiction. Remember how at the very beginning of the course we looked at Maxine Hong Kingston's *The Woman Warrior*, a modern classic of the memoir genre? It's a kind of story of her memories of growing up Chinese-American, and was the story of how she learned about some of her family's powerful secrets. The memoir begins with the tale of an aunt she never knew. This aunt is the skeleton in the family closet. *The Woman Warrior* begins with the author remembering what her mother once told her. You'll remember she writes:

> "You must not tell anyone," my mother said, "what I am about to tell you. In China, your father had a sister who killed herself. She jumped into the family well. We say that your father has all brothers because it is as if she had never been born."

It's a direct way to open a story. What we have here is a good example of a writer telling in a story, and Hong Kingston lets us know that's what she's going to do for the moment. Notice how she even uses the word "tell" in introducing the story, and the paragraph is all narrative without any description or showing. We know nothing about who the sister is, what her character might be, where the well was, or why she jumped into it; it's a straightforward and bland summary of the story outlines. This is Hong Kinsgston's point: She's reflecting on the fact that what she's been given is just the facts. The only point of suspense in this first paragraph is the fact that she's been told not to tell anyone the secret. Think back to what we said about effective beginnings: This beginning makes a promise that something else is going to be revealed.

What was this secret? As the story goes on, we learn more. This aunt was married to a man who'd been gone many years, and soon it becomes clear that she's nevertheless pregnant. In this small agricultural village, she's had a love affair with a man whose name she never reveals; and silently, the villagers had been counting. Her mother tells her what happened next; her mother tells her this story:

On the night the baby was to be born the villagers raided our house. The villagers broke in the front and the back doors at the same time, even though we had not locked the doors against them.

It's frightening, and it only gets worse. The mother goes on with her story. What happens next is a brutalizing kind of terror that's all about showing:

> Their knives dripped with the blood of our animals. They smeared blood on the doors and walls. One woman swung a chicken, whose throat she had slit, splattering blood in red arcs about her. We stood together in the middle of our house, in the family hall with the pictures and tables of the ancestors around us, and looked straight ahead.

What a powerful set of images here. The things in the room seem to be in motion. Knives drip blood; walls are smeared. There's the motion of the arc. The family photos gather in. The only motionless thing is the horrified people standing in the midst of it. But the story gets even more awful. Hong Kingston next writes:

> When they left, they took sugar and oranges to bless themselves. They cut pieces from the dead animals. … Afterward we swept up the rice and sewed it back up into sacks. But the smells of the spilled preserves lasted. Your aunt gave birth in the pigsty that night. The next morning when I went for water, I found her and the baby plugging up the family well.

It's a horrifying story, and the way that Hong Kingston tells it is gripping. Part of the reason is that she uses the technique of showing. There are vivid images of the characters and the action. Because remember: Showing isn't about loading your writing up with adjectives and description, it's about using vivid language rather than fuzzy language. It's about letting the reader experience an event. Notice how, as we talked about earlier, showing isn't about piling on adjectives and adverbs; it's about finding the right word to do the job. Less is more. Showing is the difference here between saying, "It was scary and awful," and that terrifying image of the chicken blood splattering in a murderous arc and the use of that strong and ugly word "plugging." The showing language is part of what makes this writing powerful; but the other reason—the other way that the writer creates the sense of urgency and tension—is also all in that silent juxtaposition. Here, Hong Kingston uses the gutter masterfully.

What do I mean that she "uses the gutter"? Imagine if we were to translate her sentences into frames in a graphic novel. Listen to the two sentences again. In fact, if you want to pause and try the exercise, go ahead. Listen to each sentence, and in your own comic strip rendition, sketch the frames of this story. Don't worry about how they look; the idea is just to think about what are the essential parts of the story? Here are those sentences again: "They smeared blood on the doors and walls. One woman swung a chicken, whose throat she had slit, splattering blood in red arcs about her. We stood together in the middle of our house, in the family hall …"

If this were a comic book, we would have three frames: one perhaps an image of the doors and walls; one perhaps the image of a chicken and an arc of blood; and one the image of the motionless and terrified family. Or, try again with another example from the book: "we swept up the rice and sewed it back up into sacks. … Your aunt gave birth in the pigsty that night … I found her and the baby plugging up the family well." In our comic book rendition, there would be another three images: sacks of rice, a pigsty, and a look of horror on a young woman's face over a family well.

If this were a graphic novel—or if we were to describe how the individual showing scenes move from one frame to the next—we would see that the space between the images is the essential reason why Hong Kingston can tell a moving story with such economy. Do you see how each image moves from one aspect of the story to a very different image? Do you see how in the space between those images something is left to the imagination? That's the point. As our mind moves from the gory and active image of the chicken swung in a bloody arc to the family standing motionless among the pictures—and think of the resonance there, because they're like another tragic family portrait in that moment—the reader can't help but think, "What must they have felt? What was it like to witness this destruction?" When we can engage our readers' imagination and their empathy with our characters; that's one of the hallmarks of great writing. How often have you said to yourself after reading a great book, "It was so powerful, I could feel what it was like to be there; I identified with the characters"? We want to give our readers this same experience.

But how do we learn to use this strategy in our writing? Let's try this exercise: Let's imagine three frames on a piece of paper. In the first frame, a man and a woman stand by a river, and the woman's asks coyly, "Do you like my hat?" The second frame shows a man, and he responds, "I hate how you're always thinking about your clothes." A third frame: a hat floating down the river. There's a problem with this story; or, at least, there's a way we could make it stronger. Think about it for a minute. What would make this story use the gutter more effectively?

Did you see that the thing to do is actually to remove the middle frame? The one that says, "I hate how you're always thinking about your clothes"? Sure, it gives us a detail we didn't have before; but the story here isn't about the clothing, it's about the tension in the relationship between these two characters. That's what all good stories are finally about. If we only had the first frame with the question and the final frame with the floating hat, we know everything we need to know as readers. We can fill in the blanks. We can jump in the gutter in our imaginations. We actually know more about this relationship by having to imagine the dynamic.

What do we learn from all this? The first thing to remember, then, is that if we're telling a dramatic story, we need to think about not over-narrating. Remember, the reason the gutter works is because it gives the reader two pieces of information and trusts him or her to use the imagination to transform them into a single storyline. Engaging the reader's imagination makes the reader an active participant in the story we're telling rather than a passive recipient.

It works for any personal genre, from writing the biography of a famous figure, to telling the history of our family, or writing a memoir. In fact, it works in all writing. Novelists also use it powerfully. What we want to consider is this question: To tell my story, what are the essential things a reader needs to know in order to experience it? Our instinct as writers is to tell everything. But if we tell everything, there's no room for the reader's imagination.

Or think of it another way: telling a good joke—which after all is a kind of short story—depends on holding back the punch line until just the right moment. Here's a joke for you: "What lies twitching on the bottom of the ocean floor?" "A nervous wreck" (ha ha). Do you see how the pause between the joke and the punch line is another example of the gutter? It's where the story of our joke switches the frame and changes direction. Here, the frame of the story in the joke moves from our expecting a thing to describing a person. The result is we engage the listener's emotional reaction, because hopefully they find it funny.

The writer's craft, then, is in giving what's essential and using the silence of the gutter to connect the dots of the narrative. It's all about balancing precision and concision; marrying the most vivid way of telling a story with the economy of language. It's about trusting our readers enough to let them have a role in the story we're telling.

One way to think about this is to imagine yourself telling your story as though you were a cinematographer. Think about it: When we enjoy a book immensely, we also often say how it would make a great movie or how we could see all the events happening in our heads. There's a reason books with a great story often end up making a great film. What you're doing as a writer is sketching out a series of scenes that in sequence make up the narrative arc of the story.

Of course, you might say people didn't write this way a hundred years ago; after all, back then movies and comics weren't part of the way people encountered great stories, while it's only today that films and televisions are pervasive. That's true. Writing styles change with time; and today, what we value the most is writing that balances precision (the right words to capture an image, character, or tension) and concision (the ability to use the most efficient language possible). That wasn't what writers in the 19th century valued most; after all, those writers were often paid by the word, and readers wanted epic serials. But you'll certainly find examples of the gutter in the great 19th-century novels. After all, screenwriters got the idea from somewhere.

How about a few more examples? After all, there are lots of ways the gutter can work into great writing, and you'll want to learn how to use this technique in your own nonfiction. During the Second World War, a young Jewish woman named Helene Berr spent the war living in Paris. Because her family was prominent and very rich, she was much more sheltered than many such women. In the end, however, she didn't escape the fate of so many millions. What she did leave behind is a powerful firsthand memoir of her experience as a young woman in Paris; a nonfiction account that went on to become, decades after her death, an international bestseller.

You guessed it: Helene Berr tells her story writing the silences sometimes, too. Let me give you a dramatic example:

> On Boulevard de la Gare, "there are currently two hundred people, men and women, living together in one room, with one sink between them. There is no privacy at all; men and women are being stripped of modesty with exquisite refinement. That's

> where Monsieur Kohn is. … They are all suffering, it's just that for people who are intensely sensitive like M. Kohn it must be even worse. Went to Neuilly, waste of time. To Saint-Denis at 11.30. Wept after dinner.

Neuilly and Saint Denis are neighborhoods around Paris, and the idea is that Helene and her family went looking for their friends. But that's not the interesting part for us as writers. What's interesting is to see how this young writer, in her vivid descriptions, is using the gutter; using what she's not writing, but what we can fill in as readers to tell her story.

Do you see the gutter? It's a bit more subtle than in our last example, but it's powerful. Did you hear it? If you said it's the sentences "Went to Neuilly, waste of time. To Saint-Denis at 11.30. Wept after dinner," then great work. Three short sentences, because this is also an example of using sentence variation—moving from those earlier long sentences to these three short ones—each is one frame after another. Neuilly in a desperate search; Saint Denis; and Helene doesn't say what she saw there. We don't need to know. It's far more powerful that all she says is, "Wept after dinner." Do you see how this works?

Let's look at another example of how Berr does the same thing. As you're listening, see if you can identify where she's using the technique of the gutter. This time she writes:

> At Boulevard de la Gare there are aisles for every sort of thing, furniture, sewing kits, haberdashery, jewelry. Entirely made up of things stolen from the dwellings of people who have been taken and deported, which are packed and crated by the internees themselves. The crates are sent to Germany right away.

You heard it, right? The first was the image of the street, filled with luxuries; the second is the image of the internees packing crates; the third, the crates on trains to Germany. What the reader understands, of course, is the cruel irony and how painful this experience must've been. The reader engages imaginatively and sympathetically in the scene precisely because he or she is invited to fill in the gaps. That's the central principle of the gutter.

One last example; this one from a different source. This is one of my favorite essays, by one of one of today's most talented writers of nonfiction. It's an essay—again, a memoir—by the American writer Joan Didion, from an essay called "Goodbye to All That." It's the story of how, as a young woman, she moved to New York City from California, and how she finally decided to go home. She moved into an apartment but never settled in, and she never stopped being homesick. Didion tells her readers:

> All I ever did to that apartment was hang fifty yards of yellow theatrical silk across the bedroom windows, because I had some idea that the gold light would make me feel better, but I did not bother to weight the curtains correctly and all that summer the long panels of transparent golden silk would blow out the windows and get tangled and drenched in afternoon thunderstorms. That was the year, my twenty-eighth?, when I was discovering that not all of the promises would be kept, that some things are in fact irrevocable and that it had counted after all, every evasion and every procrastination, every word, all of it.

This use of the gutter isn't quite so visual as our other examples. Have you noticed? My examples are getting progressively subtler and subtler, aren't they? After all, I want you to learn to use this technique with nuance, don't I? But do you see how there are things that Didion doesn't say; things that invite her reader to fill in the gaps in the story and to engage imaginatively in the emotional experience? We have that image of the bare apartment with the single golden curtain getting wet in the thunderstorms. It's a beautiful image. Did you see that the gold fabric is a metaphor? For what? That's right: for the golden sunlight of California, which is making this West Coast girl so homesick. But it's just a straight description of an apartment and an object on the surface, isn't it? A gold curtain in an empty apartment. Listen to what comes next. That beautiful sentence:

> That was the year, my twenty-eighth?, when I was discovering that not all of the promises would be kept, that some things are in fact irrevocable and that it had counted after all, every evasion and ever procrastination, every word, all of it.

Curtain, and emotional fallout; what the reader's invited to do is understand the connection between them. It's a wonderful example of writing the gutter.

While we're at it, think back to our lectures about rhetorical devices. Remember all those technical terms about anaphora, polysyndeton, isocolon, and parallelism? If you want to test yourself, do an analysis of that last sentence and see if you can figure out this: How does Didion craft it to create drama and climax here? What rhetorical devices is she using, along with the gutter? Because that's the idea, isn't it? We want to learn all these skills, and find new and creative ways to use them simultaneously to tell your story. The more you can think about your writing in visual terms—as a way of showing the reader—the stronger it will be.

So to recap, we've seen here another example of the difference between showing and telling. We've seen how once again beginnings establish tension and make a promise. What we've learned new in this lesson is that savvy writers don't show everything and they don't show it all at once. Holding back our punch lines, using the pregnant pause, and letting there be enough unsaid that our readers are drawn into the act of imagination are all powerful tricks of the writer's trade. If you're working on a project, can you begin to imagine the graphic scenes in one of its key moments? What does the reader have to know and what could remain implied to the imagination? Borrowing from the example of the comic book gutter, we've seen that we can use silence as a powerful tool in our writing. We'll look in the next lesson at how writers can deepen their storytelling practice by using pacing, patterns of repetition, and a whole series of other silent writing techniques within their sentences to engage and surprise their readers in other ways.

Dialogue Strategies in Creative Nonfiction

Lecture 18

Dialogue writing presents a particular challenge to a creative nonfiction writer. Not only must it adhere to the nonfiction contract and therefore be based in thorough research; it also must either reveal character or move the narrative forward—preferably both at once. Good dialogue is, above all, constructed. It does not mirror real-life speech but distills the speaker's meaning and enhances the reader's understanding.

The Challenge of Dialogue

- The nonfiction contract means we cannot make up anything, including the words we put in the mouths of our characters. We must stick to the words they said or wrote themselves. Writing dialogue in creative nonfiction requires a deft touch—and superb research skills.

- It is perfectly possible to write a great story without dialogue, but nothing builds character and connects a reader to a persona, especially a historical one, like hearing the character's own words and thoughts, whether in dialogue or interior monologue.

- Depending on your subject, you may have many or few research sources to work with. If you are writing, say, the biography of a modern public figure, you will have a greater variety at your disposal.

    - You could start with letters from, to, or about the person.

    - You could look at memoirs written by people he or she met.

    - You look at the person's own diary or journals, if any.

    - There might be speeches contained in public records or quotes in newspapers.

Dialogue in creative nonfiction must be based in fact and must serve to move the story forward or develop character—preferably both.

- o If the figure is modern enough, there might even be tape or video recordings, a particular bonus because it enables you to describe the figure's tone of voice.

- There are other strategies for researching less famous subjects. You can at least research the words of other people who lived at the same time and in the same places to set the scene and move the narrative forward, even if you cannot use what your subject said.

The Purpose of Dialogue in a Story

- Understanding what makes good dialogue in general requires understanding the purpose of dialogue in narrative, what makes it work, and what makes it fall flat.

- Like any element in storytelling, dialogue needs to do one of two things—and ideally do both at once. It needs to reveal character and move the narrative forward.

    - In daily life, what a person says and how he or she responds to a situation tells us a great deal about who they are, their intentions, their hesitations, their prejudices and convictions—in short, their character.

    - In a story, dialogue also has to be part of a context, namely the context of the narrative. It needs to show how a character responds to the conflict that is driving the story, whether that conflict is internal or external.

- What people say, just as much as what they do, can set actions into motion and can show us the consequences of actions already underway. So dialogue either has to intensify a scene or unravel an action to be really effective.

- Therefore, rule number one of writing dialogue is that it is not simply conversation; it is a way of using conversation to drive narrative action, intensify conflict, or establish character—all of which will have consequences. If you cannot say what function your dialogue serves in your story, chances are it is not working. Revise it, or cut it.

Writing Dialogue Well

- Although dialogue should be more than merely interesting, it should still be interesting. Boring dialogue that has a narrative objective is not great dialogue either. Interesting dialogue is, above all, constructed. It does not sound the way people really talk.

- Believe it or not, the way people really talk is generally pretty uninteresting, full of *ums* and *uhs*, pointless digressions, and repetition. Good dialogue leaves out the parts of a conversation that do not have a function.

- You can leave things out of your researched dialogue as long as you punctuate it properly. If you want to leave something out of a direct quote, just replace the missing material with the three-dot punctuation mark known as an ellipsis.

- You cannot take out something that changes the meaning of the quotation fundamentally. For example, you cannot replace every *not* in a sentence with an ellipsis and still be playing by the nonfiction contract rules. But otherwise, you have broad leeway.

- Therefore, rule number two of writing good dialogue is that it should not sound fake, but sounding real and sounding encyclopedic are not the same thing. Less is generally more.

- You may also correct grammar mistakes, and you should resist the temptation to emphasize regional accents or foreign words in your researched quotes. If someone has a regional accent, find a way to signal identity through description and move on.

- Making a big deal out of these features in conversation can quickly become overblown and comic unless you do it very delicately. It is akin to the problem of purple prose: It is dialogue that calls attention to itself as dialogue, rather than letting the reader focus on what the character is revealing.

- One other mistake writers often make is using dialogue as a way to have characters explain things directly to the reader. The point of dialogue is that two characters are directly engaged with each other. They should focus on each other—not on serving as extra narrators.

- For this same reason, you should use dialogue tags (*he said*, *she said*, and so forth) sparingly. Sometimes, usually at the start of dialogue, they need to be there to orient the reader. But in general, a reader should be able to follow a conversation without any difficulty; tags should only be used to smooth the process as necessary.

The Ethics of Dialogue

- What happens when you are writing a memoir and want to include a conversation that really happened, but you only have your memory of it? This is one of the trickiest situations for anyone writing a memoir and one of the places where the risks of getting it historically wrong are the most complicated.

- Temporarily setting aside the legal and interpersonal issues writers of creative nonfiction face, let's address the ethical and craft issues. The ethical issue—how this squares with the nonfiction contract—is pretty straightforward.

- If you think you might write a book, the first thing to do is start keeping notes on your conversations. Keep a daily journal. Keep your e-mails, letters, and other materials. Therefore, when the time comes, you will not have to rely on your memory.

- If you have not kept good notes and you want to use a conversation you only have in your memory, the ethical rule in nonfiction is that as long as you are reporting your experience as accurately as possible, then you are on safe ground in terms of the nonfiction contract.

- Most smart writers who are relying on memory will add a note to the beginning of their manuscript that simply states that fact and alerts the reader if there have been any changes made to the order of events or the context of the conversation.

Dialogue That Does Not Work and Dialogue That Does

- Here is a sample of dialogue that is not working. See if you can figure out why and how you would fix it.

> John came into the room and slung his briefcase in the corner. All he could see were the dishes everywhere. The kitchen was a disaster. For crying out loud, why was it always like this when he came home from a hard day of work anyhow?

"Janet," he said harshly. "What's goin' on."

"What's going on?" she said.

"Yes, what's goin' on," he said.

"I'm. … "

"I don't care watcha doing," he said. "I'm tired of this. You're always doin' this."

"I … " Janet tried to say.

"No," John interrupted, "I told you last time, when we were in the mountains in Colorado, the time your motha' was there and we argued about the children, and you were havin' fits cuz you thought I was flirting with that waitress, I told you then that if the house wuz always a mess I'd pack my bags and leave you."

"Yes," Janet said, "I remember that trip, and that argument is still a problem in our relationship, because you were flirting with that stupid waitress and you know it. But get your bag you awful man, I'm sick of this! I was cooking you a happy anniversary cake!"

And then, as the door slammed, John suddenly remembered.

- Among the problems here, it goes on too long before we get to the conflict, the slang calls attention to itself instead of to John's character, big chunks of dialogue are just backstory, every line has a mostly unnecessary tag, and the whole piece does little to develop character or move the narrative forward.

- Contrast the example above with the following excerpt from Ernest Hemingway's memoir of Paris, *A Moveable Feast*. In this scene, writer Ford Madox Ford has just "cut" another writer, Hilaire Belloc, and is bragging about it.

> "A gentleman, Ford explained, "will always cut a cad."
>
> I took a quick drink of the brandy.
>
> "Would he cut a bounder?" I asked.
>
> "It would be impossible for a gentleman to have known a bounder."
>
> "Then you can only cut someone you have known on terms of equality?" I pursued.
>
> "Naturally." …
>
> "It's very complicated," I said. "Am I a gentleman?"
>
> "Absolutely not," Ford said.
>
> "Then why are you drinking with me?"
>
> "I'm drinking with you as a promising young writer. As a fellow writer, in fact."
>
> "Good of you," I said.
>
> "You might be considered a gentleman in Italy," Ford said magnanimously.

- Here, Hemingway deftly established Ford's character, and established himself as a witty tease and a sarcastic and confident speaker. The tags are brief, and best of all, the speakers are speaking to each other, not to us.

Constructing Dialogue—A Writing Exercise

- Here are two short letters. Your job is to take the historical "facts" revealed herein and transform them into a scene with dialogue for a nonfiction book project.

> **Letter one**: Dear Eugene, it was such a pleasure to have met you at the dinner party last night at Mark's house, and thanks for giving me your business card. And for writing your message on it. … I knew from the moment we sat down over cocktails that you and I would end up seeing each other again. Did you know it too? I still remember that moment over dinner where you looked at me and asked if I liked the art of Cezanne. And of course I told you that it was my very favorite. And you said that only a wide heart could appreciate his still-life painting, and in that moment I fell in love with you. It's a foolish thing to say, but, yes, of course I'll meet you! Until soon, with a kiss, Charlotte.
>
> **Letter two [e-mail]**: Hey Mark, what a party! As always the food was great and thanks a million for the invite. Only in New York City. I mean, is it me, or were Charlotte and Eugene engaged in some serious romantic tension? All that art talk. Gag. But Mark, didn't he come there with his girlfriend?! Did I miss something? Julia just sat there like a lump on a log, so I assume she didn't much care, but then you know after she did keep winking at me, and I loved that moment in the middle of that inane Cezanne conversation that just went on forever—I love Cezanne, no, I love him more, only the gentle spirits can appreciate Cezanne, look at those blue apples. I'll never forget Charlotte saying that: look at those blue apples. Hah hah. I don't think it was about apples somehow. But I loved that moment where Julia just looked at Eugene and said "Art is stupid." And the table went silent. Hey, like I said, a truly memorable dinner party!

Suggested Reading

Card, *Elements of Fiction Writing*.

Chiarella, *Writing Dialogue.*

Hemingway, *A Moveable Feast.*

Questions to Consider

1. Where in your life could an eager historian find evidence that would help to describe you as a character? What can you do to preserve that kind of material?

2. We all reveal ourselves through dialogue and speech. What do you think your speech reveals about you as a character?

Dialogue Strategies in Creative Nonfiction

Lecture 18—Transcript

In our last lesson, we focused on learning how to shape voice in your prose, and we considered the different kinds of perspective that are available to you as a writer in your storytelling. But what about moments in our writing when we want characters to talk among themselves, rather than communicating their ideas and expressions ourselves? In other words, what about dialogue? In this lesson, we'll focus on how to write great dialogue, and we'll think especially about the challenges of dialogue in creative nonfiction. After all, the nonfiction contract means that we can't make anything up, doesn't it? That means that we can't put words in the mouths of our characters; at least not words that they didn't write or say themselves.

That's going to be a bit tricky, isn't it? After all, are you asking yourself: Where are you going to find dialogue if you can't invent it? It's a good question. Writing dialogue is definitely one of the elements in creative nonfiction that requires a deft touch and—here we are, back to this again—super research skills.

You don't have to use dialogue, of course. It's perfectly possible to write a great story without readers getting to hear two characters talking directly to each other, whether that's the author-narrator and another person, or two of the historical figures that you're writing about. You can manage it in different ways, through strong narrative and great character development and beautiful writing of your own. But it's admittedly hard not to have the opportunity to hear a character speak. Nothing builds character and connects a reader to a character, especially an historical one, as much as hearing the character's own words and thoughts, in dialogue or in interior monologue. Of course, the same nonfiction contract applies to interior monologue as it does to dialogue.

How do you go about it, then, in creative nonfiction? As you can see, it all starts with research. If you wanted to find out what Queen Victoria had to say in order to craft dialogue and interior monologue in your dazzling new biography of this 19th-century British ruler, where are you going to start looking? She did talk to people, after all; there must be records of some of what she said. You could start, of course, with her letters; what she literally wrote to the people she was in conversation with and what they said about her. You could look at memoirs written by people she met in the course of her long life, too, couldn't you? If you were writing your autobiography and once met a queen and overhead her conversation, you'd probably mention it, wouldn't you? You could also look at the queen's journals. She kept dozens of them over the decades, and surely she recorded in them herself some snatches of conversation and her own private thoughts about her experience.

What else could you look at? She's a public figure, isn't she? So what other records would there be? She gave speeches in Parliament and addresses to her people; and what she did and where she went was reported in the newspapers. There are even rare recordings of her voice, which you could use to get the information to describe the sound of it accurately. But if you don't actually hear her voice—the nonfiction contract—you can't say what it sounds like, can you? Once again, the creative nonfiction writer is an historical journalist, sleuthing out the words recorded about what someone said so you can use them to create great dialogue.

What you can see, of course, is that it's easier to write dialogue in a nonfiction book about a famous person than a less famous one, isn't it? A hundred years from now, you perhaps could locate my letters—or, more likely, emails—if you could track down my friends and relatives and if they happened to keep them. You could find a couple of interviews and other materials maybe, if someone saved them. You might stumble upon my diaries; but I doubt any of my friends think that what I said about the weather last week is among their life's most significant events somehow, and I don't they're making notes about it. I'd be surprised if in their autobiography anything I said gets mentioned; and the paparazzi aren't exactly tracking my every step and reporting them to the eager reader. Much of what I say to other people, much of what I think to myself, is only interesting to a small group of people, mostly me. A hundred years from now, writing my dialogue in your biography, that's going to be a challenge. You're going to have to work with some different kinds of creative nonfiction strategies. So your approach to less than famous characters is going to be to find out what you can about these people and the records of their lives. Then there are also some other ways we can deal with these circumstances as savvy writers. For example, you can at least use dialogue—in the mouths of other people, maybe other people who lived at the same time and in the same places I did—to set the scene and move the narrative forward, even if you can't use what I said to sketch my character.

First, let's think a bit about what makes good dialogue in general. This is true if you're writing nonfiction or if you're working on your novel. What's the purpose of dialogue in narrative? What makes it work, and when does it fall flat entirely? Here's rule of thumb number one for dialogue: Like any good element in storytelling, it needs to do one of two things, and ideally to do both, doesn't it? It needs to reveal character, and it needs to move a narrative forward. How does dialogue reveal character? Think about how we get our impressions of people in daily life. We listen to them, don't we? What a person says and how he or she responds to a situation tells us a great deal about who they are, their intentions, their hesitations, their prejudices and convictions; in short, their character. But do you see why dialogue now also has to be part of a context, and that context needs to be narrative? We just said that conversation reveals intention, hesitations. It shows how a person responds. A person is responding, after all, to something; to some conflict, internal or external. Remember how we have defined good narrative, too, in this course? It's action with consequences. What people say, just as much as what they do, can set actions into motion and can show us the consequences of actions already under way.

Dialogue either has to be part of an intensification of a scene or the unraveling of an action in order to be really effective. Dialogue isn't just interesting conversation; it's not just engaging, witty banter. Interesting conversation in storytelling is only interesting if there are consequences that come from it. So rule number one: Dialogue isn't conversation; it's a way of using conversation to drive narrative action, intensify conflict, or establish character, all of which will have consequences following from them. If you can't say what function your dialogue serves, chances are it isn't working. Revise it, or cut it.

Here's rule of thumb number two about writing dialogue: Just now I said dialogue isn't just interesting conversation. But dialogue should be interesting. It's interesting conversation with a narrative objective. Boring dialogue that has a narrative objective isn't great dialogue either, though, is it? What's the difference between dull and fascinating? Interesting dialogue is, above all, constructed. What do I mean by that? I mean that it actually doesn't sound exactly like the way people really talk. Believe it or not, the way people really talk is generally pretty uninteresting. Think about the last big argument you had with a friend, or coworker, or partner. You probably remember just a couple of hum-zingers that really captured the stakes and issues in that argument, and you probably can think of a few things the other person said that still get you riled up if you really think about them. Maybe you remember the moment you finally look at each other, too, and had a laugh; or the moment the phone rang inconveniently and drove up the temperature.

But do you remember everything that was said? Almost certainly not; and almost certainly, there were parts of that argument—if we were to make them into a story—that were just plain dull and boring, comments that didn't really have anything to do with the conflict at issue: Rehashing the details of something that even at the moment you may remember sitting there thinking, "This is completely ridiculous and irrelevant; why are we having this conversation?"; and, when we also get down to it, do we also need to hear your "ummms," "yeahs," and grumpy silences along the way to understand the story? Story, after all, is always about conflict and character. We don't, do we? This is why good dialogue leaves out the parts of a conversation that don't have a function.

Remember, as a creative nonfiction writer, one of things you're allowed to do is to not including the boring things that happen or people say just because you happen to find them in the archives. You can always leave things out, as long as you punctuate it properly. You can edit what people say strategically. If you want to leave something out of a direct quote, all you need to do is simply replace the missing material with three dots, known as an ellipsis. If you leave out the beginning of a new sentence and not just a phrase in the middle of a sentence, you use four dots. That's it. That's how a historian tells a reader, "Hey, I left out something boring." You can't take out something that changes the meaning of the quote fundamentally—in other words, you can't go dropping out the "nots" in a sentence and replacing it with an ellipsis and still be playing by the rules of the nonfiction contract—

but otherwise, you have broad leeway. After all, think about what happens when you're interviewed by a journalist. Have you ever been quoted? People are often furious when they're quoted in the news because journalists pick and choose their quotes very selectively, don't they? What you said as part of a long conversation might get placed in a context that, while not untrue, also isn't really exactly how you presented it either. That's why smart politicians learn the art of the sound bite. The sound bite is a short sentence that has the entire argument or point you that want to make completely encapsulated in it. It's how politicians hedge their bets about journalists using ellipses or a series of short quotes to drop out your boring bits. But, of course, you might not have thought they were so boring.

The rule of thumb number two is that good dialogue doesn't sound fake—it should sound like two real people talking—but real and encyclopedic aren't the same thing. With dialogue, overwriting is a danger. Less is generally more. What should be there is the part of the conversation that moves narrative, or reveals character, or intensifies a conflict. If it doesn't do that, a phrase probably doesn't need to be there.

But how are you going to know if dialogue sounds natural? Here's the thing about dialogue: It should sound like an essential part of storytelling; and that's not the same thing as sounding just like the conversation you overheard this morning in the donut shop. So drop out the "ummms," "yeahs," and "likes" unless they serve a function; that's why some brilliant editor invented the ellipsis. But also drop out the grammar mistakes and resist the temptation to emphasize regional accents or foreign words. If someone has a regional accent, find a way to signal his or her identity through description and move on. Making a big deal out of it in conversation sounds overblown and even comic unless you do it very delicately. Using endless foreign words to show a character is French has the same effect of calling attention to the fact that you're trying too hard and haven't already established this character confidently. Just because you're recording the conversation of someone who speaks with a Southern drawl, that doesn't mean you can't write the sentence truthfully in Standard American English. You don't have to try to capture how the words sounded when you know perfectly well what they were. Just because a quote is in French and you've translated it into English doesn't mean there's any good reason to leave "merci" and "a bientot" in French for flavor. It's artificial flavor and not natural, after all.

Using regional dialect, foreign words, grammar mistakes, and all those "umms" and "ahhh" that punctuate real daily speech is especially easy to fall into in fiction, where you can put the words in a character's mouth freely; but it's also true in creative nonfiction, especially if you're interviewing real people or if you're writing a memoir and describing a conversation you remember. Even when you're using quoted historical materials to shape dialogue, remember, you're always still the writer, and it's the job of the writer to take this history and make it into a great story. In creative nonfiction, we can't add materials, but we can delete them. The key to dialogue is selectivity.

How about one last rule of thumb for writing dialogue? Do you know what the problem with throwing in a lot of French words into the conversation in a text is? It's something like the problem with purple prose. What you're doing is calling attention to the writing itself; and, of course, what a reader wants in a passage of dialogue is to focus on the narrative and the characters, doesn't she? We want to be told a story; we don't want to be reminded that we're being told a story all the time.

One other way that writers can fall into this mistake is by overwriting dialogue in other ways, too. Dialogue isn't a place where the characters need to explain everything. They shouldn't have to fill in the entire back story. The point of dialogue is that two characters are directly engaged with each other. They should focus on each other, not on serving as extra narrators in a piece where they're speaking, via each other, to the reader. Dialogue should reveal information gracefully and implicitly. If your dialogue is an infomercial, it's not yet working. It's for this reason that you want to use "he said" and "she said" sparingly. Sometimes those tags need to be there. Often they need to be there. A reader should be able to follow a conversation without any difficulty, and these tags smooth that process. Few things are more annoying than reading a text and trying to figure out who's saying what in a passage. But they should be used only when necessary so the reader doesn't see them everywhere; they should function almost invisibly. You'll see what I mean in a minute when we turn to an example in this lesson.

Those are the three essential principles for writing good dialogue in fiction or nonfiction writing: It intensifies character and moves a narrative forward; it sounds realistic, but not necessarily real; and it's not overwritten. But how about that special case where you're writing a memoir and want to include a conversation that really happened, but you only have your memory of it? This is one of the trickiest situations for anyone writing a memoir, actually, and one of the places where the risks of getting it historically wrong are the most complicated. After all, if you put words in someone else's mouth in print and it's not actually what they said, and especially if the way you write it makes them looks foolish or bad in some way, then you're at risk of being accused of libel, which is a legal tangle that no writer wants to find him or herself in. If these are friends or loved ones you're writing about, how to manage this without people being furious with you is also a delicate matter, isn't it? We'll talk more about that in lesson 20. For now, let's set aside the legal and interpersonal issues writers of creative nonfiction face. How about just the ethical and craft issues?

The ethical issue—how this squares with the nonfiction contract—at least is pretty straightforward. If you think you might write a book, the first thing is: Start keeping notes on conversations. Keep a daily journal. Keep your emails, letters, and other materials so that when the time comes, you don't have to rely on memory. There's a good reason writers tend to have jam-packed file cabinets filled with the strangest things, from old birthday cards to newspaper clippings. Someday, there might be a story in something there; that was the intuition that told us not to junk it. There's a reason why the people who live with writers will tell you to be careful what you say. For a writer, everything is potential material; something that often complicates private relationships, unless you set clear and respectful boundaries.

But what if you haven't kept a journal or good notes and you want to use—and you want to use for good craft reasons—as dialogue a conversation that you only have your memory to guide you on? The ethical rule in nonfiction is that as long as you're reporting your experience as accurately as possible, then you're on safe ground in terms of the nonfiction contract. Most smart writers who are relying on memory will add a note to the beginning of their manuscript that simply states that fact, and that alerts the reader if there have been any changes made in the order of the events or the context of the conversation. After all, as we've just said, a good writer leaves out the boring bits. You can compress historical events so it seems that one follows from the other when, in fact, things evolved over a longer horizon. A smart writer will just make a note of it, cover his or her bets, and move on quickly and gracefully to tell us a story so fabulous that nothing else matters. Effectively, you're asking your reader to engage in a case of what the poet Coleridge once called "the willing suspension of disbelief." Sure, we know that probably that conversation had "ummms" in it; and we know that things in life don't happen quite like they do in narrative, with one interesting thing immediately following another; but that's what makes a great story, and as long as we tell readers the truth, their interest in being swept away in that tale and in willingly suspending their disbelief or setting aside their doubts about whether this is the whole truth without any narrative structuring is far greater than their interest in reading every "ummm" you really said in that blowup argument.

Let's try an example, shall we? Here's a passage of dialogue that isn't working. See if you can figure out why. How would you fix this? Can you identify the ways in which this dialogue isn't following our three principles? First, a quick recap. Those principles are: First, dialogue moves forward narrative and deepens character. Second, good dialogue sounds realistic but doesn't actually record real conversations with all their "umms," "ahhs," and digressions; so don't try to be encyclopedic, try to be artistic. Third, remember that dialogue is written and that adding in too many eccentricities in speech doesn't really build character effectively, but does undermine your piece by calling attention to the writing itself rather than the story you're telling; and in dialogue, your characters are talking to each other, not making speeches to the reader.

Listen to this example of dialogue, and see if you can identify where I've gone wrong in my storytelling. It's my example of our hypothetical marital disagreement, remember?

> John came into the room and slung his briefcase in the corner. All he could see were the dishes everywhere. The kitchen was a disaster. For crying out loud, why was it always like this when he came home from a hard day of work anyhow?

"Janet," he said harshly. "What's goin' on."

"What's going on?" she said.

"Yes, what's goin' on," he said.

"I'm …"

"I don't care watcha doing," he said. "I'm tired of this. You're always doin' this."

"I …" Janet tried to say.

"No," John interrupted, "I told you last time, when we were in the mountains in Colorado, the time your motha' was there and we argued about the children, and you were havin' fits cuz you thought I was flirting with that waitress, I told you then that if the house wuz always a mess I'd pack my bags and leave you."

"Yes," Janet said, "I remember that trip, and that argument is still a problem in our relationship, because you were flirting with that stupid waitress and you know it. But get your bag you awful man, I'm sick of this! I was cooking you a happy anniversary cake!"

And then, as the door slammed, John suddenly remembered.

OK, this is pretty awful. Do you see how long that beginning goes on? Do you see how awkward the slang is when I really use it? Do you ever get to see how I actually get to the real conflict between the characters? Do you see how John's story about the fight in the mountains in Colorado is just a speech? Does it go anywhere? Does that earlier argument really do anything to move this narrative forward? Are there really any consequences that follow from it? In fact, are there really any consequences that we're interested in or character development that's intriguing at all? Frankly, it's a pretty pointless piece of dialogue here?

Let's look at another example; an example of dialogue that sparkles. This is from Ernest Hemingway's memoir of Paris, *A Moveable Feast*, and it's one of the sharpest and most resonant bits of dialogue I've read in a long while. It starts in a café in Paris, where the writer Ford Madox Ford has just "cut" another writer Hilaire Belloc and is bragging about it.

> "Why did you cut him" Hemingway asks.
>
> "A gentleman, Ford explained, "will always cut a cad.
>
> I took a quick drink of the brandy.
>
> "Would he cut a bounder?" I asked.
>
> "It would be impossible for a gentleman to have known a bounder."
>
> "Then you can only cut someone you have known on terms of equality?' I pursued.
>
> "Naturally.
>
> …
>
> "It's very complicated," I said. "Am I a gentleman?"
>
> "Absolutely not," Ford said.
>
> "Then why are you drinking with me?"
>
> "I'm drinking with you as a promising young writer. As a fellow writer, in fact."
>
> "Good of you," I said.
>
> "You might be considered a gentleman in Italy," Ford said magnanimously.

It's quite a difference, isn't it? Here, Hemingway deftly established Ford's character as a man who's a bit of a fool and a poser; and it establishes Hemingway himself as a witty tease and as a sarcastic and confident speaker. The way this chapter ends emphasizes that point further, for it turns out that Ford has entirely mistaken the man he cut; it wasn't Belloc at all that he insulted. That kind of error has the potential to move a narrative forward, and it also reveals another side of Ford's character, too. The tags are brief; and best of all in this example the speakers, we really get the sense, are speaking to each other.

Alright, are you ready to try an example by yourself? Here's a bit of "historical" information for you to work with: two short "letters" that I've written. Your job: to take two of these pieces of "fact" and transform them into a dialogue and a scene in a nonfiction book project. Can you find the story? Can you turn fact into a dialogue between characters whose motivations you can begin to develop? Here they are, and they're also in your course booklet.

Letter one:

> Dear Eugene, it was such a pleasure to have met you at the dinner party last night at Marks' house and thanks for giving me your business card. And for writing your message on it. … I knew from the moment we sat down over cocktails that you and I would end up seeing each other again. Did you know it too? I still remember that moment over dinner where you looked at me and asked if I liked the art of Cezanne. And of course I told you that it was my very favorite. And you said that only a wide heart could appreciate his still life painting, and in that moment I fell in love with you. It's a foolish thing to say, but, yes, of course I'll meet you! Until soon, with a kiss, Charlotte.

How about letter two?

> Hey Mark, what a party! As always the food was great and thanks a million for the invite. Only in New York City. I mean, is it me, or were Charlotte and Eugene engaged in some serious

> romantic tension? All that art talk. Gag. But Mark, didn't he just come there with his girlfriend?! Did I miss something? Julia just sat there like a lump on a log, so I assume she didn't much care, but then you know after she did keep winking at me, and I loved that moment in the middle of that inane Cezanne conversation that just went on forever—I love Cezanne, no, I love him more, only the gentle spirits can appreciate Cezanne, look at those blue apples. I'll never forget Charlotte saying that: Look at those blue apples. Hah hah. I don't think it was about apples somehow. But I loved that moment where Julia just looked at Eugene and said "Art is stupid." And the table went silent. Hey, like I said, a truly memorable dinner party!

OK, now it's up to you. There's your reported history. Following the nonfiction contract, can you turn this into a great scene of dialogue, and into great writing?

Researching Creative Nonfiction

Lecture 19

Mastering the art of research is one of the most challenging, and yet the most important, tasks in becoming a creative nonfiction writer. First, one must understand how to find sources, both primary (firsthand, eyewitness, original) and secondary (interpreted). Then, one must learn how to evaluate these sources critically.

The Challenge of Research

- It is research, above all, that the nonfiction writer has to master with real aplomb. Therefore, it is time to think about the kinds of places nonfiction writers find their materials, what to do when you get stuck during research, how to manage first-person interviews, and how to evaluate the reliability of sources.

- The kind of nonfiction book you can write depends critically on the kind of information you can find. If you want to write something new and groundbreaking, that means you have to find that information in the difficult places.

- Let's say you want to write a biography of Queen Elizabeth I. You cannot just go to the library and call up all the books on her—or rather, you can and even should at the beginning, because unless you know what else has been written, you will not know whether you have anything new to say.

- However, if you write your book by just cobbling together materials from books that have already been published, that will not make a great piece of creative nonfiction. Creative nonfiction requires new and interesting material, a new perspective, or a new way of telling a great story. That means finding new research—either by chance or, if you are like most writers, by hard work.

Where to Begin

- Whatever your topic, you are going to have to do research—even if you are writing a memoir. For most topics, you are going start by calling up all the books at the library like the one you are imagining. You need to know what the competition is.

- Some of these books will become important secondary sources—emphasis on the word *secondary*. What a creative nonfiction writer needs is primary sources. Primary, or firsthand, sources are based on someone's direct experience or testimony. They are not someone else's interpretation or synthesis of information on a topic.

- Primary sources range from memoirs, letters, and oral histories to photographs, company records, interviews you conduct with eyewitnesses, and even your own experiences.

- Secondary sources are books and articles written by people who have done all the research, thought about it, and shaped it into a story. You are going to be writing a secondary source unless you are writing a memoir.

- There is nothing wrong with secondary sources, but if your book is just a regurgitation of the other secondary sources, then you are not doing anything creative as a creative nonfiction writer.

- One great place to start your research is with what you find at the end of any good secondary source: the bibliography. There you can not only read about other books related to your topic but also, for example, about private archives of unpublished materials, special collections in libraries and museums, memoirs, and even television specials on your topic. You can also go to the listed secondary sources and look at *their* bibliographies.

The Internet has been an enormous boon to nonfiction writers, allowing them to do huge amounts of preparation, organization, and research from home.

Tracking Down Primary Sources

- After you have made a list of all the primary materials you need to consult, then what comes next is the hardest part: tracking down those primary sources. Ultimately, you will use them as a way to find more primary sources, too.

- Your primary sources will likely be scattered far and wide, and in the end you may need to travel to see them, but that is not how you should start your research process. Before you visit any archives, you will need a clear idea of what materials you want to see, so you will need to do some preparatory work first.

- Most libraries and museums today have their catalogues online, where you can search for these materials. You can use as many related keywords as you can think up to find materials related to them as well.

- If you do need to see any materials in person, the catalogues will also give you each item's acquisition number, or call number. Before you visit the collection, you should contact its curator to explain who you are, what you want to see, and why you want to see it. In many cases, you will need permission to access the material, some of which will be fragile. There is also a chance that materials will be in special storage, in a conservation laboratory, or in a traveling exhibit when you want to visit.

From Source to Source

- How do you use one set of primary materials to find more primary materials? Let's say, for example, that you are looking at a set of advertisements for the SPAM® brand* from the 1950s kept at Harvard's library. Other university libraries might not have a SPAM® brand-specific collection, but they might have 1950s ad collections, or food ad collections, or archives related to the manufacturer of SPAM® products, Hormel Foods, and so forth.

- You might start with a quick Internet search on 1950s advertisement collections, and sure enough, you find another big collection at Duke University. Then you find that Duke has made their entire collection available online. You also learn, by way of Duke's website, that you can buy Hormel Foods ads cheaply online for your own collection. Sometimes a catalogue number for an advertisement will list the name of the advertising agency that created it, and someone at the agency can discuss their work with you. Perhaps the model or the photographer will grant an interview. All these little connections can add up to a research bonanza.

- This is why being a creative nonfiction writer is a lot like being a savvy investigative journalist—after all that is where creative nonfiction began.

---

*SPAM® is a registered trademark of Hormel Foods, LLC and used with permission.

Evaluating Secondary Sources

- How do you know whether a secondary source is reliable? After all, especially on the Internet, anyone can post anything. This is why academia places such a value on peer-reviewed work. Very little that is published in popular trade books or on the Internet is peer reviewed. Writers need to make our own judgments about veracity.

- Sources with bibliographies tend to be more reliable for one simple reason: You can check up on the author easily. Of course, if the author refers to sources that themselves do not have bibliographies—or are otherwise unreliable—all bets are off.

- Materials from certain sources tend to be more reliable than others. Sources with academic or major institutional associations—places like research institutes, the government, museums, major news outlets—tend to be more reliable.

- This is not to say that writers associated with these places do not have biases. We need to recognize the difference between facts, which should be indisputable, and interpretation of the facts, which can be spun. Academic and major cultural institutions rarely make mistakes of fact, and when they do, they will generally acknowledge and correct them. Academic authors' careers depend on their credibility. If they are wrong about verifiable facts, they will not be credible for long.

- If your source does not come with academic authority but has a good bibliography, chances are you are on a solid track. If there is no bibliography—especially for short-form online sources—it might be reliable as long as it signals the source of its information and that source is credible.

- A website might say, for example, "This article is based on private interviews with the subject." A reputable author, in this case, will give his or her e-mail address somewhere on that website so a curious historian can write and ask further questions.

- Some of the most interesting leads a writer may find may come from personal interviews. It is important to take good notes or record these conversations—but always get the interviewee's permission.

- Oral histories are a critical piece of the historical record and great sources of primary material, and a good nonfiction writer always documents his or her sources—even if only privately and especially when he or she is writing about living people.

- One other thing to look for in evaluating sources: Does the writer seem to be objective, or is there a clear **bias** to the way the story is presented? There is an important distinction between bias and interpretation.

  - Bias is when a writer has a clear agenda and all the evidence presented supports a single opinion.

  - A more balanced interpretation will present counterexamples—instances when the evidence does not fit the frame. The moments when something does not fit are the moments character is most dramatically revealed, after all. Any good writer will embrace the chance to show that his or her story is complex.

Recognizing Bias—A Research Exercise

- What would you say about this (imaginary) piece of historical information from the web as a source of information?

  https://www.elizabethanstudies.myuni.edu

  E-mail mary.oflannagn@myuni.edu

  How Elizabeth Became Queen

  By Mary O'Flannagan

Elizabeth I had an unusually tortuous path to the crown. She was not yet three when her mother was beheaded at the order of her father, Henry VIII. At Henry's death, Elizabeth's sickly half-brother Edward ascended the throne (Jones, 257). Upon his death in 1553, he bequeathed the crown to Lady Jane Grey, cutting Elizabeth out of the succession. Edward's will was set aside, however, and Lady Jane Grey was executed, allowing Elizabeth's sister Mary to ascend the throne. As a devout Catholic, "Bloody Mary" persecuted the Protestants and imprisoned Elizabeth in the Tower of London (*Letters of Queen Elizabeth*, 17). Despite these difficulties, Elizabeth learned to craft her words and fashion her behavior to gain favor and secure her own well-being. When Mary died in 1558, Elizabeth's patience and popularity paid off, and she became, at last, queen of England (Smith, 46; Newberry Library archives).

- At a quick glance, you know this source has a bibliography. We have the author's e-mail address, so you could ask further questions. Both her e-mail address and the website are .edu, meaning this information is probably part of O'Flannagan's academic work. None of this means O'Flannagan is necessarily right, but it does mean she has a professional stake in its accuracy.

- How does the following piece compare to O'Flannagan's?

    http://www.queenelizthevampire.com

    Family Tree Shows Queen Elizabeth Is Related to Dracula. By the Vampires are Real Historical Society.

    Most people think of Vampires as a vast threat to civilization as we know it, if they even believe in Vampires. But Vampires are real, and guess what—Queen Elizabeth I is related to the lineage of one of the most famous vampires of all—Vlad the Impaler. This proves that they are living today.

Lineage charts make it clear that, to quote, "this 15th century murderous count has probably contributed his seeds to the royal family tree."

Haven't you wondered about why Queen Elizabeth wears all those big hats in public? Her bloodline has been diluted, but she's obviously inherited the Vampire's sensitivity to light. I just want to point out that there aren't any mirrors in her publicity photos.

- The hints that this is unreliable material are unfortunately pretty common. The writer is anonymous and has a clear bias. There is no bibliography and no specific citations, even though there is a quotation. This author generalizes about sources but does not give you reference to any of them. The website address is a regular .com, which is not by itself a sign, but coupled with all these other hints, it confirms that that writer does not have any professional investment in his or her credibility.

- Now it is time to put your researching skills to the test. Imagine you were writing a book on Queen Elizabeth, as discussed in the lecture. Look online or at the library for five primary sources and three secondary sources on her. Then evaluate their reliability using the rules we have discussed. Which of those sources would you feel comfortable quoting in light of the nonfiction contract?

Important Term

bias: The way the perspective of the storyteller or researcher can shape his or her attitude toward evidence.

Suggested Reading

Bass, *The Associated Press Guide To Internet Research and Reporting.*

Mann, *The Oxford Guide to Library Research.*

Questions to Consider

1. What are the local research opportunities available to you in your area? Are any of them unique?

2. How do you evaluate Internet resources for reliability in other areas of your life? What makes for a reliable source of historical information?

Researching Creative Nonfiction

Lecture 19—Transcript

Throughout this course, one of the things I've emphasized over and over—from our first conversation about the nonfiction contract to our work with developing dialogue using historical sources—is how important research is for the creative nonfiction writer. In fact, I've said—haven't I?—that it's research above all that a nonfiction writer has to master with real aplomb. We've talked about some of the different ways in which you can learn to do that in your own writing in specific instances that are related to learning to master some of the skills of storytelling. In this lesson, let's take a closer look at creative nonfiction research. We're going to think today about the kinds of places nonfiction writers find their materials, what to do when you get stuck with research, how to manage first-person interviews, and how to evaluate the reliability of sources.

Do you want to know one of the most useful things about my graduate education in literature for me as a writer? It's not what I learned about literature or writing. Sure, you spend years studying for a Ph.D. in English, and you learn a lot about how to craft a sentence and about what great storytelling looks like. You learn to understand the nuances of meaning in poetry and how to make informed judgments about art. That's all true. But what's actually made the biggest difference for me as a writer? It's what I learned in graduate school about research. You can teach yourself to write if you have some good mentors and some good examples to learn from probably; and you can read poetry without a teacher if you have enough determination and spend enough time reading; and, in fact, you can learn to do research on your own, too. But having had seven years of training in how to do it sure has been useful, because learning how to do creative and complicated research is a lot more challenging than you might imagine; and the kind of book that you can write as a nonfiction author depends critically on the kind of information you can find. If you want to write a book that's new and groundbreaking, that means you have to find information in the difficult places. If the places were easy, after all, somebody else probably would've written this great story already.

Let's say you want to write the biography of Queen Elizabeth I. You can't just go to the library and call up all the books on her. Or rather, you can; and in the beginning, certainly should, because unless you know what else has been written you won't know whether you're saying anything new or whether the world even needs another biography of this famous queen. But if you write your book by just cobbling together materials from books that have already been published, that's not going to ever make a great piece of creative nonfiction; that's just retelling other people's stories. Creative nonfiction requires that you have new and interesting material; a new take; some new way of telling a great story; a new angle; something groundbreaking and fresh. That means finding new research, either by chance if you're lucky, or by hard work and design if you're like most of us as writers.

So you want to write a book of creative nonfiction and you have a subject that you think would be interesting: the biography of Queen Elizabeth; or the history of the SPAM® brand; or your memoir of a childhood in Iran during the revolution. Whatever your topic, you're going to have to do research, even if you're writing the memoir. So you find your topic and now, let's think about it, where do you start with your research? Where do you start with really creative and innovative research, in fact? As we've said, you're going to call up books at the library, all the books that are like the one you're imagining. Of course you are; you need to know what the competition is. You need to decide if you can tell a new story, or tell an old story from a new angle at any rate. Let's say you looked at the other books on the history of the SPAM® brand, and you find there aren't any; you've got a fresh topic. Sure, there are other books on the history of meat production, and there are books on the history of postwar austerity and the decline of British cooking that talk about the SPAM® brand as one element of their story; there are books on potted meat in modern literature, and there are books on the rise of processed food in America; there are books on women in World War II that talk about the touring Hormel Girls of the 1940s; and there are recent works on how unwanted email came to be known as "spam." But no one has ever written the comprehensive cultural history of the SPAM® brand. You'll be the first.

These books you've called up at the library, these are perhaps going to be important secondary sources; but we want to notice my emphasis on that word "secondary." What a creative nonfiction writer needs is sources that are primary. What do you think the difference between primary and secondary sources would be? Think about it for a moment in our imagined history of the SPAM® brand; what would be a primary or firsthand source? The obvious firsthand source would be the Hormel Foods archives, right? That would be going directly to the source. But what would be some other places you could go for information that was based on someone's direct experience?

That's what we mean by firsthand sources: It's based on direct experience or testimony. It's not what someone else who has studied the topic and synthesized the information reports to us as history, that's secondary; but it's the documents or oral testimony of people who took part in the history itself. Company records; but you could also go find and interview some of the workers who produced SPAM® products, couldn't you? Those people would have firsthand testimony. Or you could go find a memoir or letters written by a SPAM® product factory worker, an executive, a rancher who supplied meat to the Hormel Foods, or one of those Hormel Girls on tour. You could find early advertisements in newspapers, or on radio and television. You could find newspaper and magazine coverage of the SPAM® brand phenomenon. You could find records from the US government about the SPAM® brand trademark or information in government archives about the regulation and production of processed meat foods. You could find out what laws were enacted, how the industry developed. You could talk to people living in postwar Britain who ate it; and the women who wrote the SPAM® brand cookbooks, and the chefs who in the 1960s served it. You could see how it was represented in movies and on television programs; you could talk to the founders of the SPAM® fan club, and interview vegans to find out how they feel about it. You could taste it yourself and write a memoir; or maybe you grew up eating it and can find an old family photograph of a SPAM® product on your holiday table. Those are all primary sources.

Secondary sources are the books written by people who have done all the research, thought about it, and shaped it into a history or a story. You're going to be writing a secondary source when you write your history of the SPAM® brand unless you're writing a memoir of a SPAM® brand-based childhood. There's nothing wrong with secondary sources; they're wonderful. You're going to write a great one, and you already know it. But if your history of the SPAM® brand is just a regurgitation of the other histories of the SPAM®

brand out there, then you aren't doing anything creative here as a creative nonfiction writer. In fact, you're writing a book that almost certainly won't get published; or if it does, will land you in a predicament with the reviewers, who are quickly going to figure out that you didn't really do much research at all, you just cribbed from the work of other writers and journalists.

What do you need to do to write your history of the SPAM® brand to make it thorough and be creative in your firsthand research? One great place to start for any nonfiction writer is not so much with the other secondary books written as with what any good one is going to have there at the end of it: a bibliography. The very best place to start your research is by recovering the firsthand ground that others have already trail blazed. What you definitely want to do as a nonfiction writer is read the bibliographies of other books on topics related to yours so you can make a list of the firsthand sources you can start by looking at. You can learn, for example, where there might be private archives of unpublished industry materials in the special collections of libraries, or in museums, or centers related to wartime histories. You can learn what museums have exhibits of photographs of the Hormel Girls that you can go look at. You can learn about memoirs written by Hormel Foods Farmers, and you can learn on what date some nightly news special on the SPAM® brand ran across the country in the 1970s. You can learn about other secondary books; books perhaps even more closely related to particular parts of the story that you're interested in, so that you can also go look and see what's in their bibliographies.

After you've done all this—read the secondary sources and scoured their bibliographies, and the bibliographies of the books in their notes too, and made a list of all the primary materials you need to consult—then what comes next is the part that's the hardest research, but also far and away the most rewarding; because what you need to do next is to track down those primary sources, isn't it? You need to use them as a way to launch your researches so you find more primary sources, too; the sources you need to tell your story of the SPAM® brand and sources no other nonfiction writer has ever brought together to tell this fabulous and interesting history you're writing. A nonfiction writer has to have new research to be truly successful, and you're ready now to start trying to find it.

Have a look at your list of primary sources. Let's say that on it are four particularly important pieces of material: You've learned that there are a series of oral interviews that were recorded with the Hormel Girls in the 1950s; you've learned that there are a series of photographs from the Hormel Foods plant in a museum in Indiana; you've learned that the library at Harvard University has an immense collection of advertisements from the 1950s, which includes at least one SPAM® brand advertisement reproduced in a book you've found; and you know that the Hormel Foods is still in business. Take a minute and think about it. What are you going to do next? How are you going to strategize your research? How are you going to use these primary sources as a jumping off point to find out more, new, never before considered materials on the history of the SPAM® brand?

One approach is to start booking yourself some airline tickets, isn't it? But before you do that, let's have a good think about this. You might need to go to these places in the end, it's true; but you don't need to do that in the beginning, and when you go you should already have a clear idea of what materials you want to see specifically. In fact, in order to get into the archives, most librarians will require it. Researchers only rarely get to go poke around in archives, and that's almost always after they've established their expertise in this subject. You're still at the beginning of your project; you're still a SPAM® brand beginner. So what would you do next?

The good news is that most libraries and museums today have their catalogs online, and you can go and search for these materials. While you're at it, you can use as many different related key words as you can think up to find materials related to them as well, can't you? In the case of images—like for photographs and advertisements—often those are available online instantly, and maybe you'll never have to trek up to Harvard or off to that museum in Indiana in person. But if you decide you do need to see them in person, what you'll need to know is the library's acquisition number—often called a "call number"—for the precise item that you want to see. Before you go to any library or museum with special collections—definitely before you book an airline ticket—you should email the curator of the collection; tell him or her who you are, what you want to see, and why you want to see it. You need their permission in many cases; after all, historical materials are fragile. You also need to know that that box of materials hasn't just been sent off to the conservation laboratory or on a travel exhibit for 18 months, or that the library isn't closed all summer.

How do we parlay those advertisements at Harvard into more primary materials? For one thing, if there are advertisement collections at Harvard, maybe there are advertising collections at other libraries, museums, and archives, too. Now it's time for a quick internet search on 1950s advertisement collections; and sure enough, did you know there's another big collection at Duke University, and that there are websites dedicated to it? And that you can buy Hormel Foods ads cheaply online for your own collection? For some strange reason, they aren't that expensive.

Let's think a bit more from there about how to get creative, too. Sometimes a catalog number for an advertisement will list the name of the advertising agency that created it. Why would an advertising company not be willing to talk with you about one of their campaign successes and get a bit of publicity if you write about their brilliant Hormel Foods advertisements in your smashing new book? Why don't you see if you can hunt down those advertising firms and talk to their historical archivists? Maybe you can interview the person who created it. Maybe, if those advertisements were photographs, you can figure out who the model in the image was, and maybe she's someone you can talk to as well. Or maybe you can talk to her grandniece, who will tell you that Auntie Joan wrote all sorts of letters about her time as a SPAM® brand advertising model and went on to marry a big-time farmer she met on location. Who knows what interesting and compelling human stories might appear; new stories that you can write about brilliantly? This is why being a creative nonfiction writer is a lot like being a savvy investigative journalist; after all, remember, that's where creative nonfiction began, with literary journalism.

What about those websites that you find on the internet? In fact, what about those secondary sources that you find on the library shelves, for that matter? Sometimes, of course, you're going to want to use some of the information that's presented in them. That's natural; and it's okay, too. We aren't saying you can't use those books and sources; we're just saying that you have be creative and find ways to go beyond them, to do some research that's genuinely original, too. But when you're looking at them, you've also made a nonfiction contract with your own reason, and that means one of your obligations is to be as sure as you can possibly be that what you're writing is the truth and has an historical basis.

How do you know if your secondary source is reliable? After all, especially on the internet, anyone can post anything, and this is the reason in the sciences and in academics there's been such a value placed on "peer reviewed" works all these decades; that is, works that have been anonymously vetted by other experts who confirm its scholarship. Very little that's published in popular trade books or on the internet is peer reviewed, however; and as writers, we need to make our own judgments about veracity. How do we go about this?

The first thing is that sources with bibliographies tend to be more reliable for one simple reason: You can check up on the author easily. The author has said, "I'm quoting here from page 67 of this book. Go ahead, look it up." You can easily, too; so if the author's fudging things, you and other readers can know about it instantly. This is true whether it's a published book or a source on the internet, as long as the sources themselves are also reliable. After all, if someone refers to sources that themselves don't have bibliographies, or are otherwise unreliable, then all bets are off. So that's the first rule of thumb, although it's just that: Bibliographies tend to be a good sign.

Likewise, materials from certain sources tend to be more reliable than others. Sources with academic or major institutional associations—places like research institutes, the government, museums, major news outlets—all tend to be more reliable. This isn't to say that all writers don't have biases and spins. As we've already talked about earlier in this course, all writing is a matter of storytelling and representation. But there's a difference between fact and fiction; after all, that idea is at the heart of the nonfiction contract, isn't it? In that case, it means we need to find sources based on fact, and we need to learn to recognize any interpretations being given to those facts in the writing. Academic and major cultural institutions rarely make mistakes of fact; and when they do, they will generally acknowledge and correct them. Why is that? Think about it: These pieces are written by people whose careers depend on their word, on their reliability; and if they're wrong about verifiable facts, they won't be credible for long.

What about pieces on the internet especially that don't come from sources with cultural authority? How do we know if those are reliable? Again, if they have a bibliography, chances are we're on good track. But even if they don't, they might be reliable, as long as they signal to us as readers the source of their information. A website might say, "This article is written based on interviews with John Jones, a long-time factory worker, who lives in Detroit." Even without footnotes—because, after all, the footnote there would say, "Based on private interviews with the author"—this could still be reputable. But a reputable author in this case will give his or her email address somewhere on that website so that you, as a curious historian, can write and ask whether you, too, could speak with John Jones or see the interview notes.

If you're the person interviewing John Jones—and some of the most interesting leads in my research as a writer, I can tell you, have come from reaching out to living people able to tell me their version of history—then you need to keep notes, or ask John if you can record the interview. You need to be sure to let John know you're recording it and planning to write about this interview. Oral histories are a crucial piece of the record and great sources of primary material, but a good nonfiction writer always documents his or her sources, even if only privately and especially when he or she's writing about living people.

There's one other thing to look for in evaluating sources: Does the writer seem to be trying to be objective, or is there a clear bias to the way the story's presented? There's an important distinction between bias and interpretation, after all. A bias is when a writer has a clear agenda and all the evidence presented supports what's clearly his or her opinion. A reliable piece of work—and a reliable and interesting piece of creative nonfiction—will present instances of what writers call "counter-example"; that's to say, moments when the evidence doesn't fit the frame, moments when history doesn't make complete sense. After all, think about it: The moments when something doesn't fit are the moments character is most dramatically revealed, isn't it? Any good writer will embrace the chance to show the story is more interesting and complex than a simple soapbox. If it all looks look easy and if the spin is all the same—especially on a piece with no bibliography, no author contact information, and no cultural authority, which means someone doesn't have anything to lose publicly—then it's reader and writer beware.

Are you ready to try an example? What would you say about this imaginary piece of historical information from the web as a source of information?

> "How Elizabeth Became Queen," by Mary O'Flannagan (mary.oflannagan@myuni.edu).
>
> Elizabeth I had an unusually tortuous path to the crown. She was not yet three when her mother was beheaded at the order of her father, Henry VIII. At Henry's death, Elizabeth's sickly half-brother Edward ascended the throne (Jones, 257). Upon his death in 1553, he bequeathed the crown to Lady Jane Grey, cutting Elizabeth out of the succession. Edward's will was set aside, however, and Lady Jane Grey was executed, allowing Elizabeth's sister Mary to ascend the throne. As a devout Catholic, "Bloody Mary" persecuted the Protestants and imprisoned Elizabeth in the Tower of London (*Letters of Queen Elizabeth*, 17). Despite these difficulties, Elizabeth learned to craft her words and fashion her behavior to gain favor and secure her own well-being. When Mary died in 1558, Elizabeth's patience and popularity paid off, and she became, at last, queen of England (Smith, 46; Newberry Library archives).

What do you think? Is this source likely to be reliable and something you could quote with confidence in your creative nonfiction, or is it less likely to be reliable and something you would need to check up on carefully? What things did you notice? Does it have a bibliography? That's an encouraging sign—it does—because, as we said, that means you could check up on this author easily. Who is this author? We have her name and email address: Mary O'Flannagan (mary.oflannagan@myuni.edu). Did you notice that her email address is ".edu"? That means it's from an educational organization. That doesn't mean that Mary O'Flannagan is necessarily right and that we have to take her word for it—after all, all sorts of intelligent people can have different perspectives, especially on matters of historical interpretation and argument—but it does mean that if she has things very wrong, or flagrantly invented them wholesale or plagiarized them, that Mary O'Flannagan's going to have to face real professional consequences; and that means she's more likely to have been careful than, say, your next door neighbor who just decided to put up his muckraking controversial blog where he expresses all those ideas about history that everyone dreads getting trapped into listening to at the neighborhood party. The website of the address is also an academic one, suggesting that Mary is publishing this online article in a professional capacity. She's inviting that kind of scrutiny by publishing it on an academic website, and there's even a good chance this piece has been peer-reviewed.

How about a very sloppy piece of web-based source material? What would that look like? It would maybe look something like this:

> "Family Tree Shows Queen Elizabeth Is Related to Dracula," by the Vampires are Real Historical Society.
>
> Most people think of Vampires as a vast threat to civilization as we know it, if they even believe in Vampires. But Vampires are real, and guess what—Queen Elizabeth I is related to the lineage of one of the most famous vampires of all—Vlad the Impaler. This proves that they are living today.
>
> Lineage charts make it clear that, to quote, "this 15th century murderous count has probably contributed his seeds to the royal family tree."
>
> Haven't you wondered about why Queen Elizabeth wears all those big hats in public? Her bloodline has been diluted, but she's obviously inherited the Vampire's sensitivity to light. I just want to point out that there aren't any mirrors in her publicity photos.

How about that source? It's a bit comic, isn't it? But the hints that we're finding here that this is unreliable material are unfortunately pretty common. What did you notice? The writer is anonymous, and he has a clear bias. Did you notice how there's no specific bibliography and no specific citations, even though there's a quotation!? This author generalizes about sources. That should make you start to wonder as a reader about this work's reliability. The web site address is a regular .com, which isn't necessarily itself a sign, but coupled with all these other hints confirms that the writer doesn't have any professional investment in his credibility; after all, how could the writer? You don't even know who it is, and you couldn't contact him if you wanted to.

Alright, are you ready to try a bit of research and evaluation of source materials on your own? Take my idea of this imaginary book on the history of Queen Elizabeth I. Here's your assignment: See if you can find online or at the library five primary sources on the history of Queen Elizabeth I. Remember how we've said primary sources are different from secondary sources, but can often be found in their bibliographies as well as on the web. Then, your task is also to find three secondary sources on the internet and to evaluate their reliability using the rules of thumb we've talked about here. Which of those sources would you feel comfortable quoting, knowing that the nonfiction contract you have with your readers is always, as a writer, your responsibility?

How to Not Have People Hate You
Lecture 20

In the past decade, the places where we leave information about our lives has changed dramatically. With new kinds of public information about the private lives of millions of people available much more readily, our lives are richly documented—at least, for as long as these digital records last. For writers, this new digital world is either going to make things much easier or nigh on impossible. And these records raise new ethical questions as well.

Personal Records in the Digital Age

- As we have been discussing writing about others' lives, have you had a moment where you thought to yourself, "Good heavens, I hope no one ever writes a biography of me!" Privacy is a hot topic today, not least because of the rise of the Internet and social media.

- Over the past decade, the places where we leave information about our lives has changed dramatically. Digital records can be searched much more easily and without our permission in many cases, and we leave behind different kinds of information than we used to.

- Whether we realize it or not, we are leaving for posterity—and for people in the present, too—a daily diary. In the past, that diary might only be seen by a handful of people. It was also the kind of thing that a creative nonfiction writer had to hope survived … and could be located … and that the owner of it, often a family member, would grant access to it … and that it contained anything useful.

- For writers, this new digital world is either going to make things much easier or nigh on impossible. If, 20 or 30 years from now, I want to write your biography, the chances of my finding a photograph of you at some summer barbeque will be a snap—*if* all this digital information is stored long term. If it is not, if all the

The new phenomenon of digital media offers researchers a wealth of data, but it also raises a host of ethical questions about privacy.

relevant data is deleted over the next 30 years, there will be few or no hard copies to fall back on.

Respecting the Subject

- As a person, I hope for deletion of all my private digital records. But as a writer, I want just the opposite for anyone I might wish to write about.

- How would you feel if I used a digital archive of all your e-mails, texts, and photographs to write your life story? You might object that this data would only offer a partial picture of your life, or that some of that information was too private for public eyes. You might even come to the conclusion that no story can represent the vastly nuanced complexity of a human life.

- Being a creative nonfiction writer brings with it an immense responsibility. These are real people whose lives you are using to tell your story, people who surely deserve respect and to be represented accurately.

- Especially in memoir and autobiography, the line between our lives and the lives of the other people is not always clear. If your parents were abusive and you are writing a memoir of your childhood, whose story is that: yours, theirs, or both?

- You might feel it is simpler to invent characters for your narrative who had the same effect on you as the people in your real life and let the real people remain anonymous and private. But as a nonfiction writer, you cannot do this. You must not.

- One solution to the privacy dilemma is to invent a pen name. The challenge here is that authors today are brands of a sort, and readers want to know about their lives. Readers can and do seek out personal information about writers, especially online.

- If you do choose a pen name, remember that it does not exempt you from the nonfiction contract. Writing under a pseudonym may protect your privacy, but does not allow you to dodge your responsibility to the truth.

A Note about Libel

- I am not a lawyer, so in my cautious way here is a caveat: If you think you are writing something controversial, about living people especially, talk to a lawyer and get proper legal advice.

- If you write something untrue about another person, there is the possibility of being sued for **libel**. The creative nonfiction contract is not just an ethical deal we make with our readers. Breaking it can also put us into a legal bind.

- Defining libel is harder than you might think. In the United States, where libel is generally harder to prove than in many other places, it means that you wrote something untrue (or unverifiable as true) and that you did so maliciously.

- In some other countries—in much of Europe, especially—libel laws are much more liberal. In France, for example, there is a legal idea that people are entitled to their privacy. That means that even if you write something true, you could still be brought to court for libel if it is invasive.

- Smart writers, therefore, document their sources thoroughly. In the meantime, just write your book. When the time comes to publish it, you can let your **literary agent** or editor handle the legal complexities of your particular story.

- One of the invaluable things literary agents do is act as a creative nonfiction author's legal advisor. Agents let writers get on with the business of writing, which is all most of us really want to do anyhow.

The Memoirist's Worry

- How does a memoirist write a book that will not hurt people's feelings and make their friends and loved ones furious? Sometimes it is hard to predict what someone will find hurtful, but there are several rules of thumb a writer can follow.

    - Comedy should be used with care. What you may mean as gentle, another may find harsh. When in doubt, leave it out.

    - Take care not to turn real people into stock characters. If a real person comes off as a single-note figure, you have a problem in your storytelling, not to mention a guaranteed hurtful situation. You are more likely to be forgiven for saying negative things if you also say positive things, if you mention strengths as well as weaknesses.

    - Beware of sharing early drafts with the people in your story. In a draft, you are more likely to say things you might take out later, but people's memories of the offending passages will not be erased.

- On the other hand, you should show the people in your book the final draft before you publish it. If you have gotten something terribly wrong or written something that will shock or hurt them, it is better that it come out when there is time to change things than when the book is on a shelf in the store.

- You can avoid some of these last-minute shocks by engaging the people in your book in your research process from the beginning. Instead of relying on your memories of Uncle Joe, ask your cousins about their father. You will get a fuller picture of your uncle and be able to share your vision of the character with them ahead of time.

Character Sketch—A Writing Exercise

- Write a character sketch of someone you know in which he or she does or says something characteristic. Here is the catch: There must be something negative about the person in this character sketch.

- Once you have written it, read it again and ask yourself: Have I fallen into any of the pitfalls of writing character—not just stock characters and rash comedy mentioned in this lecture, anything we have talked about throughout the course?

- Finally, ask yourself, how would the subject of this character sketch react upon reading it? That is what it is going to feel like to write a memoir or the biography of a living person. It is a sensation at the heart of creative nonfiction.

Important Terms

libel: The legal term for having written something untrue and malicious about another person.

literary agent: A person who acts as an intermediary between an author and a publisher and represents the author's interests legally.

Suggested Reading

Frey, *A Million Little Pieces.*

Telushkin, *Words That Hurt, Words That Heal.*

Questions to Consider

1. Would you want your digital records and private e-mails recorded for posterity, or would you like to see them deleted? How might this change how history is written in the future?

2. Can you imagine writing under a pseudonym, or would that take all the fun out of writing? If you were to adopt a pen name, what would it be, and why?

How to Not Have People Hate You

Lecture 20—Transcript

As we've been talking about all the ways in which a creative nonfiction writer needs to be creative—above all, in how he or she goes about doing research and ferreting out the details of other people's lives—have you had that moment where you thought to yourself, "Good heavens, I hope no one every writes a biography of me"? I wouldn't want people writing about some of the private parts of my life; in fact, the idea fills me with a certain kind of horror. Are you having that same thought yourself at this moment?

In fact, this feeling of exposure is one of the central concerns in the current debate about privacy and the internet really, isn't it? After all, in the last decade, the places where we leave information about our lives have changed dramatically. Not only do we leave information behind in different places—in digital records that can be searched much more easily and without our giving our permission in many cases—but we leave behind different kinds of information today, too. Whether we realize it or not, we're leaving for posterity—and for people in the present, too—a daily diary. In the past, that diary was the kind of thing only a handful of people might see. Hopefully not very many people, because the whole idea was to keep for oneself something private. It was the kind of thing that, if you're a creative nonfiction writer, you had to hope survived—and could be located—and that you could get the owner of it, often a family member, to give you access to it. After that—and this is something we'll talk more about here—you had to hope that once you had access, you'd also be given the right to quote from it.

Today, with new kinds of public information about the private lives of millions of people available much more readily in a way that's keyword searchable and that's digitally archived, our lives are richly documented, for a moment or two at least. Gone, some say, are the days of paper diaries and letters. After all, how often these days do you get a proper letter in your post box any longer? It's emails and social network sites where we chronicle our lives. For writers, this new digital world is either going to make things much easier or nigh on impossible. If I want to write your biography, the chances of my finding 20 or 30 years from now a photograph of you at that summer BBQ where you met the famous artist or writer so-and-so is easier than it ever was, assuming digital information is stored that long. But if it's archived long term, then your private life is going to be laid out for historians in a way it never has been before. On the other hand, if it's not archived—if all your emails 30 years from now are deleted—there will be no manuscript letters for many of those historians in another century to fall back on.

Personally, I hope for deletion of all my private digital records. Can you imagine if all your personal emails were one day the subject of examination? Someone once told me that the best idea was never to write anything in an email that you wouldn't want to see on the front page of *The New York Times.* But who does that, really? I'm probably in luck. It's hard to imagine why anyone would bother to save them once all those internet companies out there have abstracted from them the information about how to market their products to me. I'm rooting for their destruction; but the writer in me, the writer wants just the opposite. If I were writing a hundred years from now my own biography, wow, I really, really, really want to see that decade-worth of emails. From it, I'd be able to piece together an incredibly rich archive of materials to tell a story from.

If you were the subject of this biography that I'm writing now, and if I had access to all your emails, can you see what the problem might be? Think about it for a moment: How would you feel if I used that archive to write your story? It's uncomfortable, isn't it? But maybe you'd say to me, "But wait, that's only a partial picture of my life. You're just looking at things from one perspective. Creating a sweeping narrative of my life out of my emails? Wait, no, there are private things in there. Sometimes I was grumpy and irritated with my mother and wrote to my sister what a pain in the butt she is. But I didn't have to write how much I loved her, because my sister knew that. My mother would be heartbroken to know I said something unkind. It would put my sister in a difficult spot. It wasn't really how I felt in general, just a moment's irritation! It's not fair!" That's how many of us would feel if our private lives were taken and crafted into a narrative, with all the things we've learned in this course about what a narrative needs to have and do, with arcs, and cliffhangers, and conflict, and dramatic tension. We'd feel exposed, that we'd been turned into characters; that no story can represent the vastly nuanced complexity of a human life in its totality; that people's feelings might get hurt, ours especially. All of that's true.

Yet we're writers, and we write stories. Being a writer brings with it a kind of responsibility; and for creative nonfiction writers, that responsibility's immense. Because think about how you would feel, and then remember, you're writing nonfiction: There are real people whose lives you're using to tell your story; people who surely deserve to have the rich complexity of their lives honored; who, no matter what they've done or not done, deserve more than being reduced, especially, to stock characters. They deserve to be represented accurately; to not have words put into their mouths; to not have their passions and private thoughts misrepresented or invented. You, as a writer, want to tell the story because, of course, especially in memoir and autobiography, the line between our lives and the lives of the other people who impact us isn't always a clear one. If your parents were cruelly abusive and you're writing the memoir of your childhood, whose story is that, yours, or theirs, or everyone's? It's a difficult position; and remember how I said way back at the beginning of the course, when we were talking about the nonfiction contract and the scandal surrounding James Frey's *A Million Little Pieces*, how I said maybe some of the reason he made things up was exactly because of this? Because it's hard to write a story about your own addiction and to talk about the other people you met with your illness and how they impacted you without exposing their private lives in a way that you know is going to be hurtful. How much simpler to invent characters who had the same effect on you in the narrative as happened in real life, and let the other people—those people whose only error was in becoming your friend and knowing you—remain anonymous and private.

As a nonfiction writer, you can't always do this. You must not. The result is scandal. But the temptation is one any creative nonfiction writer understands. It's one you might find yourself struggling with. After all, you want to tell your story; but you don't want your entire family to hate you afterward. Worse, you don't want your entire family to sue you, either; and you'd be amazed how writing even something as simple, let's say, as your family history—you know, how your amazing family emigrated to Katmandu, or tamed the wildebeests, or had secret love affairs in the 17th century with a dozen princes, or sailed the seas as pirates—how even that history can send some members of your family into fits of irritation with you. People are often just as invested in history as they are in the present.

What are you going to do here as a writer of nonfiction? How are you going to tell your story—and tell it both truthfully and dramatically, with a great, dazzling narrative and well-developed characters—and still be allowed to come to family holidays? Of course, you could just invent a pen name. That's one solution; and actually, this is a serious proposition. Here's the thing about being a writer: Ten years ago, maybe even five years ago, before I started building my career as a writer publicly, I was happy with the fact that there was no photograph of me on the internet. I was still anonymous. I also had my privacy. Once you become a *New York Times* bestselling author, however, that changes. Today there are dozens of photographs; some of them ones I dislike heartily and over which I have no control. If you want to write a book that will hit the Times list—and why shouldn't you—it's something you want to think about. Authors today are brands of a sort, and readers want to know about the lives of their favorite authors. I'm always curious myself to see those magazine articles where you see an author's home, aren't you? It's the reason why thousands of people flock to Ernest Hemingway's home in Key West each year, or Jack London's estate in northern California. It's neat to see where an author lived and worked, isn't it? That's great, except sometimes when you're the author and when someone gets angry about how you represented some obscure 18th-century duke who happens to be his great-great-great uncle's second cousin thrice removed; and then, the fact that someone can find out a good deal of information about your private life on the internet—maybe even your home address—is unsettling. It's one of the reason authors spend a fair amount of time at cocktail parties talking about creative ways to protect their basic privacy.

If I had it to do all over again, I think I might've started my writing career under a pen name. Many writers do it; but you don't know that they do, because, well, that's the whole point of the pseudonymity, isn't it? Maybe if you're married to a high-profile executive whose career would be jeopardized by your writing, or maybe if you're writing about stories so sensitive but compelling that your privacy seems especially important, you'll want to consider adopting a pen name. If you do it, it makes sense to do it in the beginning of your career as a writer. In order for it to work for you, however, you have to be very good at keeping secrets; and for many writers, half the fun of being an author is having people know you've written something wonderful. If you do choose a pen name, remember that a pen name doesn't mean you don't have to honor the exact same nonfiction contract as any writer. Writing under a pseudonym is a way to protect your privacy, but it can't be a way of dodging our responsibility as authors.

Let's say you want to write that family history under your own name, but you're still worried. What can I write? What can't I write? How do I prevent my family from disowning me? What do I do especially when I think I'm showing someone in a good light, in a way that's affectionate and comic, but when there's a good chance they'll see it differently and perhaps even be hurt by it?

First, let's think just about some of the basic legal parameters. This isn't a legal course and I'm not a lawyer, so in my cautious way here's the caveat: If you think you're writing something controversial, about living people especially, talk to your own lawyer and get proper legal advice. This isn't that. But what in a general way any writer wants to think about is that fact that if we write something that's untrue about another person, there's the possibility of being sued for libel. The creative nonfiction contract, then, isn't just an ethical deal we make with our readers—though it is that—but breaking it can also put us into a whole other kind of mess. We can't make up things about other people; we can only write what's true. As we've seen, sometimes the truth is a hard thing to nail down. This is why, in the last lesson, we talked about how important it is to have verifiable sources for any truth statements that we make in our writing. In fact, journalists are often required to have more than one source for each piece of information.

What is libel? That's a harder question than you might think it is, too. In the United States, where libel is generally harder to prove than in many other places, it means that you wrote something untrue—or unverifiable as true—and that you did it in order to be mean-spirited. This is why the divorce revenge memoir is a challenging genre, tempting though the idea of writing a hum-zinger is. It's why you want to be especially careful to document all your facts if you're writing a book that shows your ex-husband's famous grandfather was an undiscovered Nazi, or that that your sister-in-law is a brothel madam. That's why you want to be careful as you're writing a terrible childhood memoir, which is a surprisingly popular genre. Because even if you get the details of Nazi activities or the brothel address correct, if someone is furious with you and you got something else wrong, even something seemingly trivial, the possibility of libel exists all the same. Here's something even trickier: In some other countries—in much of Europe, especially—it's much easier to get sued for libel. In France, for example, there's a legal idea that people are entitled to their privacy. That means even if you write something true that you could still be brought to court for libel if it is invasive. So what does a smart writer do? Document, document, document your sources.

For now, just write your book. When the time comes to publish it, you'll have all your sources well documented. From there, when you get that big book contract, you can let your agent or editor handle the legal complexities of your particular story. Have you ever wondered why writers have literary agents and rely on them and often thank them so enthusiastically in their acknowledgements? It's because one of the invaluable things literary agents do is to act as a creative nonfiction author's legal advisor. Agents let writers get on with the business of writing, which is all most of us really want to do anyhow.

Now you know about libel, and agents, and the marketing of authors and pen-names. But for most writers, in most cases, you aren't going to have to worry about anything like this. Chances are your real worry is the one that all writers worry about, especially if we're writing memoir: How do I write a book that won't hurt people's feelings and make everyone in my life furious with me? It's especially hard because sometimes what someone's going to find hurtful is hard to predict. If you're writing about other people, then it's a good question to ask yourself. But from there, what are you actually going to do in your writing? How will you manage this? The first thing is you have to write the truth and write it accurately, of course; but what do you do beyond that?

Here are some of the places where other people tend to get more upset with us as writers. The first is when we use comedy. Comedy has an important role in narrative, right? It can bring a scene alive. It can establish wonderful character. It can draw a reader into the story and set the tone brilliantly. So you're writing your family memoir. Let's say you're writing a family memoir about Uncle Joe, who fought in the Second World War as a soldier.

And you admire Uncle Joe; it's a story about his heroism. But you also remember him from when you were a child, how he wore purple polyester trousers and didn't bathe enough; and how your Aunt Nancy nagged him and they bickered. So you start your memoir with a funny scene of how you remember Uncle Joe. You think it's sweet; it's comic; I'm showing my readers the intimate and awkward side of this man that I'm going to go on to show is a real hero. It's a way to draw the reader into the story; and darn it, it's true, he did wear those pants.

So you write your scene, and you share it with your cousin, Joe Junior. Guess what? That's right; Joe Junior is livid. "How could you mock my father like that? How could you make fun of a hero?" "But Joe Junior," you try to explain, "it's sweet and comic. That's how I remember Uncle Joe. And you didn't keep reading, to the part where I said what an amazing hero Uncle Joe was." But Cousin Joe has already hung up on you, and you aren't going to get invited to his daughter's wedding all of a sudden. In fact, Joe Junior tells everyone at the wedding how you're writing a book that makes fun of Uncle Joe the war hero. What a jerk you are, everyone says.

This is not what every author hopes for, is it? So writer's rule number one for avoiding conflict in memoir: Use comedy very carefully. It requires the lightest touch imaginable. When in doubt, leave it out; or let it come across in dialogue, where someone can either pick up on the humor or miss it entirely. Sometimes the funniest things are the things you don't explain to people. As every comedian knows, sometimes the funniest guy in the room is the straight man. In memoir, you want to be that guy.

Know what will make Cousin Joe even angrier with you, though, than a bit of humor? That's turning Aunt Nancy—or any person in the memoir—into a stock character. Remember how we talked about stock characters earlier in the course? How these are characters who are basically stereotypes of a sort? How they serve just a structural function in a narrative but never come alive as characters? If we turn Aunt Nancy here in our imaginary memoir into the "Shrewish Wife" who never does anything other than nag and is the kind of person who's the butt of all those tasteless nagging wife jokes, here's the trouble: First, Aunt Nancy doesn't really do much for us as writers. We'd want to ask ourselves very clearly: Do I have a character here who is really part of a great narrative arc, or is she just a flat and unnecessary element? If she's not part of a great story, then we've got a bigger problem than Cousin Joe; we've got a problem with our storytelling. Maybe we realize that later in our revision; but we made the mistake of showing Cousin Joe the draft. What's his response going to be? He's going to be furious. Now he's going to write you the email and say, "How dare you! You make my mother look like a terrible person! How could you do then when she was so kind to you? She and my dad loved each other, and you're not showing what a complicated and wonderful person she was. No wedding invitation for you!"

So writer's rule of keeping friends and family number two: Beware of turning living people into stock characters. People's lives are complex, and you're more likely to be forgiven for saying negative things if you also say positive things and give a sense of the complicated and nuanced character who, like all of us, has private struggles and character strengths as well as weaknesses.

Rule number three: Beware, too, of sharing the draft of your manuscript with the people in it early in the process. A draft says, "Weigh in, I'm still revising, what do you think?" You'll likely find people weighing in rather emphatically once you invite it; and in a draft, you're more likely to say things you might take out later, on colder consideration, as your narrative comes together and you see the story clearly in your own mind at the end. The trouble with writing something in a draft that upsets someone, even if you were going to revise it out anyhow, is that you still have an upset person; someone who's not likely to forget what you wrote the first time. Share your draft with your writing group, with friends, with strangers in cafés if you must; but resist the temptation to share it with the people intimately connected to it until the end.

But you say to me, "Wait, wouldn't it be better to get them in on the ground floor and to just talk about all of this?" It's a good point; and here's rule number four for memoir especially: You'll have to show the people in your book the final draft before you publish it if you care about these relationships. After all, once you publish it, everyone's going to be able to read it. There's no point in trying to hope they won't notice; and if you've really got something terribly wrong or have written something that ends up being terribly hurtful, without intending it, it's far, far better to know when you still have a chance to make a change rather than when it's there on a shelf in a bookstore.

In the end, anyone portrayed in your book, you're going to have to show the book to this person in the final stages. One of the best ways to lay the groundwork for that final moment absolutely is to engage the people who are going to be portrayed in the book—or whose family members will be—in the process at the very beginning. Interview Cousin Joe. Say to him, "Hey, Cousin Joe, do you remember how your dad wore those polyester pants? What else do you remember about him? Tell me about your mom. I know sometimes she nagged. What do you think was her real anxiety?" Or you might ask Cousin Joe to look at a photo album with you; an album where, no surprise, Uncle Joe is in polyester once again. Ask Joe tell you his stories about those photos. Ask him to send you an email with his character sketch of his dad; and ask his brothers and sisters and all those other cousins who are going to be at that wedding that you might not get invited to if they would do the same: to share stories, memories, and images of what that time was like.

Remember that part of the great skill of a creative nonfiction writer is research; and part of doing great research is learning to be a great interviewer. In an interview, as in life, the truth is that most of us just want our stories and experiences to be heard and affirmed as valid. Once Cousin Joe knows how you remember Uncle Joe—and once he knows that you were interested in and hopefully able to incorporate into your family memoir some of the details of his memories—there's a context for Cousin Joe to read your final story in. He can say, "Ok, that's not how I would've told that story; but I believe that this is true to my cousin the author's experience of the family story, and let's hear how he or she tells it." You know, you might learn some amazing things you didn't know about Uncle Joe's wartime heroism, too. As we've already seen, details of people's lives and historical moments get tucked away in all sorts of odd places, and maybe Second Cousin Jemina has a whole drawer full of his wartime letters that she's just never mentioned to anyone in the family.

So beware of sharing work in progress with the people being portrayed in your memoir, but welcome them enthusiastically into your research process in the beginning. Promise them that before you publish the history of our amazing family, you'll show them the final manuscript. In between, welcome to the sometimes lonely life of a writer, where much of what happens, happens only between you and the page anyhow; where you learn to rely on other writers and writing groups; where you revise in private and where you struggle with all those questions of: Is this the best way to tell this story? Are my characters compelling, is the scene dramatic, is the prose beautiful; and have I kept the nonfiction contract and always remembered that, if I'm writing nonfiction, that I'm writing about the lives of real other people?

In the next lesson, we'll talk about how sometimes that lonely process of drafting goes, and how to make it feel less lonely by finding those writers' groups and friends who can read drafts for you. We'll talk, too, about learning how to take and give feedback, especially the most useful kind: the critical kind.

Here at the end of the lesson today, here's your assignment: Write a character sketch of someone you know in which you introduce your reader to this person by describing a scene in which you remember them doing or saying something characteristic. There's just one other rule: There must be something negative about the person in it. Then, once you've written it, read it again and ask yourself: Have I fallen into any of the pitfalls of writing character? Not just the ones we've talked about here today about stock characters and rash comedy, but that we've talked about throughout the course. Think of this as a moment to review everything we've learned so far about what makes for good character in a narrative. After you've written your character sketch, ask yourself one last question: What would happen if this person were to read this? You don't have to send it; just ask the question and see what the answer feels like. That's what it's going to feel like to write a memoir or the biography of a living person. It's a sensation at the heart of creative nonfiction.

Revising Your Work

Lecture 21

There are moments in our process when we might want to share our work with people other than our subjects. Three of the toughest questions any writer has to face are how to find good readers for work in progress, how to give and receive feedback usefully, and how to revise the work. A large part of understanding good feedback comes from recognizing poor feedback, and the best way to get good feedback is by being the sort of reader who gives good feedback to fellow writers.

Why Writers Need Feedback

- We all get invested in our writing. Writers worked hard on their work. They put something of their hearts and souls and egos into it, and they know it is not perfect; if it were perfect, they would not be calling it a draft and looking for feedback. The draft stage is a vulnerable period for any writer.

- As painful as it may be, receiving feedback on a draft is a necessary part of every writer's process. Most of us get too close to the writing at some point to know exactly what needs to be done.

- The challenges of finding good feedback are many: How do you manage all these complicated feelings? How do you find good readers? How do you learn what advice is worth taking and what you should ignore? How do you know when you are ready to share your work—and when you are not?

Choosing the Moment

- When you look at your writing, do you know what the problems are already and do you know how to fix them? If so, then you should fix them before sharing your work. The most valuable moment to share your work is when you know the problem but do not know the solution or when you cannot quite pinpoint the problem.

- Sometimes, writers seek feedback not because they are having problems but because we are frustrated with the hard work that writing involves and what we really want is encouragement. This is a completely natural impulse, but this is not a respectful use of someone's time. You are also likely to be disappointed; if you ask someone to read and give you criticism, they may say they love your work, but they will also give you the criticism you asked for.

- If what you really want is a pep talk, you should look for—or start up—a writers' support group. Get a group of hardworking writers together once a month for the explicit purpose of cheering each other on, sharing stories of triumph and disappointment. You can often find contact information for writers' support groups on bulletin boards in libraries, through book clubs, or in cafes. If you cannot find one in your area, you can put a notice up yourself.

- If you really do need and want constructive criticism, this is still difficult terrain for many writers. You know there are problems *x*, *y*, and *z*; you must be prepared for a reader to identify problems *a* and *m*, too. You have to be genuinely open to receiving whatever criticism the reader offers and to revising your work, too. Otherwise, the process is futile.

Good feedback is essential for all writers, from beginners to seasoned professionals.

- The result of good feedback is always going to be learning that you have more work to do. It is easy, even natural, to get defensive, but it is not productive. So here is the best way to set yourself up for success:

- First, do everything you can think to do on that piece of work, so it is in the best possible shape.
- Second, be honest with yourself about whether you are ready to hear criticism and do not ask for it until you are ready.
- Third, count on the fact that, after you get the feedback, you will need to invest time and energy in revising.

- If possible, time your feedback so it does not coincide with major life events, big work obligations, or other inevitable distractions. The time when most of us have the energy to undertake a big revision is when the reader's comments are fresh. If we have questions, it also helps if the reader still has our work clearly in mind.

- Professional etiquette is either to return the favor of a careful reading when asked or to buy your reader a nice dinner. A good reader will have spent hours on your work, and it is a big favor. Among writers, in fact, it is the biggest favor of all.

The Right Reader and the Right Feeback

- There are better readers and worse readers, and sometimes even when we are ready to hear feedback, the criticism we get is not terribly useful. How do you tell the difference between good and less good feedback, and how can you increase your chances of getting the good stuff?

- The worst kind of feedback actually is the kind that says, "This is perfect! Don't change a thing!" It feels good for about 90 seconds, and you are getting it because the reader thinks you want a pep talk. But you already knew there were problems, so being told it is perfect is pretty useless.

- The second-worst kind of feedback is what writers and writing professors call unconstructive criticism. This kind of feedback has two flaws: First, it tends to criticize the writer, rather than the writing, and second, it tends to be vague and meaningless. The hallmarks of such criticism are phrases like, "*Your* problem is … " and "This just didn't interest me."

- The personal nature of unconstructive criticism is unhelpful because it connects you and your work. What we all need to learn to do as writers is to separate our egos from our prose. Those two things have nothing to do with each other. Statements about broad sweeping problems with your work are pretty unhelpful because they do not help a writer think about ways to fix the problems.

- **Constructive criticism** talks about the work, not the person. It addresses specific problems and makes concrete suggestions about how to solve them. It also points out what is strong about the piece. Finally, it acknowledges how complicated fixing a problem is, because sometimes by fixing one problem, we create others.

- You will not get ideal criticism very often. Most of the time, you will get something between the extremes of unconstructive and ideal. But there are things you can do to increase your chances of getting good feedback, and part of that includes giving good feedback to your writing partners.

- One of the best ways to get useful feedback is to ask for it. Send a letter with your writing calling out the specific problems you see in the work, mentioning any solutions you have already tried, and asking for advice. You should also mention that you are open to hearing about other problems the reader might identify. Do not forget to thank the reader for his or her time, too!

- This kind of letter accomplishes three things: First, it says I am talking about my work as a piece of writing—not as part of my personal identity. Second, it says I have done some thoughtful work already; I am not wasting your time. Third, requests concrete ideas, thereby shaping the reader's response. It looks professional and helps the reader focus his or her efforts.

The Rules of Revision

- Once you have the feedback, it is time to get to work. Good feedback will make you feel energized and excited to get back to the project, because you will know that you have some tools to make your piece better.

- You should never feel obligated to take your readers' advice. Often, a reader's good suggestion will lead you to an even better one—one you might not have come upon if someone had not helped you to see your work differently.

- There are just two rules to the revision process:

  - First, be willing to change anything and everything. Be willing give it a try at least. Nothing in the world is harder for a writer than cutting whole pages—or whole chapters But there are times when that is the best solution.

  - Second, always save a copy of your original. In fact, save copies of everything at every stage in the process. Save what you cut. Save your files before you made changes. Sometimes you were right the first time. Back up everything. Back up often.

Giving Feedback—A Writing Exercise

- Try writing a wonderful feedback letter to yourself. You can use your current work in progress, or if you do not have one, use one of the exercises you wrote earlier in this course. (If you really do not have any work of your own, you may write something for a friend instead.)

- After writing your feedback, take an honest look at it. Is it objective, frank, and balanced? If so, maybe you are ready to ask someone to read your draft. That letter to yourself is the basis of a letter you can write to your reader, inviting the kind of response that you would find most useful.

Important Term

constructive criticism: Criticism of a piece of writing that works to help the writer imagine improvements rather than putting down the writer and his or her abilities.

Suggested Reading

Levine, *The Writing & Critique Group Survival Guide*.

Prose, *Reading Like a Writer*.

Questions to Consider

1. What kind of feedback would you most like to receive on a piece of your writing?

2. What is your writing style? Do you write many drafts, or do you plod slowly through a single draft, revising each sentence carefully as you work? How will this affect your revision strategies?

Revising Your Work

Lecture 21—Transcript

In our last lesson, we started talking about the writing and drafting process, and about how there are moments in our process when we might want to share our work with people other than our subjects. In this lesson, let's think a bit more about those process issues; about how to find good readers for our work in progress, how to give and receive feedback usefully, and how to think about the part of writing that for many writers is the most difficult part: revising our work. We'll do a hands-on exercise together to review some of the skills we've learned together so far to give you a chance to try your hand at some revision and feedback.

I just said that revision, and all that comes with it, is the hardest part for many authors of the writing process. Let's think about why that might be. By the time you've got to the point of revision and getting editorial comments on your work from a reader, you've necessarily written something; you have some sort of manuscript. The simple truth is this: We all get invested in our writing. You've worked hard on it; you've put something of your heart, soul, and ego into it, and you know it's not perfect. If it were perfect, it wouldn't be a draft, would it? You wouldn't be looking for a reader to give you suggestions for how to improve it. But it's still hard to imagine taking it all apart and rearranging it. It's hard after all that work to hear what the weaknesses of something are when what we want at that moment to celebrate, maybe get a bit of affirmation.

So a draft is a vulnerable state for a writer. You're invested enough that criticism is going to sting. You're honest enough with yourself to know that it still needs work. But chances are at this point you're too close to the piece of writing to know exactly what needs to be done; and that's why we turn to readers, isn't it? To get fresh eyes on our writing and to get an idea of how a real reader is going to respond to our story. So we ask for some feedback, and we're trying to deal with how criticism makes us feel. How do you manage all these complicated emotions and investments? How do you find good readers? How do you learn what advice is worth taking and what you should ignore? How do we help our readers give us useful criticism and good suggestions? How do you know when you're just not ready to share your work with anyone at all because it wouldn't be useful for you? Those are questions every writer, from the beginning amateur to the most seasoned professional, struggles with.

Let's think about first things first: Sometimes you aren't ready to share your work with anyone. Sometimes anything someone says is going to push you over that edge to where you just throw in the towel or find yourself too frustrated to even imagine continuing. We need to respect above all our own process as a writer. How do you know if you're ready? Here are two questions to ask yourself. The first one is: When I look at this piece of writing, do I know already what the problems are already, and do I know how to fix them? Do you know, for example, that there's a missing transition on page 16 of your manuscript, and that it's just a matter of sitting down to fill that in? Do you know that there are sentence fragments and you need to fix them? Do you know that you have an underdeveloped character, but you see, of course, how you're going to shape the voice in your next revision? If so—if you know the problem and the solution—then you shouldn't be sharing your work with readers; not with readers who you're asking to give you any serious feedback at any rate.

Why is that? Because good readers—people who will read your work and go to the effort of really thinking about your draft and helping you to see things differently—are hard to find and extremely valuable. If you ask someone to read work that you already know has problems that you already know how to fix, you're wasting the time and good will of that reader. What's going to happen? The reader will come back to you and chances are say, "This transition isn't working. This character isn't developed," and your response will be, "Oh, yeah, I know that." The reader thinks, "Great, you gave me something sloppy and you don't really need me to read this, why are you wasting my time?" The next time—the time when you really do need that great reader to help you with a problem—you're going to find someone less willing. If you know the problem and the solution, then do the revision that has to happen. A manuscript that's ready to share with a reader and to receive real feedback is one on which you've already done everything you know how to do on it already.

That doesn't mean that you've solved all the problems in your writing. The most valuable moment to share your work with other writers is the moment where you know what the problem is, or that there's one here somewhere and you can't quite pinpoint it, and you don't know how to fix it. You're stuck trying to figure out what a revision would look like. Those are the moments when someone else can most usefully help you. Another writer can say, "Hey, did you know there's a transition missing here? I think that's why you've got this character problem, actually. You could fix it by doing something like this." That kind of advice in the writing process is invaluable, and the reason is because it helps you solve a problem that you weren't seeing or weren't seeing the solution to. It allows your reader to offer you help and ideas that you're genuinely going to be able to welcome, rather than dismiss as obvious. That's a fair and respectful use of another writer's time; and as you know from our conversations about how hard it is to find the time in our busy lives to write at all, a writer's time is precious.

That's the first question to ask before deciding to share your work: Is this work really ready for readers, or am I jumping the gun? Do you know why most of us jump the gun? It's because we're frustrated with the hard work that writing involves, and what we really want isn't feedback but encouragement, don't we? Sometimes, when we share our work with a reader, what we really want this person to say is, "Wow, this is great; you're a fantastic writer, keep writing. It's all worth the effort, really it is." It's a completely natural thing to want, a bit of an occasional pep talk. But do you know what? If that's what you want, then you probably aren't ready to share your manuscript either. When you ask someone to read your work and when you tell them, "This is a draft, what do you think?" 99 percent of the time your reader is going to come back to you and say, "Wonderful work in progress; here and here and here and here are the problems I see, though." Why? Because you invited criticism; that's what we're doing when we ask someone to read our manuscripts, whether it's our friends, our writers' group, our classmates in a creative writing workshop, our professors, our editors, or our agents.

So question number two to ask yourself before you ask someone to read your work is this: What do I really want from this person right now? Let's say you aren't really ready to share your work and that what you want is a pep talk. There's nothing wrong with that. But where would you go to find this? The creative writing workshop isn't the place, and neither is the craft-based writer's circle. Instead, what you need to find or start on your own is a writers' support group. A friend of mine who's a wonderful writer started a great one of these in the town we live in, and she named it the "Toast and Boast." The idea was to get together a hardworking group of writers once a month for the explicit purpose of cheering each other on. We had wine; we ate cheese and crackers and chocolate; and each person went around and said what she was working on, what manuscript she'd finished drafting or had sent out to an editor or what she had published, and we raised a glass to toast the writer. Sometimes, of course, the writers would admit to being discouraged. A manuscript gets stuck; a parent or a partner gets sick; an editor turns you down flat and you get some mean and unhelpful feedback. The purpose of the group was the commiseration of colleagues. It was a wonderful group and very useful and supportive.

But do you notice what we didn't do in the Toast and Boast? We didn't read and comment on each other's work. If what you really need is encouragement rather than smart criticism, what you need is to set up your own Toast and Boast, or your own writer's circle, or your tongue-in-cheek fan club. You need a supportive spouse who asks you at the end of the day, "So how did the writing go?" or a mother who'll brag about you to all her friends and make sure you know about it. You can find writer support groups in local communities everywhere—on bulletin boards in libraries, through book clubs or in cafes—and if you don't find one, you can put up the notice yourself on the bulletin board yourself inviting like-minded writers to contact you. But you don't need feedback on your manuscript at that moment. If you're ready to share your manuscript and do really need and want constructive criticism, it's still difficult terrain for many writers. You know there are problems x and y and z, and you have to be prepared for a reader to identify problems a and m, too. When you ask for feedback, you have to find a way to make yourself genuinely open to receiving it and to revising your work, too. Otherwise, it's futile. It's harder than it sounds, isn't it? After all, the result of good feedback is always going to be learning that you have more work to do. It's easy to get defensive; in fact, it's natural. But it's not productive.

Here's my advice for how to know when you're ready for some writerly criticism: First, do everything you can think to do on that piece of work. Work to your limits as a writer so you can welcome someone else's solution to the problems that stump you. Two, be honest with yourself. "Am I ready to hear criticism?" Three, count on the fact that after you get the feedback, the result's going to be returning to this piece fresh and prepared to invest time and energy in it. Sometimes that means you have to put a manuscript in a drawer for a few weeks before you pass it along to a reader and work on something else. It means you probably want to time your feedback so it doesn't coincide with major life events, or big work obligations, or other inevitable distractions; because the time when most of us have the energy to undertake a big revision is when the reader's comments are fresh and when, if we have questions, the reader still has our work clearly in mind and can help to answer them. Professional etiquette is either to return the favor of a careful reading when asked or to buy your reader a nice dinner. A good reader will have spent hours on your work, and it's a big favor. Among writers, in fact, it's the biggest favor of all; and when someone offers to read your work for you, it's a mark of generosity and respect for your art.

That said, there are, of course, readers who are better and worse than others; and sometimes even when we're ready to hear feedback, the criticism that we get is more or less useful. How do you tell the difference between good and less good feedback? How can you increase your chances of getting the former and decrease your chances of getting the latter? Just as importantly, how do you give good criticism, too? The worst kind of feedback actually is the kind that says, "This is great, perfect, don't change a thing!" It feels good for about 90 seconds, and you're getting it because the reader thinks you want a pep talk and not a conversation. But you already knew there were problems you needed to solve, didn't you? So being told something is perfect that you know has problems is officially useless. Nice; but useless.

But the second worst kind of feedback to get is what writers and professors call "unconstructive criticism"; and you already know its hallmarks, don't you? Think about it for a moment: What would you least like to hear someone say about your work? What would be the most destructive feedback you could get? Think about it for a minute, because I'll bet you already know what I'm going to say.

What did you come up with? Feedback that makes a personal judgment on the writer is awful, isn't it? After all, it's the polar opposite of the pep talk. This is the kind of criticism where the reader connects the writing and the writer. Telltale sentences begin, "This piece doesn't work for me, and your problem is …" Your problem? That's connecting you and your work; and that's not helpful at all, because what we all need to learn to do as writers is to separate our egos from our prose. Our prose can always be better, always; but I'm sure you're a perfectly wonderful human being. Those two things have nothing to do with each other, and unhelpful criticism is the kind that suggests they do, even if it's meant to be intimate and friendly.

What else? Statements about broad, sweeping problems with your work are pretty unhelpful, too, aren't they? How does it help anyone to hear, "I don't think this piece is working right now; it just didn't interest me. I think you need to do a major revision." That's so general that it's perfectly useless. It doesn't help you understand the problem, and it doesn't help you to think about ways to fix it; it's a general condemnation. It would be enough to make any writer think about throwing in the towel or strangling the reader. But if you get this kind of feedback you need to think, "OK, this isn't helpful. How can I change that dynamic?"

So unconstructive criticism: It's personal and it's vague. Those are its worst features. That means useful criticism, the kind you're going to write when you're a great reader, is going to be the opposite. It's going to talk about the work and not the person. It's going to be precise about the problems you see and why they're emerging; and if at all, as generously as possible, it's going to give the writer concrete ideas about how to solve them. It's also going to point out what's strong about the piece; and it's going to gesture toward how complicated fixing problems is, because sometimes by fixing one problem in a narrative we create others.

Let me give you two examples. Here's what an unconstructive peer review looks like:

> Dear Jane,
>
> Well, I see why you needed a reader. This piece isn't working for me yet, and I think your problem is you don't really know if there's an interesting narrative arc in here yet. I thought the main character was undeveloped and (sorry!) boring. You really

> need to fix that I think to keep the reader's interest. At least, you lost mine. Also, that long section in chapter 4, where you talk about the history of the Inquisition, I'm not seeing what that gets you. I imagine you see it as somehow related to the main character's motivations, but, well, I don't think it works. And a whole lot of the other problems in this manuscript are a result of that mistake. The title's okay. Good luck revising.

Ouch; and more than ouch, do you see why this is perfectly useless to a writer? Would you know where to begin revising if you received this feedback? Me, I'd like to begin by revising who I asked to give me feedback in the future.

Now here's an example of what would be useful, but honest and direct feedback, from that same reader.

> Dear Jane,
>
> Thanks for sharing this piece with me. It was such a pleasure to see what you've been working on. As I think about my own writing, what I found most useful to see you managing so deftly in this piece is the shift between third and first person perspectives in the descriptive passages (pages 56 and 101 especially). In terms of the places in the text where you could strengthen the narrative arc for your reader (as you mention in your note), here is what I am noticing. Let me know if you have any questions about what I'm seeing. It's a tricky subject, I can see. This manuscript has to balance a lot of concrete historical detail and a compelling narrative arc, and it's a complex negotiation. The moments where I think the manuscript tilts toward too much detail and where the reader risks losing the narrative momentum are usually passages where the characterization comes too late to guide us. So, for example, on page 81, where you are writing about the Inquisition. The manuscript starts with historical detail and some dramatic events (for example, the execution of that scientist in the castle on page 82), but the main character that frames this section doesn't

> appear until 5 pages later. What about thinking about moving that section from page 86 to page 92 to the front of the chapter and reshaping from there? I think what this would achieve is to give the reader a character to hang onto and to identify with as the narrative moves forward. Also, by the by, I'm overall in favor of but not in love with the title, that's my feedback. Good luck with the revisions, and congratulations on a complete draft! That's a fabulous achievement. Fred.

Wow, now this; this is dream feedback. Concrete suggestions; a clear line between the writer and the work. It identifies problems and solutions. It gestures toward the complexity of the project. It encourages the writer, but is direct and honest, and frankly rather critical. But this is the kind of criticism only a generous reader can give you, and it's worth more than a hundred pep talks to a writer. This is the kind of criticism, I won't kid you, you aren't going to get very often. You're more likely to encounter most of the time something in between those two extremes. But this is the kind of criticism it would be great if you can learn to write for your colleagues. It's the kind of criticism that it would be even better if you can learn to give yourself as a writer, in your own internal conversations. And it's the kind of criticism we want you to be able to set yourself up to get and have the best chances of receiving; because there are things you can do to make this kind of response more likely.

Any idea what you can do? Did you notice in my second example—the example of the good feedback—the reader mentions the letter the author wrote and sent along with the manuscript? That's a great idea. In fact, that's what any writer can do at any time to increase the chances of getting the kind of feedback that's going to be the most useful. After all, this is a conversation, isn't it? That's what we all want as writers: an informed and intelligent conversation about our work. That means, since it's our work after all, we should be the ones to begin it and set the tone. So write a letter to your reader. Say to Fred, "Hey, Fred, thanks for taking the time to do this. I really appreciate it. Here's where I'm stuck right now. Here's how I've tried to fix it, but I'd really appreciate any fresh ideas about what's working, what's not working, and ways you can see to help me out of my writerly predicament. And I'm open to other things I haven't seen, too. Concrete suggestions about changes you would make; wow, that would be so useful. Let me know if I can return the favor."

But do you see that what that letter to the reader says is three things? First, it says, "I'm talking about my work as a piece of writing, not as part of my personal identity. You can do that, too, don't worry. I'm not overly sensitive; I'm a professional." Second, it says, "I've done everything I can think to do here. Let me tell you what I've tried, how I've conceived of the problem, where I'm stuck trying to manage it. I'm not wasting your time. If you take the extra time to help me think through how to solve this craft dilemma, I'm ready to take on board good suggestions." Third, it says, "What I'd love are concrete ideas, about this or other problems you see." It shapes the response. After all, most people who are nice enough to do us this favor want to give us what we're looking for. Communicate your hopes, and make it clear that you know there are strengths here as well as weaknesses. You don't need a pep talk; though, of course, we all appreciate a genuine compliment. But you know, it's not half bad either. You're calm, cool, confident, collected, at least in your authorial presentation. Deep down, maybe you're an artistic wreck. So what; every artist is sometimes. But wrecks don't get the kind of advice that artists really need and deserve to move their work forward.

Where do you find this kind of reader, and what do you do once you've received this dream letter? That's actually the easy part of this whole equation. You find these readers by making friends with other writers, by joining your local writers' group, by setting up your own, or by taking a creative writing class. What do you do once you have the feedback? You get back to work, don't you? Good feedback will make you feel energized to get back to the project because you'll know that you've been given some tools to make your piece better, even if you don't take the advice. Because you never need to; it's always your piece of writing in the end. You're the author; it's your decision. But often a good suggestion about how to solve a problem will lead you to recognize an even better one; one you wouldn't perhaps have come upon if someone hadn't helped you to see this piece differently. Sometimes the process of revision will take you in entirely unexpected places.

There are just two rules to thinking about revision: One is, be willing to change anything. Be willing to try it out. Sure, we all get invested in sentences. Nothing in the world is harder for a writer than cutting out whole pages, maybe even sometimes whole chapters that aren't working; but there are times when that's the only best solution. Writers are ruthless with themselves. All that matters in the end has to be the story: writing the best one possible. Time doesn't matter. That you spent six week going down a blind alley is part of what happens even to the most experienced writers among us. Ego can't matter. The work has to be more important than our feelings of frustration, regret, or urgency. The most successful writers learn to be their own best critics; and just think, isn't that much better? Far better that you say to yourself, "Blimey, this isn't working, I need to fix it," than hear it from an agent when you've only got maybe one chance to impress him, or from an editor when you have only one chance to get a contract, or from a reviewer in the *New York Times* when it's far too late to fix it; and you know in your heart of hearts it's true, you should've revised that section. So rule one of revision: Be willing to consider changing absolutely anything in the revision process. Be willing to see from vastly new perspectives.

Rule two: Always save a copy of your original. Save copies of everything at every stage of the process. Save what you cut out, and save your files before you made changes. Sometimes, you were right the first time. Back up everything, back up often. If you want to see a writer in despair, look at one in a computer repair shop trying to recover lost files. Don't be that writer.

Your assignment? Write one of those wonderful feedback letters. Take out your current work in progress and write it to yourself. It's the best gift a writer can give him or herself, actually: an honest accounting of the strengths and weaknesses. If you don't have a work in progress, write one for a friend; and if you don't have a friend, write one on one of the exercises you've written so far in this course. If you wrote the feedback for yourself, look at it again clearly, too. Is it objective, frank, and balanced? If it is, maybe you're ready to ask someone to read your draft. That letter to yourself is the basis of the letter you can write to your reader, inviting the kind of response that you'd find most useful.

Building Your Audience
Lecture 22

Believe it or not, getting published in creative nonfiction does not begin with writing a book; it begins with writing a book proposal. Book proposals follow a strict formula that allows a writer to show off his or her skills, ideas, and research while simultaneously allowing an agent or editor to evaluate the sales potential of a work. Even if you are not ready to write your book, learning to write a proposal is an invaluable skill for a beginning nonfiction writer.

Setting Realistic Expectations

- Now that you have learned how to write your work of creative nonfiction, the question that remains is, how do you get your work published? What you will learn quickly as a professional writer is that a good story counts for more than anything—more than connections, more than reputation, more than any other factor.

- That said, there are other elements at play, and some great stories never get published because the writer did not know how to pique the interest of readers in the beginning. A beginning writer needs to understand how the professional writing world is structured.

- One thing a new professional writer must have is realistic expectations. Most professional agents and editors will tell you that today, in a country as large as the United States, maybe a few hundred writers make a comfortable living from the art alone. The vast majority supplement their writing incomes in other ways.

- The most important thing is to define the reason you write and the idea of success. The essential measure of success is writing a great book. If you find someone else who reads your book and likes it well enough to publish it, then you have, by any measure, reached the top of the field in writing. Beyond this, anything else is extraordinary good fortune and huge talent.

The Book Proposal

- Like any professional world, there are rules, traditions, and protocols in the world of publishing. You will need to learn to speak the language of your agent and editor.

- The good news is, if you are bound and determined to make a living at writing, creative nonfiction is one of the strongest literary markets out there.

- Also, unlike fiction writing, where a first-time writer has to finish a novel before he or she can attempt to sell it, you do not have to write the book before approaching an agent or editor. In fact, you probably should not!

- You still have to think through your narrative arc and characters, you still have to do your research and other preparatory work, and you still have to hone your writing skills so that you can do a great job on the manuscript and to meet your deadlines because you probably will not get a second chance at a book contract if you drop the ball on the first one. But when you know you have a great story and are ready to tell it, instead of writing the book, you need to write a **book proposal**.

- To write a proposal, you only need three things: You need a great story. You need to be ready to tell it. And you need to have an audience in mind. You need to be able to explain to an agent or a publisher why your book is going to sell at least enough copies to break even—and preferably make a profit.

- An audience should consist of more than your family, friends, and colleagues. There should be a group of people who will accept you as an expert on your chosen topic. This is what agents and editors call an **author platform**—your track record in an area that has enough people who are interested in it.

© iStockphoto/Thinkstock.

Giving public lectures on your specialty subject is a good way to develop a platform for your future nonfiction book.

- You can develop a platform by giving lectures to local community groups on your subject, writing columns for a newspaper, or developing a following for your blog. If you have a business or client list already that is related to your topic, those customers or clients are also a potential audience.

What Goes into a Proposal?

- These days, unless you are publishing with a small, local press, you need a literary agent. Acquiring an agent is actually the hardest part of the whole process because agents are paid only on commission. If they do not sell your book, they do not get paid. Therefore, an agent is only going to agree to represent a book that he or she thinks can really sell.

- Agents are essentially the gatekeepers of the publishing world, and a fabulous book proposal is the key to that gate. Writing a book proposal is also a fabulous way to test yourself on everything you have learned in this course.

- A book proposal must demonstrate your book's narrative arc. It showcases your great beginning and develops captivating characters, all in your scintillating prose. In short, it is a virtuoso exercise in great writing. Writing a practice book proposal is a great exercise, even for a book you do not plan to write.

- A book proposal contains three parts and runs 30–50 pages, as follows.

    - A pitch and chapter summaries. The pitch is one or two pages where you describe the big picture of the story. It requires a great beginning that launches the narrative arc; quickly and powerfully sketched characters, and a series of actions that demonstrate complications and consequences. It should have tight pacing, good momentum, and—above all—great writing. Chapter summaries are exactly what they sound like. Together, they will show the narrative form of the book, demonstrating the ebb and flow of the story.

    - A sample chapter. This is usually the first chapter, which should be 4,500–6,000 words. This is where you pull out all the stops. You make it a great piece of storytelling so that readers end it just plain wanting to read more.

    - A market section. This is, for most writers, the most challenging section, where you discuss your platform and who you envision buying this book. It is where you say who you are, how you have established your expertise, and what kind of audience you have. You should also address who else, if anyone, has written a book on this topic and why your book is different. If your story is unique, tell the reader why now is the time to tell it.

Practice Makes Perfect

- What if, as you begin to think about writing a book proposal, a whole book begins to look like a daunting place to start? Whether you are a beginning writer or an experienced writer looking to develop an author platform, starting out with smaller publications is a great idea. It is a way to hone your craft, get your work out there, get some experience with editors, and start to think of yourself—no matter what you do for a day job—as a "real" writer.

- Writing is hard work. Every writer out there will tell you so. But like all good work, it is also a great pleasure, and that is what we want to have you learn to enjoy.

Important Terms

author platform: The way in which the general public associates the name of the author with certain kinds of books or stories; also, the author's expertise and credentials for writing on certain topics.

book proposal: A brief outline of a book that is sent to a publisher as part of the contract process.

Suggested Reading

Eckstut and Sterry, *The Essential Guide to Getting Your Book Published.*

Rabiner and Fortunato, *Thinking Like Your Editor*.

Questions to Consider

1. What are your goals as a writer, and how does the market for books affect your goals?

2. What do you think about the change in our reading habits in today's multimedia world? Do you think people will read paper books 20 years from now? Have new technologies changed your reading habits?

Building Your Audience
Lecture 22—Transcript

We've come a long way together, haven't we? You've learned how to find your story; how to find a narrative structure to fit it; how to develop character, craft your prose, find your voice, create vivid descriptions, and profound silences. You've learned how to revise your story; how to encourage good readers; and what to do with the criticism that's part of any writer's life. You know the genres that are possible; how to hunt down great sources in a creative fashion; and above all, how to keep the nonfiction contract while taking your readers on a great ride in your story. In short, you've learned how write your fabulous work of creative nonfiction.

Now the question that every writer wants the answer to is: How do you get this published? After all, who doesn't want to be the next bestselling writer, right? Somebody has to make it big; heck, it might as well be you. You know, there's no one to say you won't make it; first-time writers do break through into the world of publishing. What you learn quickly as a professional writer is that a good story counts for more than anything—more than connections; more than reputation; more than anything—a great story told well. If you want the secret of making a living as a writer, that's the most essential element.

But, of course, there's more to the process than that, too, isn't there? There are other elements at play; and it's also true that some great stories never get published because the writer didn't know how to pique the interest of readers in the beginning. After all, remember what we said about writing a great story: You need to start with a sentence that makes your reader want to read the next one, and then you need to write another and another. Pitching your story to an agent and an editor is more or less the same thing.

In a minute, we're going to talk about all of this; about how the professional writing world is structured and what to do if you want to see if your story can find its way to millions of readers, or even just thousands. But first, let's talk about why to be a writer and realistic expectations. After all, if you're going to measure your success as a writer, you might as well have some sense of where the goalpost is, right? So think about this statistic: Most professional agents and editors will tell you that today, in a country as large as the United States, maybe a few hundred writers make a comfortable living from the art alone. The vast majority, myself included, supplement our incomes as writers in other ways. The poet Wallace Stevens spent his days working in an insurance agency, and he's gone down in history as one of the 20th century's great poets. The famous novelist of the Jazz Age, F. Scott Fitzgerald, wrote magazine articles; and let's not forget, he and so many of his friends went off to Paris because back then, Paris was an absolute bargain for writers and you could live there cheaply. Ernest Hemingway was poor enough that he and his wife poached pigeons in the parks of Paris to eat them for dinner, even when Paris was a bargain. Myself, I teach at a college and find time for writing in between my other responsibilities. Among my friends in the world of writing—many of whom have won important literary prizes and have published well-reviewed and important novels, screenplays, poems, and memoirs—they do things like rehab houses, ghostwrite the autobiographies of rich industrialists, proofread doctoral dissertations, or work out deals house sitting winters in drafty summer cottages.

This isn't to discourage you. After all, maybe you'll be one of the lucky hundreds. I hope so, so I can say I knew you when. But chances are you'll find another way to pay the rent or meet the mortgage, and the most important thing is to redefine the reason you write and the idea of what it means to succeed. The essential measure of success is writing a great book, one that you know is beautifully and smartly written; one that respects nonfiction and storytelling as an essentially human art; one that treats the story and the reader with respect, which makes them promises and keeps them; one that engages the hearts and minds of your readers, whoever and however many they happen to be. When John Milton wrote his great epic poem *Paradise Lost*, he had just one hope for his masterpiece: that it would "find fit audience, though few." What he meant was that what he really wanted most for his poem was for it to find the readers who'd most appreciate it, even if it wasn't very many of them; and in the end, Milton would've been pleasantly surprise to know that his work went on to become one of history's greatest works of literature. But it wasn't how he defined success for himself as a writer.

Finding your "fit audience?" That, in itself, is success; and there are many, many writers who, in their lives, learn to be content with this. If you find someone else who reads your book and likes it well enough to publish it—who believes that there are people who want to read it—then you have, by any measure, reached the top of the field in writing; and book publishing is a difficult business, so this isn't easy. Beyond this, anything else is extraordinary good fortune and huge talent. To be honest, it's a lot of the former.

Ok, are you still thinking about quitting your day job? Maybe you will in the end; but let's think this through. If you're early in your career or in transition, you want to think sensibly about the prospects. In the next lesson, we'll talk about how to hold down a job and still make a fabulous career as a writer. People do it all the time. I do it; you can, too. So don't chuck it all in, at least not quite yet. Pragmatically speaking, writing for three or four hours a day is a lot of time writing. Writing takes an incredible amount of emotional and intellectual energy and stamina. Many of literature's most famous novelists and poets wrote less than a few hours a day; and most of us, if we're passionate enough, can find a few hours a day to write if we really set our minds to it. It seems impossible until you commit yourself to doing it, and then you'll be amazed.

So separate your art from how you make a living, at least at first. That's my best advice to you, born from long experience. Then, commit yourself with no reservations to the art. Write the great memoir or biography in you. Write the family history. Writers are people who write, and it's as simple as that. Only the lucky make a living from it. I can say without any hesitation: Writing eight hours a day is far, far more exhausting than you might imagine. So we've set the goalpost here: Write a great book. Find your fit audience, however many people might be in it. From there, if you're very ambitious, see if you can get it published by a press. And from there, a wise writer lets go of any other expectations.

So far in this course, I've shared with you what I can tell you about how to do the first thing: how to write a great book; and a great book will always find its own audience. But how about that third part of the writer's ambition? How to get it published; that's where it starts to seem like a secret society here, doesn't it? I see what you're thinking: It's true; like any professional world, there are rules, traditions, and protocols. There are things you can do to speak the language of your agent and the language of your editor. In this lesson, we'll talk about how to learn to ropes in this dizzying world of nonfiction publishing. Are you ready?

The good news, if you're bound and determined to be one of those writers who make a living at it—and great for you to be so determined—is that creative nonfiction is one of the strongest literary markets out there. Making a living as a nonfiction writer is much easier than making it big as a literary novelist or a poet. Why? It's simple. Think about what you read when you buy a book. Not many of us buy books of poetry, do we? It's a shame, because there are lots of fabulous poets out there. We should be buying books of poetry. But the numbers unfortunately tell a different story. And sure, we read novels. But most of us read commercial novels: mysteries, thrillers, the women's novels known as "chick lit," that sort of thing; things like Dan Brown's novels, or John Grisham's, or most of those big-named, fast-paced novels you find in airport bookshops. Literary novels sell far fewer copies. Literally thousands and thousands are published a year, and far more are written, but only a handful each year end up becoming popular books. The market for nonfiction, however, is much larger. Most of us read biographies, memoirs, true crime, business books, history books, and travel writing, to name just a few nonfiction genres, and we read it far more often than we read contemporary poetry. Because so many more of us read them, that means more of us buy them, and that means publishers are more willing to publish them; and making a living as a writer means getting published. So here's the great news: Nonfiction is a good market to try to break into.

Want another piece of great information about nonfiction? Let's say you're writing your first novel. It's going to be great. But if you want to get it published, you first need to write it; all of it. Maybe down the road, when you're an experienced writer—when you've got a publication track record—you can get a publishing deal without the whole manuscript of a novel ready to send off at a moment's notice. But as a first-time writer, you have to write the novel and then you can, as we say, shop it. With creative nonfiction—how's this—you don't have to write the book first. In fact, you probably shouldn't if you're serious about getting it published. Now that doesn't mean you don't have to think the entire narrative arc and characters through; it doesn't mean you don't have to do all the research. You do have to do all of that, and you have to be sure that when the time comes, you're an experienced enough writer to be able to do a great job on the manuscript and able to meet your deadline, because you probably aren't going to get two chances at a book contract if you drop the ball on the first one. But when you know you've got a great story and are ready to tell it and—this is crucial—when you've found yourself some readers, then what you need to do isn't start writing. How's that for nuts? What you need to do is to put together a book proposal.

Ok, let's back up a minute here before we talk about that book proposal. Are you ready to write it? There are three things I just said you need: You need a great story; you need to be ready to tell it; and you need readers. Let's boil it down: that's story, craft, and audience. Story and craft we've learned about; but how do you find an audience before you write your book? It's a quandary, isn't it? Welcome to the real world of publishing. This is why most beginning writers need to break into the world of publishing with small steps.

You need an audience because one of the critical parts of that book proposal we're going to talk about here in a minute is marketing. After all, a publisher wants to know that you can find that "fit audience" and have reason to believe it's going to be large enough to cover the costs of producing, marketing, and distributing your great work of creative nonfiction. You need to be able to explain to an agent and to your publisher after that why your book is going to sell at least enough copies to break even. After all, publishing houses are businesses. Even nonprofit presses need to break even. Breaking even means selling your book, and that means you need to be able to show that there are people out there who are going to be interested in your books. Not just your family and friends, though they can help; real people who already see you as an expert at something. An expert on the life of Marie Antoinette, or the history of beer making, or on how to do genealogical research, or on the history of Flint, Michigan. Whatever the topic of your book is, you need to have what agents and editors call a "platform," some established track record in that area and enough people who are interested in it.

So what does that mean? Let's say you want to write that history of Flint, Michigan; how do you generate an audience? Maybe you start by giving lectures to local community groups on interesting local history. If you can pack the audience, you're on your way. Or maybe you offer to write a column on the city's history in your local newspaper. Or perhaps you start a webpage where you blog—keep an online log or journal, that is—about life in Flint; or the history of Flint; or, even better, a site for people from Flint now scattered around the world who want to feel connected to home. You know, I grew up in the state of Maine, and I once came across a funny web page started by a couple of people from Maine who were homesick, and they made these t-shirts they sold with the logo "Born in Maine, Living in Exile." Here's what they write on their website today:

> We're back in Maine now, but we remember EXILE vividly—lonely—frustrating—no wicked good anything in sight. So we created a website just for you MAINE EXILES.
>
> Then they go on to say:
>
> Take a look at messages from your fellow M.I.E.'s (Mainers In Exile) on the Messages from Exile board, and then post one of your own.
>
> While you're here, scroll down through the guestbook and add your name and current place of Exile. You might even find an old prom date—or chaperone—listed there.

Think of it: They have an audience, don't they? They can go to an agent or a publisher and say, "Hey, we want to write a memoir about living away from home." Ok, so they need a great story here, and they need craft; but if they figured that out, they could also say, "Hey, guess what, we also have 6,000 people who read our webpage." See how smart they are about asking you to leave your name and email? When that book comes out, they can let you know about it. That's what a publisher wants to see.

In short, that's the first thing you need to do before you sit down to write that book proposal: You need to build an audience for the project. You need to figure out the story; that means you need a great arc. You need characters, you need to do the research. You need to write enough to know, in your heart of hearts, that if you get the big book contract, you're ready—really ready—to write it. You've worked on your craft; you've written; you've learned how to write a great story. When you have all those things in place, then you're ready to think about seeing if you can become a published author. In nonfiction, that means the book proposal.

To understand what a book proposal does, you have to understand how the publishing world works. These days, unless you're publishing with a small, local press, you need a literary agent. This is actually the hardest part of the whole process; and here's why: A literary agent gets paid only on commission. If they don't sell your book to a publisher for a contract—which comes with what's known as an advance or some upfront money to write the book based on how many copies a press thinks it could sell—then your agent doesn't get paid. As you can imagine, that means that a literary agent is only going to agree to represent a book proposal that he or she thinks can really sell. That means that agents are essentially the gatekeepers of the publishing world. Why would a busy editor look at a book proposal that a professional agent doesn't think has a chance of selling when books an agent does think could be bestsellers are coming across his or her desk dozens at a time? You need an agent as a first-time writer; and the only way to get an agent is to write a brilliant book proposal. Got it?

Writing a book proposal is also a fabulous way to test yourself on everything you've learned in this course, too; because you know what a book proposal essentially does? It pitches to an agent your narrative arc. It writes a great beginning that makes the agent want to read more. It develops captivating characters. It demonstrates scintillating prose. In short, it's a virtuoso exercise in great writing in which you also explain what this amazing book you're going to write is all about. It's actually a great exercise, even if you don't plan to publish your memoirs or that family vacation travelogue, because you can't write a book proposal unless you've really thought through what the best way to tell whatever your story is. Now you see why agents and editors ask writers to send them, don't you?

How do you write a book proposal? There are basically three parts; and a professional one—one you would really send off to an agent to see if you could get representation—usually runs 30–50 pages. It's not a little thing, is it? The first part of the book proposal is what writers and editors talk about as the pitch and the chapter summaries; and you can guess immediately what this is, can't you? That's right: It's a page or two where you describe (or pitch) the big-picture of your story. It's a pitch because it's a ballgame metaphor, isn't it? Your agent and editor are batters waiting at the plate. Everyone wants a home run. This is one case where you, the pitcher, don't want to be throwing out sliders or fastballs. You don't want to be out of the strike zone especially. What you want to do—contrary to all your sporting impulses—is lob a nice, slow, beautiful ball right across that plate; the kind of ball where an agent and editor look at it and say, "Now that one, that one we can have over the fence easy."

What happens in one of those slow, beautiful pitches? It's simple: great storytelling. Think about it here for a minute (stop the course if you have to mull it over): Thinking back on everything you've learned in this course, what's going to happen in those first few pages where you pitch your book idea? What did you come up with? You're going to have a great beginning, aren't you? Did you remember that what a great beginning does is launch narrative arc and establish character tension? You're going to have to sketch, quickly and powerfully, some great character, too. No stock characters here. We'll want multifaceted characters who make us believe in them and care about their struggles. We want a narrative arc that grabs us. We want actions where we can begin to imagine—with a bit of foreshadowing perhaps—a series of complications and consequences. We need to have great writing. We need paragraphs that build momentum; sentences that control pacing; parallelism, metaphor, scene, setting, dialogue, voice; a great narrator. Research we can trust; material that's fascinating; the promise of a great story, and a few pages that makes us believe it's all just right there waiting, if only we could turn the page. But wait, you haven't written this book yet. You want your readers—those agents and editors here—to say, "Not yet written? We need to correct that."

But even if you don't need to publish that book, even if you write it only for personal pleasure, to record a family history, or to inspire a local community, do you see why this exercise is one that every reader should do anyhow before sitting down to write a full-length book?

Ok, so that's the pitch; the first page or two. Then come the chapter summaries; and these are just what they sound like. Together, they sketch out the narrative arc of the story. Together, they explain how the character conflicts collide and tangle, and unravel and resolve. It'll show a reader what the narrative form of your book will be, linear or circular? Those chapter summaries mean you have to know the answer. Then—because remember we learned how each chapter has its own narrative arc—the paragraph for each chapter will also tell a story of its own; or it'll end with a cliffhanger; or with an elegant transition. It'll move the lives of the characters forward; and because this is nonfiction, it'll tell an interesting history, too. If you're thinking about your book with an eye toward getting the big contract, something else to know: The average nonfiction book is 90,000 words, including any notes or a bibliography. Most of them have 15–20 chapters. You're looking at each chapter being about 4,500–6,000 words. When you're sketching out your story, then—which is the same outlining any writer does at the beginning of a project—see if you can break it into 15–20 chapters.

The second part of a book proposal—hey, it's something else every writer does as part of the drafting process, too—is called a "sample chapter." Usually it's the first chapter; and you already know how long a chapter should be now, too, don't you? This is where you give your reader the first chapter of a book and pull out all the stops. You make it a great piece of storytelling so that readers end it just plain wanting to read more. It's everything you've learned here in this course, and it's the story you want to tell. At the end of the book proposal exercise, you know what else? Even if you never send that proposal off, you have a draft of the first chapter of your work of creative nonfiction. All you have to do now is keep on writing. After all, now that you have chapter summaries, you know what the next chapter's going to be already, don't you?

Then the third part of a book proposal; this is the part most writers have the hardest time with: It's the market section. This is the place where you want to be able to say, "I have 6,000 followers on my webpage. I've given community lectures to excited crowds. I've got my colleagues all abuzz with interest and a thousand friends on my book topic Facebook fan page." It's where you say who you are, how you've established an expertise, and what kind of audience not only this book has, but you have, too. It's also the moment where you see who else has written a book on your topic and you explain, to yourself and your readers, what's new about this story; why it needs to be told right now. If there are three biographies of George Washington already out there, it doesn't mean you can't write a new and better one, but it does mean you need to be able to say why yours is different. What makes it new, and better, and timely? If it's not new and timely, think of all the work you've saved yourself writing something that's already been written.

This all, too, is a useful exercise, no matter what your goals. After all, the market section is really about thinking through what your narrative voice is going to be—the part about how you're going to tell the story and present yourself to the reader—and thinking through who your reader is. After all, we need to know our audience. As we've learned in this course, creative nonfiction at its heart is about making a contract with our readers. In fact, all storytelling, we've learned, is about creating and meeting our readers' expectations by telling a well-wrought tale with new and timely information that rewards a reader's investment of time and energy in the world you're creating.

What if, as you begin to think about this, the whole book begins to look like a daunting place to start? A book is quite an undertaking. If you're a beginning writer—or even if you're an experienced writer looking to develop an author platform before you pitch that great book idea that you know is someday going to be a bestseller—starting out with smaller publications is a great idea. It's a way to hone your craft, get your work out there, get some experience with editors, and start to think of yourself—no matter what you do for a day job—as a real writer. You'll be in good company.

In the next lesson, we'll talk about lots of smaller ways in which you can get started as a writer: in contests, magazines, in travel writing. We'll also talk about prewriting exercises and outlining; because are you thinking that coming up with even one chapter summary is harder than it looks? You'd be right. Writing is hard work; every writer out there will tell you that same thing. But like all good work, it's also a great pleasure; and that's what we want to have you learn to enjoy.

Getting Published

Lecture 23

Many great creative nonfiction writers start their careers not with books but with shorter writing pieces. In this lecture, we discuss how to get your feet wet in the professional nonfiction writing world, with particular focus on travel writing, and how to write a feature article proposal much the way one writes a book proposal.

Starting Small

- Starting your career in creative nonfiction by writing a book is a bit like learning how to climb a mountain by attempting to scale Mount Everest. Most successful professional writers start out smaller.

- There have never been so many great opportunities for breaking into publishing as there are today. There are local history societies, club newsletters, creative nonfiction journals, and writing contests. To find them, you only need to do a quick Internet search or check announcements in journals like *Creative Nonfiction* or *Poets & Writers*.

- Travel writing is a huge market with a lot of opportunities. Have you ever wished you could write about your vacation to share it with friends and family? Have you ever wished that one of your older relatives, who saw amazing things and went interesting places, had written down those stories? Those are all different kinds of travel writing.

- Thinking about what it takes to prepare to write a travel piece is also a wonderful way to practice the research preparation and narrative outlining that goes into creating any great work of creative nonfiction.

A World of Opportunities

- On the publication side, there are travel-writing contests, hundreds of travel blogs and travel-related websites, and you can always start your own blog in a matter of minutes with a minimum of technological know-how. If you start writing a blog that other people are interested in reading, you will gain new fans—and that is also an important step toward establishing platform.

- If you are writing for family and friends on your blog, you probably will not need to do a lot of research in advance. But what if you ultimately want to write a feature article for *Travel and Leisure* or *National Geographic*? Before you write for those major magazines, you will have to have published other pieces of travel writing for smaller venues.

- In the publishing world, your previous writing credits are called clips; they are your credentials, proof that you can deliver good work. After you are published in a few small venues, you break into the next level by writing an amazing pitch letter to the editor of a magazine—or by writing an amazing travel book proposal to an agent.

- Most of the writing in commercial creative nonfiction is **under contract writing**—work where you do the research, pitch the idea in detail, lay out the narrative arc, and hopefully get a contract to go ahead and do the piece for payment before writing the entire piece.

- What does a pitch for an article look like, as opposed to a pitch for an entire book? It is usually in the form of a letter addressed to a specific editor by name. Grammar and proofreading count for a lot here. You must also target the type of story you want to write to how the magazine views itself—the kinds of articles that interest its readers.

- The best way to figure out if a magazine is a good fit for your idea is to read a couple of current issues. You need to figure out what the "classic" feature article for this magazine looks like—How long are they? What voice are they written in? How do they hook the reader? Is there character? How do they develop narrative arc? What kinds of topics are they on?

- Once you can answer these questions, your letter should tell the editor your story and the source of your information in 100–150 words.

Writing the Feature Article Proposal

- Imagine you were a single woman taking a trip to Marrakech, Morocco, for a spa vacation and wanted to pitch this subject as an article for *National Geographic.* The first thing to do would be to study the magazine's features. You will note that it does not generally focus on luxury travel—this is more of a *Travel & Leisure* subject.

- *National Geographic* is mostly interested in human culture, society, science, and history. The role of women in modern North African culture would be of interest. Perhaps this article can be about the history of women-only spas and the hamman—the Moroccan baths—and how modern culture—especially Western culture—is reshaping them.

- While there is often a personal element to stories for *National Geographic*, the author is rarely a character. These articles are usually told in the third person. You will probably want a linear narrative because you are going to describe changes in culture. And since a linear narrative is plot driven, you will need a strong set of dramatic events to structure the narrative arc.

- So, how do you pitch this plot-driven narrative about what is going to happen on a trip you have not taken yet? You will need to do a lot of research. That is where you will "find the story." You will have to look for a set of facts that are interesting enough to suggest the possibility of a good story narrative, even before you buy a plane ticket.

© iStockphoto/Thinkstock.

There might be a dozen different interesting stories to be written on the hammams of Morocco, but which one is *your* story?

- If you paused the lecture to do some quick research, you may have come up with some or all of the following possibilities: The hammam is historically associated with fertility, and women go to the baths as part of birth and marriage rituals, so one angle could be a story on wedding customs in Morocco. Another angle could be on the belief in the genii said to haunt baths in Marrakech and the rituals to protect against them. You could write a historical piece on how the idea of removing body hair was introduced to European culture by Europen women visiting the Moroccan hammam in the 18th century.

- Whichever angle you choose, you need enough research to convince an editor that there is not just interesting information but an entire story in it—a story the readers will want to read. You need to make enough connections to sustain a story of the proposed length. Finally, you need to give the editor a confident sense that, even if the final story is something a bit different than what is proposed, you are a great storyteller and there is a great story waiting to be told.

Pitching an Article—A Writing Exercise

- Imagine the travel piece that you would most like to write. Research it. Find the story. Find the characters. Find the narrative arc. Plan how you would complete your trip or your research.

- Once your plan is in place, write a 100-word pitch—maximum! Tell an editor the heart of this story you would tell. Craft those sentences. Build paragraph moment. Pull out all the stops. Show off everything you've learned in this course.

Suggested Reading

George, *Lonely Planet Travel Writing.*

Mayle, *A Year in Provence.*

Powell, *Julie and Julia.*

Questions to Consider

1. What trips have you taken that would make a great piece of travel writing? How would you pitch that idea to make it a great story? Where would you pitch it?

2. If you were going to start a blog—an online writing website with your work in progress—what topic would you choose? Would you be comfortable making your work public? Who would you want to be your audience?

Getting Published

Lecture 23—Transcript

We've talked a lot in this course about what it takes to think about writing a book-length project in creative nonfiction—a biography, cultural history, memoir, or other work—where what you're always balancing as a writer is the creative part of writing with the nonfiction part of your contract with the reader. So we've talked about developing character and launching narrative arcs, and about how to shape chapters and think cleverly about research. But starting out as a writer by writing a book is a bit like learning how to climb a mountain by attempting to scale Mount Everest, isn't it? Most successful professional writers start out smaller, with a few shorter published pieces; and they get the feel for writing for publication one step at a time. It's very much the normal way to go about making a career for yourself as a writer and building a track record of publications.

For a new writer, there have never been so many great opportunities to breaking into the world of publishing—so many opportunities for seeing your first work of creative nonfiction in print—even if you never intend to make your living as an author and only write for the sheer pleasure of sharing your experiences and stories. There are local history societies, club newsletters, creative nonfiction journals, and writing contests. To find them, you only need to do a quick internet search of the words "creative nonfiction" and "contest." Or you can subscribe to the journal *Creative Nonfiction* or to the magazine *Poets and Writers*, which every month at the end has announcements for different writing opportunities. Or if you get stuck, you can go to your public library and ask the reference librarian to help you find opportunities for writers. Contests and calls for submissions are a great way to give yourself a challenge—and a deadline—as a writer. Another great way to practice writing great creative nonfiction is to craft something as simple as your family's holiday letter. A good one will tell a story and develop wonderful characters. A bad one; we've all read bad ones before, haven't we? It's a wonderful way to get feedback on your writing, too, because if you write a good one, you'll hear about it.

But there's one other kind of writing that falls under the category of creative nonfiction that we haven't talked a lot about yet and that's also a fabulous place to get your start, both as a writer in this genre and perhaps in print for the first time: travel writing. In fact, travel writing's a huge market. Think of books like *A Year in Provence* or *Under the Tuscan Sun*. Those are travel memoirs that have gone on to be feature films. But also look at your bookshelves. Chances are you have at least one guidebook sitting there from a vacation, don't you? Or look at the stack of magazines on your coffee table. Is there one that has a travel article? *National Geographic*, *Travel and Leisure*; maybe even your favorite fly-fishing magazine that tells you great spots for planning a fishing vacation? Have you ever thought how you wished that you'd been able to write about your vacation to share it with friends and family? Have you ever wished that one of your older relatives, who saw amazing things and went interesting places, had written down those stories so you could know a bit more about firsthand history? Those are all different kinds of travel writing.

Thinking about what it takes to prepare to write a travel piece is also a wonderful way to practice thinking about the kind of research preparation and narrative outlining that goes into creating any great work of creative nonfiction. Let's think about the publication side of things briefly, if that's your interest. Where are the publishing opportunities? There are travel writing contests you can find online or in magazines; that's one opportunity. There are also literally hundreds of travel blogs and travel-related websites online. They're changing all the time, so there's no point in naming any of them; but you can find them in seconds if you search online with terms like "travel blog" and "how to contribute," or "contest." They won't pay much—$50 maybe, often not at all—but it can be a great way to get your first piece of travel writing published.

Here's another idea: If you want to write about your travels regularly, you can also start your own blog in a matter of minutes online for free on sites like wordpress.com or blogger.com. Even those of us who are only technologically just so-so can do it, and it can be a great way, for example, for you to keep family and friends updated about your adventures on the road on your next vacation. You know what's even better? If you start writing a blog that other people are interested in reading, you'll gain new fans, and that's also an important step toward becoming a published writer. Many popular books—things like *Julie and Julia*, for example—started out as blogs that gained a lot of followers, enough that a publisher suggested the author turn them into a book. Your travelogue might be the next bestseller; and even if it's not, it's a great way to practice writing creative nonfiction, to share your work publicly, and to entertain your new fans with some great writing.

If you're writing for family and friends on your blog, you probably won't need to do a lot of research in advance. After all, this is the kind of thing where you just need access to a computer and an internet connection, and you can write in the moment from anywhere in the world. You can see what it is you experience today and write about in compelling detail. But what if you want to write one of those feature articles for *Travel and Leisure* or *National Geographic*? The first thing, of course, is to know that before you write for those major magazines, you're going to have to have published a couple of other pieces of travel writing on blogs or for smaller venues. These are also, in the world of travel writing, the Mount Everests. When you propose an article for these kinds of magazines, the editor is going to ask you to submit with it usually three other "clips"—that's three other published writing samples—ideally ones that are in progressively more prominent places. It's a bit of a catch-22: Most places want you to have written for a place at the same level before you write for them.

But how do you get your first piece published? The answer is by doing two things: by getting your feet wet in places like blogs and small venues, so that you can work your way up to the print travel writing market and get three strong clips; and after that, you break into the next level by writing an amazing pitch letter to the editor of your dream travel magazine, or by writing an amazing travel book proposal and sending it to an agent.

Remember how we said that one great thing about creative nonfiction was not just that there's a good market for it but also that, unlike fiction or poetry, you don't actually have to write the article or book before someone agrees to publish it? Most of the writing in commercial creative nonfiction is what we call "under contract" writing: work where you pitch the idea in detail, do the research, lay out the narrative arc all in a brief synopsis, and hopefully get a contract to go ahead and do the piece for payment and publication. The thing is, even if you never intend to publish your feature travel article, writing a pitch is still a fantastic prewriting exercise, just like writing a book proposal is. If you're stuck at the beginning of a project, this is a great way to think through your idea. In fact, when I get stuck as a writer, I find writing an imaginary pitch much more useful than outlining. Because think what a pitch is: It's a short summary that explains to a reader who the characters are, what the narrative arc is, why the topic is newsworthy, and what the content's going to be. Those elements are essential to any good story.

What's a pitch, for, say a feature travel article? It's going to be a letter; it's going to be addressed to the editor; and if you're really sending this pitch it's very important that you look at the masthead of the magazine—the front page where it gives the names of the editors of the different departments—and that you address the correct one. Because it's a business letter where you're trying to convince someone that they should give you a couple of thousand dollars to write an article they haven't seen, what do you think: Is grammar and proofreading going to matter? It sure is; critically.

Here's the trick about magazine writing: Every magazine has a clear idea of what its kind of story is; what kinds of articles interest their readers and fit their niche in the magazine market. Unfortunately, there's no way to go and look it up. In fact, magazine editors I've talked to often don't know themselves precisely what they're looking for in a story idea. They'll say, "Oh, you know, it has to be newsworthy; a great story; of interest to our readers; not something we've done or a competitor has done recently. It has to be a good 'fit.' " This more or less boils down to that old adage about pornography: "They'll know it when they see it."

How are you going to figure out what the editor of your dream magazine is looking for? You're going to look at a couple of current issues, aren't you? You're going to be a bit of a sleuth. What you need to do is figure out is: What does the classic feature article for this magazine look like? How long are these travel articles? In what voice are they written? How to they hook the reader? Is there character? How do they develop narrative arc? How do they transition from one paragraph to another? How do they end? What's their narrative structure? What kinds of topics are they on? How many pictures are there? How much dialogue is there? Do you see what all of this means? Do you see that this is all just another way of asking: What kind of storytelling does this magazine want? Do you see how now, here at the end of our course, you know what all those things mean and how to identify them? This is all you're doing when you research for a magazine pitch: You're teaching yourself to understand what the particular style of storytelling the editors want for their publication is. Then, you're going to write a letter where in maybe 100 or 150 words you start to tell that story. You tell how the arc will develop and where your research comes from.

How about an example? Remember that piece I said that I wrote for *Food and Wine* magazine on my travels in Napa Valley? You can read it online if you want; but in a general way, let's imagine you're using this as your *Food and Wine* example. I started it out by telling the reader how I used to live in Sonoma, got a divorce, and moved to the East Coast, but had to go back to work on a wine guide in Napa. I'm filled with trepidation. What will it be like to go back to the wine country? What will be like to be in Napa rather than Sonoma? I tell the reader I'd expected Napa to be flashy and commercialized, but I was wrong. That's the gist of how the article opens.

Let's ask the most basic question: What kind of narrative is this going to be? Do you remember the main kinds? There are two: linear or circular. Which is this article going to be? What is the editor of *Food and Wine* probably looking for? You know that I'm going to write about how vibrant and unassuming Napa really is, don't you? That's going to be the narrative arc here, or at least part of it. But you know, because I tell you, that this isn't my perception of Napa at the beginning; so this is going to be a narrative about the main character—the "I"—changing her perspective, right? That's what kind of narrative? That's right, it's circular. So we have a circular narrative; and it's a personal narrative, too, isn't it? It's in the first person, and I'm telling you, "This is going to be the story of my trip and how it changed my mind about Napa."

What else do you know about what the editor at *Food and Wine* might be looking for? You know that this magazine wants glamorous pieces, written for sophisticated travelers interested in food and wine; but it wants articles that shake up the norms and outdated perceptions, right? There has to be something newsworthy. You also know that there has to be something pretty personal about the story. I tell you a bit about my private life; why do you think a writer does that? What's the narrative function of it? It creates character for the "I," doesn't it? So here's another one of those examples of the author as character in creative nonfiction. I tell you about my love life particularly; and do you know what, that tells you something else, too, about the narrative structure of this article, doesn't it? Can you guess how this story has to end? Remember, we said at the beginning of the course that the narrative arc we launch in the beginning will shape what the possible endings will be. Love goes wrong in Sonoma. I go to Napa. It's more fun than I thought it would be. What must the ending of this circular narrative be? I'd better either fall in love with Napa or fall in love in Napa, hadn't I? That's exactly how it ends: I fall in love with Napa. That's what structures the narrative arc. Slowly I realize I'm falling in love with the Napa; that's what's going to let me move in the article, from paragraph to paragraph about offbeat tourist things you, too, can do in Napa, with a narrative direction.

Let's take another example, one of yours maybe. Let's imagine a trip together. Let's say that I'm going to go off as a single woman to Marrakech, in Morocco, for a spa vacation. Let's imagine that I want to pitch this trip as a magazine article for *National Geographic*. That would be aiming high; for most writers, that would be a dream publication. But once you're an established travel writer, why not? Let's imagine you're sending that pitch to *National Geographic*. What's the first thing you'll do? You'll go to back issues of the magazine and study their features. You'll learn that this magazine doesn't really care about fancy spa vacations, or that it doesn't think its readers care about that, more precisely. *Travel and Leisure* might, but not *National Geographic*. In fact, if you want to try an exercise, stop the course and have a look at a copy of *National Geographic* before we continue. See if you can figure out how you'd pitch them.

If you were to look at a copy of *National Geographic*, what you'd see is that this magazine wants travel articles that talk about human culture, society, science, and history. The role of women in modern North African culture would be of interest. The history of women-only spas and the *hamman*—the Moroccan baths—and how modern culture is reshaping them. The experience of a Western woman in Islamic North Africa at this precise moment in world history might be of interest. But this isn't going to be an article on where the fanciest spas and most outlandish cocktails, or the best pick-up scenes for the high flier in Marrakech are to be found, is it? We might learn that while there's often a personal element to stories for *National Geographic*, here we don't use the author as character. Instead, these articles are often told in the third-person primarily, and the emphasis is on interesting characters, local or international.

Because these aren't typically first-person travel narratives, what do you think? Will it be likely a circular or a linear narrative? Circular narratives are well-suited to stories where the characters change; and while maybe a writer for *National Geographic* could use one effectively to describe changes in culture, chances are the linear narrative is going to be more effective. Since a linear narrative depends more on plot than on the changing perspective of the narrator, what does that mean? Did you see it? It means we're going to need a strong set of dramatic events to structure the narrative arc, aren't we? I went to dinner at a neat wine bar in Napa and really saw a different side of the county; that's not going to be what the editor at *National Geographic* wants to hear in a story.

I want to write my story for *National Geographic* on the spas of Marrakech, and now I know how I have to pitch it to the editor. Because I'm a professional writer, and because I know major magazines always expect a pitch before I write a story anyhow—because, after all, they want a role in shaping it—I know I'm going to send this query letter to the editor, the right editor, well before I take off on my adventure; probably before I buy my plane ticket, and certainly before I plan my itinerary. But how are we going to pitch a story, especially a plot-structured narrative, about what's going to happen on a trip we haven't taken? That's the tricky part of pitching any work of creative nonfiction for a contract. What's the answer?

It's going to be the research, isn't it? In order to pitch a story, just like to write a book proposal or start writing any piece of creative nonfiction, you're going to need to do a lot of research. Remember, there's the creative side, and there's the nonfiction side. The most important thing to learning how to write great creative nonfiction, maybe even especially in the first-person pieces, is how to do smart and interesting research; because it's by doing research that you'll learn how, as journalists say, to find the story. That means you need to find where the information you discover opens up possibilities for great narrative, great character, and fabulous storytelling. There are fabulous stories all around us. We can't all write all of them; we have to find the stories that interest us and resonate with us, of course. But there are more than enough stories out there for all of us to be writing for an entire lifetime.

Let's think some more about my Marrakech pitch. We know that I'm a woman going to Morocco alone. We know that it's a tense political and historical moment in the world and that will shape my experiences as a woman in North Africa, and will make part of what I'm writing about potentially newsworthy. We know that I speak French but not Arabic, so that's going to shape the kind of interviews and research I can do once I get there. You know I want to write about Marrakech and not Casablanca. We know, if you know me, that I'm old and wise enough to not be foolish as a woman traveling alone in a place I've never been before; so I'm probably not going to be able to write a story that involves solo hiking in the Atlas Mountains. I'm too big of a wimp to take on something that adventurous. In fact, if you know me, you know that culture interests me; luxury interests me; spas, now those interest me. Rocks in my shoes and sleeping out in a rainstorm? Not my forte, however. I know that *National Geographic* is a magazine about culture and history; it's not a magazine that gives out hotel recommendations, is it? So I'm going to structure my research accordingly. What I need to research is a story that brings together Marrakech, women, culture, and spas in a way I can pitch to *National Geographic*.

If you want to work along with me in this lesson, you can also stop here in the course and try it yourself. Give yourself 20 minutes to do the research on the internet. Remember, what you're looking for is a set of facts that are interesting enough to suggest the possibility of a good story narrative.

What do we come up with if we look into story ideas for Marrakech? We learn that women attending *hammam* is historically associated with the idea that it increases fertility, and that women go to the baths as part of many of life's rituals, including births and marriages. One angle could be a story on wedding customs perhaps in Morocco, the North African equivalent of the bachelorette party. Or, we learn there's the idea that there are supernatural genii said to haunt baths in Marrakech, and there are rituals one uses to protect against them. An article on "The Best Haunts of Marrakech"? Or how about the fact that in the 18th century, what fascinated European travelers was the fact that in Moroccan *hammam* the women—unheard of in Europe then—removed their body hair? The beginning of the bikini wax? What's the story of how women ended up shaving their bodies, anyhow? It makes you wonder, doesn't it? That's the idea: You're looking for the kernel of an idea that you can use to tell a story and to capture the attention of your readers and the editor who can help you reach them.

Are you getting the idea? This is a how a writer of creative nonfiction, and travel writing especially, works out the concept for an article or a book. You find a promising idea; you do some research; you try to find the story or find the angle. You do a check to make sure someone else hasn't already written this story recently; because if someone has, then no magazine is going to want to publish yours, and there's no point in doing any more research on this idea. Then you think to yourself, "Ok, what if I write that article on the 'Best Haunts of Marrakech?' Where am I going to go back to find some more research, enough to make a narrative out of this? Enough to find some characters? My *hammam* history is one part of that story. Where do I go to find other haunted locations in this ancient North African empire?" Because I need enough to convince an editor that there's not just interesting information here, but there's a story in it; a story his or her readers will want to read. I need to find a haunted hotel and go stay in it, don't I? I need to read up on the legends of genii in Morocco; and if genii live in bottles, I need to go find someone who sells antique bottles for goodness sake. I need to figure out: Is there any connection between the genii and the spirits and all those famous snake charmers and fortunetellers in the public squares of Marrakech? Who can I interview? Before I ever get there: How can I find out enough about the many fascinating characters out there to give an editor a confident sense that, one, I'm a great storyteller; and two, there's a great story in here waiting to be told. It's story and research and a bit of writing, followed by looking for the story, doing more research, and a bit more writing. Repeat. In fact, repeat until you know as a writer that you have all the elements of story that you've learned about here.

Are you ready for your final course assignment of "Writing Creative Nonfiction?" Here it is: Imagine the travel piece that you'd most like to write. Where would you like to go and what would be your first idea for a topic? Now here's your task: Research it; think about it; poke around; and see if you can do what any journalist or writer of creative nonfiction needs to do. Can you find the story? Is there a fresh angle? Who's your audience? Can you find characters? What will the arc be? Where will you go for more research? Before you get too far into the process of putting together this story idea, also check to make sure this story hasn't just been published. After all, maybe if you're really serious, you'll even think about where you would send this dream feature article if you could get someone to pay you to write it. Maybe you'll even go ahead and write it someday. For now, in 100 words—your maximum limit—write a pitch. Tell us, your reader and your editors, what's at the heart of this story you'd tell? If you only had 100 words to tell it, what would you say? Craft those sentences; build paragraph moment; use climax, sentence variation. Give us a fabulous beginning line; use character; pull out all the stops. In those 100 words, show off everything you've learned in this course.

Think of this as your 100-word final assignment; the chance to put everything you've learned in this course in motion simultaneously. At the beginning of our next—and last—lesson, I'm going to give you a checklist and ask you see how many of the things we've covered together you remembered to think about actively in your writing; because if you've learned one thing from this course, above all, I hope it's that a good writer is an active and thoughtful writer more than almost anything.

Being a Writer
Lecture 24

There is one thing that all writers have in common—they write. Sounds simple, but writing can be a challenging task for all sorts of reasons. This lecture will discuss how to overcome some of the most common challenges that keep writers from writing, such as the ever-daunting writers block and the modern menace of time management.

Writers Write

- Think back for a moment over everything we have covered in the past 23 lectures, from narrative arc and finding the right kind of structure for your book to developing character, beginning and ending chapters, writing cliffhangers, using sentence variation and pacing, and writing effective metaphors.

- You already know everything you're going to need to write your first substantial work of creative nonfiction—except for one thing: Whether or not you have the self-discipline to do it.

- Here is one last secret all writers know: Writers are people who write. Teachers can teach people *how* to write, but you cannot be a great writer unless you write something to start with.

- Every writer—from beginners to seasoned pros—dreads writer's block. But what *is* writer's block really? Perhaps if we can figure out where it comes from, we can figure out how to conquer it.

When Writer's Block…Isn't

- What are the things that prevent the words we want to write from making their way onto paper? Typically, writer's block occurs when writers worry so much that worrying is the only thing that is occupying the imagination. Life overtakes art, and you just cannot focus.

- The moment that I decided to write *The Widow Clicquot* was a moment of complete desperation. I was in a job that I really did not like, and I was afraid that I was trapped. I was living 1000 miles apart from my husband. I was coming up on a significant birthday without a lot of enthusiasm. And I decided that I was going to write the book I always wanted to write. I was going to commit to my writing. I turned back to my writing at a moment of crisis.

- That time I was lucky: The words came easily in crisis. But the next time—when I was writing my second book and dealing with my divorce—I was not so lucky. At the beginning of writing *The Secret of Chanel No. 5*, I spent a whole summer staring at a computer screen, unable to write a word that I did not delete by mid afternoon.

- The problem was not my writing. The problem was my life, but it did not feel that way at the time. The risk of linking writing and stress is that if we connect that turmoil to our identity as writers, we can create blocks that last long after the problem has been solved.

- When you experience writer's block, make sure it is actually your writing that you are struggling with. If not, remember, you will write again when you are ready, when you are on the other side of the crisis.

Silencing Your Inner Doubts

- Sometimes writer's worry really is writer's worry. That is the kind of writer's block that you can do something about, because it really is all in your head.

- The trick to writing for the long haul, the trick to *being* a writer, is learning how to silence that little voice in the back of all of our heads that says, "You are not a good writer. This is a stupid book. Put that pen down and walk away from the table." That little voice is the enemy of all writing.

- All of the famous writers I know are familiar with that little voice. If people who write amazing books that the world agrees are wonderful have that voice, then that voice does not know anything. Its judgment is completely uninformed.

- Sometimes, things are not working in your writing. Sometimes we do go a long way down dead ends and discover that we have to delete the words we sweated over. Sometimes, we are not doing our best work. But writer's worry mostly comes from getting frustrated and mixing up the difference between a paragraph that is stumping us and our ability to fix it.

- There are three concrete steps you can take to silence the voice and work your way out of writer's worry.

  - Keep writing. If the words will not come, sit for 15 minutes and make yourself write without stopping, even if all you write is "This is such a stupid exercise. I have nothing to say. I have writer's block. I can't believe I have to do this for 15 minutes." Sooner or later, you will find something better to say.

  - Set smaller goals. If you are consistently failing to meet your own expectations, you will only increase your worry. Be gentle on yourself. Even if you have to reduce your goal to one good sentence a day, that one good sentence will start to feel good and make you want to write another. Taking the pressure off will get the creative juices flowing.

  - Cultivate the seven habits of a writer, which you will find below. Writing is a habit that, if you let it, grows on you.

- Finding time to write is harder than it sounds in our busy modern lives. After you account for talent and imagination, writing really does come down to hard work and perseverance.

- In fact, the more you write, the more you submit your writing, the more rejections you will receive. What successful writers know is that when you get a rejection, you should not put that piece into a drawer and forget it. Revise it and send it out again.

The Seven Writers' Habits

- What are the seven habits you can adopt to make space in your life for your writing?

  - Throw out the TV: Most of the writers I know do not own televisions, not because they do not enjoy them but because they are distractions. Let yourself be hungry for stories, so hungry that you write them yourself.

  - Find a time and a place to write. Make your writing space and writing time sacrosanct. It does not need to be anything so grand as a real office; it can be the corner table at the diner down the street, where you go at 5 am every day. But it must be yours, and it must be a priority.

  - Set concrete, realistic goals, and reward yourself for meeting them. To do this, you will need to figure out how you write best. Are you a quick first-drafter? Are you an outliner? Are you a slow plodder? Maybe your goal is a draft in three months, then plenty of time to revise. Maybe you want to write one perfect page per day. Do whatever works for you, but make sure it is doable. It is also important to reward yourself for meeting your goals.

  - Write like clockwork: I write six days a week. Does that sound crazy? Do you watch television six days a week? Do you drink coffee every morning? Those are all just habits. Writing can be the same.

  - Read more. Words are your tools, and you want to become more and more familiar with what they can do and how writers can use them.

- Keep a journal. This is not the same thing as a diary, although it can be that, too. A journal is just a centralized place to keep all your writing-related ideas: books you are interested in reading, bits of conversation you overhear, story ideas, to-do lists, and so forth.

© iStockphoto/Thinkstock.

There is only one rule: Writers write.

- Make friends with other writers. Find or start a writing group. Take a course or find a retreat. Talking to other writers will help you think of yourself as a writer. People who think of themselves as writers are more likely to write.

- Feeling uncertain? Does writing your book seem like a daunting process? Of course it does! Writing is hard. But you are ready. There is just one thing left for you to do. Write!

Suggested Reading

Hill, *Napoleon Hill's Keys to Success*.

Straw, *Unstuck*.

Questions to Consider

1. Which of the seven writer's habits do you already have? Which habits can you imagine starting now?

2. Have you ever had writer's block? What do you think created it, and how did you get over it?

Being a Writer

Lecture 24—Transcript

Here we are at the end of our course together on writing creative nonfiction. You've learned a lot already about how to tell a great story. Think back for a moment over everything we've covered, from narrative arc and finding the right kind of structure of your book, to developing character, beginning and ending chapters, writing cliffhangers, using sentence variation and pacing, writing effective metaphors, and many other things as well. You already know everything you're going to need to write your first substantial work of creative nonfiction, except for one thing: What you might not know yet is just whether you have the self-discipline to do it.

But here's one last secret for you that all writers know; are you ready for it? It's just this: Writers are people who write; it's as simple as that. Let me say it again: Writers are people who write. We can teach people how to write; I can show you the tricks of the trade, and you can learn to master them. But in the end, writing is hard work. Back in the 1930s, an author named Napoleon Hill wrote a series of early bestselling self-help books with titles like *Think and Grow Rich* and *The Law of Success*. When it came to writing, he had just one piece of advice: "Reduce your plan to just writing."

You know what, he's right: "Reduce your plan to just writing." That, maybe more than anything, is the secret to becoming a great writer, because you can't be a great writer unless you write something to start with. A bit later, we'll talk about what you can do to create for yourself great writer's habits—the kinds of habits that maximize your chances of writing not just that first story you already have in mind, but all the stories after that, too—because there are habits that can help you to become a person who writes.

But let's talk first about something that every writer, whether you're just a beginner or a seasoned pro, dreads. You know what I'm going to say, don't you? That's right: writer's block. We all know that writer's block is when the words won't come and you can't think of anything to say. It's that horrible experience when a writer wants to write but he or she simply can't. But what is writer's block, really? After all, if we can figure out where it comes from, maybe we can figure out how to conquer it, right? If you think about the term, where does the idea of being "blocked" come from? It's the language of psychology isn't it? That means that writer's block is in our head; and since that happens to be the same place ideas and the imagination come from, you can see the problem.

What are the kinds of things that block us as writers? What are the things, in other words, that trip us up in our heads and prevent the words we want to write from making their way onto paper? I sometimes think that we should really call writer's block "writer's worry." It's when writers worry so much that worrying is the only thing that's occupying the imagination; and that's not a happy story for a writer. What kinds of things worry a writer? Sometimes life worries us, and when crises happen, to be honest there's not much you can do besides keep working and trying to just get through. If you're dealing with a family tragedy, a personal crisis, or an illness, sometimes writing can be very therapeutic. But sometimes life overtakes art, and you just can't focus. It can get tricky, because many of us turn to writing for the first time—we decide to give it a real try—when other parts of our life are in moments of great transition. After all, I know that's how it started for me.

Want to know the day that I decided to write *The Widow Clicquot*? It was a moment of complete desperation. I later wrote about it in the prologue to the book. I was in a job that I really didn't like, and I was afraid that I was trapped. I was living in a marriage where our new jobs were now a thousand miles apart. I was coming up on a significant birthday without a lot of enthusiasm. What did I do? I decided that, darn it, I was going to write the book I always wanted to write; I was really going to take a chance on committing to my writing. It was a great story, both the biography I wanted to tell and for me personally. Maybe, like you, I turned back to writing at a moment of crisis. That time I was lucky; the words came easily in crisis.

But the next time, when I was writing my second book and dealing with the divorce that followed from that long-distance lifestyle, I wasn't so lucky at all. At the beginning of *The Secret of Chanel No. 5*, I spent a whole summer staring at a computer screen, unable to write a word that I didn't delete by mid-afternoon and absolutely despairing. You know what? The problem wasn't my writing. I didn't have writer's block, or writer's worry; I had life giving me a serious run for my money. But it didn't feel that way at the time. Life was making writing hard. Do you know the feeling? Don't worry; every real writer knows the feeling. We've all been there. The risk of linking writing and stress is that if we connect that turmoil to our identity as writers, we can create blocks that last long after the problem has been solved. That's the first thing about writer's block: Make sure it's actually your writing that you're struggling with. If not, remember: This moment of transition is what made you dedicate yourself again to the idea that you have something important to say. You'll say it when you're ready, when you're on the other side of the crisis. Meanwhile, don't add writing to your list of worries.

But sometimes writer's worry really is writer's worry. Sometimes there's something stressing us out or blocking us that really is about our writing or our process. That's the kind of writer's block you can do something about, because this is the kind that really is all in your head. There's something I always tell writers in my classes at the university when they're feeling stuck, and I'll share it with you, too. It's a secret every writer I know understands immediately: The trick to writing for the long haul, the trick to being a writer, is learning how to silence that little voice in the back of all of our heads that says, "You are not a good writer, this is a stupid book, put that pen down and walk away slowly from that table." That little voice is the enemy of all writing; and it's the enemy of all art, actually, because painters, actors, and musicians have it, too. All of the famous writers I know—writers whose names you'd recognize—know about that little voice. If people who write amazing books that the world agrees are wonderful have that voice, do you know what this must mean? It has to mean that that voice doesn't actually know anything. It doesn't know whether you're a good writer or not. It doesn't know whether this book is working yet or if you need to reimagine the structure. Its judgment is actually completely uninformed. That voice does just one thing: It tells you to quit. It tells you to put the pen down and doubt yourself. It's one of those negative characters—I'm sure you've met them—who finds the bad in everything. It doesn't mean to, but it can't help it. It's just a negative little voice; but the great thing is you don't have to live with it unless you choose to.

But that little voice is what writer's block—or, as we're going to rename it, writer's worry—is all about. It's about worrying that you're wasting your time and that no one will ever want to read what you're writing anyhow. Sometimes, things aren't working. Sometimes we do go a long way down dead ends as writers and then discover that, in fact, the only solution is to push the delete button on words we sweated over. Sometimes the story we want to tell demands it. Some writing is better than other writing. We don't want to kid ourselves, because we want to be good writers, and sometimes we all make mistakes and just have to start over again in the morning. But writer's block mostly comes from getting frustrated or feeling under pressure to do something too quickly, and mixing up in our heads the difference between a paragraph that's stumping us and our ability to fix it and make it work beautifully; they're two different things.

Ever wondered why writers talk about the craft of writing? It's interesting actually, isn't it? Readers talk about the art of a writer. Writers talk about craft; and writer's worry is part of the reason why. What writers know is that learning the tools of storytelling, working slowly and carefully over the period of years to become masters in this craft of wordsmithing, that's the way to keep putting pen to paper and the way to dismiss that little voice and to keep it quiet.

What can you do? I mean, what can you do concretely? There are three steps you can take to silence the voice and to work your way out of writer's worry. The first is: Keep writing. This sounds crazy, doesn't it? After all, you're going to say to me, "I'm blocked! I can't write; that's the problem." But actually, you can; so if you get stuck, try this exercise. Sit for 15 minutes and make yourself write without stopping. It doesn't matter if what you write is "This is such a stupid exercise, I have nothing to say, I have writer's block, and I can't believe I have to do this for 15 minutes." Sooner or later, you're going to get tired of writing that sentence, and you'll start to write ones like "Okay, what I'm really trying to say here is," and then soon you'll come up with an idea that gets you going. If you do it for 15 minutes, you will. Then, that's not everything: Then you need to give yourself another 15 minutes to write just one paragraph, or to sketch out one section of the setting, or whatever it is your idea suggests; but 15 minutes to get yourself started again in the right direction.

Number two is: Set yourself smaller goals. The way to work yourself out of this writer's worry is not to set yourself hugely ambitious goals that you can't meet. Setting goals that you can't meet only adds to that stress and worry, doesn't it? So take a step back. Tell yourself, "Okay, today, I'm going to write just one good sentence." After you do that for a few days, you'll start to get enthusiastic. If there are deadlines, you need to tackle extending them. Take the pressure off; that's the way to get the creative juices flowing. Any editor would rather extend a deadline before it's passed rather than after. Be that editor for yourself, too.

The third thing: Cultivate the seven habits of a writer; because writing is a habit that, if you let it, grows on you. Writer's worry often comes from doing something that we could make a more natural part of our lives if we work at it, and find the time for it. Finding the time to write is harder than it sounds in our busy modern lives, especially in a world where the commercial reality is that few writers—even great ones—will make their livings as writers alone. You can marry for money; you can win the lottery; or you can go to work, clean the house, and pursue your career, and in a few hours each day dedicate yourself to writing as an art and a passion. To be honest, the last approach is the normal route, even if it's difficult for most of us. But it takes self-discipline, and self-discipline is largely a matter of habits.

Here at the end of the course, let's talk about what the writerly habits are. What do people who are writers do to keep themselves writing? I have a friend who's a wonderful writer, and she told me not too long ago about a dinner party she was at. Around the table were all other writers. One of them was a writer who'd written one beautiful literary novel that had won high praise and several prizes. One of them was a writer who'd written a half-dozen popular books over the last couple of decades. One of them was a prolific and famous writer whose last work was an international bestseller. The conversation turned to, "How do you write?" What struck my friend most was one simple fact: There was a direct relationship between how celebrated and prolific the writer was and one basic thing, how often and how regularly he or she wrote. After you account for talent and imagination, after that it really does come down to hard work.

And to perseverance; because rejection, it happens to all writers. In fact, the more you write, the more often you'll get rejected. After all, if you don't write anything, how can anyone ever say no? What successful writers know is that when you get a rejection, there's one thing you don't want to do: Don't put that piece that you think is ready to go out in a drawer and think about it. Revise it; work on it; and send it out again, and again, and keeping working to make it better, too. Remember those old dolls from the 1970s, the Weeble Wobble dolls? They were egg-shaped dolls, and the advertisement for them was a catchy tune with the lyric, "Weebles wobble but they don't fall down." That's the habit successful writers learn to cultivate: wobbling but not falling down. Sure, no one likes criticism or rejection. It doesn't derail a professional writer, however. Those writers at that dinner party, they all worked hard, all had been rejected, and all kept at it.

What kinds of other habits do writers have? What are the seven habits you can adopt to make space in your life for your writing? One is: Throw out the TV. Most of the writers I know don't own televisions. I'm among them. This isn't because writers don't like televisions; we do. If I owned one, I'd watch it, even if for only an hour or two a day. The trouble is that televisions do two things: They take up an hour or two a day, when most of us are trying to eke out just a bit of time for our writing. Perhaps worse than this, televisions are storytelling instruments. We sit and watch a story being told, and it satisfies that desire; a desire without which few of us will ever write our own books. Let yourself be hungry for story; hungry enough that you'll write them yourself. I know it's a radical idea; but time and time again, I've asked writers: "Do you have a television?" and more often than not, they recognize it as simply too easy a temptation.

How about another one? Find a time and a place to write. What can you do if your spouse and children would mutiny at the idea of a television-free home? You can do something many other writers also do: You can find yourself an office, and you can go to it every day, at the same time, no matter what. Rome could be burning; you go to your office for two hours in the morning as a writer. You make it sacrosanct. That office doesn't need to be anything so grand as a real office. It can be the corner table at the diner down the street at 5 am, where after a few days you'll be the regular in the back and they'll keep your coffee cup filled for you silently. It can be a desk at a public library. It can be your spare bedroom, or the office you decide to rent across town, too. I have one friend who has three young children and not much money, and her office is the front seat of her station wagon. She drives down the street, parks under a tree with her coffee, and locks the doors on the world for an hour every morning. It doesn't have to be morning; it can be every day at 5 am or every evening at midnight. It can be the hour your kids are playing soccer, as long as it's the same hour every day and nothing except flood, famine, and emergency room visits are allowed to interrupt it. When you set up your office, wherever it is, there's one other writerly habit, too: Leave the cell phone off. Don't let there be internet. You need an hour or two with no disruptions and no temptations, because writing is hard. Even the most experienced writer will sometimes do almost anything to avoid it.

A third: Set concrete goals. To do this, you first need to decide what kind of writer you are. It will help you set goals that you'll feel satisfied meeting. As writers, we want to reward ourselves with feelings of success regularly; ideally daily. Are you a quick first-drafter? Are you an outliner? Are you a plodder? I'm the last type of writer. That means I rarely revise something after I've written it, but it can take me 10 or 15 minutes sometimes if I get stuck on a sentence to work my way through a problem. I work sentence-by-sentence, writing carefully, and I don't move on until I'm happy. In fact, my regular schedule for myself is very modest even as a full-time writer: I start work at the same time each day, six days a week, and I set myself the goal of 1,000 words when I'm writing seriously. That's only two single-spaced pages, but in six months you can write a book like that. I reward myself by creating a rule that I live by: I have to write 1,000 publishable-quality words. I set myself a goal and reward myself for accomplishing it. That's a writerly habit. In fact, it's just basic human conditioning: We do most regularly the things that we get rewards for doing. In fact, some writers swear that the best strategy of all is to follow up your writing time with some exercise. Write for an hour and then go do your workout. The exercise floods our body with physiologically feel-good hormones, and we start to associate writing with a sense of health, well-being, and relaxation that comes with mental and physical exercise.

Our fourth rule of habits of writers: Write like clockwork. You'll also notice that I said I write six days a week. Does that sound crazy? But it isn't, really, and it's another writerly habit. Do you watch television six days a week? Do you drink coffee every morning? Those are all just other habits. You don't have to be a full-time writer to write every day; you just need to find yourself one hour. If you can find more, that's a true indulgence. But in one hour, six days a week, you can be a writer. Do you know why writing regularly is so important? It's not just because, like anything, it's easier to do things that are part of our regular habits, though that's true, too. It's because here's the thing about chaos, our lives, and writing: If you're in the habit of writing daily—if you're used to that being time when you enter a world of the imagination, where things are calm and quiet—writing becomes a little escape from the world. If you set that up as a regular habit when things in life are normal, then you have a huge advantage. There are times in all our lives when things aren't normal and a few more that are unusually stressful. But if you're in the habit of writing, then writing sometimes can hold the chaos at bay for a little while each day. But if you try to start writing in a period of complete turmoil, or if you don't write regularly, then when the periodic stresses of life intrude, one of two things is likely to happen: Either you'll struggle to concentrate on your writing during whatever time you've found for it and it'll become a frustrating experience and feel like failure, or you'll stop writing. Both of those are things that, as a writer, you're trying to create habits to avoid.

Our fifth habit: Read more. Being a bookworm, that's another writerly habit. If you're a writer, then words are your tools, and you want to become more and more familiar with what they can do, how writers can use them, what they look and feel like in our hands as authors. But there's another important reason to read as much as you can as a writer, too. Think back here to everything we've said that needs to be happening at once, like a dozen balls we're juggling in the air simultaneously, to make a great story. Everyone gets stuck sometimes. You'll sit there writing and you'll find yourself thinking, "Now how the devil am I going to solve this problem?" Often, by reading things that remind you of the project you're working on, you'll see how someone else solved that same problem; or you'll see how someone did something that has nothing at all to do with your problem, but would be exactly what you need to fix it anyhow.

Our sixth habit: Keep a journal. A journal isn't the same thing as "Dear Diary," though it can be that if that's what you want it to be. Your journal can be just a notebook. That's all mine is, and it's completely disorganized. In fact, mine is a pile of notes written on the back of envelopes, and beat up notebooks, and Post It notes all jammed into an old leather binder. It's where I write down books that I'm interested in, bits of conversation that I overhear on the street and would make the beginning of a great story, to-do lists, random business cards I've collected, research notes, and the printouts of the paragraphs that sometimes in the process of writing I end up deleting. Those are often paragraphs that simply belong somewhere in a book other than the one I happen to be writing. Someday maybe I'll return to them, or maybe never; but it's there if I ever need it.

The seventh habit: Make friends with other writers. Start the writing group; put up a sign at the coffee shop; take a course or find a retreat that you can head off for. Talking to other writers will help you think of yourself as a writer. People who think of themselves as writers are more likely to write,

That's everything. Follow these habits, and maybe along the way you'll invent one or two others yourself, and you know what? You'll be on your way to being the writer you imagine you can be.

Except you need to do this one other thing on top of this, don't you? You need to write what's in you, in your mind and in your imagination; and you need to tell a great story. That's what you've learned to do in this course. You are ready to do this.

Feeling uncertain? Does writing that book seem like a daunting process? Of course it does; writing is hard. But you're ready.

There's just one thing left for you to do. Remember how we started this lesson? I said there was only one thing more you needed to know, didn't I? It's that writers are people who write. Or, take that advice from Napoleon Hill: Reduce your plan to just writing. After all, you're ready. You know what to do once you begin it; and what you don't know, you'll learn along the way like all writers do. That's why writing is a craft, after all. You have all the tools you need, and there are great stories out there that your readers are going to look forward to enjoying. So go ahead, just begin it.

Glossary

alliteration: The repetition of the same sound at the beginning of successive words.

anadiplosis: The repetition of the word that ends one clause at the beginning of the next clause.

anaphora: The repetition of the same word or phrase at the beginning of successive clauses.

antagonist: The character who is in central conflict with the main character of a narrative.

antimetabole: The repetition of phrases in successive clauses in which their order in the first clause is reversed in the second clause.

antithesis: The expression of opposing ideas in parallel grammatical structure or clauses.

assonance: The repetition of the same vowel sound in successive words.

asyndeton: The strategy of omitting normally used conjunctions in writing.

author platform: The way in which the general public associates the name of the author with certain kinds of books or stories; also, the author's expertise and credentials for writing on certain topics.

bias: The way the perspective of the storyteller or researcher can shape his or her attitude toward evidence.

book proposal: A brief outline of a book that is sent to a publisher as part of the contract process.

circular narrative: A narrative structure where the end and the beginning meet and where the story focuses on the transformation of the character during the experience of the events in it.

cliffhanger: A strategy for building suspense and anticipation in a narrative by leaving the reader at a moment of crisis.

consonance: The repetition of the same consonant sound in successive words.

constructive criticism: Criticism of a piece of writing that works to help the writer imagine improvements rather than putting down the writer and his or her abilities.

creative nonfiction: The art of bringing all the strategies of storytelling to the narration of factual events.

direct discourse: Quoted speech in a narrative that is attributed to a speaker.

displacement: A kind of metaphoric thinking in which one idea is substituted for another. *See* **metonymy**.

dramatic conflict: Conflict, either internal or external, that characters experience that moves a narrative forward.

epanalepsis: The repetition of the same word or group of words at the beginning and end of the same clause or sentence.

epistrophe: The repetition of the same word or group of words at the end of successive clauses.

first-person narrative: A narrative that uses an *I* or *we* point of view.

flashback: The moment in a narrative where a character or narrative jumps back in time to an earlier moment in the story.

foreshadowing: A strategy for building suspense and anticipation in a narrative by giving the reader hints of things to come.

frame narrative: A narrative structure in which the essential story is bracketed at the beginning and end by a second perspective on it.

free indirect discourse: Speech in a narrative that is not quoted and is not attributed to a specific speaker.

hypotactic: A sentence structure characterized by subordination.

implied author: The personality of the author that the reader gleans from the narrative, as distinct from the narrator's or point-of-view character's personality.

indirect discourse: Speech in a narrative that is attributed to a specific speaker but is not directly quoted.

inversion: Reversing the normal subject-verb-object order of expression in English.

isocolon: Creating successive clauses of a similar length.

libel: The legal term for having written something untrue and malicious about another person.

linear narrative: A narrative structure where events follow on events to build to a climax and resolution and where the plot is emphasized over the character who experiences it.

literary agent: A person who acts as an intermediary between an author and a publisher and represents the author's interests legally.

market: The potential number of readers and book buyers interested in certain kinds of publications.

metaphor: An implied comparison that allows readers to see things in a new light.

metonymy: A kind of metaphor in which one object is described by reference to another object somehow associated with it. *See* **displacement**.

minor character: A character who plays a smaller role in a story or in developing the central conflict of the main character(s).

mixed metaphor: When the implied comparison of a metaphor is awkward, ineffective, or incongruous.

multiple perspectives: A narrative strategy that involves using more than one point of view in a story.

narrative arc: The idea that a story has a natural forward trajectory and that conflicts move toward complication and resolution.

narrative voice: The perspective through which a story is told.

negative character: A character—not necessarily the antagonist—with unpleasant or off-putting traits.

nonfiction contract: The implied agreement between a reader and a writer that the author of creative nonfiction does not invent any facts in his or her storytelling.

objective mode: A mode of writing that purports to report the facts unemotionally.

omniscient mode: A mode of writing in which the narrator is assumed to have complete knowledge of all events.

pacing: The writer's ability to influence the reader's experience of a story's drama by speeding up or slowing down the narrative.

parallelism: Expressing parallel or antithetical ideas in similar sentence structures to heighten the comparison or the contrast.

paratactic: Sentence structures characterized by a lack of subordination.

pen name: An assumed name, different from the author's real name.

pitch: A short proposal outlining the narrative of a magazine article or essay sent to an editor before a writing assignment is given.

point of view: The perspective from which a story is told; may be first (*I/we*), second (*you*), or third person (*he/she/it/they*).

polyptoton: The repetition of words of the same root in successive clauses or sentences.

polysyndeton: Using more conjunctions than one would normally expect in a clause or sentence.

prewriting exercises: Exercises authors use to prepare for a larger writing project.

protagonist: The main character of a narrative, whose conflict is central to the story.

purple prose: Writing that is overwrought or self-consciously written and calls attention to itself and away from the narrative; generally seen as negative.

quest narrative: A narrative structure in which the main character goes on a journey in search of knowledge, experience, or some concrete object.

revision: The process of reworking a piece of writing to strengthen the finished product.

sample chapter: Part of a book proposal in which the author includes a sample of the project being proposed to the publisher.

second-person narrative: A narrative that uses the *you* point of view.

sentence variation: A strategy of mixing sentence types to influence the reader's experience of the narrative pacing, drama, and intensity; an element of strong writing.

simile: An explicit comparison using the words "like" or "as" that allows readers to see things in a new light. See *metaphor*.

stock character: A character who represents a familiar type of person, rather than an individual.

story starter: The combination of character, conflict, and narrative that sets a story in motion—an essential element of a great beginning.

subjective mode: A mode of writing in which the narration is presumed to be filtered through the subjective opinions and experiences of a particular consciousness or character.

synecdoche: A kind of metaphor in which a part of an object represents the whole.

third-person narrative: A narrative that uses a *he*, *she*, *it*, or *they* point of view.

under-contract writing: Writing of a book or essay that begins after the publisher or editor has agreed to publish the work; often involves an advance payment or an agreement to cover expenses.

unreliable narrator: A narrator who is revealed either to not have all the information or to not be entirely truthful in what he or she related to the reader.

writing the gutter: Using juxtaposition and untold aspects of a story to heighten a reader's drama and interest.

Bibliography

Arabian Nights: Tales from a Thousand and One Nights. Translated by Richard Burton. New York: Modern Library, 2001. A classic example of storytelling that uses a frame narrative and cliffhangers.

Austen, Jane. *Northanger Abbey*. Oxford: Oxford University Press, 1998. A classic work of fiction, used as an example of free indirect discourse.

Bass, Frank. *The Associated Press Guide to Internet Research and Reporting.* New York: Basic Books, 2002. An excellent handbook to evaluating the quality of research sources on the Internet.

Berr, Hélène. *The Journal of Hélène Berr.* New York: Weinstein Books, 2009. The diary of a young Jewish woman living in Paris during the Second World War, used as an example of strong memoir-writing techniques.

Brown, Dan. *The Da Vinci Code*. New York: Anchor, 2009. The best-selling novel, used as an example of strong character development and chapter control.

Calvino, Italo. *If on a Winter's Night a Traveler.* New York: Everyman's Library, 1993. The experimental novel by an Italian author, used as an example of innovative narrative structures.

Card, Orson Scott. *Elements of Fiction Writing: Characters & Viewpoint.* New York: Writers Digest Press, 1999. An excellent handbook with more information on working with point of view in storytelling.

Chiarella, Tom. *Writing Dialogue.* Cincinnati, OH: Story Press, 1998. An excellent handbook with more information on writing effective dialogue.

Corbett, Edward, and Robert J. Connors. *Style and Statement*. Oxford: Oxford University Press, 1998. The classic handbook on rhetorical devices and their effects in storytelling.

Didion, Joan. "Goodbye to All That." In *The Art of the Personal Essay*, edited by Phillip Lopate. New York: Anchor, 1997. An essay by a renowned nonfiction author, used as an example of excellent paragraph pacing and sentence variation, as well as rhetorical writing.

Eckstut, Arielle, and David Sterry. *The Essential Guide to Getting Your Book Published: How to Write It, Sell It, and Market It … Successfully*. New York: Workman Publishing, 2010. An excellent handbook on the nuts and bolts of getting a book published in the current marketplace for aspiring authors.

Ensign, Georgianne. *Great Beginnings: Opening Lines of Great Novels*. New York: HarperCollins, 1993. An excellent handbook for writing great opening lines and chapter beginnings.

Fandel, Jennifer. *Picture Yourself Writing Nonfiction: Using Photos to Inspire Writing*. Mankato, MN: Capstone Press, 2011. An excellent handbook for using photographs as prompts for creative nonfiction writing and research.

Faulkner, William. *Sanctuary*. New York: Vintage, 1993. The novel by an American author, used as an example of foreshadowing and character development.

Fish, Stanley. *How to Write a Sentence: And How to Read One*. New York: HarperCollins, 2011. An excellent guide to the different ways of reading and writing sentences, written by a famous English professor.

Fisher, M. F. K. "Once a Tramp, Always." In *The Art of the Personal Essay,* edited by Phillip Lopate. New York: Anchor, 1997. Essay by a renowned food writer, used as an example of paragraph climax and effective rhetorical writing.

Frey, James. *A Million Little Pieces.* New York: Nan A. Talese, 2003. The scandalous "nonfiction" memoir of drug abuse and desolation, revealed to have broken the nonfiction contract.

George, Don. *Lonely Planet Travel Writing.* Oakland, CA: Lonely Planet, 2009. An excellent hands-on guidebook to writing and publishing travel articles, written by a respected travel publisher.

Glass, Charles. *Americans in Paris: Life and Death Under Nazi Occupation.* New York: Penguin, 2010. Creative nonfiction account of life in Paris during the Second World War, used as an example of excellent narrative nonfiction writing.

Hacker, Diana. *A Writer's Reference.* New York: Bedford/St. Martin's, 2010. A standard grammar and research handbook, for writers wishing to refresh their understanding of syntax and common errors.

Hemingway, Ernest. *A Moveable Feast.* New York: Scribner, 2006. Ernest Hemingway's classic memoir of life in Paris, used as an example of excellent life writing in the creative nonfiction genre.

Hill, Napoleon. *Napoleon Hill's Keys to Success: The 17 Principles of Personal Achievement.* New York: Plume, 1997. A guide to creative good habits for success, many of which are also useful for writers.

Homer. *The Odyssey*, translated by Robert Fagles. New York: Penguin, 1999. The classic quest narrative, an example of the most famous early circular narrative.

Hong Kingston, Maxine. *The Woman Warrior: Memoirs of a Girlhood among Ghosts*. New York: Vintage, 1989. The haunting memoir of life in America as a Chinese American woman, learning about her family's past in China, used as an example of excellent narrative nonfiction writing and of writing the gutter.

Hood, Ann. *Creating Character Emotions.* Cincinnati, OH: Story Press, 1998. An excellent handbook for more exercises on character development.

Janzen, Rhoda. *Mennonite in a Little Black Dress: A Memoir of Going Home*. New York: Henry Holt, 2009. The memoir of a woman returning to her Mennonite childhood home after a divorce, used as an example of strong creative nonfiction strategies.

"James Frey and the *Million Little Pieces* Controversy." *Oprah*. 2006. http://www.oprah.com/showinfo/James-Frey-and-the-A-Million-Little-Pieces-Controversy. Discussion of author James Frey breaking the creative nonfiction contract on Oprah's Book Club.

Joyce, James. *Ulysses*. New York: Vintage, 1990. A novelistic updating of Homer's *Odyssey* and one of the great works of modern literature, used as an example of innovative narrative structure.

Krakauer, Jon. *Three Cups of Deceit: How Greg Mortenson, Humanitarian Hero, Lost His Way*. 2011. http://byliner.com. Journalist and creative nonfiction writer Jon Krakauer's expose of how Greg Mortenson broke the creative nonfiction contract in his bestselling book.

Levine, Becky. *The Writing & Critique Group Survival Guide: How to Make Revisions, Self-Edit, and Give and Receive Feedback.* New York: Writers Digest Books, 2010. A practical, hands-on guide for writing and responding to critiques of your work by other writers.

Lewis, C. S. *The Voyage of the Dawn Treader*. New York: HarperCollins, 2005. A 20th-century children's novel, used as an example of excellent character development.

Lounsberry, Barbara. *The Art of Fact: Contemporary Arts of Nonfiction*. Westport, CT: Greenwood Press, 1990. An excellent primary guide to the world of writing creative nonfiction.

MacKay, Marina. *The Cambridge Introduction to the Novel.* Cambridge: Cambridge University Press, 2011. An academic guide for readers interested in learning more about the history of the novel and the history of narrative structure and characterization.

Mann, Thomas. *The Oxford Guide to Library Research.* New York: Oxford University Press, 2005. An academic guide for readers interested in serious research for their creative nonfiction projects.

Marquez, Gabriel Garcia. *A Hundred Years of Solitude.* New York: Harper Perennial, 2004. The innovative "magical" novel, used as an example of writing great beginnings.

Mayle, Peter. *A Year in Provence.* New York: Vintage, 1991. The bestselling memoir of a year in France, used as an example of how authors find their market.

Mazzeo, Tilar. "The Author as Character in Narrative Nonfiction." In *Write Now! Nonfiction. Memoir, Journalism and Creative Nonfiction Exercises from Today's Best Writers*, edited by Sherry Ellis. New York: Penguin, 2009. An essay and additional writing exercise on using the author as a character in creative nonfiction, by your course professor.

———. *The Widow Clicquot: The Story of a Champagne Empire and the Woman Who Ruled It.* New York: HarperCollins, 2008. Best-selling biography and narrative nonfiction on the life of the world's first international businesswoman, by your course professor.

Miller, Brenda, and Suzanne Paola. *Tell It Slant: Writing and Shaping Creative Nonfiction.* New York: McGraw-Hill, 2004. An excellent primary overview on the art and craft of writing creative nonfiction.

Mortenson, Greg. *Three Cups of Tea: One Man's Mission to Promote Peace … One School at a Time.* New York: Penguin, 2006. The best-selling memoir of one man's charity mission—ultimately and scandalously revealed to have broken the creative nonfiction contract.

Perl, Sondra, and Mimi Schwartz. *Writing True: The Art and Craft of Creative Nonfiction*. Boston: Wadsworth Publishing, 2006. An excellent primary overview on the art and craft of writing creative nonfiction.

Plath, Sylvia. *The Bell Jar*. New York: Harper Perennial, 2000. A 20th-century novel, used as an example of how to write great beginnings.

Pollack, Eileen. *Creative Nonfiction: A Guide to Form, Content, and Style, with Readings*. Boston: Wadsworth Publishing, 2010. Another excellent primary overview on the art and craft of writing creative nonfiction.

Powell, Julie. *Julie and Julia: My Year of Cooking Dangerously.* New York: Little, Brown and Company, 2009. The best-selling memoir of one woman's obsession with Julia Child's classic cookbook, used as an example of how an author can find his or her audience in the current marketplace.

Prose, Francine. *Reading Like a Writer: A Guide for People Who Love Books and for Those Who Want to Write Them.* New York: Harper Perennial, 2007. A personal and profound reflection on reading and writing by an award-winning author.

Pynchon, Thomas. *The Crying of Lot 49*. New York: Harper Perennial, 2006. Contemporary novel, used as an example of the excellent use of the quest narrative in modern writing.

Rabiner, Susan, and Alfred Fortunato. *Thinking like Your Editor: How to Write Great Serious Nonfiction—and Get It Published.* New York: Norton, 2003. The best book on the market for helping aspiring writers draft a successful book proposal.

Raisley, Alicia. *The Power of Point of View: Make Your Story Come to Life.* New York: Writer's Digest Books, 2008. An excellent additional resource for working with point of view in your writing.

Richardson, Samuel. *Clarissa; or, the History of a Young Lady*. New York: Penguin, 1986. An 18th-century epistolary novel and one of the so-called great works of English literature, used as an example of how narrative and characterization work in classic texts.

Rilke, Rainer Maria. *Letters to a Young Poet*. New York: W. W. Norton, 1993. One of the last century's most celebrated authors writes letters of advice to a young writer that are still moving and relevant.

Shakespeare, William. *Romeo and Juliet*. Oxford: Oxford University Press, 2008. The classic tale of young love and family betrayal, used as an example of how narrative structure creates powerful story.

Shelley, Mary. *Frankenstein*. New York: Bantam Classics, 1984. The classic story of Victor Frankenstein and his monster, used as an example of a celebrated frame narrative.

Straw, Jane. *Unstuck: A Supportive and Practical Guide to Working Through Writer's Block*. New York: St Martin's, 2004. A good guide for writers struggling with writer's block and looking for additional strategies for getting back to writing successfully.

Strunk, William, E. B. White, and Roger Angell. *The Elements of Style*. New York: Longman, 1999. The updated classic text, still short but sweet, on what makes beautiful prose style.

Telushkin, Joseph. *Words That Hurt, Words That Heal: How to Choose Words Wisely and Well*. New York: William Morrow, 1998. A somewhat spiritually focused book on choosing our words carefully; relevant for authors writing about the lives of other people.

Truss, Lynne. *Eats, Shoots & Leaves: The Zero Tolerance Approach to Punctuation*. New York: Gotham, 2006. A humorous and instructive guide to grammar and common errors, relevant for writers looking to refresh their memory.

Ueland, Brenda. *If You Want to Write: A Book About Art, Independence, and Spirit.* St. Paul, MN: Graywolf Press, 2007. A more spiritually and holistically oriented book on the writer's life, with some excellent prewriting exercises and self-assessment ideas.

Wallace, Benjamin. *The Billionaire's Vinegar: The Mystery of the World's Most Expensive Bottle of Wine*. New York: Crown, 2008. The best-selling creative nonfiction account of a bottle of wine once owned by Thomas Jefferson, used an as example of excellent writing in the genre.

Wolfe, Thomas. *The Bonfire of the Vanities.* New York: Bantam, 1988. The celebrated 1980s novel about the life of high-flying bankers in New York City, used as an example of prose style.

Woolf, Virginia. *Mrs. Dalloway*. New York: Mariner, 1990. A classic novel, used as an example of working with free indirect discourse and getting inside a character's head.

Zinsser, William Knowlton. *On Writing Well: The Classic Guide to Writing Nonfiction.* New York: Harper Reference, 1998. A superb book on what it means to write beautifully and how to do it in creative nonfiction.